INTERNATIONAL SANCTIONS

Targeted sanctions have become an established practice in international relations since the end of the Cold War. Such sanctions – directed at certain leaders or concerning particular commodities or services – have been used by both international organizations and individual states. This book examines this new instrument of international diplomacy, and analyses what such sanctions require in terms of capacity building by the UN and by member states to be effective. It furthermore investigates how the sanctions are used by new actors in international political affairs, notably the EU, African countries and the WTO. Finally, through a legal analysis and a study of individuals listed by the UN, the book highlights the new problems targeted sanctions give rise to, notably issues of human rights, and draws attention to the potential of incentives as part of an international sanctions strategy.

Contributors to this book include international scholars from social and legal sciences as well as practitioners from international organizations.

This timely book will appeal to advanced undergraduate and postgraduate students of peacekeeping and conflict resolution, national and international policy makers and professionals in NGOs.

Peter Wallensteen holds the Dag Hammarskjöld Chair in Peace and Conflict Research, Uppsala University, Sweden. He leads the Uppsala Conflict Data Program, which publishes annual data on armed conflict in the world, and coordinated the Stockholm Process on targeted sanctions. This process presented *Making Targeted Sanctions Effective: Guidelines for the Implementation of UN Policy Options* to the Security Council in February 2003.

Carina Staibano is Senior Research Assistant at the Department of Peace and Conflict Research, Uppsala University. She is working on international sanctions and United Nations system reform issues.

THE CASS SERIES ON PEACEKEEPING
General Editor: Michael Pugh

This series examines all aspects of peacekeeping, from the political, operational and legal dimensions to the developmental and humanitarian issues that must be dealt with by all those involved with peacekeeping in the world today.

1. **Beyond the Emergency: Development within UN Missions**
   edited by Jeremy Ginifer

2. **The UN, Peace and Force**
   edited by Michael Pugh

3. **Mediating in Cyprus: The Cypriot Communities and the United Nations**
   Oliver P. Richmond

4. **Peacekeeping and the UN Agencies**
   edited by Jim Whitman

5. **Peacekeeping and Public Information: Caught in the Crossfire**
   Ingrid A. Lehman

6. **US Peacekeeping Policy under Clinton: A Fairweather Friend?**
   Michael MacKinnon

7. **Peacebuilding and Police Reform**
   edited by Tor Tanke Holm and Espen Barth Eide

8. **Peacekeeping and Conflict Resolution**
   edited by Oliver Ramsbotham and Tom Woodhouse

9. **Managing Armed Conflicts in the 21st Century**
   edited by Adekeye Adebajo and Chandra Lekha Sriram

10. **Women and International Peacekeeping**
    edited by Louise Olsson and Torunn L. Tryggestad

11. **Recovering from Civil Conflict: Reconciliation, Peace and Development**
    edited by Edward Newman and Albrecht Schnabel

12. **Mitigating Conflict: The Role of NGOs**
    edited by Henry F. Carey and Oliver P. Richmond

13. **Ireland and International Peacekeeping 1960–2000: A Study of Irish Motivation**
    Katsumi Ishizuka

14. **Peace Operations after 11 September 2001**
    edited by Thierry Tardy

15. **Confronting Past Human Rights Violations: Justice vs. Peace in Times of Transition**
    Chandra Lekha Sriram

16. **The National Politics of Peacekeeping in the Post-Cold War Era**
    edited by Pia Christina Wood and David S. Sorenson

17. **A UN 'Legion': Between Utopia and Reality**
    Stephen Kinloch-Pichat

18. **United Nations Peacekleeping in the Post-Cold War Era**
    John Terence O'Neill and Nicholas Rees

19. **A Velvet Fist: The Military and Negotiation**
    Deborah Goodwin

20. **NATO and Peace Support Operations 1991–1999: Policies and Doctrines**
    Henning-A. Frantzen

21. **International Sanctions: Between Words and Wars in the Global System**
    edited by Peter Wallensteen and Carina Staibano

INTERNATIONAL SANCTIONS

Between words and wars in the global system

Edited by
Peter Wallensteen and
Carina Staibano

FRANK CASS
London and New York

First published 2005
by Frank Cass
2 Park Square, Milton Park, Abingdon, Oxon, OX14 4RN

Simultaneously published in the USA and Canada
by Frank Cass
270 Madison Ave, New York, NY 10016

Frank Cass is an imprint of the Taylor & Francis Group

© 2005 Peter Wallensteen and Carina Staibano editorial matter and selection;
individual chapters, the contributors

Typeset in Times by Keystroke, Jacaranda Lodge, Wolverhampton
Printed and bound in Great Britain by
St Edmundsbury Press, Bury St Edmunds, Suffolk

All rights reserved. No part of this book may be reprinted or reproduced or utilized in any form or by any electronic, mechanical, or other means, now known or hereafter invented, including photocopying and recording, or in any information storage or retrieval system, without permission in writing from the publishers.

British Library Cataloguing in Publication Data
A catalogue record for this book is available from the British Library

Library of Congress Cataloging in Publication Data
International sanctions : between words and wars in the global system /
[edited by] Peter Wallensteen and Carina Staibano.–1st ed.
p. cm. – (The Cass series on peacekeeping ; 21)
Includes bibliographical references and index.
1. Sanctions (International law). I. Wallensteen, Peter 1945–. II. Staibano, Carina.
III. Title. IV. Series.

KZ6373.I58 2005
341.5'82–dc22
2004018303

ISBN 0–415–35596–6 (hbk)
ISBN 0–415–35597–4 (pbk)

CONTENTS

List of illustrations   ix
Notes on contributors   xi

Introduction: new challenges for international sanctions   xv
PETER WALLENSTEEN AND CARINA STAIBANO

PART I
New sanctions: emerging patterns   1

1 **Trends in economic sanctions policy: challenges to conventional wisdom**   3
   KIMBERLY ANN ELLIOTT

2 **Consensus from the bottom up? Assessing the influence of the sanctions reform processes**   15
   THOMAS J. BIERSTEKER, SUE E. ECKERT, AARON HALEGUA AND PETER ROMANIUK

3 **Trends in UN sanctions: from ad hoc practice to institutional capacity building**   31
   CARINA STAIBANO

PART II
New sanctions capacity: emphasizing implementation   55

4 **Targeted sanctions and state capacity: towards a framework for national level implementation**   57
   THOMAS J. BIERSTEKER, SUE E. ECKERT, AARON HALEGUA AND PETER ROMANIUK

CONTENTS

5   A sanctions coordinator: options for enhancing compliance   65
    DAVID CORTRIGHT AND GEORGE A. LOPEZ

6   International armament embargoes and the need for end-use
    documents   75
    BJÖRN HAGELIN

PART III
New actors: empowering organizations   93

7   The EU as a new actor on the sanctions scene   95
    ANTHONIUS W. DE VRIES AND HADEWYCH HAZELZET

8   EU sanctions: three cases of targeted sanctions   108
    MIKAEL ERIKSSON

9   African sanctions: the case of Burundi   126
    LENNART WOHLGEMUTH

10 Implementing targeted sanctions: the role of international
    agencies and regional organizations   144
    DAVID CORTRIGHT, LINDA GERBER AND GEORGE A. LOPEZ

11 The World Trade Organization: sanctions for non-compliance   159
    STEVE CHARNOVITZ

PART IV
New targeting: enhancing legality and effectiveness   165

12 The Counter-Terrorism Committee: its relevance for
    implementing targeted sanctions   167
    CURTIS A. WARD

13 Protecting legal rights: on the (in)security of targeted sanctions   181
    IAIN CAMERON

14 Examining targeted sanctions: are travel bans effective?   207
    ERICA COSGROVE

CONTENTS

15 Positive sanctions: on the potential of rewards and target differentiation **229**
PETER WALLENSTEEN

Selected bibliography 242
MIKAEL ERIKSSON

Index 247

ILLUSTRATIONS

Figures

1.1	Trends in the use of economic sanctions	5
1.2	Sanctions trends in the 1990s	5
1.3	Effectiveness of foreign policy sanctions, 1914–99	9
1.4	Use and effectiveness of unilateral US sanctions	9
6.1	A holistic approach to end-use controls in support of international arms embargoes	79

Tables

1.1	Senders and targets in sanctions cases initiated 1970–99	6
1.2	Use and effectiveness of economic sanctions as a foreign policy tool	8
2.1	United Nations Security Council Resolutions imposing sanctions, 1990–2004	20–1
3.1	United Nations Security Council sanctions, 1966–2004	32–4
9.1	Exchange rates in central Bujumbura	131
15.1	Positive sanctions: possible measures	233
15.2	Targeted positive sanctions in internal conflicts	239

Boxes

6.1	List of end-use assurances	77
6.2	Example of an end-use document	86

CONTRIBUTORS

Thomas J. Biersteker is Director of the Watson Institute for International Studies and Henry R. Luce Professor of Transnational Organizations at Brown University. The author of seven books, his research focuses primarily on international relations theory and international political economy, and his recent activities include work with the UN Secretariat and the government of Switzerland on targeting sanctions. He received his PhD and MS from the Massachusetts Institute of Technology and his BA from the University of Chicago.

Iain Cameron is Professor in Public International Law at the University of Uppsala. His research interests lie in human rights, international criminal law and civil liberties. He is a member of *inter alia* the Advisory Board of the *Nordic Journal of International Law*, and a Rapporteur for the journal *European Public Law*. He holds an LLD and an LLM in International Law. He has published extensively in the fields of international law and constitutional law, particularly on international criminal law and human rights issues. He was an expert adviser to the Badinter Commission and to the Swedish government commission of inquiry proposing legislation on UN sanctions (Statens Offentliga Utredningar/Swedish Government Official Reports series 1995:28). He is the author of the report to the Swedish Foreign Office on Legal Safeguards and UN Targeted Sanctions (October 2002). His most recent books are *National Security and the European Convention on Human Rights* (Kluwer, 2000) and *An Introduction to the European Convention on Human Rights* (fourth edition, Iustus, 2002).

Steve Charnovitz practices law at Wilmer, Cutler and Pickering in Washington, DC, and serves as an adjunct professor at the Georgetown University Law Center. He is a member of the Board of Editors of the *American Journal of International Law* and the *Journal of International Economic Law*.

David Cortright is President of the Fourth Freedom Forum in Goshen, Indiana and a Research Fellow at the Joan B. Kroc Institute for International Peace Studies at the University of Notre Dame, USA. He has served as consultant or adviser to various agencies of the United Nations, the Carnegie Commission on Preventing Deadly Conflict, the International Peace Academy, and the John D. and Catherine T. MacArthur Foundation. Along with George A. Lopez he has provided research and consulting services to the Foreign Ministry of Sweden, the Norwegian Institute of International Affairs and the Foreign Ministry of Germany. He has written widely on nuclear disarmament, nonviolent social change, and the use of incentives and sanctions as tools of international peacemaking.

Erica Cosgrove is currently a Lecturer at the Woodrow Wilson School of Public and International Affairs at Princeton University in the United States where she teaches courses on public policy, international law and international relations. She has been involved in several studies and policy projects on sanctions and international security and has published articles, book chapters and policy briefs on these issues. She is writing a book on sanctions.

Sue E. Eckert is Senior Fellow and co-director of the Targeting Terrorist Finances and Targeted Financial Sanctions projects at the Watson Institute for International Studies, Brown University. Previously, Ms Eckert was US Assistant Secretary of Commerce where she was responsible for economic sanctions and export control policies, and also served on the professional staff of the Committee on International Relations of the US House of Representatives dealing with international trade and security issues.

Kimberly Ann Elliott is a Research Fellow at the Institute for International Economics, Washington, DC and has a joint appointment with the Center for Global Development. She is the author or co-author of numerous books and articles on a variety of trade policy and globalization issues. Much of her work focuses on the uses of economic leverage in international negotiations, including both economic sanctions for foreign policy goals and trade threats and sanctions in commercial disputes. She has co-authored two books on the costs of trade barriers in the United States and in recent years has turned to broader globalization issues, including the causes and consequences of transnational corruption, international labour standards, and the backlash against globalization.

Mikael Eriksson is currently involved in a research project focusing on EU (European Union) targeted sanctions. The project is sponsored by the Swedish Research Council. He has previously been the project leader of the Uppsala Conflict Data Project at the Department of Peace and Conflict Research, Uppsala University.

Linda Gerber is Research Director of the Fourth Freedom Forum in Goshen, Indiana. She received her Masters of Library Science degree from the School of Library and Information Science at Indiana Univesity, Bloomington. She participates in the joint Fourth Freedom Forum/Kroc Institute Sanctions and Security Project and has helped write and edit various reports and books produced by the Fourth Freedom Forum.

CONTRIBUTORS

Hadewych Hazelzet works as an official for the General Secretariat of the Council of the EU, Directorate General for External Relations, Directorate for United Nations and Human Rights.

Aaron Halegua is Research Assistant for the Targeted Financial Sanctions and Targeting Terrorist Finances projects at the Watson Institute for International Studies, Brown University. He will complete his undergraduate studies in International Relations in 2004. He is co-author of *Targeted Financial Sanctions: A Manual for Design and Implementation – Contributions of the Interlaken Process* (2001).

Björn Hagelin is Associate Professor in the Department of Peace and Conflict Research, Uppsala University. Since 1998 he has been the project leader on international arms transfers, Stockholm International Peace Research Institute (SIPRI). He worked for more than fifteen years as security analyst at the National Defense Research Institute (FOA), Stockholm. He has held guest research positions in the USA, UK, Australia and Norway.

George A. Lopez is Director of Policy Studies and Senior Fellow at the Joan B. Kroc Institute for International Peace Studies at the University of Notre Dame, USA. He has written extensively on human rights, repression and coercion, and in 2000 received the Choice Academic Book Award for *The Sanctions Decade*, co-authored with David Cortright. Between 1998 and 2003 he served as chair of the Board of Directors of the *Bulletin of the Atomic Scientists*.

Peter Romaniuk is Senior Research Assistant for the Targeted Financial Sanctions and Targeting Terrorist Finances projects at the Watson Institute for International Studies, Brown University, where he is a PhD candidate in Political Science. He is co-author of *Targeted Financial Sanctions: A Manual for Design and Implementation – Contributions of the Interlaken Process* (2001).

Carina Staibano has been at the Department of Peace and Conflict Research at Uppsala University since 2002 where she is Senior Research Assistant. She is the co-editor of *Making Targeted Sanctions Effective: Guidelines for the Implementation of UN Policy Options* (2003). Her most recent publication is on dialogue and international strategies in Burma (2004). Currently, Ms Staibano is working on United Nations system reform issues.

Anthonius W. de Vries is presently the Special Envoy of the Commission of the EU to the Republic of Azerbaijan; before that he was the economic and financial sanctions coordinator at the European Commission.

Peter Wallensteen, Professor, holds the Dag Hammarskjöld Chair in Peace and Conflict Research at Uppsala University, Sweden. He leads the Uppsala Conflict Data Program, which publishes annual data on armed conflict in the world and coordinated the Stockholm Process on targeted sanctions. This process presented *Making Targeted Sanctions Effective: Guidelines for the Implementation of UN Policy Options* to the Security Council in February 2003. In 2002 he published *Understanding Conflict Resolution: War, Peace and the Global System* (Sage).

Curtis A. Ward is an independent Adviser to the UN Security Council Counter-Terrorism Committee on Technical Assistance. He served as Chair of Working Group II in the Stockholm Process on the Implementation of Targeted Sanctions, 'Supporting Member State Capacity to Implement Targeted Sanctions'.

Lennart Wohlgemuth has been the Director of the Nordic Africa Institute in Uppsala, Sweden, since 1993. Prior to this he worked for many years for the Swedish International Development Cooperation Agency (Sida), most recently as Assistant Director General and head of the Sectoral Department. For the past few years he has been working actively as an expert on the Great Lakes region, and has published extensively.

INTRODUCTION
New challenges for international sanctions

The end of the Cold War removed the restraints on joint action for international peace and security that had been imposed by major power rivalry for more than four decades. From then on the United Nations (UN) was activated in ways that hitherto were politically inconceivable. This was also reflected in the practice of sanctions. This instrument of collective security was brought to use not only as a gesture or a recommendation but as a mandatory measure for all member states. During the decade and a half that has passed, the instrument has been gradually refined. The development of targeted sanctions is one aspect of this. This comes after unfortunate experiences with more comprehensive approaches. Also, it is noteworthy that other institutions have been engaged, and applied sanctions for new purposes.

This means that sanctions now are put to work in new situations. Obviously, issues of international peace and security figure prominently. There are, however, also other sanctions regimes. One of the novelties is the World Trade Organization (WTO) and its sanctions mechanism for upholding fair international trade practices. Indeed, WTO includes a prohibition against discriminatory trade measures that makes it difficult for other institutions (apart from the UN Security Council, whose mandatory decisions override all other commitments) and states to impose sanctions. For instance, the European Union has already earned a record for having sanctions for the protection and promotion of human rights and democracy, a new issue area for sanctions. However, EU sanctions have to be carried out within WTO rules. These concerns have also contributed to the development of sanctions measures in areas other than general trade. The targeting of resources of particular individuals in government and/or power positions are novel ways of making sure international legal frameworks are not disturbed. At the same time, those responsible for policy decisions are expected to reflect the impact of world opinion in concrete actions. This, furthermore, relates to matters of suspected war crimes. Individuals who are indicted or fear they might be indicted now refrain from travelling, as they might being brought to international courts. To be indicted or even suspected, thus, in effect could function as a form of travel restriction, a self-imposed sanction.[1]

INTRODUCTION
New challenges for international sanctions

The end of the Cold War removed the restraints on joint action for international peace and security that had been imposed by major power rivalry for more than four decades. From then on the United Nations (UN) was activated in ways that hitherto were politically inconceivable. This was also reflected in the practice of sanctions. This instrument of collective security was brought to use not only as a gesture or a recommendation but as a mandatory measure for all member states. During the decade and a half that has passed, the instrument has been gradually refined. The development of targeted sanctions is one aspect of this. This comes after unfortunate experiences with more comprehensive approaches. Also, it is noteworthy that other institutions have been engaged, and applied sanctions for new purposes.

This means that sanctions now are put to work in new situations. Obviously, issues of international peace and security figure prominently. There are, however, also other sanctions regimes. One of the novelties is the World Trade Organization (WTO) and its sanctions mechanism for upholding fair international trade practices. Indeed, WTO includes a prohibition against discriminatory trade measures that makes it difficult for other institutions (apart from the UN Security Council, whose mandatory decisions override all other commitments) and states to impose sanctions. For instance, the European Union has already earned a record for having sanctions for the protection and promotion of human rights and democracy, a new issue area for sanctions. However, EU sanctions have to be carried out within WTO rules. These concerns have also contributed to the development of sanctions measures in areas other than general trade. The targeting of resources of particular individuals in government and/or power positions are novel ways of making sure international legal frameworks are not disturbed. At the same time, those responsible for policy decisions are expected to reflect the impact of world opinion in concrete actions. This, furthermore, relates to matters of suspected war crimes. Individuals who are indicted or fear they might be indicted now refrain from travelling, as they might being brought to international courts. To be indicted or even suspected, thus, in effect could function as a form of travel restriction, a self-imposed sanction.[1]

INTRODUCTION

By now, the international community has gathered considerable experience in operating sanctions. In this volume the focus is on sanctions carried out by a collectivity of states in international global or regional frameworks, since the end of the Cold War. The interest is in targeted sanctions, their development, impact, requirement for effective action and new problems that may arise as part of the targeting of individuals. Targeted sanctions, some even call them 'smart' sanctions, provide new challenges to the international community.

This book is organized along the lines of four primary challenges. The first is to study if such sanctions are effective, compared to other sanctions, and whether their performance can be improved. Kimberly Ann Elliott (Chapter 1) writes, based on the data collected in a project at the Institute for International Economics, Washington, DC, on trends in government uses of sanctions, thus also including actions by the USA. Thomas J. Biersteker, Sue E. Eckert, Aaron Halegua and Peter Romaniuk (Chapter 2) look at the attempts to reform the sanctions regimes of the United Nations and what these actually have led to. This reform process has involved initiatives from countries such as Switzerland, Germany and Sweden. Finally, Carina Staibano (Chapter 3) studies trends in the UN application of sanctions with a focus on implementation measures. She argues that considerable improvement has been made, but on an ad hoc basis that now needs to be converted into sustained capacity.

Second, the effective use of targeted sanctions requires improved capacities within international organizations, member states and local societies. Simple comprehensive sanctions, isolating an entire country, are administratively easier to implement. The more sophisticated forms of sanctions that we are now witnessing demand new capacities, in order to be effective. Such needs are addressed in Part II of this volume. It is not only a matter of resources. It also calls for training in a new mindset and the development of new routines. The issue is concretized by David Cortright and George A. Lopez (Chapter 5) who examine the possibilities of sanctions coordinators at national and UN levels. Thomas J. Biersteker, Sue E. Eckert, Aaron Halegua and Peter Romaniuk (Chapter 4) study ways of developing the legal framework for national implementation. In an attempt to improve implementation Björn Hagelin (Chapter 6) discusses end-use certificates for arms transfers in order to enhance the impact of arms embargoes. This technique could have a potential also for other commodities.

A third challenge is the use of sanctions by new governmental actors. Noteworthy is the frequent uses by the European Union. Thus, contributions to this volume bring attention to EU procedures, decision making and experiences. Anthonius W. de Vries and Hadewych Hazelzet (Chapter 7) study the EU from a decision-making point of view, while Mikael Eriksson (Chapter 8) examines three different sanctions cases the EU has been engaged in. There are also other regional bodies and neighbouring countries that have undertaken sanctions. Lennart Wohlgemuth (Chapter 9) illustrates this through the example of Burundi. In some instances, international organizations are needed for the support of UN sanctions (e.g. in cases of financial freezes, aviation bans, etc.). There are also experiences in sanctions by international organizations themselves, and David Cortright, Linda Gerber and George A. Lopez (Chapter 10) show the mechanisms that have been developed to deal with situations of member state non-compliance. Steve Charnovitz (Chapter 11) elaborates on the same theme by scrutinizing the World Trade Organization's mechanism for making member states fall in line with the demands of the organization.

Finally, targeted sanctions have met some challenges which have to do with the targeting itself. Such sanctions aim at hitting particular individuals and units. At this time (February 2004) there are 515 persons and 109 entities worldwide on UN sanctions lists (financial sanctions and/or travel bans). Since the establishment of the lists now in place, in 1998 for Sierra Leone, in 1999 for the Taliban, in 2001 for Liberia and the Al-Qaida and in May 2003 for Iraq, there has been a steady increase in the number of listed individuals and entities. However, the decision on Liberia (December 2003) meant a reduction in numbers. The European Union has similar experiences. Curtis A. Ward (Chapter 12) examines how a UN innovation, stemming from the counter-terrorism activities after September 11, 2001, has worked. Furthermore, there are important legal ramifications for the individuals listed. These measures require legal instruments and concerted international action, something that is dealt with by Iain Cameron (Chapter 13) in an innovative way. This theme is further expanded by Erica Cosgrove (Chapter 14) in her study of the psychological effects, building on interviews with targeted individuals. Finally, Peter Wallensteen (Chapter 15) explores the theoretical approach of positive sanctions and incentives in differentiating between various segments of a country.

This work has been made possible through a grant from the Swedish Ministry for Foreign Affairs. It constitutes part of the Stockholm Process on the Implementation of Targeted Sanctions that was set in motion in 2001. The Stockholm Report with practical ideas for improving sanctions was handed over to the Security Council in February 2003. The present volume contains more elaborate – academic as well as practical – conclusions on the function of targeted sanctions.

Peter Wallensteen
Carina Staibano
Uppsala, June 2004

Note

1 This point has been made by Dr Krystyn Sikkink of the University of Minnesota.

Part I

NEW SANCTIONS
Emerging patterns

1
TRENDS IN ECONOMIC SANCTIONS POLICY
Challenges to conventional wisdom

Kimberly Ann Elliott

According to the conventional wisdom, one consequence of the more complex, less ordered environment following the end of the Cold War was a proliferation of US economic sanctions in response to demands to "do something," about ethnic conflict, human rights violations, drug trafficking, terrorism, or nuclear proliferation. In this conventional wisdom, US sanctions policy also became more unilateral, with Congress in the driver's seat and ethnic and other special interests doing the navigating. Evidence collected for the third edition of *Economic Sanctions Reconsidered* suggests that the conventional wisdom, while not entirely wrong, misses some important nuances.[1]

The frequency of US sanctions increased in the 1990s, but not as much as many people think, if a longer view is taken, and US sanctions have not been nearly as unilateral as in the past. Moreover, there was far more activity by the European Union than is generally recognized, often in cooperation with the United States but sometimes not. Also contrary to the conventional wisdom, Congress does not appear to have intervened more often than before, but the nature of that intervention has changed in important ways. Finally, the really big changes in sanctions policy have been in the United Nations (UN), not in the United States. The collapse of the Soviet Union freed the UN from its Cold War straitjacket and allowed it to intervene more aggressively in international affairs, including the imposition of mandatory economic sanctions ten times compared to just twice prior to 1990.

At the same time, the international economy has become increasingly integrated over the past two decades, with international trade and capital flows outpacing global output. This is a double-edged sword for economic sanctions, since interdependence increases potential vulnerability to disruption of these flows while also increasing the opportunities for evasion. These trends suggest that unilateral sanctions should become less effective, all else equal, and multilateral measures more effective. But the mechanisms for translating "economic pain into political gain" are still not well understood. The backlash against the humanitarian consequences of the broad UN sanctions against Iraq and Haiti resulted in a search for "smart" or targeted sanctions that dominated UN discussions of the sanctions tool into the new century.

Proliferation of economic sanctions in context

Figure 1.1 gives a snapshot of foreign policy sanctions launched in the twentieth century. Our study does not cover normal commercial reprisals, and our coverage probably misses several cases between countries of the second and third rank. That said, we have recorded 193 episodes, starting with World War I and extending through the UN sanctions against the Taliban regime in Afghanistan in 1999.[2] Nearly 60 new instances of sanctions were recorded in the 1990s and, of these, 42 involved the United States, usually in cooperation with other countries.[3] Contrary to conventional wisdom, less than a third of the cases involving the United States were unilateral initiatives. To be sure, several high profile cases launched in the 1990s (such as the sanctions against India and Pakistan over their nuclear weapons tests), as well as a few inherited from the past (notably Cuba, Libya, and Iran) were unilateral endeavors. But in episode-count terms, the United States was less a Lone Ranger in the 1990s than in the 1970s and 1980s. It is also notable that, while the number of new sanctions imposed nearly doubled in the 1990s compared to the 1980s, the increase is less dramatic when compared to the previous 1970s peak. Moreover, Figure 1.2 shows that the proliferation of cases slowed markedly after the first part of the decade.

Table 1.1 shows the changes in the distribution of sanctions users in the 1990s, as well as the changing geography of those most likely to be targeted with economic sanctions. It shows clearly the relative decline of the United States as a user of sanctions (though it remains at the top in absolute terms), as well as the sharply increased sanctions activity by the European Union, Russia, and the United Nations. It must be noted, however, that several of the UN sanctions are weakly enforced arms embargoes, designed to curtail civil strife and genocide, and most European sanctions involve relatively minor aid cutoffs.

The targets of choice have also changed in the 1990s, reflecting in various ways the end of the Cold War. The Soviet Union or its allies were targets of Western sanctions (mainly US-led) nine times in the 1970s and 1980s. In the 1990s, Western sanctions against the Former Soviet Union (FSU) sharply diminished, but the new FSU states were subject to six sanctions initiatives by Russia in attempts to induce more favorable economic or political terms from its newly independent neighbors (using our definition of a foreign policy sanction).[4] The other striking changes are the decline in new cases targeting Latin American countries and the rise in new cases targeting African countries. In broad terms, this reflects the swing of Latin America to democratic governance and the rising incidence of civil strife, despotic leadership, and large-scale killing in Africa. This shift in locus – from the US backyard to the European backyard – appears to be one factor in the decline in unilateral US sanctions and the rise in European initiatives.

TRENDS IN ECONOMIC SANCTIONS POLICY

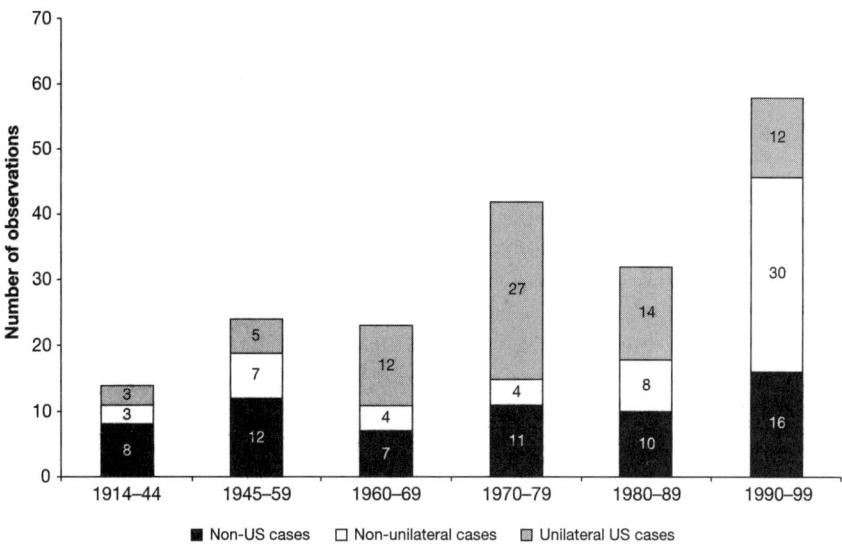

Figure 1.1 Trends in the use of economic sanctions

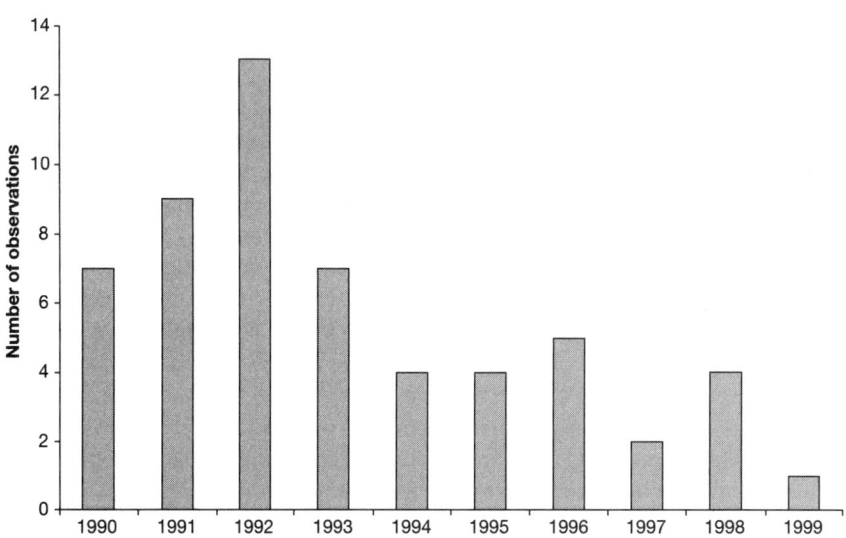

Figure 1.2 Sanctions trends in the 1990s

Table 1.1 Senders and targets in sanctions cases initiated 1970–99

	1970–89	1990–99
Primary senders[a]		
United States	48	25
Western Europe	9	19
USSR/Russia	0	6
United Nations	0[b]	11[c]
Targets by region		
Africa	11	18
Asia	15	6
Western Europe	7	7
Latin America	18	9
Middle East	6	4
USSR/FSU[d]	9	8

Notes
a These numbers are based on cases in which one or more sender country played a leadership role. They do not include senders that cooperated in a sanctions effort but without taking a leading role. UN cases are not included in the count of cases initiated by individual sender countries.
b Two UN cases initiated in the 1960s were ongoing in this period: Rhodesia and South Africa.
c This count includes the threat of UN sanctions against North Korea in the mid-1990s and the authorized but not mandatory actions against the Khmer Rouge faction in Cambodia.
d FSU = Former Soviet Union; this category also includes Soviet bloc members.

Congress and the role of domestic politics in US sanctions policy[5]

Another piece of the conventional wisdom about economic sanctions in the 1990s is that the US Congress became much more involved in imposing sanctions. This trend purportedly reflects a relaxation of national security constraints with the end of the Cold War and an increased role for domestic political motives. A careful analysis of US sanctions cases over time, however, suggests that the role of Congress in sanctions policy began changing well before the Cold War ended and that détente and other political and institutional changes in the US government were nearly as important as the collapse of the Soviet Union.[6]

In the 1970s (and 1980s), Congress was quite active on foreign policy issues, but it intervened in relatively limited fashion, passing laws to encourage the executive to impose sanctions in pursuit of Congress's goals, but not mandating it, or restricting economic or military aid, often for relatively short periods of time. Perhaps the most striking change between the 1970s and 1990s is the increase in country-specific sanctions legislation and the related increase in presidential sanctions intended to head off more severe, or less flexible, congressional action. The hand of narrow special interest groups (not necessarily ethnically based) is also more apparent in many of these cases than in earlier periods. There were just two country-specific congressional sanctions actions in the 1970s (the boycott of Ugandan goods) and 1980s (the Comprehensive Anti-Apartheid Act against South

Africa). There were five in the 1990s: new sanctions against Burma (investment and aid bans that were extended in 2003 to include a ban on all imports) and Romania (denial of most favored nation (MFN) status), and the expansion of sanctions against Cuba, Iran, and Libya.

Whether or not they served the national interest, the Helms-Burton bill targeting Cuba and the Iran–Libya Sanctions Act (ILSA) were both strongly influenced by special interest lobbying – the American Israel Political Action Committee in the case of Iran, the families of the Pan Am bombing victims in the case of Libya, and the Cuban-American community with respect to Helms-Burton. These bills also brought American policy to a new level of unilateralism by threatening sanctions against firms in third countries that do not cooperate with US sanctions against the primary target – even though their home governments have imposed no such sanctions against Iran, Libya, or Cuba. A similar bill, pushed by African-American groups concerned about slavery and religious groups concerned about persecution of Christians in Sudan's civil war, would have barred companies investing in Sudan's petroleum industry from issuing securities on US financial markets. It passed the House of Representatives overwhelmingly in early 2001 and was put aside only when Sudan offered to cooperate in the war on terrorism after the September 11 attacks. Nevertheless, the public pressure has caused some western oil companies to disinvest in Sudan, though they have been replaced by companies primarily from India and Malaysia.[7]

In addition, the lifting of some sanctions against Sudan, Pakistan, and Azerbaijan suggests that the war on terrorism could help to break the political logjam that has kept some sanctions in place for decades with no discernible benefit for US interests. More generally, it might induce the Congress to grant more flexibility and discretion to the executive branch in the conduct of foreign policy. As of early 2003, however, the relative bipartisanship that initially surrounded the war on terrorism began to fray amid concerns over the war in Iraq and the Bush administration's embrace of a preventive, rather than pre-emptive, war policy for protecting American interests. Still, amid international and domestic debates over how quickly political control should be turned over to the Iraqi people, the American takeover of Iraq did result in an end to the much-criticized UN embargo against that country (except for continuing controls on military goods and the seizure of Saddam Hussein's personal assets).

Sanctions effectiveness in the 1990s

Preliminary findings from the data collected for the third edition of *Economic Sanctions Reconsidered* suggest that, in terms of achieving their foreign policy objectives, sanctions in the 1990s were about as successful (or unsuccessful, depending on your perspective) as those imposed over the previous two decades. Our success scale has two components, both judgmental: was the objective achieved, at least in part? How much did the sanctions contribute to a positive outcome? By this scale, sanctions contributed to positive foreign policy outcomes

Table 1.2 Use and effectiveness of economic sanctions as a foreign policy tool

	Total number of observations	Number of successes	Successes as a percentage of the total
All cases			
1914–44	14	7	50
1945–69	47	20	43
1970–79	42	13	31
1980–89	34	8	24
1990–99	51	16	31
1914–99	188	64	34
1970–99	127	37	29
All cases involving the United States			
1945–69	28	16	57
1970–79	31	8	26
1980–89	22	3	14
1990–99	38[a]	10	26
1970–99	91	21	23
Unilateral US sanctions			
1945–69	17	12	71
1970–79	27	5	19
1980–89	14	1	7
1990–99	12	2	17
1970–99	53	8	15

Note
a Total differs from Figure 1.1 because success–failure assessments for all of the cases in Figure 1.1 were not available when this table was compiled.

(from the perspective of the sender government) 31 percent of the time, identical to the success rate in the 1970s and a slight recovery from the trough of the 1980s (Table 1.2).[8]

As in the second edition, the United States continued to perform more poorly with its sanctions policy than other senders, particularly when it acted unilaterally. As shown in Table 1.2, US unilateral sanctions succeeded in only 17 percent of cases in the 1990s and in only 15 percent for the entire 30-year period 1970–99. The latter is barely half the success rate for all cases of sanctions in this period and just a third of the 44 percent success rate for all other senders (calculated from figures in the Table; see Figure 1.3). The lack of a correlation between frequency of use and foreign policy effectiveness is one of the factors many observers point to in asserting that domestic politics must be driving US sanctions policy (Figure 1.4). The discussion above suggests that, while these critics may have a point, domestic politics is hardly the only factor in US sanctions policy.

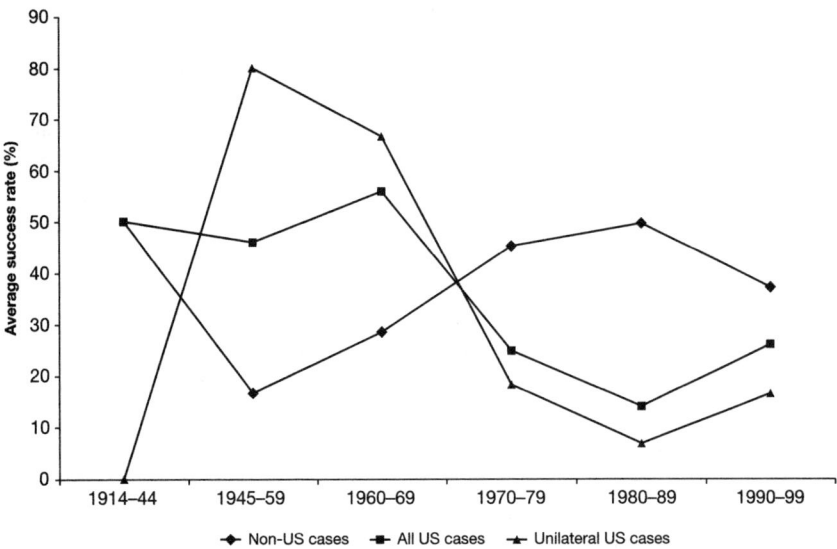

Figure 1.3 Effectiveness of foreign policy sanctions, 1914–99

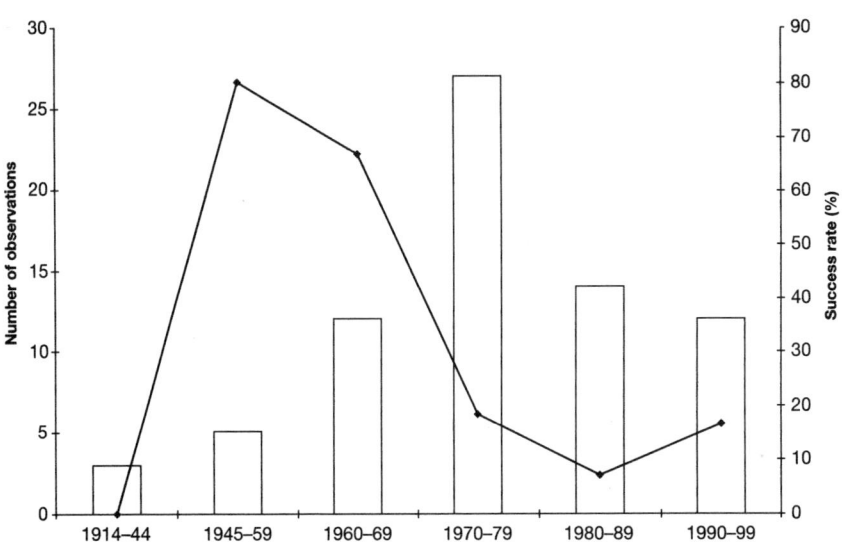

Figure 1.4 Use and effectiveness of unilateral US sanctions

The United Nations enters the sanctions scene

The end of the Cold War dramatically increased the latitude available to the United Nations Security Council (UNSC) when confronted with international threats to collective peace and security. That, combined with an evolving and expanding definition of collective peace and security, led the UNSC to become far more active in imposing economic sanctions than in the previous 45 years. After the initial burst of enthusiasm, however, disillusionment quickly set in. The embargo of Iraq dragged on for more than a decade, reducing living standards to levels not seen for decades, and the economic embargo of Haiti, one of the poorest countries on the earth, led hundreds of desperate refugees to risk their lives in attempts to flee to the United States. Moreover, the threat or use of military force was necessary in both cases to achieve the initial goals – reversing the Iraqi invasion of Kuwait and restoring the democratically elected government in Haiti. Comprehensive economic sanctions against Yugoslavia seem to have contributed to the peace settlement in Bosnia, but, again, at very high costs to the civilian population.

Thus, in these early cases, the economic and humanitarian pain inflicted by broad multilateral sanctions often seemed to outweigh the political gain. Over the course of the 1990s, the UN maintained a relatively higher level of sanctions activity than during the Cold War, but the nature of that activity has changed sharply – away from the comprehensive embargoes of the early decade to more limited measures:

- arms embargoes against Somalia and Rwanda; and
- arms embargoes plus travel restrictions and limited assets freezes against Afghanistan, Liberia, Libya, the UNITA faction in Angola, and the rebels in Sierra Leone.

Other than arms, the only restrictions on trade were limited restrictions on strategic commodities – lucrative diamond exports from rebel-held areas of Angola and Sierra Leone, respectively (as well as transshipments through Liberia in the latter case), an oil embargo against Sierra Leone for a short period when the rebels controlled the capital, and, in mid-2003, restrictions on timber exports from Liberia to deny the Taylor government revenues that might be used to fuel the renewed civil conflict there.

These sanctions have not been particularly effective. The civil war in Angola ended only after rebel leader Jonas Savimbi was killed and those in Sierra Leone and Liberia were disrupted by external military intervention. The only case with some degree of success was Libya but in that case, targeted UN sanctions were buttressed by comprehensive US sanctions and, still, it took years to gain the surrender for trial of the suspects in the Pan Am bombing case.

Nevertheless, continuing ethnic conflicts in the Balkans, Africa, and elsewhere, as well as the new war on terrorism, continue to generate interest in improving economic sanctions as a tool to promote international peace and security. In addition to looking for ways to ameliorate the costs of sanctions for innocent civilians and third parties, those interested in making multilateral sanctions more effective are questioning whether the UN has sufficient resources, authority, or expertise to monitor and enforce multilateral sanctions. Many in the UN and academic communities are also analyzing whether targeted sanctions such as those used in Africa and Afghanistan, in particular freezing the personal assets of political, military, and economic leaders in rogue states, can be made more effective.[9]

Rising interest in targeted sanctions

There has been extensive study in recent years of various types of targeted sanctions and many useful suggestions for how the United Nations could better organize itself to effectively use economic sanctions tools.[10] It is not yet clear, however, whether this particular circle – more effectiveness with less civilian impact – can be squared. More targeted impact also often means more limited impact, even for those targeted. Given the nature of most "rogue" targets, it is not always easy to find weapons that hurt them.

Travel and transportation sanctions fall at the mild end of the spectrum of targeted countermeasures, though how targeted they are depends on whether they affect individuals or sectors. Visa bans targeted at individual leaders or policy-makers impose primarily psychological and diplomatic costs, though they could interfere with efforts by nongovernmental actors to raise money or acquire arms if that required travel abroad. Somewhat broader transportation sanctions, such as the ban on air travel to and from Libya, clearly make international travel more difficult and costly and may, therefore, impede foreign direct investment or certain types of trade – in perishables, for example. But the economic costs are still likely to be relatively small.[11] Similarly, the costs of restrictions on cultural, scientific, or sports exchanges will be mainly psychological. This suggests that targeted travel and transportation sanctions are likely to be useful primarily as symbolic or punitive measures.

Arms embargoes are another tool in the panoply of targeted measures. They may have economic effects, by raising the price of military hardware and squeezing budgetary resources, but the major objective of these sanctions is to prevent conflict or at least reduce the level of violence by denying protagonists the means to carry it out. In theory, timely implementation and vigorous enforcement of an arms embargo might achieve these goals. But the obstacles to effective arms embargoes are numerous and the logistical challenges are compounded by the strategic fact that nominally even-handed arms embargoes may lead to highly inequitable results on the ground. This, in turn, can undermine support for the embargo, as happened in the former Yugoslavia where the UN arms embargo effectively favored local Serb forces, who had access to indigenous arms production that was denied to the Bosnians. Unfortunately, arms embargoes often appear to be part of an effort to conduct foreign policy on the cheap. Declaring an arms embargo is often an easy and obvious action to take when violent conflict breaks out. Equally often, however, the political will does not exist to apply the diplomatic and material resources necessary to make it effective.

One of the most frequently mentioned targeted sanctions is a freeze of the overseas assets of key individuals in the target country. The rationale behind this is two-fold: to hit those responsible for undesirable behavior and to spare those who have no power to change it. Financial sanctions in general do offer the potential for greater effectiveness than trade sanctions as a foreign policy tool because they are relatively easier to enforce, harder to evade, and may spur market-reinforcing effects. But broad financial sanctions are not necessarily more humane or more likely to affect elites. The question, then, is whether financial sanctions can be targeted in a way that both retains their relative utility and reduces the collateral damage.

Analysis detailed elsewhere[12] suggests that for financial sanctions targeted against individuals to have any chance of success,

- regime leaders must hold assets abroad;
- the assets must be identifiable;
- and, in cases where compliance rather than punishment is the goal, the assets must be a large enough proportion of the targeted individuals' total assets that the costs of defiance – the value of the blocked assets – must be perceived as being larger than the political, economic, or other costs of complying with the sender's demands.

Thus, the first challenge is to find and identify the assets to be blocked, no mean feat when targeting corrupt dictators who have an incentive to hide their ill-gotten gains even before being targeted for sanctions. Moreover, analysis suggests that, even if successfully carried out, the economic and political effects of an asset freeze would be limited in many cases without complementary controls on flows. That is, if the targeted leadership can replenish their assets through additional theft and corruption, an assets freeze may have little impact.

These caveats suggest that targeted assets freezes, assuming that such assets can be found, will have the most utility,

- against corrupt dictators in poor countries with few resources or options for accumulating new wealth;
- when the goal is punitive or symbolic; or,
- when the sender seeks only modest changes in policy or behavior that do not threaten the regime's ability to hold power.

More ambitious goals relating to conflict prevention or abatement, or the restoration of democracy following a coup, would appear to be out of reach unless financial *flows* are also disrupted, such as by restricting the ability of Jonas Savimbi to sell diamonds or of Charles Taylor to sell tropical timber. Even then, however, that may not be enough because the costs of compliance – in some cases, imprisonment, exile, or even death – will exceed the costs of any economic sanction.

Summary

Economic sanctions were used more frequently in the 1990s, but not only by the United States and not with any more success on average than the previous two decades. US sanctions in general became less rather than more unilateral as the focus turned from Latin America to Africa. But the level of unilateralism was ratcheted up in a few prominent cases – especially Cuba, Iran, and Libya – where US policymakers failed either to bring the targets to heel or to convince allies to cooperate in imposing sanctions. Frustrated with the lack of success on either score, Congress, pushed by narrow but powerful constituencies, took matters into its own hands in these cases. Because of their prominence and the disputes that arose with key allies and trading partners, however, these cases disproportionately color the view that most people have of US sanctions policy in the 1990s. Far bigger changes occurred in United Nations sanctions policy and the European Union also became more active as the locus of so much foreign policy concern turned to its backyard in Africa.

But at least some of these trends seemed to be reversing themselves within just a few years as the costs and limitations of economic sanctions as a policy tool once again revealed themselves. Overall, the frequency of use declined after the initial surge in the early 1990s. Still the search for ways to make sanctions both more effective and less costly for innocent civilians, particularly at the United Nations, continues.

Notes

1 G. C. Hufbauer, J. J. Schott, and K. A. Elliott, assisted by B. L. Oegg, *Economic Sanctions Reconsidered*, 3rd edition, revised (Washington, DC: Institute for International Economics, forthcoming 2004).
2 This figure is higher than the 171 case studies that will be included in the book because some cases have multiple targets (10), goals (4), or distinct phases (8). Also note that all numbers in this chapter are preliminary and subject to change, as the database for the third edition of *Economic Sanctions Reconsidered* was still being finalized at the time this was written.
3 This figure is significantly lower than the 61 instances of new laws or executive actions authorizing sanctions catalogued in a 1997 National Association of Manufacturers study. In addition to including environmental and worker rights sanctions, which are excluded from *Economic Sanctions Reconsidered*, the NAM catalogue also includes actions that do not result in sanctions actually being imposed. See National Association of Manufacturers, "A Catalogue of New U.S. Unilateral Economic Sanctions for Foreign Policy Purposes, 1993–96," Washington, March 1997.
4 See D. W. Drezner, *The Sanctions Paradox: Economic Statecraft and International Relations* (Cambridge: Cambridge University Press, 1999).
5 This section draws on K. A. Elliott and B. L. Oegg, "Economic Sanctions Reconsidered – Again," presented at the International Studies Association, Annual Meetings, New Orleans, March 2002.
6 Tony Smith notes that the rise in social activism, which began in the 1960s, coincided in the 1970s with a number of institutional changes that weakened the seniority system in Congress and eroded party discipline more broadly. Congress also responded to

overreaching by presidents Johnson and Nixon in Vietnam by passing the War Powers Act in 1973. Events in this period both led Congress to intervene more than previously in foreign affairs and made it more open to special interest influence. See T. Smith, *Foreign Attachments: The Power of Ethnic Groups in the Making of American Foreign Policy* (Cambridge, MA: Harvard University Press, 2000), p. 91.

7 See Human Rights Watch, *Sudan, Oil, and Human Rights,* New York, 2003.

8 As shown in Figure 1.1 and Table 1.2, both the use and the effectiveness of sanctions declined in the 1980s, relative to the decades just before and just after. While we have not yet examined the explanatory variables in the database, one hypothesis to explain this might be that the Reagan administration was both more selective in its use of sanctions and more ambitious in the goals it sought to achieve, thus offsetting any benefits from greater selectivity.

9 On the humanitarian consequences of economic sanctions, see T. G. Weiss *et al.* (eds) *Political Gain and Civilian Pain* (Lanham, MD: Rowman & Littlefield, 1997); on UN sanctions, see D. Cortright and G. A. Lopez, *The Sanctions Decade: Assessing UN Strategies in the 1990s* (Boulder, CO: Lynne Rienner, 2000) for the International Peace Academy.

10 For detailed proposals on how to make targeted UN sanctions more effective, see the reports produced by the "smart sanctions" processes: P. Wallensteen, C. Staibano, and M. Eriksson (eds) *Making Targeted Sanctions Effective: Guidelines for the Implementation of UN Policy Options*, Uppsala University, Department of Peace and Conflict Research (Stockholm: Elanders Gotab, 2003); T. J. Biersteker, S. E. Eckert, A. Halegua, N. Reid and P. Romaniuk, *Targeted Financial Sanctions: A Manual for Design and Implementation – Contributions from the Interlaken Process*, organized by the Swiss Confederation in cooperation with the United Nations Secretariat and the Watson Institute for International Studies, Brown University (Providence, RI: Watson Institute, Brown University, 2001); M. Brzoska (ed.) *Design and Implementation of Arms Embargoes and Travel and Aviation Related Sanctions, Results of the "Bonn-Berlin Process,"* organized by the Bonn International Center for Conversion in cooperation with the Auswärtiges Amt (German Foreign Ministry) and the United Nations Secretariat (Bonn, FRG: Bonn International Center for Conversion, 2001).

11 An exception is countries where tourism is important. In such cases, restrictions on transportation to the target, or on the issuance of visas to residents of the sanctioning country who might want to visit the target country, could have severe economic effects. In such cases, however, it may also be difficult to disentangle the effects of the sanctions from the depressing effects on tourism of whatever instability or disturbance triggered the sanctions in the first place.

12 K. A. Elliott, "Analyzing the Effects of Targeted Sanctions," in D. Cortright and G. A. Lopez (eds) *Smart Sanctions: Targeting Economic Statecraft* (Lanham, MD: Rowman & Littlefield, 2002).

2

CONSENSUS FROM THE BOTTOM UP?

Assessing the influence of the sanctions reform processes

Thomas J. Biersteker, Sue E. Eckert, Aaron Halegua and Peter Romaniuk

In response to criticisms of comprehensive sanctions imposed by the United Nations Security Council in the post-Cold War period, especially those imposed against Iraq, the 1990s saw an increase in calls for sanctions to be directed against the individuals responsible for reprehensible policies and the elites who benefit from and support them. The idea of targeting sanctions has attracted much attention within the Council, and in the academic and NGO communities. Acknowledging the importance of this innovative approach to imposing sanctions, the governments of Switzerland, Germany, and Sweden took the lead in examining targeted sanctions, and advancing our understanding of the design and implementation of such measures. Through the three sanctions reform processes that they sponsored – the Interlaken (1998–2001), Bonn–Berlin (1999–2001), and Stockholm (2001–02) processes, respectively – these governments brought together practitioners, experts, and academics to consider targeted financial sanctions, travel and aviation bans, arms embargoes, and implementation issues in depth. As a result of these initiatives a range of specific recommendations for imposing and administering targeted sanctions have been advanced, and the normative shift away from comprehensive sanctions has matured further.

While these achievements are noteworthy of themselves, there exists no assessment of whether and how the sanctions reform processes have affected sanctions policy and practice within the Security Council. What evidence is there that consensus has been achieved around the idea of targeted sanctions? Further, if it can be shown that the recommendations of Interlaken, Bonn–Berlin, and Stockholm have been adopted at least in part, does this represent a lasting trend in reforming UN sanctions? What constraints upon further sanctions reform remain, notwithstanding the progress achieved in the past five years?

We argue that, through the sanctions reform processes, the broad normative shift away from comprehensive sanctions has influenced the policy and practice of sanctions imposed by the Security Council. We show this by reviewing the recommendations made in the three processes and noting their adoption in three important areas: procedures for the listing and de-listing of targets, procedures for permitting exemptions, and Member State reporting practices. While these influences manifest the normative preference against comprehensive sanctions, we caution that, under certain conditions, the apparent consensus around the idea of targeted sanctions may yet be challenged. For this reason, further research regarding the design, implementation, and effects of targeted sanctions is critical.

We present this argument in three parts. First, we summarize the proceedings and findings of the three sanctions reform processes. Second, we show how the recommendations of these processes have been adopted in (at least) three areas of sanctions policy. Finally, we reflect upon the conditions under which normative consensus around the idea of targeted sanctions may be questioned and challenged.

The Interlaken, Bonn–Berlin and Stockholm processes

The Interlaken Process

Because of increasing criticism of the effects of comprehensive sanctions directed against Iraq, and reflecting a growing interest in the potential use of targeted sanctions, the Swiss Government convened in March 1998 and again in March 1999 seminars of experts to explore ways of making United Nations targeted financial sanctions more effective. The sessions gathered representatives of governments, the private sector (financial community), the United Nations and other international organizations, as well as academia to discuss the challenges of designing and implementing targeted financial sanctions. The purpose of the sessions was to elaborate the specific requirements of financial sanctions, and to develop new options to refine the tool for exerting pressure directly on a targeted country's decision-makers through freezing their assets in the world financial markets. The results of the Interlaken Process significantly advanced the collective understanding of the promise and feasibility of targeted financial sanctions.[1]

The first meeting (Interlaken I) focused on the specific technical requirements of financial sanctions and identified a number of preconditions necessary for targeted sanctions to be effective: clear identification of the target, ability to identify and control financial flows, and strengthening the UN sanctions instrument. The first order challenge concerned the target, and the need for analysis regarding the vulnerability of targeted governments and elites; success of targeting depends to a large extent on the characteristics of the targeted country. In addition, a clear delineation of parties covered by the sanctions, as well as the nature of the sanctions themselves (extending to all financial assets, including property, or just blocking financial transactions) is necessary. Participants also noted that speed and discretion in determining targets and the specific sanctions – which are often difficult to accomplish in a multilateral setting – are critical to success.

The second Interlaken (Interlaken II) meeting further developed recommendations on the technical aspects of targeting, but most importantly, addressed issues arising from differences in implementation of financial sanctions among States. Experts noted that many Member States lack the legal authority necessary to implement the requirements of Security Council resolutions, and even among those with such capacity, great variation exists among implementation and enforcement – undercutting the overall effectiveness of UN sanctions.[2] In response, Interlaken II examined the basic elements required for national implementation, and developed a model law that would enable States to implement UN-authorized targeted financial sanctions quickly, fully, and consistently. Also, to promote more uniform implementation across Member States, common definitions of core terms (such as "assets" and "to freeze") and standardized texts or building blocks of language were developed, such that the Security Council could draw upon these in drafting sanctions resolutions. Overall, the Interlaken seminars concluded that targeted financial sanctions are *technically* feasible, but that concrete measures at the national and international level are necessary for the instrument to be developed more fully and made effective.

To consolidate the contributions of the Interlaken Process into practical tools to refine the use of targeted financial sanctions, the Swiss Government asked the Watson Institute's Targeted Financial Sanctions Project to develop a manual for practitioners. *Targeted Financial Sanctions: A Manual for Design and Implementation* provides draft language for those developing Security Council resolutions imposing targeted financial sanctions (with options for different scenarios), and identifies "best practices" for the implementation of those measures at the national level. The manual, which was presented to the Security Council in October 2001, is intended to serve as a guide for both Security Council members and national officials responsible for designing and implementing targeted financial sanctions.

The Bonn–Berlin Process

Following the model of the Interlaken Process, the German Foreign Office, in cooperation with the United Nations Secretariat and Bonn International Center for Conversion, led an effort to examine the use of travel bans, aviation sanctions, and arms embargoes by the Security Council. These measures, like the targeted financial sanctions in conjunction with which they are often used, can also be tailored to target certain groups, economic sectors, or individuals. To explore ways of improving such sanctions, the First Expert Seminar in Bonn in November 1999 brought together experts from governments, academia, and NGOs to achieve three objectives. First, experts analyzed the deficiencies of the concerned sanctions, noting weaknesses at the UN level and implementation problems on the ground. Second, experts discussed a broad range of proposals to increase the effectiveness of arms embargoes and travel and aviation bans. The third task was to select a number of proposals from the broader list that would benefit from a more thorough examination by an Expert Working Group.[3]

In selecting which proposals to focus on, the preference was for "technical" (rather than "political") issues that would be useful to those working on these issues at the UN and in national capitals. Four Expert Working Groups were established: the first group focused on developing model resolutions and proposals for the national implementation of travel and aviation sanctions; the second group concentrated on how to make arms embargoes more effective "on the ground"; the third group developed model text for Security Council resolutions on arms embargoes; while the fourth suggested ways to improve monitoring and enforcement of arms embargoes at the UN level.

The Expert Working Groups met throughout 2000 and each produced draft reports, which were discussed at the Final Expert Seminar in Berlin, 3–5 December 2000. Participants in this seminar not only commented upon the work of the groups, but placed their proposals in the wider context of the sanctions debate. The final reports are published along with relevant commentary from the expert discussion in *Design and Implementation of Arms Embargoes and Travel and Aviation Related Sanctions: Results of the "Bonn–Berlin Process."* This document was presented along with the Interlaken Report to the Security Council at its special meeting devoted to targeted sanctions in October 2001.

The Stockholm Process

Recognizing the continued need to refine targeted sanctions to maximize their effectiveness, the Swedish Government continued the initiative which the Swiss and German governments began. The Stockholm Process, conducted in cooperation with the UN Secretariat and Uppsala University's Department of Peace and Conflict Research, was organized in a format similar to that of the Interlaken and Bonn–Berlin processes, and involved some 120 experts to focus on making targeted sanctions effective. Recognizing that "implementation" is essential for targeted sanctions to work, the Stockholm Process sponsored three Working Groups to make recommendations on different aspects of implementation – which can be found in the published outcome, *Making Targeted Sanctions Effective: Guidelines for the Implementation of UN Policy Options.*[4]

The first Working Group (responsible for Part II of the report) made recommendations on ways to improve implementation, particularly in terms of strengthening the role of the UN Secretariat. Proposals include designing sanctions with implementation in mind, maintaining support internationally for the sanctions regime, consistently monitoring and improving the regime, and building the Secretariat's capacity.

Working Group 2 (responsible for Part III) focused on implementation at the national level. For all targeted sanctions, the group stressed the importance of capacity-building and training programs, and noted that a Model Law can enhance implementation. The group also examined various types of targeted sanctions (financial, arms embargoes, aviation, etc.) and argued that they require different national measures, which were summarized in a series of tables.[5]

The third Working Group (authors of Part IV) took an in-depth look at aspects of targeting and discussed how to overcome the evasion of sanctions. The group noted the need for accurate targeting and procedures to maintain an up-to-date target list, as well as emphasizing the need for improving the way States report to the UN.

Through these three different sanctions reform processes, the normative rejection of comprehensive sanctions has been consolidated. What is less clear, however, is whether this normative shift has made a difference in the policies and practices of sanctions imposition in the Security Council.

Sanctions reform in practice

Table 2.1 illustrates the extent to which the Security Council has preferred targeted over comprehensive sanctions in the post-Cold War period. At a broad level, this record reflects the influence of the reform processes. At the level of Security Council procedures, recommendations of the Interlaken, Bonn–Berlin, and Stockholm reform processes have made several important contributions to the design and implementation of sanctions. In the areas of the listing and de-listing of targets, exemptions, and Member State reporting practices, innovations resulting from the reform processes have had concrete effects on the policy and practice of sanctions implementation.

Procedures for the listing and de-listing of targets

Prior to the Interlaken and Bonn–Berlin processes, the need for procedures to enable the de-listing of individuals erroneously targeted was recognized but mechanisms to address them had not yet been developed. Three central questions relating to procedures for de-listing were identified: first, who is entitled to submit requests for removal from the list? Should individuals affected be permitted to do so, or should Member States do so on their behalf? Second, on what grounds should appeals be permitted? Beyond erroneous listing, how might a target show that his/her behavior has changed sufficiently to warrant removal from the list? And third, how should appeals be decided? Given that lists are operationalized only through implementation by Member States, how should their interests in de-listing be considered by sanctions committees with the authority to remove names from the list?

Each sanctions reform process addressed these questions. Bonn–Berlin's Expert Working Group on Travel and Aviation Sanctions debated the desirability of a procedure for allowing individuals to petition sanctions committees for removal from a list of targets.[6] Although opinion was divided, the group concluded that individuals ought to be able to make submissions for their removal from the list of

Table 2.1 United Nations Security Council Resolutions imposing sanctions, 1990–2004

Cases (chronological)	Comprehensive	Targeted financial sanction	Arms embargo	Travel ban	Aviation-related sanction	Oil embargo	Ban on trade in diamonds	Ban on trade in timber
Iraq	Res 661 (1990)	Res 1483 (2003)						
Yugoslavia	Res 757 (1992); Res 942 (1994)	Res 820 (1993)	Res 713 (1991); Res 1160 (1998)					
Somalia			Res 733 (1992)					
Libya		Res 883 (1993)	Res 748 (1992)	Res 748 (1992)	Res 748 (1992); Res 883 (1993)	Res 883 (1993) (limited to oil-transporting equipment)		
Liberia		Res 1532 (2004)	Res 788 (1992); Res 1343 (2001); Res 1521 (2003)	Res 1343 (2001); Res 1521 (2003)			Res 1343 (2001); Res 1521 (2003)	Res 1478 (2003); Res 1521 (2003)
Haiti	Res 917 (1994)	Res 841 (1993); Res 917 (1994)	Res 841 (1993); Res 873 (1993)	Res 917 (1994)	Res 917 (1994)	Res 873 (1993)		
UNITA (Angola)		Res 1173 (1998)	Res 864 (1993)	Res 1127 (1997)	Res 1127 (1997)	Res 864 (1993)	Res 1173 (1998)	
Rwanda			Res 918 (1994); Res 997 (1995)					

Sudan		Res 1054 (1996)	Res 1070 (1996) (although ban never went into effect)
Sierra Leone		Res 1132 (1997); Res 1171 (1998)	Res 1132 (1997)
Afghanistan (Taliban and Al-Qaida)	Res 1267 (1999); Res 1333 (2000); Res 1390 (2002); Res 1452 (2002); Res 1526 (2004)	Res 1333 (2000); Res 1390 (2002); Res 1526 (2004)	Res 1267 (1999); Res 1333 (2000)
Eritrea/Ethiopia		Res 1298 (2000)	
Democratic Republic of Congo		Res 1493 (2003)	

Note

This table summarizes those resolutions *imposing* sanctions only (amendments that do not impose new measures are not included) and is current to April 2004. Sources: Office of the Spokesman for the Secretary-General, "Use of Sanctions Under Chapter VII of the UN Charter" http://www.un.org/News/ossg/sanction.htm; the various sites of the Sanctions Committees available at http://www.un.org/Docs/sc/committees/INTRO.htm and Security Council Resolutions available at http://www.un.org/Docs/sc/index.html (all accessed 20 April 2004).

targets. To reserve this power to Member States would be problematic in cases where leaders were targeted, or where non-state actors in conflict with states (e.g. the targeted sanctions against UNITA in Angola) were targets. The group considered that individuals ought to be able to petition committees for removal on grounds that a genuine mistake has been made, or that the targeted individual has changed his/her behavior. However, regarding the question of how such decisions should be made, the group noted that a change in behavior could be difficult to assess, and that political considerations are likely to dominate the committee's decision-making. The Group codified this approach by reference in the "Sanctions Committee" section of the mock resolution presented.[7]

The Interlaken Report builds upon the Bonn–Berlin Expert Working Group in asserting that individuals should be able to petition for removal from the list on the basis that their listing is unfounded, or that their behavior has changed. However, the mock resolution included in the Interlaken Report elaborates a more detailed process for deciding upon petitions for removal from target lists. In a separate paragraph, the Interlaken Report suggests that, upon receiving a request for removal, the committee may gather information, including from states and international organizations, in order to facilitate decision-making. Following consideration of this information, the committee should indicate whether the prohibitions imposed against the target should continue to apply.

Subsequent to Bonn–Berlin and Interlaken, the Working Groups of the Stockholm Process generally endorsed existing approaches, adding that guidelines should be established by sanctions committees to ensure transparency regarding de-listing procedures. Beyond this, in light of concern resulting from the listing of Swedish citizens as part of the revised sanctions against the Taliban, Al-Qaida and affiliates, the issue of legal safeguards for those targeted by sanctions was the subject of a separate study,[8] and is addressed in Chapter 13 of this book. We return to discuss this study, below.

The influence of the de-listing debate is most clearly seen in the work of the sanctions committee established pursuant to Resolution 1267 (1999) concerning the Taliban. Although the 1267 Committee initially found it difficult to form a list,[9] intervening events and subsequent resolutions have had the effect of improving the list of individuals and entities to whom the measures apply. The list establishes categories of detailed information about those targeted, recognizing that some information may not be available for each target.[10] It is updated periodically and sent to Member States at least every three months (Resolution 1455 (2003), para. 4), and is also available on the Committee's website.[11]

The Committee first circulated guidelines for the conduct of its work in November 2002, including a formal mechanism for considering requests for inappropriate inclusion on the target list.[12] Under this procedure, listed individuals, groups or entities may petition their government of residence and/or citizenship to request a review of the case. The target him or herself is responsible for establishing the grounds upon which such an appeal is based. The petitioned government is then asked to review all relevant information and begin bilateral discussions and information exchanges with the State originally responsible for inclusion, who may consult the chair of the Committee. The petitioned government may then, preferably but not necessarily with the designating State, submit a request for de-listing to the Committee, who will reach a decision by consensus of its members.[13] At the time of writing, four individuals and eleven entities have been de-listed.[14]

This procedure reflects the influence of the sanctions reform processes insofar as it addresses the three central questions regarding de-listing, set out above, and is articulated in formal guidelines. Contrary to the recommendations of the sanctions reform processes, however, the Committee denied targeted individuals from petitioning the Committee directly, did not clearly identify the grounds of appeal, and deferred to bilateral discussions between states the issue of resolving requests for de-listing. Although experience with the Committee's procedure is limited, the recommendations of the sanctions reform processes may yet have an influence on the Committee. As noted in Iain Cameron's October 2002 report to the Swedish Foreign Office, the inability of individuals to petition the Committee directly may give rise to concern, especially where their state of residence and/or citizenship is not interested in intervening on their behalf.[15]

In contrast to the 1267 Committee, the 1343 Committee (on Liberia) allows appeals for removal from individuals, in exceptional circumstances.[16] These appeals may also come from the state of which the target is a citizen, or from a UN office. While this Committee does not establish the grounds upon which appeals may be considered, the procedures for deciding upon such appeals are specified, as suggested in the sanctions reform processes.

Therefore, both Committees' consideration of the de-listing issue have been informed by the sanctions reform processes. While neither Committee's approach follows the Interlaken and Bonn–Berlin models precisely, those models specify three important questions (who is entitled to submit a claim that a target be removed, on what grounds, and how should such appeals be decided?) that have guided policy developments.

Exemptions[17]

Until recently, virtually all resolutions dealt with exemptions to financial and travel prohibitions in a similar manner, with the Council authorizing the Sanctions Committee to make exceptions to the prohibition for humanitarian, medical, or religious reasons. Paragraph 7(b) of Resolution 1343 (2001) concerning Liberia, authorizing exemptions to a travel ban established in the previous subparagraph, is quite typical: "*Decides* that measures imposed by subparagraph (a) above shall not apply where the Committee established [by this resolution] determines that such travel is justified on the grounds of humanitarian need, including religious obligation." Thus, two areas were left vague: first, the exact criteria for granting exemptions; and second, how the exemptions process was to be administered.

The Interlaken Process tackled the first of these issues by developing a menu of fifteen specific exemptions to a financial sanction that the Council could include in the resolution.[18] On the second point, the Interlaken Report also suggested that to avoid overburdening the Sanctions Committee, some (or all) of these exemptions could be left to States to administer.[19] Sharing a similar mission, the Bonn–Berlin Expert Working Group on travel bans said the "thrust of the work of the Expert Working Group is to develop options and arguments for greater specificity in Security Council Resolutions,"[20] and supported the development of criteria and a process for administering exemptions. The Stockholm Process, while not suggesting specific text or procedures, did note the importance of the Council providing "clear and complete mandates" to sanctions committees, and called for greater transparency of the exemptions process.[21] The impact of both the general call for greater clarity, as well as of the specific suggestions made in these processes, is evidenced by the recent activities of two sanctions committees.

Resolution 1452 (2002) establishes separate procedures for three different kinds of transactions excluded from the assets freeze against Usama bin Laden, Al-Qaida, the Taliban and associated individuals and entities. First, paragraph 1(a), offers a list of specific purposes for which an exemption may be granted, many of which are suggested in the Interlaken Report – namely, foodstuffs, rent, medicines, taxes, insurance, utility charges, legal services, and the maintenance of funds. Moreover, such exemptions are granted by a State notifying the 1267 Committee of its intention to do so and not receiving a negative decision by the Committee within 48 hours of notification – the amount of time recommended in the Bonn–Berlin Report.[22] Alternatively, the second exemption, which permits payments from frozen accounts for "extraordinary expenses," requires a positive statement of approval by the Committee (subparagraph 1(b)).

Resolution 1452 also establishes two cases under which adding funds to a targeted account is acceptable. The first allows for payments of "interest or other earnings due on those accounts" to be added (subparagraph 2(a)) and the second permits "payments due under contracts, agreements or obligation that arose prior to the date on which those accounts became subject to the" prohibitions (subparagraph 2(b)). Again, both of these exemptions are included in the Interlaken Report. Further, the Committee is not involved in the administration of this exemption, as the authority remains entirely with Member States.

The Council has also responded to the call for greater transparency in the administration of exemptions. Subparagraph 3(a) of Resolution 1452 (2002) charges the Committee with the task of maintaining "a list of the States that had notified the Committee of their intent to apply the provisions of paragraph 1(a) above . . . and as to which there was no negative decision by the Committee." Maintenance of such a list may mark the emergence of a trend among sanctions committees. The Liberia Committee, established pursuant to Resolution 1343 (2001), also maintained a list of the exemptions to the travel restrictions that it approved with the authority granted to it by Resolution 1343 (2001) para. 7(b). That Committee granted eighteen exemptions to the travel ban.[23]

Consistent with the recommendations of the Interlaken, Bonn–Berlin, and Stockholm processes, the Liberia Committee in 2003 went far beyond the 1267

Committee by establishing a clear and detailed procedure for the administration of exemptions to the travel ban (imposed by Resolution 1343 (2001), paragraph 7(a)). The procedure calls for any request to be submitted in writing to the Chair of the Committee, establishes a deadline for the submission of such applications, and notes the Committee's right to attach conditions to any exemptions it may grant. The Committee also specified exactly what information must be included in an application for an exemption to the travel ban, which includes information on the proposed traveler, the purpose of the travel, a complete itinerary, and the modes of transportation to be used.[24]

Member State reporting practices

As a result of the Security Council's Counter-Terrorism Committee (CTC) established pursuant to Resolution 1373 (2001), the quality and quantity of reporting by Member States to the Council has increased dramatically.[25] While this record of compliance reflects enhanced political will surrounding the issue of terrorism, the substance of the reporting requirements set out by the CTC owes much to the sanctions reform processes.

Traditionally, the quality of reports submitted by most Member States to sanctions committees have been poor, typically consisting of no more than one sentence indicating that States had "taken all necessary steps to comply with the requirements of the resolution." Many states failed to submit reports at all. Sanctions experts in both the Interlaken and Bonn–Berlin processes suggested measures to improve Member State reporting, without which monitoring of sanctions at the UN level is made more difficult.

The Interlaken Report[26] enumerated specific categories of information that sanctions committees should require from states in order to monitor effectively the implementation of financial sanctions, and suggested the types of information to be elaborated in the text of the resolution itself, along with specific time periods at which reports are to be submitted. Further, the use of templates was endorsed as a means of ensuring that States are appraised of the information sought by committees. Similarly, the Bonn–Berlin Expert Working Group advanced the idea of a questionnaire for States to respond to regarding implementation that could form the basis of their reports.[27]

To facilitate Member States' preparation of reports on actions to implement Resolution 1373, the CTC adopted detailed guidance along the lines suggested in the Reports regarding the format and substance of reporting requirements. In a guidance note issued in October 2001, the Chairman of the CTC requested that Member States structure their reports to the Committee as responses to a series of specific questions that relate to the paragraphs of Resolution 1373.[28] This was particularly important in establishing a threshold for substantive reporting, and helped to serve as a basis for dialogue with States. Under CTC procedures, reports are evaluated by experts, who then provide formal responses to Member States. For the most part this expert feedback is not public,[29] although the exchange between the CTC and a Member State can be gleaned by reading successive reports.

In light of these developments, and the high rate of compliance with 1373 reporting requirements, the Stockholm Report took note of lessons from the CTC process and sanctions regimes. Working Group 3 developed "Guidelines to Assist States in Preparing Reports on Sanctions Implementation,"[30] with detailed questions concerning the implementation of different types of targeted sanctions. Subsequent developments have further reinforced more detailed reporting by establishing clear criteria against which states are to report. The text of Resolution 1455 (2003) calls for States to report on, "[A]ll . . . investigations and enforcement actions, including a comprehensive summary of frozen assets of listed individuals and entities with Member States territories" (para. 6). The Sanctions Committee also issued guidance for Member State reports, including the specification of 26 items against which states are to report, broken down by type of sanction.[31] Beyond the 1267 Committee, the Liberia Panel of Experts referred directly to the outcomes of the Stockholm Process in developing a model questionnaire for Member State reporting on the implementation of the targeted measures against the Liberian leadership.[32]

In summary, the sanctions reform processes have had a very important and positive influence on reporting by Member States to the Security Council. As a result of specific guidance, questions, and the dialogue between Member States and the sanctions committees/CTC, reports on national measures to implement sanctions have improved dramatically and resulted in an unprecedented amount of information. While it is too early to determine if the Council has the resolve to act on such information to compel compliance with sanctions, enhanced reporting requirements appear to be a lasting innovation that will be part of future sanctions regimes.

Other influences

The sanctions reform processes have influenced Council action in other ways. For example, regarding the targeted financial sanctions against UNITA, the Monitoring Mechanism suggested that Member States ought to investigate the movement of targeted funds "before and after" the location of those funds, and proposed that evidence of "such exhaustive investigations, applied retroactively, have been made on all identified accounts should be provided."[33] The idea of such "retroactive reporting" was initially proposed in similar form in the Interlaken Report, which also offered resolution draft text to require such investigations.[34]

The Bonn–Berlin Report noted that effectively implementing a travel ban requires collecting "as much information as possible about the individuals concerned," or listed – a point also stressed in the Interlaken Report for targeted financial sanctions.[35] The list of travel ban targets maintained by the Liberia (1343) Sanctions Committee utilized five types of identifying information (name; alias; date of birth; passport number; and designation)[36] – all but the last of which can be found in the target information the Bonn–Berlin Report recommends collecting for a travel ban. The list developed by the 1267 Committee seeks to provide an even greater number of "identifiers" for each target, including all the Interlaken suggestions[37] as well as others (such as national identification number and the date placed on the list). This Committee's list of targeted entities follows Interlaken's recommendations as well, asking for any known aliases, addresses, and other relevant information.[38] Finally, this information must not only be collected, but efficiently disseminated – causing the Bonn–Berlin Expert Working Group to suggest the "increased use of the Internet," and making all "relevant information ... available on a website,"[39] which is exactly what these two committees have done.

The recent contributions of the Stockholm Process regarding Expert Panels have also influenced UN policy. For instance, Working Group 1 identified the need not only to provide specific mandates to these bodies, but also clear guidance on how to proceed in achieving them and methods to be used.[40] In drafting Resolution 1474 (2003), which renews the Somalia Arms Embargo Panel of Experts, the Council appears to have followed this advice. Eight specific subparagraphs (paragraph 3 (a-h)) are offered that clearly detail the mandate and operations of the group.

Conclusion: whither comprehensive sanctions?

In this chapter, we have presented evidence that the sanctions reform processes have influenced policy and practices regarding sanctions, reflecting a broader normative shift away from comprehensive sanctions. Indeed, we find it difficult to envision a return to the use of comprehensive sanctions by the Security Council in the near future. However, it remains the case that the move toward targeted sanctions has occurred in a historical context conducive to such normative change. On the one hand, the deleterious consequences of the comprehensive sanctions against Iraq required that the Security Council develop alternatives if sanctions were to remain a viable policy tool. On the other hand, the apparent failure of armed multilateral humanitarian interventions meant that responses to post-Cold War crises not involving the use of force remain desirable. Therefore, in a period of increased Security Council activity, targeted sanctions offered an appealing alternative. Still, there are two scenarios under which the consensus forged through the sanctions reform processes may come under pressure.

First, enduring implementation problems and successful strategies of evasion may give rise to the perception that targeted sanctions are unlikely to achieve their aims, or have been tried and failed. All sanctions create incentives for evasion, which are felt keenly by states sharing close relationships with targets, and these problems are acute in targeted sanctions regimes. In each sanctions reform process, participants noted that targeted sanctions are difficult to implement, often requiring an administrative capacity and resources beyond many states. Therefore, measures to enhance implementation and counter evasion are necessary to maintain consensus around the efficaciousness of targeted sanctions. The sanctions reform processes, as well as the experience of the CTC, provide useful proposals for improving effectiveness through assistance to Member States facing implementation problems. In this regard, capacity-building initiatives to ensure that targeted measures are as effective as possible are critical to the long-term viability of targeted sanctions.

Second, the battery of critics that claim "sanctions don't work" may find evidence to extend their argument to cover targeted sanctions. Such an argument asserts that targeted sanctions can have comprehensive effects in some cases. After all, most targets (whether individuals, groups, or economic sectors) are embedded in a larger network of suppliers, service sector providers, and/or consumers, such that the effects of targeted sanctions cannot be entirely limited to targets. Also, targeted elites often possess the means to pass on the burden of sanctions to their populations.[41] The possibility that the economic effects of targeted sanctions may not be limited to the intended targets alone warrants careful consideration by scholars and practitioners. Additional work to improve targeting and understand evasion tactics is necessary.

For these reasons, among others, optimism regarding targeted sanctions must be qualified.[42] However, we should not be overly cautious in reflecting on the advances in targeted sanctions policy resulting from the sanctions reform processes. Rather, as we have discussed, the initiatives of the Swiss, German, and Swedish governments have had demonstrable effects and have further reinforced the normative shift away from comprehensive sanctions. While these developments occurred in a specific historical context, and may be challenged under certain conditions, it is difficult to imagine a return to comprehensive sanctions in the near future.

As important as the reform processes have been, however, in refining the sanctions instrument, more analysis is required. The continued utility of targeted sanctions will depend on the ability of States to effectively implement them, and of the UN to effectively monitor and enforce them. We need to continue to explore targeted sanctions to consolidate goals of efficiency and effectiveness, and provide policymakers a genuine option "between words and wars."

Notes

1 The Interlaken Process website – http://www.smartsanctions.ch – provides the findings and discussions of the Process, including the published outcomes of Interlaken I and II.
2 See N. Reid, S. E. Eckert, J. Chopra and T. J. Biersteker, "Targeted Financial Sanctions: Harmonizing National Legislation and Regulatory Practices" in D. Cortright and G. A. Lopez (eds) *Smart Sanctions: Targeting Economic Statecraft* (Lanham, MD: Rowman & Littlefield, 2002), pp. 65–86.
3 The Bonn–Berlin Process website – http://www.smartsanctions.de – provides comprehensive information on the Process.
4 The Stockholm Process website – http://www.smartsanctions.se – provides complete information on the deliberations of the Working Groups, and other relevant documents.

5 Stockholm Report, pp. 67–81. This argument is explored in greater depth in Chapter 4 in this volume.
6 See Bonn–Berlin Report, pp. 55–58.
7 Bonn–Berlin Report, p. 55.
8 See, I. Cameron, "Targeted Sanctions and Legal Safeguards," Report to the Swedish Foreign Office, October 2002. Available at: http://www.jur.uu.se/arkiv/sanctions.pdf
9 Resolution 1267 was passed in October 1999. A modest list of targets was not circulated until April 2000 (see press release SC/6844, 13 April 2000).
10 For individuals, the Committee seeks the name(s), title, designation, date and place of birth, aliases, nationality, passport number, national identification number, address, and other supplementary information of those listed; while for entities, it seeks the name, aliases, former names, address, and other supplementary information. As we mention below, the kinds of information now requested about targets may represent the further influence of the sanctions reform processes. Compare "New Consolidated List of Individuals Associated with the Taliban and Al-Qaida Organisation" (available at http://www.un.org/Docs/sc/committees/1267/1267ListEng.htm) with the Interlaken Report, p. 8.
11 The list is available at: http://www.un.org/Docs/sc/committees/1267/1267ListEng.htm
12 "Guidelines of the Committee for the Conduct of its Work" (adopted on 7 November 2002 and amended 10 April 2003). The de-listing procedure is set out in Section 7 of the amended guidelines, available at:
http://www.un.org/Docs/sc/committees/1267/1267_guidelines.pdf
13 For further information, refer to Section 7 of the Guidelines document:
http://www.un.org/Docs/sc/committees/1267/1267_guidelines.pdf
14 See http://www.un.org/Docs/sc/committees/1267/1267ListEng.htm
15 See Cameron, p. 19. Cameron is skeptical of de-listing procedures generally, preferring legal assurances over political ones. Consistent with Cameron's later discussion (p. 39), our pragmatic view is that such political measures as de-listing and exemption procedures (see below) are a valuable way of ameliorating the unintended consequences of targeted sanctions, given that alternative legal solutions to erroneous targeting are unlikely to be adopted.
16 See "Procedures for updating and maintaining the list of persons subject to travel restrictions pursuant to resolution 1343 (2001)," 18 March 2003. Available at:
http://www.un.org/Docs/sc/committees/Liberia2/Proced_TBL.pdf
17 The Bonn–Berlin Report offered a definition to distinguish "exemptions" (not requiring the approval of the Sanctions Committee) and "exceptions" (requiring approval of the Committee). This definition is followed in the Interlaken Report, but has not been observed in practice. For present purposes, the use of the terms should be understood on a case-by-case basis.
18 Interlaken Report, pp. 72–75.
19 Interlaken Report, pp. 20–21.
20 Bonn–Berlin Report, p. 48.
21 Stockholm Report, pp. 24–25.
22 Bonn-Berlin Report, p. 58.
23 See: http://www.un.org/Docs/sc/committees/Liberia2/Liberia2waiverEng.htm
24 See http://www.un.org/Docs/sc/committees/Liberia2/waiver_proc_en.pdf
25 For example, there is now evidence of universal compliance with the "first round" reporting requirement of 1373. See "Letter dated 15 July 2003 from the Chairman of the Security Council Committee established pursuant to resolution 1373 (2001) concerning counter-terrorism addressed to the President of the Security Council," S/2003/710, p. 2.
26 See pp. 30–32.

27 See Bonn–Berlin Report, pp. 34–35, 61, 81–82.
28 Note from the Chairman, "Guidance for the submission of reports pursuant to paragraph 6 of Security Council resolution 1373 (2001) of 28 September 2001," 26 October 2001. Available at: http://www.un.org/Docs/sc/committees/1373/guide.htm
29 The exception is the general expert commentary by Dr Walter Gehr, "Recurrent Issues," Briefing for Member States, 4 April 2002. Available at: http://www.un.org/Docs/sc/committees/1373/gehr.html
30 Stockholm Report, pp. 129–132.
31 Guidance for reports required of all States pursuant to paragraphs 6 and 12 of resolution 1455 (2003). Date not specified. Available at: http://www.un.org/Docs/sc/committees/1267/guidanc_en.pdf
32 See S/2003/779, pp. 37–38.
33 See Report of the Monitoring Mechanism on Sanctions against UNITA, S/2002/486, 26 April 2002, p. 37, para. 235.
34 Interlaken Report, pp. 17–18.
35 Bonn–Berlin Report, p. 58; Interlaken Report p. 8.
36 http://www.un.org/Docs/sc/committees/Liberia2/1343_list.htm
37 Interlaken Report, p. 8.
38 http://www.un.org/Docs/sc/committees/1267/1267ListEng.htm
39 Bonn–Berlin Report, p. 58.
40 Stockholm Report, p. 56.
41 Norrin Ripsman raises a similar point in discussing the literature on "smart sanctions": "The Challenge of Targeting Economic Sanctions," *International Journal*, Vol. 57, No. 4 (Fall 2002), pp. 647–651.
42 See A. Tostensen and B. Bull, "Are Smart Sanctions Feasible?" *World Politics*, Vol. 54 (April 2002), pp. 373–403.

3
TRENDS IN UN SANCTIONS
From ad hoc practice to institutional capacity building

Carina Staibano

This chapter presents an overview of trends and practices in United Nations sanctions policy with a special focus on implementation measures mandated by the Security Council. It also examines trends and changes in the *use* of sanctions by the United Nations Security Council. Based on these past practices some recommendations on how to improve the implementation of targeted sanctions are then presented.

First, a discussion over changes in the use of sanctions by the UN will be introduced. Each sanctions regime will then be presented chronologically and analysed from the implementation perspective. From this, some general and case-specific observations are made on innovations in the UN system. In the final part the author argues in terms of the necessity to go from more or less ad hoc practice to systematic capacity building with regard to improving the implementation of UN sanctions.

UN sanctions and threats to international peace and security[1]

The primary function of the UN is to maintain international peace and security. During the Cold War, the Security Council imposed mandatory sanctions only twice, on Southern Rhodesia and South Africa. Depending on the coding criteria, we could say that after the end of the Cold War another 17 cases, under Chapter VII of the UN Charter, have now been added: Iraq I (Iraq vs Kuwait), Yugoslavia I, Somalia, Libya, Liberia I, Haiti, UNITA (Angola), Rwanda, Sudan, Sierra Leone, Yugoslavia II, Afghanistan/Taliban and Al-Qaida, Ethiopia and Eritrea, Liberia II, Democratic Republic of Congo (DRC), Iraq II and Liberia III. Data on these 19 cases are presented in Table 3.1.[2]

Mostly sanctions have been imposed in connection with ongoing or threatening armed conflicts. During the Cold War, such situations were normally described as

Table 3.1 United Nations Security Council sanctions, 1966–2004[a]

Country	Type of sanction	I – date imposed L – date lifted Exp – expiration	UN sanctions decisions	Monitoring/enforcement
Southern Rhodesia	Comprehensive economic sanctions	I 16 Dec. 1966 L 21 Dec. 1979	232 (1996) 460 (1979)	
South Africa	Arms embargo	I 4 Nov. 1977 L 25 May 1994	418 (1977) 919 (1994)	
Iraq I	Comprehensive economic sanctions	I 6 Aug. 1990 L 22 May 2003	661 (1990) 1483 (2003)	MIF (1990–2003) UNSCOM (1991–1999) UNMOVIC (1999–)
Iraq II[b]	Arms embargo, financial sanctions	I 22 May 2003	1483 (2003)	
Yugoslavia I	Arms embargo	I 25 Sep. 1991 L 18 June 1996	713 (1991) 1021 (1995)	Sanctions Assistance Missions (OSCE/EU) (1992–96)
	Comprehensive economic sanctions	I 30 May 1992 L 22 Nov. 1995	757 (1992) 1022 (1995)	
	Comprehensive economic sanctions	I 23 Sep. 1994 L 1 Oct. 1996	942 (1994) 1074 (1996)	
Yugoslavia II	Arms embargo	I 31 May 1998 L 10 Sep. 2001	1160 (1998) 1367 (2001)	UNPREDEP (1998–99)
Somalia	Arms embargo	I 23 Jan. 1992	733 (1992)	Expert Panel (Aug.–Nov. 2002, Apr.–Oct 2003, Dec. 2003–May 2004)
Libya	Arms embargo, flight ban, diplomatic restrictions	I 31 Mar. 1992 L 12 Sep. 2003	748 (1992) 1506 (2003)	
Liberia I	Arms embargo	I 19 Nov. 1992 L 7 Mar. 2001	788 (1992) 1343 (2001)	

Haiti	Arms and oil embargo, targeted financial sanctions	I 16 June 1993	841 (1993)
		L 27 Aug. 1993	861 (1993)
	Arms and oil embargo, targeted financial sanctions	I 18 Oct. 1993	873 (1993)
	Comprehensive economic sanctions	I 21 May 1994	917 (1994)
		L 16 Oct. 1994	944 (1994)
Cambodia[c]	Oil and log exports embargo	I 30 Nov. 1992	792 (1992)
		L 4 Nov. 1994	880 (1993)
UNITA/Angola	Arms and oil embargo	I 15 Sep. 1993	864 (1993)
		L 9 Dec. 2002	1448 (2002)
	Travel and flight ban	I 28 Aug. 1997	1127 (1997)
		L 14 Nov. 2002	1439 (2002)
	Targeted financial sanctions, diamond embargo	I 12 June 1998	1173 (1998)	Expert Panel/Monitoring mechanism (1999–2002)
		L 9 Dec. 2002	1448 (2002)
Rwanda	Arms embargo	I 17 May 1994	918 (1994)	UNICOI (1996–98)
		L 16 Aug. 1995	1011 (1998)[d]
Sudan	Diplomatic and travel restrictions	I 10 May 1996	1054 (1996)[e]
		L 28 Sep. 2001	1372 (2001)
Sierra Leone	Arms and oil embargo	I 8 Oct. 1997	1132 (1997)	ECOMOG (1997–99)
		L 5 June 1998	1171 (1998)[f]	Expert Panel (Sep.–Dec. 2000)
	Travel ban	I 5 June 1998	1171 (1998)
	Diamond embargo	I 5 July 2000	1306 (2000)
		Exp 5 June 2003	SC/7778–AFR/634
Afghanistan/ Taliban/Al-Qaida	Targeted financial sanctions (Taliban), flight ban	I 14 Nov. 1999	1267 (1999)	Monitoring Group (2001–) Analytical Support and Sanctions
	Arms embargo, targeted financial sanctions (Bin Laden and associates), flight ban	I 19 Dec. 2000	1333 (2000)	Monitoring Team (2004–05)
	Targeted financial sanctions (Al-Qaida), arms embargo, travel ban	I 16 Jan. 2002	1390 (2002)

continued

Table 3.1 continued

Country	Type of sanction	I – date imposed L – date lifted Exp – expiration	UN sanctions decisions	Monitoring/enforcement
Eritrea/Ethiopia	Arms embargo	I 17 May 2000 Exp 16 May 2001	1298 (2000) S/PRST/2001/14	
Liberia II	Arms and diamond embargo, travel ban Log/timber exports embargo	I 7 Mar. 2001 I 6 May 2003	1343 (2001) 1478 (2003)	Expert Panel (2001–03)[h]
Liberia III[i]	Arms and diamond embargo, travel ban, log/timber exports embargo and targeted financial sanctions[j]	I 22 Dec. 2003	1521 (2003)	Expert Panel (Jan.–May 2004)
Democratic Republic of Congo	Arms embargo	I 28 July 2003	1493 (2003)	Expert Panel (Mar.–July 2004) MONUC[k]

Source: Use of sanctions under Chapter VII of the UN Charter, www.un.org/News/ossg/sanction.htm

Notes

a The data in this table is current as of May 2004.
b In November 2003 a Sanctions Committee pursuant to Resolution 1518 was established to monitor the implementation of the sanctions.
c The sanctions against Cambodia were not mandated under Chapter VII of the UN Charter, but under Chapter VI (i.e. not mandatory measures).
d The sale and supply of arms to non-governmental forces remain prohibited under sanctions.
e This embargo never went into effect because of the expected humanitarian consequences.
f The arms embargo remained in place for members of the former military junta and the RUF.
g After the establishment of UN Assistance Mission for Sierra Leone (UNAMSIL) in 1999 by S/RES/1270, ECOMOG contingents started to withdraw from Sierra Leone, see S/RES/1289 (2000).
h Expert Panels on Liberia, April–October 2001, February–April 2002, July–October 2002, February–April 2003, May–October 2003, December 2003–April 2004, June–October 2003.
i Due to revised basis for action under Chapter VII of the Charter to reflect the changed circumstances in Liberia, the Council dissolved the Committee established under Resolution 1343 (2001) (see Liberia II) and established the 1521 Committee.
j The Security Council decided to impose targeted financial sanctions against former president Charles Taylor and individuals associated with him by adopting Resolution 1532 in March 2004.
k By Resolution 1533 (March 2004) the Security Council authorised the UN Mission in the Democratic Republic of Congo (MONUC) to monitor, collect and dispose of arms in violation of the arms embargo.

interstate or colonial conflicts. Thus, the question of Rhodesia was seen as a matter of an organized decolonization of Rhodesia, with the requirement that the majority should rule, not the minority that unilaterally declared the country independent. Similarly, the issue with respect to South Africa was – at the heart of the matter – a question of majority rule and decolonization, although the argument in the UN contest was one of the threat posed by South Africa to neighbouring states. However one looks at these two situations, the reality was one of a question of government control in the country: who should rule? The strong objection to raising matters essentially within the jurisdiction of sovereign states precluded an explicit statement of this fact.

The preoccupation with internal affairs has continued with respect to the uses of sanctions. Thus, 14 of all UN sanctions regimes have dealt with internal wars or internal matters of governance or territory, i.e. more than 70 per cent of all sanctions regimes. Those that did not fit this category were 'classical' interstate situations in two instances (Iraq vs Kuwait, Eritrea vs Ethiopia) and new types of threats in three cases, relating to issues of terrorism (Libya, Sudan and Afghanistan). It means that UN uses of sanctions have closely followed the global security agenda since the end of the Cold War, where issues of internal wars and terrorism have gained a stronger significance than previously was the case. In that way sanctions have been regarded as an instrument among others available to the UN Security Council. It contrasts the more expressive uses of sanctions during the Cold War, when the instrument was seen more as a way of communicating a stand, rather than expecting it on its own to achieve significant political change.

Several of these sanctions measures have had the aim of reducing or controlling overall economic activity of the targeted state. This was the case with Rhodesia, as well as Iraq I and Yugoslavia I. These situations have also been among the most debated in the sanctions literature and have had an important effect of initiating the search for more refined measures.

During the 1990s, however, more defined types of targeted measures have emerged. Most notably are financial sanctions, where particular leaders and significant individuals are exposed to sanctions, rather than the full nation. This means that the sanctions aim at affecting the internal balance of power in conflict situations. It reflects that the international community does not necessarily see its role as one of being a neutral third party but, rather, may define conflicts in terms of one or the other party being more responsible for the threat to international peace. This can be observed in most of the sanctions cases. Often the measures were aimed at the government, in order to force it to change. In some instances, however, the reverse was true, the measures aimed at strengthening the incumbent government by targeting opponents (UNITA (Angola), Rwanda, Sierra Leone, Iraq II and DR Congo). Only in the Horn of Africa has this not been the case. The arms embargo on Somalia included the entire territory and did not discriminate between different actors. The same was true for the arms embargo on Ethiopia and Eritrea (an interstate war). In these cases, it meant that the international community was not prepared to take sides. In both instances it was coupled to mediation efforts by the UN and other international actors.

UN sanctions 1966–2003 and international implementation measures

Southern Rhodesia

The unilateral declaration of independence by the Smith regime in Southern Rhodesia in 1965 resulted in the first UN application of mandatory sanctions as a main tool of the world body. The sanctions were initiated immediately after the declaration of independence by the colonial power, Great Britain. Then the measures were recommended by the UN Security Council, became mandatory in 1966 and remained in force until the end of 1979. The UN sanctions on Southern Rhodesia were aimed at the illegal racist minority regime of Southern Rhodesia and its prevention of the country's independence under majority rule.[3] The Security Council imposed sanctions on export commodities such as tobacco and copper in addition to oil and arms imports. A UN Sanctions Committee tasked with examining the reports from the Secretariat and of seeking information from Member States about implementation and possible sanctions-breaking activities was not set up until two years after the adoption of the sanctions, i.e. May 1968.[4]

The Sanctions Committee received a great number of reports of sanctions violations but the networks of illegal trade were often too complex to track and expose for a committee with limited resources. Governments were reported to be slow and reluctant to reply or follow-up on enquiries. It seems safe to say that the cases actually dealt with represented no more than the tip of an iceberg of sanctions evasions. An attempt was made to establish a manual of documentation and procedures to assist governments in detecting and dealing with sanctions violations but this was considered an issue too much of a 'technical nature' to be dealt with by the Committee and its delegates.[5] This is a remarkable reaction as the work of the sanctions committees (implementation, monitoring, exemptions, etc.) is more of a technical than diplomatic nature.

In the initial phase of the sanctions regime a Commonwealth Sanctions Committee was set up to maintain surveillance over trade and to attempt to monitor the sanctions (the Committee was renamed the Commonwealth Committee on Southern Africa in 1976). In practice, however, the Committee had a very limited impact on the overall sanctions implementation as well as the evasion strategies.[6] After the Lancaster House agreement on the future of Rhodesia in 1979 the sanctions were removed and the Committees dissolved.

South Africa

Sanctions on South Africa were imposed as a response to the government of South Africa's acts of repression, its continuance of the system of apartheid and its attacks against neighbouring states. It had taken almost thirty years for the Security Council to reach common understanding that the apartheid regime and its attacks against neighbouring independent states constituted a threat to international peace and security. Resolution 418 in November 1977 imposed an arms embargo. A Sanctions Committee was set up one month later.

As the resolutions did not include any provisions for monitoring implementation, the Committee took the initiative to establish contacts with a number of non-governmental organizations. These provided information and input concerning the effects of sanctions. There were also contacts with other actors and experts in the field, including journalists, trade union leaders, academics and parliamentarians, and a number of hearings were held. In theory, this arrangement can be seen as a successful example of how NGOs and civil society can contribute to the monitoring and enforcing of sanctions. However, in the case of South Africa the arms embargo was not respected by all Member States and seems to have failed to restrict the government's access to arms.[7]

The sanctions were terminated as South Africa's first non-racial government was inaugurated in May 1994. Seventeen years of unsuccessful UN sanctions were ended.[8]

Iraq

The Security Council in its Resolution 661 (1990), following Iraq's invasion and illegal occupation of Kuwait in August 1990, imposed economic sanctions on Iraq. This included a full trade embargo barring all imports from and exports to Iraq, exempting only medical supplies, foodstuffs and other items of humanitarian nature. By the same resolution a Committee of the Security Council was established to monitor compliance with the sanctions. In addition, Resolution 670 (1990) introduced a ban on flights destined to land or take off in Iraq, again with humanitarian exemptions.

A novel device was contained in Resolution 665 (1990) which called upon states with maritime forces in the area to halt all inward and outward maritime shipping to ensure implementation of the sanctions and to prevent smuggling. To that end, a Multinational Interception Force (MIF) was set up by interested member states, which operated in the area until 2003. The force began as a bilateral effort by the United States and the United Kingdom in 1990. Later it was endorsed by the Western European Union (WEU) and gained support from Argentina, Australia, Bahrain, Belgium, Canada, France, Greece, Italy, New Zealand, the Netherlands, Spain and the UAE. Member states of the Gulf Co-operation Council (GCC) provided logistical and personnel support to MIF, and accepted that vessels diverted for violating UN sanctions against Iraq entered their waters. MIF was not mandated under Chapter VII of the UN Charter but was recommended by the Security Council.[9]

In 1991 a Special Commission on Monitoring (UNSCOM) was established, which was to carry out immediate on-site inspection of Iraq's biological, chemical and missile capabilities. UNSCOM was mandated by Resolution 687. Five years later in March 1996 the sanctions enforcement was further enhanced when an export and import monitoring system was established. Iraq and countries exporting to Iraq had to notify UNSCOM and the IAEA (International Atomic Energy Agency) in the supply of 'dual-use' items to Iraq. In 1999, the United Nations Monitoring, Verification and Inspections Commission (UNMOVIC) replaced UNSCOM and took over its functions.[10]

After widespread international criticism of the humanitarian situation in Iraq under comprehensive sanctions, the Security Council in 1995 adopted the Oil-for-Food Programme (OFFP), with the first humanitarian supplies arriving in 1997. Under the OFFP the Iraqi government was enabled to sell oil and use the revenues for humanitarian supplies. The programme was initiated as a temporary solution to alleviate the humanitarian crisis in the country and it quickly became the sole source of food for 60 per cent of Iraq's population.

In May 2002, the Security Council decided to approve a new revised list of commodities in its sanctions against Iraq. In short, this meant that weapons imports continued to be banned, and dual-use technologies on the GRL (Goods Review List) would be subject to review, but all other civilian imports would be allowed to flow freely into Iraq.[11] However, the difficulties remained with the Sanctions Committee's case-by-case review of applications for humanitarian imports and the frequent holds placed on items that could be considered dual use. As a consequence the reconstruction of the Iraqi economy and of necessary civilian facilities remained severely restricted.

Since the departure of UNSCOM from Iraq in 1998, no new weapons monitoring had been conducted until after the passing of Resolution 1441 in November 2002. In this decision the Council strengthened the inspection regime and provided Iraq with a final opportunity to comply with its disarmament obligations. Following this, inspections were taken up again and UNMOVIC and IAEA were allowed into the country. However, the inspections came to an end in March 2003 before they had been concluded, just prior to the US–UK military action against Iraq.

Since May 2003, after the fall of the Iraqi government, comprehensive economic sanctions are no longer in place against the country. The Sanctions Committee established in 1991 was terminated at the end of 2003. However, an arms embargo is still ongoing and in addition targeted financial sanctions against former members of the Iraqi government have been imposed.[12] In November 2003 a new Security Council Committee was established to update and identify individuals and entities subject to financial sanctions.[13]

Federal Republic of Yugoslavia

As part of an effort by the UN, the European Union (EU) and the Organization for Security and Co-operation in Europe (OSCE) to restore peace and dialogue in the Federal Republic of Yugoslavia (FRY), the Security Council imposed a general and complete arms embargo against the country in September 1991. A subsequent resolution set up a Sanctions Committee.[14] In May 1992, in response to the FRY's involvement in the war in Bosnia–Herzegovina, the Council imposed full trade sanctions, a freeze on the FRY government's financial assets, a ban on maritime and air traffic, and a ban on participation in international sporting and cultural events. Belgrade's diplomatic status was also downgraded.[15]

In response to numerous reports of violations, the Security Council took a proactive approach and in November 1992 decided to strengthen the sanctions regime, for instance by prohibiting the trans-shipment through the FRY of petroleum, coal, steel and other products. In addition, the EU and OSCE started a programme, Sanctions Assistance Missions (SAMs), to implement, monitor and enforce the sanctions regime.

Sanctions assistance missions were set up in October 1992 in Hungary, Romania and Bulgaria; in Macedonia in November 1992; and in Croatia, Ukraine and Albania in early 1993. They operated jointly with the EU sanctions monitoring missions. In each of these countries the SAMs consisted of a European, a United States and a Canadian customs official, led by a representative of one of the participating OSCE countries and supported by a small staff. Each SAM filed reports and sent information relating to suspected violations to the SAM Communication Center (SAMCOMM) in Brussels, which, in turn, forwarded these to the relevant national authorities for further investigation. The SAMCOMM developed a system of computerized satellite communications linking its headquarters in Brussels with the UN Sanctions Committee in New York. The system was maintained by the United States and the purpose was to enable customs officials in the field to verify shipping documents and prevent the use of forged or falsified documents.

Other European organizations contributed further to the enforcement of sanctions against FRY. The WEU and NATO established in 1993 a naval task force in the Adriatic Sea, checking all vessels entering or leaving the Adriatic and inspecting cargoes and documents.[16] Major regional organizations contributed with financial resources and political will to enforce UN sanctions, in what many regard as a unique example of correctly enforced sanctions. Sanctions were also imposed against the Bosnian Serbs facing their refusal to accept the territorial settlement proposed in the peace plan in August 1994.[17]

As a result of the signing of the Dayton peace accord and the certification by the OSCE of the 14 September 1996 elections in Bosnia and Herzegovina, the Security Council decided to lift and terminate sanctions against the Federal Republic of Yugoslavia and the Bosnian Serbs.[18] Following that decision, the EU/OSCE Sanctions Assistance Missions also started to conclude their activities.[19]

However, in response to the mounting repression and violence in another part of the region, Kosovo, the Security Council in March 1998 adopted Resolution 1160, imposing an arms embargo on Yugoslavia. All countries were prohibited from selling or supplying arms or weapons related material to Yugoslavia. By Resolution 1186 (1998) the mandate of the UN Preventive Deployment Force (UNPREDEP) was widened to include the tasks of monitoring and reporting the flows on illicit arms and other activities prohibited under Resolution 1160.

The widening of UNPREDEP's mandate was due to the fact that the overall resources pledged by UN Member States would not allow for a comprehensive monitoring regime as envisaged in the resolution. The inclusion within UNPREDEP's mandate of monitoring of the arms embargo reveals an innovative side in UN sanctions implementation. UNPREDEP's mandate was not renewed beyond February 1999 as an extension was vetoed in the Security Council.[20] That meant that the arms embargo would not be monitored during a crucial phase of the Kosovo crisis.

The fall of Slobodan Milosevic in October 2000 resulted in the withdrawal of all UN sanctions on the country.[21]

Somalia

In January 1992 the Security Council imposed a comprehensive arms embargo on Somalia in response to the bloody factional fighting resulting in heavy loss of life, widespread material damage and a refugee crisis. Subsequently a resolution called for a Committee of the Security Council to monitor the implementation of the arms embargo.[22] As no on-ground monitoring mechanism was mandated, the Security Council and the Sanctions Committee limited activities to appealing to Somalia's neighbouring states and others in the region for information on reported or suspected violations. The problem with this arrangement was that many of Somalia's neighbours were themselves involved in violations of the arms embargo. For instance, eleven years later, in 2003, a report from the Expert Panel charged with the on-ground monitoring of the arms embargo cites Ethiopia as a country that has played an overt military role in Somalia. Eritrea and Djibouti are also reported to have been major suppliers of arms and ammunition.[23]

There has so far been only a marginal progress towards establishing any kind of widely recognized national government. Somalia, still characterized by anarchy and widespread lawlessness, is divided into fiefdoms run by clan leaders and warlords. More than ten years after the imposition of the arms embargo, in May 2002, the Security Council decided to act. First, the Council set up a team to prepare an action plan to assess the requirements for a Panel of Experts. The Panel's mandate was to investigate violations of the arms embargo and also to provide recommendations on possible practical steps and measures for giving effect to and strengthening the arms embargo.[24] Then, an Expert Panel was constituted. Its report to the Security Council came in March 2003 and one of its key findings is that there is a consistent pattern of breaches of the arms embargo against Somalia. The report states that the embargo has no normative value as it has not been enforced in any way and as none of the Somali faction leaders or their regional sponsors have been held accountable. There is an attitude of 'business as usual' prevailing among these groups.[25] It is the opinion of the Panel that the sanctions regime should be enhanced and implemented with increased determination.

The Security Council made no enforcement decision based on the findings of the Expert Panel. However, in April 2003 the Panel was re-established for a further period of six months to continue the investigations of sanctions violations.[26] The monitoring efforts continue as a monitoring group was established by the Council in December 2003, this time to focus on the ongoing arms embargo violations.[27]

Libya

In 1992, the Security Council imposed a total air and arms embargo in response to Libya's continuing refusal to extradite the suspects in the bombings of the Pan Am flight 103 which exploded over Lockerbie, Scotland. Resolution 748 also established a Sanctions Committee. In the resolution, it is stated that sanctions will be lifted if Libya agrees to extradite to the UK the two suspects in the Pan Am 103 bombing.[28]

Subsequent resolutions tightened sanctions on Libya by, among other measures, freezing Libyan funds and financial resources in other countries and banning the export to Libya of equipment for oil refining and transportation.[29] The sanctions on Libya were not comprehensive but target key sectors and particular commodities. In March 1999, it was announced that Libya had agreed to hand over the suspects for trial. On the basis of this development, the Security Council noted that the conditions for suspending the wide range of aerial, arms and diplomatic measures against the Libyan Arab Jamahirya had been fulfilled. All UN sanctions against Libya were suspended and the Committee dissolved.[30] In September 2003 the sanctions on Libya were terminated after the Libyan government had agreed to financially compensate the families of the bombing victims.[31]

Haiti

The Security Council threatened Haiti with an oil and arms embargo in June 1993 in order to ensure the departure of the de facto authorities and the restoration of the legitimate institutions in Haiti. In particular, this referred to the return from exile of the democratically elected president, Jean-Bertrand Aristide, who had been ousted by a military coup in September 1991. The same resolution also established a Sanctions Committee.[32] The sanctions included the freezing of foreign assets of the government or authorities in Haiti, or of entities, owned or controlled by the Haitian authorities. This action marked a shift in the practice of the Security Council when imposing sanctions, from the freezing of assets of governments to closing accounts of specific entities and individuals, making sanctions more targeted. This would be repeated in the sanctions against UNITA in Angola, the Taliban regime in Afghanistan and follow-on Al-Qaida sanctions and those on the Taylor regime in Liberia.

A few days before sanctions were to take effect the military junta agreed to enter into negotiations with Aristide. The sanctions were suspended in August 1993 by Resolution 861. However, delays in implementation and the preventing of the deployment of UN peacekeeping troops by the Haitian military led in May 1994 to the re-imposition of sanctions. At the same time Resolution 917 (1994) expanded the embargo to include all commodities and products (with the exemption of medical supplies and foodstuffs) and a travel ban.

Sanctions experts claim that the sanctions on Haiti were weakened considerably by the mixed messages from the United States and other major actors. The administration in Washington exempted, for example, US-owned export assembly factories from sanctions so that US businesses could maintain their operations in Haiti. The Dominican Republic undermined sanctions enforcement by opposing sanctions against its neighbouring country and as a consequence flows of goods continued to cross the Dominican borders on their way to Haiti. Little was done to monitor and enforce the sanctions on the ground. An attempt was made with a naval blockade but the effort was quite modest and did not have any real impact on the illicit trade. The naval blockade and the efforts to close the Dominican border to Haiti came at the very end of the crisis. These measures have been seen more as acts of desperation and improvisation by the Security Council to do something about the failing sanctions enforcement.[33] In September 1994, after the Security Council had authorized a military operation to depose the regime, but before any deployment, Aristide was returned to power.[34]

Angola

An arms and oil embargo was imposed on UNITA (União Nacional para a Independência Total de Angola) in September 1993, following UNITA leader Jonas Savimbi's refusal to honour the results of UN-supervised elections, and the rebel group's return to war. The same resolution also established a Sanctions Committee.[35] Despite repeatedly threatening to impose additional sanctions, the Security Council did not act until August 1997, when it introduced travel and diplomatic sanctions.[36] Fighting nonetheless escalated in 1998, prompting the Council in June to freeze UNITA's financial assets, ban all financial transactions with the group, and prohibit the trade of Angolan diamonds not certified by the government.[37] The Security Council took this action to strengthen the sanctions because UNITA refused to abide by the 1994 Lusaka Protocol and was continuing to wage war for control over the country's vast natural resources. With the sanctions against UNITA, the Council imposed sanctions directly on a non-state actor. The freezing of UNITA's financial funds and the prohibition of the trade with diamonds made the sanctions more targeted.[38] A marketing and certification programme to guarantee the origin of diamonds from non-UNITA sources was established. However, despite this system and industry participation, illegal diamond exports from Angola continued.[39]

After several efforts to improve the implementation of the measures imposed on UNITA,[40] the Council decided to establish an Expert Panel to trace violations on the ground. Of particular concern were areas such as arms trafficking, oil supplies, diamond trade, international representation and travel, as well as the moving of UNITA funds.[41] The Expert Panel owed much to Ambassador Robert Fowler who chaired the Angola Sanction Committee in 1999–2000. The mandate of such monitoring mechanisms has since then been extended. From 2000 to 2002 the monitoring body issued eight reports on the status of the Angola sanctions. This makes the Angola sanctions one of the more investigated.[42] In one of its last reports, it was concluded that a complex network of criminals, industry and government officials constantly violated the sanctions. Without this UNITA would not have been able to sustain the conflict on the level of military intensity that it did. The report also states that monitoring of violations enhanced the international compliance as it increased the risks and costs of those involved in sanctions busting.[43]

In December 2002, following the death of UNITA leader Jonas Savimbi, the sanctions against UNITA were terminated and the Sanctions Committee dissolved.[44]

Rwanda

In May 1994, one month after the genocide began in Rwanda, the Security Council imposed an arms embargo against Rwanda. The resolution also established a Sanctions Committee.[45] However, the attempt by the UN to stop arms from reaching the country came too late as major suppliers did not promptly incorporate the arms embargo into their domestic law. As a result, arms and ammunition continued to enter and cross the country.[46]

In response to widespread allegations and international speculation on the sale and supply of arms to former Rwandan government forces involved in the genocide, the Security Council decided to establish an International Commission of Inquiry (UNICOI). This was the first appointment ever of an independent monitoring mechanism to review the implementation of sanctions by the Security Council. The Commission's mandate was to collect information and to investigate breaches of the arms embargo in the Great Lakes region.[47] UNICOI issued six reports from 1996 to 1998, thoroughly documenting the supply routes and underground networks used to arm the rebels in eastern Zaire.[48] The Commission described fund-raising efforts of Rwandan rebels in Kenya, arms flows from southern and central Africa, and military co-operation between the governments of the Democratic Republic of Congo and Sudan. The Commission also found evidence of arms flows to the region from Eastern Europe even after the imposition of the arms embargo. The commissioners complained about the lack of co-operation from governments and officials in the region but also from states in Western and Eastern Europe.[49] The Security Council did not use these findings to enforce the arms embargo. No decision was taken on continued monitoring of the arms embargo, despite UNICOI's reports of violations. Since 1998 the ongoing arms embargo against Rwanda has neither been monitored nor enforced through specific implementation measures.

Sudan

In April 1996, in response to Sudan's lack of compliance with the Security Council's demand to extradite three suspects wanted in connection with the attempted assassination of President Hosni Mubarak of Egypt in June 1995 and the country's support of terrorist activities, the Council imposed limited diplomatic sanctions on Sudan.[50] More far-reaching travel sanctions and the setting up of a Sanctions Committee were provisionally approved by the Security Council but never implemented, due in part to Egypt's reluctance to support stronger actions, as well as a UN pre-assessment report on the likely humanitarian impact of such measures.[51]

In September 2001, the Security Council decided to lift and terminate the travel and diplomatic restrictions against Sudan and to dissolve the Sanctions Committee.[52]

Sierra Leone

In May 1997, the Armed Forces of the Revolutionary Front (AFRC) overthrew the civilian government of Ahmed Kabbah. Five months later, the Security Council, concerned over the military violence following the military coup, imposed an oil and arms embargo against Sierra Leone and established a Sanctions Committee. At the same time, it introduced travel restrictions on members of the military junta.[53] The Council also authorized the Nigeria-led military observer group (ECOMOG) of the Economic Community of West African States (ECOWAS) to enforce these measures, by force if necessary. This is the first UN example of regional organizations *authorized* by the Council to enforce sanctions. In reality, lack of resources severely undermined the effectiveness of these measures.[54]

Shortly after the sanctions were imposed, the junta accepted an agreement that called for the restoration of the elected civilian government and the demobilization of Sierra Leone's armed forces and rebel groups. However, as the junta leaders failed to implement the agreement, the ECOMOG troops in February 1998 toppled the military regime and Kabbah was returned to power. Although the civilian government was reinstalled, much of the country remained in rebel hands. The Security Council decided to lift all remaining sanctions against the government of Sierra Leone. Instead, it targeted the measures on leading members of the military junta and the Revolutionary United Front (RUF).[55] As RUF leader Sankoh, like Savimbi in Angola, had cornered a substantial part of Sierra Leone's diamond trade, the Security Council also imposed a ban on the direct import of rough diamonds from Sierra Leone. This was done through a certificate of origin regime.[56]

Resolution 1306 (2000) established a Panel of Experts to conduct on-ground monitoring of sanctions violations and to make recommendations to the Council. One of the key findings of the Panel was that the arms and diamond embargoes were repeatedly being broken. The government of Liberia with its president Charles

Taylor was found to be a major supplier and supporter of the RUF guerrillas in Sierra Leone. On the basis of the conclusions in the Expert Panel report a new sanctions regime was imposed against Liberia.[57] Despite the utility of the Expert Panel its mandate was not renewed. The mandate expired in December 2000. No further efforts were made to monitor these sanctions.

In June 2003 the Council chose not to renew the diamond embargo. The diamond sanctions were terminated as the Council believed that the Sierra Leone government could now control the diamond industry.[58]

Afghanistan/Taliban and Al-Qaida

In October 1999, the Security Council demanded the Taliban regime in Afghanistan close all terrorist training camps in the country and turn over Usama bin Laden to appropriate authorities. As these demands were not met, the Council imposed an aviation ban and a freezing of funds directly or indirectly owned or controlled by the Taliban. The same resolution also established a Sanctions Committee, known as the 1267 Committee.[59] The sanctions were widened in December 2000, when the Council established an arms embargo, as well as a ban on Taliban and Ariana Afghan Airlines offices abroad and financial sanctions aimed at Usama bin Laden and the Al-Qaida network.[60] A mechanism to monitor the arms embargo and the closure of terrorist training camps was established in July 2001.[61]

The attacks of September 11, 2001 led to a new level in the struggle against international terrorism. The counter-terrorism measures mandated in Resolution 1373 (2001) and subsequent resolutions were directed against individuals and entities involved in the financing of international terrorism. The resolution also established a new committee, the Counter-Terrorism Committee (CTC) to deal with such measures and to monitor and assist Member States in the implementation of the resolutions. As a consequence, the mandate of the monitoring group was widened and became more comprehensive. This was specified in Resolution 1390 (2002). Interestingly, the mandate for this monitoring group is extended for a period of one year at a time, compared to the practice seen in other cases where the Council seem to have preferred periods of 3–6 months. This reflects the higher degree of political will and commitment to counter terrorism after September 11, 2001.

Resolution 1390 from January 2002 targets Usama bin Laden, the Taliban and other individuals, groups, undertakings and entities associated with them, including the Al-Qaida organization as such. A travel ban was added and the arms embargo was amended to target the specified individuals and entities rather than an entity controlling a specific territory.

In January 2004 the monitoring regime was strengthened by the creation of an Analytical Support and Sanctions Monitoring Team to report on the implementation of measures by Member States.[62] In an effort to further revitalize the efforts to fight international terrorism the Security Council decided in March 2004 to restructure its Counter-Terrorism Committee. In Resolution 1535 it was decided that the CTC would consist of a Plenary – comprising the Security Council's 15 Member States and focusing on wider strategic and policy decisions – and a Bureau, which would be comprised of expert and Secretariat staff, known as the Counter-Terrorism Executive Directorate (CTED), headed by an Executive Director. Although originally conceived of as sanctions on Afghanistan, the regime now has a global reach.

Ethiopia and Eritrea

In May 2000, due to the continuing fighting between Eritrea and Ethiopia, the Security Council imposed an arms embargo against both states. The resolution's duration was for one year. The same resolution also established a Sanctions Committee.[63] With the setting of a twelve-month period for the arms embargo, time limits were introduced for the first time by the Security Council. If the sanctions were not renewed at the end of that period, they would expire and be automatically terminated. After the passing of that year the Council decided not to extend the measures, largely due to the commitments made by the two governments to abide by the agreement signed in Algiers (2000). The sanctions expired in May 2001.[64] No study of their impact was made by the UN.

Liberia

In November 1992, in response to the deteriorating conflict in Liberia, the Security Council imposed a general and complete arms embargo against Liberia. A Sanctions Committee to monitor the implementation of the sanctions was not established until three years later, in April 1995. No measures were taken by the Security Council to enforce the arms embargo or to monitor its implementation, until the establishment of the new sanctions regime on Liberia in 2001.[65]

In March 2001, the arms embargo was terminated and replaced by a renewed and tightened weapons and military equipment embargo, as part of a wider package of sanctions against Liberia. These new sanctions were adopted as the country was recognized as the primary supply base for the RUF guerrillas in Sierra Leone. As the government of Liberia did not cease its support for the RUF and other armed rebel groups in the region, the sanctions went into effect.[66] This was the first time the Council threatened and imposed mandatory measures against one country for its defiance of sanctions against another (secondary sanctions). Due to lack of compliance from the government of Liberia, the new sanctions entered into force in May 2001. The measures included, in addition to the arms embargo, a ban on the import of Liberian rough diamonds as well as a travel ban. The Council also decided to ban all Liberian registered aircraft. This stemmed from the conclusions of the Sierra Leone Expert Panel (S/2000/1195) that Liberian aircraft were used in violation of the arms embargo against Sierra Leone. In addition, the resolution established a five-member Panel of Experts, for a period of six months, to monitor the implementation of the sanctions and to investigate any violations.[67]

According to Expert Panel reports on the situation in Liberia the government in Monrovia continued actively to support the rebel groups. It was found that the arms embargo was being broken through a network of Serbian arms dealers and Chinese timber companies using fake documents.[68] In May 2003 the Council decided to extend the sanctions against Liberia for one year and in addition place a ban on the import of Liberian timber as the Taylor government continued to support rebel groups in the region.[69] The monitoring was also continued.

In December 2003, as a response to the changed circumstances in Liberia with President Charles Taylor leaving the government, the Council dissolved the Sanctions Committee and terminated the sanctions. Instead it imposed a new sanctions regime with revised prohibitions in connection with arms, diamonds, timber and travel, for a period of twelve months. It was also decided to re-establish the Expert Panel for a period of five months to monitor the situation on the ground.[70]

From case-specific innovations to general trends

The developments since the early 1990s have marked a shift in the practice of the Security Council when imposing sanctions. The Council has shown more flexibility when designing and updating sanctions. Its practice has moved away from the use of comprehensive trade sanctions towards more targeted and selected measures. Since 1994, no general sanctions have been imposed. Only four cases, Southern Rhodesia, Iraq I, Haiti and Yugoslavia I were comprehensive UN trade sanctions. The following 15 cases have concerned a limited number of sectors of a state's economy. Furthermore, the practice has changed from sanctions imposed on governments to measures also imposed on non-state actors, entities and individuals.

The sanctions innovations that can be seen were derived from unique political contexts, and were, at the time, seen as specific solutions to specific problems. When new situations arose these innovations again were useful and thus we can see them as trends, notably expert panels charged with the on-ground monitoring of sanctions, targeting of non-state actors, sanctions aimed at individuals, etc. Some innovations remained case-specific and were not repeated, for instance far-reaching monitoring and implementation systems like SAMs (in the case of FRY) and secondary sanctions (in the case of Liberia).

General trends

In 1992, the Security Council imposed sanctions on areas of Cambodia controlled by the PDK (Party of Democratic Kampuchea). Sanctions were thus for the first time targeted against a non-state actor, the Khmer Rouge. This was followed in 1993 by the targeting of a particular actor, UNITA, in Angola, as this party did not follow the internationally recognized agreements. In the case of Haiti, in 1993 measures were targeted against members of the Haitian military junta. In 1994, specific sanctions were imposed on Bosnian Serb areas. The practice of targeting non-state actors inside countries continued in the sanctions against Rwanda, Sierra Leone and Taliban/Al-Qaida. Although no specific evaluation has been made of the impact and efficacy of actor-specific targeting, this approach has gained general political support.

Initially, financial sanctions were imposed only on government assets, as in the cases of Iraq, Libya and Yugoslavia. Since 1994, however, beginning with the case of Haiti, the Council ordered the closing down of bank accounts of non-state entities and individuals. Assets freezes were imposed against the Haitian military junta members, UNITA leaders in Angola, the Taliban in Afghanistan, members of the government in Liberia and, of course, on a range of individuals and organizations in the counter-terrorism activities mandated in Resolution 1373 (2001) and subsequent resolutions (Al-Qaida sanctions). Also travel and flight bans have increasingly been applied on specified targets (Sudan 1996, UNITA 1997, Sierra Leone 1998, Taliban/Al-Qaida 1999/2002 and Liberia 2001).

The Security Council has imposed arms embargoes 17 times since 1991, most often as elements of larger economic sanctions. However, in Somalia (1992), Liberia (1992), Rwanda (1994), FRY (1998), Eritrea and Ethiopia (2000) and the Democratic Republic of Congo (2003) the Security Council imposed stand-alone arms embargoes. That is, in almost half of the cases.

The first monitoring mechanism to be established by the Security Council was the International Commission of Inquiry on Rwanda (UNICOI) in 1996. Following that, expert panels and monitoring mechanisms were set up in six cases, that is, Angola (1999), Sierra Leone (2000), Afghanistan/Taliban/Al-Qaida (2000), Liberia (2001), Somalia (2002) and in DR Congo (2004). This means that in the most recent cases some form of monitoring has accompanied the sanctions. It seems that this monitoring is also connected to the use of commodity sanctions.

Another step towards more targeted sanctions is the imposition of sanctions on specific commodities, in particular diamonds. Trade with conflict diamonds[71] was widely known to be used to fund military rebellion and human rights abuse. In 1998, the Security Council imposed, *inter alia*, an embargo on Angolan diamonds not controlled by the Angolan government.[72] The case of Sierra Leone also drew attention to the connection between diamond trade and war. This led the Security Council to decide on a diamond embargo on Sierra Leone in 2000.[73] It required a certificate of origin system, through which legal diamonds could be exported. In response to the findings that the Taylor government in Liberia used the revenues from the export of RUF diamonds, the Security Council imposed a diamond embargo also on Liberia in 2001.[74] Interestingly, in 2003 this was followed by a ban on Liberian timber exports as a number of reports indicated that revenues from timber exports were used by the Liberian government to continue to fund rebel groups in the region.

The embargoes on arms, diamonds and other commodities have now become an established practice, which may also require a closer monitoring of their implementation.

Case-specific innovations

With the imposition of sanctions against Liberia in March 2001, the Council for the first time introduced mandatory measures against one country because of its defiance of sanctions against another. Recognizing Liberia's role as the primary supply base for the RUF in neighbouring Sierra Leone, the Council imposed sanctions against the government of Liberia. Although reports have revealed a number of other sanctions cases where Member States have violated UN mandated sanctions, secondary sanctions have only been used once.

The use of regional and non-governmental organizations in the enforcement and monitoring of sanctions is an interesting development in UN sanctions policy and, as the overview shows, perhaps not fully explored. The first example was in Sierra Leone in 1997, where the Council authorized the Nigeria-led ECOMOG to enforce the sanctions. However, lack of financial resources undermined the group's work considerably. With better results, owing much to international and regional support and adequate financial resources, was the network of Sanctions Assistance Missions (SAMs) organized by OSCE and the EU in the case of the Yugoslavia sanctions.

Going from ad hoc practice to systematic capacity building

Adequate monitoring

The experience from the 1990s confirms that sanctions have little chance of succeeding without credible enforcement, monitoring efforts and concerted international co-operation. Continuous on-ground monitoring enhances the flexibility of the Security Council and helps sanctions committees respond with changes in the sanctions regimes. While the use of monitoring mechanisms has increased during the last decade, the monitoring mechanisms are still not integrated as a regular feature in UN sanctions policy. In Somalia (1992), Liberia (1992), Rwanda (1994), in the FRY (1998), in Eritrea and Ethiopia (2000) and in the Democratic Republic of Congo (2003), the Security Council imposed stand-alone arms embargoes. With the exception of the SAMs experience in the FRY, no serious international effort was made to enforce the embargoes. In Liberia (1992), the Sanctions Committee mandated to monitor the implementation of sanctions was not established until three years after the sanctions went into effect.

It is recommended that all sanctions regimes should have an independent, active monitoring mechanism as long as the sanctions are in force. The monitoring group for the Taliban/Al-Qaida sanctions is a model case as it was set up from the very beginning. In the Somalia case, a monitoring mechanism could in fact have contributed with recommendations on how to improve the current sanctions regime at an earlier stage. It took ten years of continued conflict and poorly implemented sanctions before the measures were evaluated. Still no decision has been taken by the Security Council to enforce the embargo at the time of writing.

Enhanced implementation through regional co-operation and assistance

The sanctions assistance missions (SAMs) were part of the sanctions against former Yugoslavia. Clearly, they contributed significantly to the success of the sanctions against former Yugoslavia and actually placed them among the more rigorously enforced UN sanctions. More than 200 customs officers and other experts were engaged in monitoring and enforcing sanctions in seven SAMs located in Yugoslavia's neighbouring states.[75] This is an experience that should be further explored by the UN in future sanctions implementation. The ECOMOG experience in the case of Sierra Leone also provided assistance to the region to facilitate the implementation of sanctions, although the assistance was limited. ECOMOG lacked the financial resources and technical capacity necessary for effective implementation. The Multilateral Interception Force (MIF) in Iraq should also be seen as an important initiative to enforce sanctions by the international community. In this case, the United States played a major part in the force. Another example comes from South Africa where the Sanctions Committee established contacts with a number of non-governmental organizations and other civil society actors to monitor and evaluate the sanctions. These experiences show that regional organizations, as well as NGOs, can play a significant role in the monitoring and enforcement of sanctions if political will as well as sufficient financial resources are available.

The sanctions committees

The sanctions committees are created by the Security Council to monitor the implementation of sanctions. These committees are administrative bodies and do not have on-site monitoring of the sanctions. They vary greatly in extent and effectiveness, depending both on the extent of the cohesion (or division) within the Security Council (international pressure and Member State interests) and the political and geographic circumstances of the target country and the leadership provided by the committee chairs. Sanctions committees seem to be more reactive than systematic in their work (see, for example, Rwanda, Somalia and Sierra Leone where the sanctions committees are quite passive compared to those for Iraq, FRY and Haiti). This results many times in decisions and strategies in the sanctions committees that are not always easy to understand for the general public. Why, for example, did it take the Security Council more than ten years of failed sanctions in Somalia to decide on a monitoring mission to the country?

Building capacity and expert knowledge

A question linked to the problem of highly politicized sanctions committees is the need to update and brief the delegates in the committees in a variety of expert areas necessary for sanctions implementation. Expertise of a more technical or operational nature needs to be present to facilitate the daily work in the committees. The policymakers and decision-takers at headquarter level need to have knowledge on how the decisions can be translated in practice and how they will be implemented in a given context. In 1977 the South Rhodesian Sanctions Committee rejected a proposal to establish a manual on procedures and documentation to assist governments in detecting and dealing with sanctions violations, on grounds that this was too technical an issue to be dealt with by the Committee. This is today no longer a valid or credible argument.

During the last decade sanctions have been used more frequently, compared to the period prior to 1990. Though the administration of sanctions has improved, the UN Secretariat needs to be further strengthened in response to this augmented burden, in terms of staff, resources and mandate. The UN Secretariat should be able to respond to the increasing demands stemming from an increase in sanctions work by providing information and meaningful analysis and assistance and support to other auxiliary mechanisms in their work to enforce and monitor sanctions. This increased workload should be made part of the regular work plan and budget, and should not be subject to temporary ad hoc solutions. Along with the increased reliance on sanctions by the Security Council, the establishing of monitoring mechanisms (expert panels) has also increased during this past decade.

The monitoring mechanisms need administrative, budgetary and logistical support and also some kind of institutional memory/database on information collected that could be of use to other monitoring groups. The mechanisms also require some kind of minimum co-ordination.[76] Regardless of the focus of this enhanced support, it is important that adequate resources are allocated.[77]

Stand-alone sanctions, with little or no enforcement, have very limited possibilities of altering the behaviour of targets. As it has been shown in this chapter, these 'low activity' sanctions cases, like Rwanda, Somalia and Sierra Leone, run the risk of becoming protracted without serious enforcement; they are left on their own. This affects sanctions efficacy and ultimately the legitimacy of sanctions in the eyes of the international community.

Notes

1 This section has benefited from the work of Patrik Johansson, Research Assistant at the Department of Peace and Conflict Research, Uppsala University during 2003.
2 In addition there is one case of a sanctions regime under Chapter VI, on Cambodia in 1992.
3 See United Nations Security Council Resolution S/RES/232(1966), P. Wallensteen, *A Century of Economic Sanctions: A Field Revisited*, Uppsala Research Paper, no. 1 (Uppsala: Department of Peace and Conflict Research, 2000), p. 2.
4 See S/RES/253 (1968).
5 M. Doxey, *Economic Sanctions and International Enforcement* (London: Macmillan, 1980), pp. 103–104.
6 Doxey, 1980, p. 102.
7 'The Experience of the United Nations in Administering Arms Embargoes and Travel Sanctions', in M. Brzoska (ed.), *Smart Sanctions: The Next Step: The Debate on Arms*

Embargoes and Travel Sanctions within the 'Bonn–Berlin Process' (Baden-Baden: Nomos Verlagsgesellschaft, 2001), p. 48.
8 See S/RES/919 (1994).
9 See for example D. Cortright, G. A. Lopez and A. Millar, *Smart Sanctions: Restructuring UN Policy in Iraq*, Policy Brief Series, Fourth Freedom Forum and the Joan B. Kroc Institute for International Peace Studies (2001), pp. 17–18.
10 See S/RES/1051 (1996) and S/RES/1284 (1999).
11 See S/RES/1409 (2002), for the Revised Goods List see document S/2002/532, for the revised procedures see document S/2002/515.
12 See S/RES/1483 (2003).
13 See S/RES/1518 (2003).
14 See S/RES/713 (1991) and S/RES/724 (1991).
15 See S/RES/757 (1992).
16 R. Garfield, *Economic Sanctions, Health, and Welfare in the Federal Republic of Yugoslavia 1990–2000*, issued by OCHA and UNICEF (Belgrade, 2000), pp. 16ff. For further reading on the SAM experience see D. Cortright and G. A. Lopez, *The Sanctions Decade: Assessing UN Strategies in the 1990s* (Boulder: Lynne Rienner, 2000), pp. 68ff. and the Annual Report 1995 on OSCE activities, www.osce.org/docs/english/misc/anrep95e.htm
17 See S/RES/942 (1994).
18 See S/RES/1074 (1996).
19 Annual Report 1996 on OSCE activities, www.ocse.org/docs/english/misc/anrep96e.htm
20 United Nations Peacekeeping Operations, UNPREDEP, www.un.org/Depts/DPKO/Missions/unpred_b.htm#BACKGROUNDER
21 See S/RES/1367 (2002).
22 See S/RES/733 (1992), S/RES/751 (1992).
23 See S/2003/223, pp. 20–31.
24 See S/RES/1407 (2002).
25 See S/2003/223, pp. 6–10.
26 See S/RES/1474 (2003).
27 S/RES/1519 (2003).
28 G. C. Hufbauer, J. Shott and K. Elliot, *Economic Sanctions Reconsidered, Case 92–12, United Nations v. Libya*, 3rd edition, revised (Washington, DC: Institute of International Economics, forthcoming 2004). Furthermore see S/RES/748 (1992).
29 See S/RES/883 (1993).
30 See S/PRST/1999/10.
31 See S/RES/1506 (2003).
32 See S/RES/841 (1993).
33 See Cortright and Lopez, 2000, pp. 87–103; see S/RES/875 (1993) for the naval blockade.
34 See S/RES/944 (1994).
35 See S/RES/864 (1993).
36 See S/RES/1127 (1997).
37 See S/RES/1173 (1998).
38 Wallensteen, 2000, p. 11.
39 See S/RES1173 (1998). D. Cortright and G. A. Lopez, *Sanctions and the Search for Security: Challenges to UN Action* (Boulder, CO: Lynne Rienner, 2002), p. 183.
40 See for example the Secretary-General's report on improving the measures imposed against UNITA, S/1999/49.
41 See S/RES/1237 (1999).
42 See S/2002/1339 (final report), S/2002/1119 (add. report), S/2002/486 (add. report),

S/2001/966 (suppl. report), S/2000/1225 (final report), S/2001/363 (addendum), S/2000/1026 (interim report) and S/2000/203.
43 See S/2002/1119, para. 16.
44 See S/RES/1448 (2002) and for the final report from the Monitoring Mechanism see S/2002/1339.
45 See S/RES/918 (1994).
46 B. Wood and J. Peleman, *The Arms Fixers: Controlling the Brokers and Shipping Agents*, BASIC Research Report, 1999, chapter 3.
47 See S/RES/1013 (1995).
48 For the UNICOI reports see documents S/1996/67, S/1996/195, S/1997/1010 – the report was issued in November 1997 but was not released until one year later in December 1998 – S/1998/63, S/1998/777 and S/1998/1096.
49 See Commission's report S/1998/1096 and Wood and Peleman, 1999, chapter 3.
50 See S/RES/1054 (1996).
51 See the Secretary-General's report S/1996/940 and S/RES/1070 (1996).
52 See S/RES/1372 (2001).
53 See S/RES/1132 (1997). The Council feared the sanctions could easily create a humanitarian disaster in Sierra Leone. Therefore, shortly after the sanctions were imposed, the UN dispatched an assessment team to measure the humanitarian effects of sanctions. See *Inter-Agency Assessment Mission to Sierra Leone: Interim Report* (New York: OCHA, 1998).
54 See C. De Jonge Oudraat, 'Making Economic Sanctions Work', *Survival*, 42, 3 (2000), pp. 9–10 and Cortright and Lopez, 2000, pp. 68–70.
55 See S/RES1171 (1998).
56 See S/RES/1306 (2000).
57 The final report of the Expert Panel on Sierra Leone (S/2000/1195), for secondary sanctions on Liberia see S/RES/1343 (2001), and following section on Liberia.
58 See UN press release SC/7778AFR/634.
59 See S/RES/1267 (1999).
60 See S/RES/1333 (2000). The report from the Committee of Experts was submitted in May 2001 (S/2001/511).
61 See S/RES/1363 (2001). The five-member monitoring group, established by Resolution 1363 (2001), submitted its first report in January 2002 (S/2002/65). Its second report was submitted in May 2002 (S/2002/541), and the third report in December 2002 (S/2002/1338).
62 See S/RES/1526 (2004).
63 See S/RES/1298 (2000).
64 See Presidential Statement S/PRST/2001/14.
65 See S/RES/788 (1992) and S/RES/985 (1995).
66 See S/RES/1343 (2001).
67 The Expert Panel reports were published as S/2001/1015, S/2002/470 and S/2003/498.
68 See the Expert Panel reports S/2001/1015, para. 321–350 and S/2003/498. For the role of the timber industry as an income for the Liberian government to continue to fuel conflicts see 'The Usual Suspects: Liberia's Weapons and Mercenaries in Côte d'Ivoire and Sierra Leone: Why it's Still Possible, How it Works and How to Break the Trend', *Global Witness Report* (March 2003).
69 See S/RES/1478 (2003).
70 See S/RES/1521 (2003).
71 Conflict diamonds means rough diamonds used by rebel movements or their allies to finance conflict aimed at undermining legitimate governments described in relevant UNSC resolutions. For a further discussion on the definitional issues see C. Dietrich, 'Hard Currency: The Criminalized Diamond Economy of the Democratic Republic of

Congo and its Neighbours', The Diamonds and Human Security Project, Occasional Paper no. 4, Partnership Africa Canada (2002), p. 45.
72 See S/RES/1173 (1998).
73 See S/RES/1306 (2000).
74 See S/RES/1343 (2001).
75 See for example Cortright and Lopez, 2000, p. 69.
76 For the role of a UN sanctions co-ordinator see Chapter 5 in the present volume.
77 For more on how to enhance the capacity of the UN Secretariat and UN Security Council see Part II in P. Wallensteen, C. Staibano and M. Eriksson (eds) *Making Targeted Sanctions Effective: Guidelines for the Implementation of UN Policy Options*, Department of Peace and Conflict Research, Uppsala University (Stockholm: Elanders Gotab, 2003), pp. 48–55.

Part II

NEW SANCTIONS CAPACITY
Emphasizing implementation

4

TARGETED SANCTIONS AND STATE CAPACITY

Towards a framework for national level implementation

Thomas J. Biersteker, Sue E. Eckert, Aaron Halegua and Peter Romaniuk

What are the general requirements that states must possess to enable them to implement targeted sanctions effectively? What specific capabilities are necessary to implement the range of targeted sanctions addressed in the Interlaken, Bonn–Berlin and Stockholm processes? What are the key challenges in national level implementation? How should the international community respond?

Building on the work of Working Group 2 of the Stockholm Process, this chapter summarizes a framework for implementation of targeted sanctions on the national level, identifying general elements that pertain across different types of targeted sanctions, as well as the specific requirements of each type. The utility of such a framework is underscored by ongoing challenges to national-level implementation, such as the need for parallel standards of implementation across states, refining and developing new targeted measures, addressing the unintended consequences of sanctions (especially for neighboring states), and the necessity of sustained efforts to build state capacity. In response, we suggest that these challenges be prioritized on the agenda of ongoing sanctions reform debates. In this way, the advances in our knowledge about the implementation of targeted sanctions that have been made through the three sanctions reform processes can be consolidated and extended.

A framework for implementing targeted sanctions at the national level

In drafting *Targeted Financial Sanctions: A Manual for Design and Implementation* (known here as the Interlaken Report)[1] we developed a framework to describe the requisite legal and administrative mechanisms for the implementation of targeted financial sanctions at the national level. As Part 2 of the Report establishes, targeted financial sanctions require that states: possess the legal authority to implement UN Security Council resolutions; designate an administering agency to oversee implementation; disseminate information to those affected by sanctions; undertake compliance activities; decide upon exemptions and exceptions as appropriate; administer frozen assets; and pursue enforcement actions where sanctions are breached. In elaborating on a framework with Working Group 2 of the Stockholm Process, we found that some of these elements pertain to other kinds of targeted sanctions, while others were specific to targeted financial sanctions. Delineated below are five general aspects of implementation of targeted sanctions at the national level that hold across different types of targeted sanctions, as well as an elaboration of requirements unique to sector-specific sanctions.

General aspects of targeted sanctions implementation

First, a necessary precondition to the implementation of sanctions at the national level is domestic legal authority to act. Put simply, without appropriate authority, national governments are powerless to implement resolutions passed by the Security Council. It is worth recalling that, under the terms of the UN Charter (Article 25), Member States are bound by decisions of the Council, having agreed to "accept and carry out" those decisions.

In the course of the sanctions reform processes, experts have discussed a variety of ways in which this legal requirement can be fulfilled. For example, states may amend existing legislation in specific sectors affected by UN targeted sanctions, or rely on generic constitutional authority enabling them to give automatic effect to Council resolutions.[2] In some cases, such as the European Union, regional organizations with competence over sanctions implementation may provide the necessary legal authority.[3] While approaches may vary, the idea of a "Model Law," first proposed through the Interlaken Process, has been recognized by experts as the most straightforward and efficient means of giving effect to Security Council resolutions imposing targeted sanctions.[4] The Model Law developed at Interlaken suggests national enabling legislation to provide governments with the appropriate powers to adopt secondary legislation to give effect to decisions under Article 41 of the UN Charter. As such, the Model Law obviates the need to pass legislation for each sanctions regime, contributes to the consistent implementation of sanctions across Member States, and provides the ability to implement *all* Article 41 measures.

Beyond possessing the domestic legal authority ("primary legislation"), states must also undertake administrative action to implement sanctions. Here, the terms "secondary legislation" or "national measures" have been used by sanctions experts to describe the kinds of regulatory, executive or administrative instruments that states need to adopt in order to give effect to sanctions. Whether secondary legislation or national measures are undertaken, acknowledging the different administrative traditions around the world, it is necessary for states to promulgate regulatory or administrative measures for effective implementation at the national level.

A second general component of the implementation of targeted sanctions at the domestic level is that states must designate an administrative agency or agencies to be responsible for the various tasks required in implementing targeted sanctions at the national level. Depending on the range of prohibitions imposed by the Security Council, it is likely that agencies with sector-specific expertise (such as the treasury or central bank in the case of targeted financial sanctions, and aviation authorities in the case of an aviation ban, etc.) will be centrally involved in sanctions implementation. The expertise of functional specialists is critical. In addition to detailed knowledge about how best to adopt measures within a particular jurisdictional setting, they may have contacts within their networks (i.e. private banks, air traffic controllers, etc.) who will be called upon to assist in sanctions implementation. While specialized expertise is vital, there is also a strong need for coordination and cooperation across different branches of government. Here, domestic agencies closest to the UN itself, such as the foreign ministry or equivalent, have played a key role in implementation in some states. Importantly, such agencies may be best placed to communicate with missions and UN bodies (most likely the Sanctions Committee and the Secretariat) in New York. Domestically, they are often the head of an interdepartmental committee on sanctions implementation – a mechanism that has been used to good effect in a number of countries. This is especially valuable where targeted sanctions involve the designation of a list of targeted individuals and entities. While this list is developed within a UN sanctions committee, a variety of domestic agencies must rely upon such designations in identifying targeted persons, freezing their assets or denying their travel. In determining administering agencies, states should ensure as a matter of priority that communication between the UN in New York and domestic agencies is effective. As a corollary, these domestic agencies play a critical role in providing information to UN bodies, fulfilling states' reporting requirements to sanctions committees.

Third, as alluded to above, agencies responsible for sanctions implementation must disseminate information to domestic actors, especially those in the private sector. This range of actors – banks and financial institutions, airlines, arms and commodity brokers, etc. – are on the frontlines of targeted sanctions implementation. While general public information about the imposition of sanctions is useful (some foreign ministries issue press releases for this purpose), specific information provided to those affected by and called upon to take action to implement targeted sanctions is vital. This information should include: the scope and requirements of the prohibitions (as set out in secondary legislation); the list of individuals, entities, and/or commodities targeted by sanctions; information regarding monitoring and enforcement measures (see below); and contact points in relevant administrative agency for queries that may arise. Where government agencies have an ongoing relationship with key private sector actors, this information should be raised in the course of routine interactions. Further, workshops and on-site information seminars have been successfully utilized by some states to ensure that necessary information reaches the appropriate parties.

Fourth, a national program for monitoring the implementation of sanctions is required to ensure compliance with the prohibitions. Although monitoring activities reflect the practices of the individual implementing agencies, these activities usually consist of reporting and information-sharing to ensure compliance. Requirements imposed upon private sector actors typically consist of periodic reports identifying actions taken to implement the prohibitions, as well as notifications when targets attempt to evade sanctions. Compliance may be facilitated through on-site audits and inspections, where domestic actors can be evaluated against an articulated standard of implementation. In some cases, the use of technology may assist in monitoring activities; however, this varies dramatically depending on the type of sanctions imposed as discussed below.

Finally, the effective implementation of sanctions requires that enforcement measures be pursued at the national level. These measures include penalties for breaches of sanctions sufficient to deter circumvention, and which are broadly consistent with other states (the importance of parallel implementation is explored in greater depth below). Penalties may be civil proceedings such as monetary fines and/or criminal measures such as imprisonment. The second key element of enforcement is the investigation and prosecution of violations. Procedures for doing so should be established by administering agencies. Where possible, information on enforcement activities should be reported to the relevant sanctions committee.

Sector-specific requirements for targeted sanctions implementation

Beyond these five core elements are more detailed requirements for the effective implementation of sanctions that are specific to each type of targeted sanction. Implementation requirements may be "sector-specific" in two ways: first, there may be additional measures unique to the type of sanction; and second, existing governance structures in each sector affected by the imposition of targeted sanctions provide a different context for implementation. This section provides a brief overview of these requirements across the different types of targeted sanctions imposed by the Security Council. It is important to note that developments in individual sectors may have positive spillover effects for sanctions implementation more generally.

Arms embargoes According to the Bonn–Berlin Report,[5] arms embargoes require a number of more detailed measures than the five general aspects articulated above. For example, specific information must be developed and disseminated by states regarding a list of goods subject to the prohibitions, as well as requirements to track and verify movement of those goods through licensing arrangements (including end-use certification). Further, as part of their monitoring and enforcement efforts, states must develop procedures for seizing arms in breach of the embargo, and may require forfeiture of goods in these circumstances. The context of implementation is notable in this regard, as numerous regional and international agreements deal with the trade in arms. Established multilateral agreements such as the Wassenaar Arrangement require countries to develop procedures and standards for trade in arms and dual-use goods. While these requirements were not developed for the purpose of implementing UN arms embargoes, such procedures may help facilitate more effective implementation on the national level.

Targeted financial sanctions In addition to the general aspects of implementation, targeted financial sanctions require that states develop procedures to address requests for exemptions to the prohibitions and exceptions permitted by the sanctions committee. Further, states must consider policies for administering frozen assets, and the Interlaken Report addresses standard practices of crediting interest to, and debiting charges from, frozen accounts that are commonly used. In addition, the Report notes the connection between the implementation of targeted financial sanctions and the emergence of international norms to counter money laundering through institutions such as the Financial Action Task Force (FATF). While targeted financial sanctions and anti-money laundering initiatives differ, advances in one area could reinforce the other. This view remains compelling in light of the mobilization of international cooperation to counter terrorist financing, for example, through the Security Council's Counter-Terrorism Committee (CTC) and the re-fashioned mandate of the FATF itself (extending to terrorist financing). While the similarities and differences between terrorist financing and money laundering have been discussed elsewhere,[6] these closely related developments leave states better placed to implement targeted financial sanctions in the future, for example, by enhancing the legal and technological capacity of states to impose such measures.

Travel bans Similar to targeted financial sanctions, travel bans require that states develop procedures for processing and implementing exemptions to the prohibitions. Also, states need to maintain a database of listed individuals to ensure that those targeted are not granted a visa or otherwise permitted to enter the country. Although international cooperation in the area of civil aviation is well established, and Resolution 1373 (2001) addresses travel of terrorists, the positive spillover effects from these measures are not as apparent in this case.[7]

Aviation bans Specific to this sector, aviation bans require that states develop procedures for barring aircraft from takeoff and landing, including measures to seize aircraft. In implementing aviation bans, access to central databases such as the ICAO register of aircraft will facilitate implementation. Finally, states ought to elaborate policies to give effect to exemptions.

Bans on the trade in rough diamonds As with arms (and other commodities), the specific requirements for effective bans against the trade in rough diamonds include certification that particular shipments do not contain diamonds covered by the prohibitions. The Kimberley Process establishes a certification scheme whereby the origin of each shipment of rough diamonds is indicated. While the Kimberley Process is still in an early phase of implementation,[8] the potentially beneficial effects of the Process are likely to be that sanctions targeted on the trade in rough diamonds will be implemented more effectively by those who observe its standards in the future.

Bans on the trade in conflict timber The Panel of Experts established pursuant to Resolution 1343 (2001) to assess the humanitarian and socio-economic impact of the sanctions subsequently imposed on timber products from Liberia recognized the utility of the Kimberly Process. In their report,[9] the experts specifically note that no mechanism such as the Kimberley Process exists in the timber sector. Further, the experts refer to the many difficulties that NGOs and international financial institutions have in attempting to certify forest products and improve regulation of this sector, concluding that, "Until legal wood can be segregated from illegal wood, it must be assumed that illegal wood will enter the supply chain and that combatants may gain revenue from the illegal exploitation of timber resources."[10] Whereas in other sectors existing administrative mechanisms facilitate the implementation of targeted sanctions, the absence of such measures in the timber sector represents an obstacle to effective implementation.

Ongoing challenges in implementing targeted sanctions at the national level

Despite the considerable progress in the design and implementation of targeted sanctions in recent years, important challenges remain with regard to ensuring consistent implementation across different national jurisdictions, refining and developing new targeted measures, mitigating the unintended consequences of targeted sanctions and addressing the need for capacity building.

Parallel standards of implementation Participants in the Stockholm Process concluded that sanctions implementation is "only as strong as its weakest link."[11] As it may only take a handful of sanctions-busters to undermine a sanctions regime, broad international implementation consistent across different national jurisdictions is necessary for targeted sanctions to be truly effective. Inconsistent implementation across states permits jurisdictional arbitrage, creating loopholes in the regime and undermining its effectiveness. Therefore, variations in the willingness and capacity of Member States to implement sanctions measures remain a fundamental challenge.

Refining and developing new targeted measures In order to exert maximum pressure on targets, the international community needs to identify the means by which targets maintain their ability to pose a threat to international peace and security. Where targets are susceptible to those measures addressed by the

Interlaken or Bonn–Berlin processes (i.e. financial sanctions, travel and aviation bans, and arms embargoes), knowledge about the design and implementation of targeted measures is well advanced. Increasingly, however, targets are utilizing sectors and commodities that have received less attention to date – diamonds, gold, tanzanite, and other natural resources. While Working Group 2 of the Stockholm Process undertook a preliminary survey of sanctions on the trade in diamonds and timber, in these and other sectors the lack of experience and expertise in developing and implementing such targeted measures represents a significant challenge. In the case of the timber sanctions imposed by Resolution 1478 (2003) concerning Liberia, the framework articulated by the Working Group has proven to be a useful way to approach Member State implementation.[12] While past experience is a useful guide, additional research and debate regarding new types of targeted measures is necessary to fill current gaps in our understanding and to improve the overall development and implementation of targeted sanctions.

Mitigating the unintended consequences of sanctions To the extent that unintended consequences of sanctions have been addressed by scholars and practitioners in the past, they tend to focus on the negative humanitarian effects of comprehensive sanctions. However, all sanctions, including targeted sanctions, are likely to exert a range of unintended effects and prompt new strategies for evasion. Further, the burdens of imposing sanctions are likely to fall disproportionately on neighboring countries who share close relationships with the target. This latter effect has been particularly evident in UN sanctions regimes, where all Member States are obliged to implement Security Council resolutions, the effects of which are distributed unevenly. As the Article 50 mechanism for the consideration of claims by those particularly affected by sanctions has to date been inadequate, other options for addressing the claims of these states need to be considered. One means includes technical assistance efforts such as those initiated by the CTC and the 1267 Committee.

Sustained capacity building As demonstrated by the CTC's experience implementing Resolution 1373 (2001) and the reports of the Monitoring Group of the 1267 Committee, even when political will exists by states to implement Security Council sanctions, they will not be effective without a systematic and sustained means to create greater national capacity. Enhanced attention has been focused on the significant needs of many states lacking even a basic legal framework, let alone administrative mechanisms to implement targeted sanctions, and important efforts to organize and provide such assistance in the past year have been initiated.[13] Substantial suggestions in this regard were proposed by Working Group 2 in the Stockholm Process, including consideration of financial assistance to those needing help in implementing the required measures.[14] Such capacity-building initiatives need to be enhanced, however, and addressed systematically in a sustained manner for future targeted sanctions to be implemented effectively.

Conclusion

This chapter has outlined a framework for implementing targeted sanctions at the national level. Important advances have been made in sanctions reform through the Interlaken, Bonn–Berlin and Stockholm processes, but additional work is necessary for national level implementation of targeted sanctions to be effective. Fundamental to successful implementation are effective international efforts to assist Member States in building the necessary domestic legal and administrative capacity. In addition, to consolidate and extend the achievements of these initiatives, ongoing inquiry regarding new means to develop and refine targeted sanctions is necessary.

Notes

1. T. J. Biersteker, S. E. Eckert, P. Romaniuk, A. Halegua and N. Reid, *Targeted Financial Sanctions: A Manual for Design and Implementation – Contributions from the Interlaken Process* (Providence, RI: Watson Institute for International Studies, 2001). The Report is available at www.smartsanctions.ch and www.watsoninstitute.org/tfs
2. For a more detailed discussion of these options, see Interlaken Report, pp. 82–89.
3. For example, see Chapter 7 in this volume.
4. For a more detailed discussion of the Model Law, see the Stockholm Report, P. Wallensteen, C. Staibano, M. Eriksson (eds) *Making Targeted Sanctions Effective: Guidelines for the Implementation of UN Policy Options,* Department of Peace and Conflict Research, Uppsala University (Stockholm: Elanders Gotab, 2003), pp. 81–89.
5. See Bonn–Berlin Report, M. Brzoska (ed.) *Design and Implementation of Arms Embargoes and Travel and Aviation Related Sanctions: Results from the "Bonn–Berlin Process"* (Bonn: BICC, 2001), pp. 99–109.
6. See E. Aninat, D. Hardy and R. B. Johnston, "Combating Money Laundering and the Financing of Terrorism," *Finance and Development*, Vol. 39, No. 3, Sept. 2002.
7. Rather, in a recent report, the Monitoring Group established pursuant to resolution 1373 (2001) and extended by resolutions 1390 (2002) and 1455 (2003) noted that the travel ban in place against the Taliban and Al-Qaida is for political purposes only (see S/2003/69). A more detailed analysis of the effects of counter-terrorism initiatives on migration controls is beyond the scope of this chapter.
8. For example, see I. Smillie, *The Kimberley Process: The Case for Proper Monitoring*, Occasional Paper No. 5, Partnership Africa Canada, Sept. 2002.
9. See S/2003/779, Annex II.
10. S/2003/779, p. 29.
11. Stockholm Report, p. 10.
12. See "Report of the Secretary General in pursuance of resolution 1478 (2003) concerning Liberia," S/2003/793, 5 August 2003. This report endorses the recommendations of the Stockholm Process, especially those regarding, "processes of certification, as in the Kimberley Process, and listing of approved traders" (p. 12).
13. See "Guidelines for reports required of all States pursuant to paragraphs 6 and 12 of resolution 1455 (2003)," issued by the 1267 Committee, undated, p. 5. Available at: http://www.un.org/Docs/sc/committees/1267/guidanc_en.pdf (accessed 21 September 2003).
14. See Stockholm Report, Part III.

5

A SANCTIONS COORDINATOR

Options for enhancing compliance

David Cortright and George A. Lopez

The implementation of Security Council sanctions would benefit greatly from greater coordination efforts. At present when sanctions are imposed, no one is in charge of implementation. The Security Council usually creates a sanctions committee, with a chair and vice chair, and the Secretariat staff provides valuable support services, but no single office or individual is charged with managing and coordinating implementation. There is no leadership or focal point for mobilizing the international community in support of Security Council purposes. It's like sending an army into the field without a general. The army here is a very broad array of individual government agencies, regional organizations, specialized international agencies, and private actors – all of whom must be contacted and organized into a coordinated international effort to assure sanctions implementation. Without a general, or in this arena a sanctions coordinator, efforts to mobilize these diverse interests into collective action are more difficult. With greater leadership, the prospects for coordinated action will improve.

This chapter provides a brief introduction to the issues associated with creating a position of sanctions coordinator and makes a succinct case for the utility of such a role. We begin by defining the functions required for special sanctions coordination. We review the precedent established for this role by Ambassador Robert Fowler, former permanent representative of Canada to the UN Security Council, during his tenure as chair of the Angola Sanctions Committee. We consider lessons learned from the experience of Special Representatives of the Secretary General (SRSGs) and from the workings of the UN Counter-Terrorism Committee. We discuss the relationship of a sanctions coordinator to the sanctions committee chair (and vice chair) and examine options for how the different roles might complement one another. We discuss political and institutional requirements that would be necessary to assure the effectiveness of a sanctions coordinator – including a sanctions budgeting process and the creation of a permanent monitoring mechanism. We conclude by presenting options for structuring the proposed coordinator role either on a case-by-case basis or as a permanent feature of the UN Secretariat.

Purposes

The principal justification for creating a sanctions coordinator is to enhance the cooperation of UN member states in the implementation of Security Council sanctions. In the UN system, where the powers of the central organization are strictly limited, individual member states bear the primary responsibility for implementing Security Council resolutions. At present, member states receive little guidance or support from the Security Council or the Secretariat on the implementation of sanctions. Coordination efforts have improved in recent years, as the Security Council and the UN Secretariat have become more sophisticated in the design and execution of sanctions, but additional improvements are necessary.[1] A more concerted effort to encourage and assist member states in fulfilling their compliance obligations is essential to improving the effectiveness of UN sanctions. The purpose of a sanctions coordinator would be to act on behalf of the Security Council to assure greater international cooperation in the implementation of sanctions.

The proposed coordinator role would enhance international sanctions leadership. Presently member states with a vested interest in a particular episode or the chairs of the relevant sanctions committees attempt to provide guidance for implementation efforts. This often places a special burden on the particular member state or Security Council ambassador involved. It may also raise issues about the foreign policies of particular member states excessively influencing UN policy. The effectiveness of the present sanctions committee chairs could be enhanced through the additional leadership functions of a sanctions coordinator.

Creating the position of sanctions coordinator would strengthen the institutional and policy framework for sanctions implementation. The proposed coordinator could be either a temporary appointee established for a particular sanctions case, or a permanent post created within the Security Council division of the UN Secretariat. Three distinct functions would be associated with the sanctions coordinator position: political outreach, special assistance, and policy guidance. The first would enable the Security Council to engage with member states, regional organizations, and other actors to communicate the purposes of sanctions resoluions and encourage greater compliance and enforcement. The second would provide feedback to the UN system on the support services member states and regional organizations may require to fulfill their obligations. The third would include organizing and coordinating the delivery of such services. A special sanctions coordinator could fulfill the following functions:

Public diplomacy

- meeting with front-line states and principal trading partners of a targeted regime to ensure effective implementation;
- coordinating compliance efforts among relevant regional organizations and specialized inter-governmental agencies;

- traveling to regions affected by sanctions to increase public awareness of the political objectives of UN policy and the compliance obligations of member states;
- meeting with private companies and trade associations to review compliance needs and remind public and private actors of their legal responsibilities to comply with Security Council mandatory measures.

Special assistance

- identifying necessary forms of technical and administrative assistance for member states and international organizations;
- making recommendations to the Security Council, individual member states, and other relevant organizations for the provision of special assistance.

Policy guidance

- recommending to the Security Council any adjustments in the terms of sanctions that may be necessary to enhance effectiveness;
- enhancing coordination of sanctions support activities within the UN Secretariat and improving liaison with various regional organizations and specialized agencies;
- assuring effective coordination between sanctions committees and the UN Counter-Terrorism Committee in the provision of assistance and the implementation of Security Council mandates;
- improving liaison and coordination between the Security Council and expert panels, humanitarian monitoring missions, and third-party impact assessments; and
- facilitating liaison between the Security Council and non-governmental organizations.

Supporting sanctions implementation

Despite significant advances in sanctions design, there is often inadequate follow-up and implementation of Security Council resolutions. An aggressive effort to put sanctions into operative form soon after Security Council resolutions are adopted is generally lacking. Member states may feel little obligation to fulfill their enforcement responsibilities. Front-line states and principal trading partners often lack information about specific sanctions mandates. Legitimate concerns about mitigating humanitarian consequences and reducing third-party impacts may receive inadequate attention. These difficulties can be addressed by providing focused and clearly defined leadership in the implementation of sanctions and by offering greater communication and coordination services through a sanctions coordinator office.

Many member states and regional organizations lack the legal authority, administrative means, and institutional capabilities for effectively enforcing UN sanctions. Until very recently, few UN member states had the necessary legislative authority, administrative capacity, and institutional capability to implement the often demanding provisions of Security Council resolutions. Since the creation of the Counter-Terrorism Committee following the September 11 terrorist attacks against the United States, many UN member states have taken action to improve their capacity for implementing financial controls and restrictions on the travel and supply of terrorists. These improvements also enhance sanctions implementation capabilities. Nonetheless, a great deal of support is still necessary, especially for developing nations. The proposed special sanctions coordinator could serve an important function in identifying the needs of these states and recommending specific forms of help to strengthen implementation capacity, in coordination with the assistance efforts of the Counter-Terrorism Committee.

A greater effort to communicate the purposes of Security Council sanctions and the obligations of member states would contribute to effective sanctions implementation. A political representative empowered to speak on behalf of the Security Council would provide a focal point for press relations and help to build public understanding and support for the goals of UN policy. Establishing visibility for sanctions implementation would be especially critical in neighboring states and among principal trading partners. Specialized communications efforts with relevant trade groups and regional organizations would ensure that necessary information is received by those who bear the greatest responsibility for sanctions implementation.

Visits to the regions affected by sanctions can be effective in reminding key players of their compliance responsibilities. The Security Council has adopted the practice of sending missions to regions affected by conflict to gain first-hand information about political, military, and humanitarian conditions, and to assess the impact of UN peacekeeping and sanctions policies. Examples include Security Council missions to Somalia and surrounding countries in support of the arms embargo in that region, and to Afghanistan and Pakistan in support of sanctions against Al-Qaida and the Taliban. A sanctions coordinator could supplement and enhance the effectiveness of such missions by helping to advance and provide follow-up. The sanctions coordinator would have the responsibility of identifying specific needs and problems that local governments and regional organizations may encounter in attempting to implement Security Council resolutions. The very presence of a senior UN official in the affected region would help to raise awareness and increase the visibility of UN policy. By mandating additional visits to regions affected by sanctions, the Security Council would provide encouragement and support for local implementation efforts.

Precedents and models

A model for sanctions coordination is the leadership provided by Robert Fowler while he was chair of the Angola Sanctions Committee in 1999 and 2000. Fowler developed a new, proactive approach to the role of sanctions committee chair. Previously these committees and their chairs played a rather passive role, receiving reports from member states but taking little action to mobilize international compliance. Fowler took a different approach, adopting a more assertive monitoring and enforcement role for the Sanctions Committee. In May 1999 Fowler traveled to central and southern Africa to meet with governments, regional organizations, and private officials affected by the sanctions against the UNITA rebel movement. In July 1999 he visited Europe and northern Africa to continue his consultations with relevant parties on strengthening sanctions implementation. Fowler traveled widely during the remainder of his term as chair of the Sanctions Committee in a ground-breaking effort to breathe new life and vitality into the Security Council sanctions in Angola.

Fowler engaged neighboring governments, principal trading partners, private companies, regional and international organizations, and non-governmental experts in a wide-ranging series of meetings and consultations to facilitate sanctions enforcement. He issued reports on his initial missions that contained a series of recommendations for improving the implementation of sanctions.[2] He received pledges of cooperation and support from many member states and specialized agencies. This extensive effort by a representative of the Security Council was unprecedented, and injected a greater degree of seriousness into the sanctions enterprise. The reports from Fowler's missions led to the appointment of the Angola Panel of Experts, and then to the Angola Monitoring Mechanism. These investigative bodies in turn produced a series of reports which provided information on sanctions violations and helped to turn promises of cooperation into actual compliance.[3]

The institutionalization of a sanctions coordinator role would build upon the ad hoc experience of the Angola Sanctions Committee. It would make the proactive approach pioneered by Fowler a regular feature of Security Council policy. The sanctions committee chair or vice chair would be authorized to act on behalf of the Council to fulfill the identified coordination functions. This could help to improve the effectiveness of Security Council measures.

Lessons for a special sanctions coordinator role can be gleaned from the experience of SRSGs in UN peacemaking missions. In recent years, the Secretary General has appointed special representatives for dozens of peace missions. These have ranged from the highly visible role of Algerian ambassador Lakhdar Brahimi in the UN mission to Afghanistan in the fall of 2001, to the more recent efforts of Senegalese ambassador Ibrahima Fall in settling the conflicts in West Africa. Some of these special representatives operate in settings where UN peacekeeping forces are deployed. Others function where individual member states, such as the United States in Afghanistan or Australia in East Timor, have played a dominant role in carrying out military enforcement operations.

The functions performed by these SRSGs are different from those that would be required of a sanctions coordinator. The special representatives often serve in conflict zones, where even if a ceasefire has been agreed, hostilities may be continuing. The special representatives provide leadership for peacekeeping and verification missions. They are responsible for helping to negotiate and implement peace settlements, which in some cases includes the organization and administration of UN-supervised elections. They help to coordinate the full range of UN field operations, including humanitarian relief and refugee assistance missions. A sanctions coordinator serving in the midst of a conflict situation would have different duties, but at least some of the functions, including verification and coordination, would be the same.

Some of the lessons learned from the UN experience with SRSGs are relevant to the proposal for a special sanctions coordinator.[4] If the Council decides to establish a special sanctions coordinator for a particular case, it should provide that coordinator with written terms of reference that specify the required responsibilities and duties and that clarify the relationship of the coordinator to other UN actors and to other international agencies and organizations. The Security Council, acting through its relevant sanctions committee chair, should inform all concerned UN agencies, international organizations, and member states of the appointment of the special sanctions coordinator. The announcement should identify the coordinator's duties and responsibilities and relationship to other actors and should encourage maximum cooperation with the sanctions coordinator.

Although not a sanctions committee, the UN Counter-Terrorism Committee (CTC) serves as a model for coordinating and assisting member state compliance with Security Council mandates. Established pursuant to UN Resolution 1373 (2001), the CTC is charged with implementing the far-reaching, multiple requirements of UN Resolution 1373. The resolution directs member states to cut off the financing of terrorist groups and those who harbor or support them, and to impose a series of restrictions on the travel, recruitment, and supply of terrorist groups. The mandates of UN Resolution 1373, if fully implemented, would mobilize the entire world community in a concerted campaign to drive terrorist organizations out of business.

Sanctions cases generally do not have the urgency or command the broad international support that exists in the campaign against terrorism, but lessons can be learned from the CTC experience that are applicable to the challenge of enhancing sanctions implementation. In asking member states to report on their compliance efforts, the CTC provided detailed and specific guidelines for the kind of information being sought. Nearly all UN member states replied to these requests, far exceeding the usual level of response to requests for compliance information. The CTC hired a team of international experts to analyze the reports and categorize the responses. The committee also established a special assistance office, headed by former Jamaican ambassador Curtis Ward, to consult with member states and regional organizations about ways of enhancing their capacity to comply with CTC mandates. Assistance needs range from help with the drafting and adoption of legislative and regulatory authority, to the provision of financial support for the expansion of law enforcement capabilities. Part of the job of the assistance office is to match states and regional organizations that are capable of providing assistance with those that need such help. The CTC has also worked with regional organizations and specialized international agencies to coordinate implementation efforts by region (for example, strengthening counter-terrorism staff capacity within regional organizations) and by function (for example, building cooperation among financial agencies for interdicting terrorist funding).

In all of these functions the CTC has benefited from a high degree of political commitment from member states and regional organizations, and from a substantial commitment of resources from member states and the UN system. The requirements for effective sanctions implementation are similar. A more proactive committee process, increased levels of member state response, a greater use of specialized experts, new mechanisms for identifying and addressing assistance needs, and a greater commitment of financial resources – these are the factors that make the CTC a distinctive element in the global campaign against terrorism, and that are needed to improve sanctions implementation.

In the case of the CTC, coordination functions have centered on the Committee chair and vice chairs. Sir Jeremy Greenstock, then British ambassador to the UN, was the first chair of the Committee, and he set a precedent of engaged leadership that was crucial in gaining international cooperation with the CTC process. Greenstock drove the Committee to play a greater leadership role, creating two vice chair positions to assist with managing the Committee's multiple mandates. He mobilized resources within the UN system and beyond to hire experts and a special CTC staff. He met frequently with other UN representatives and the press to communicate the Committee's mission and report on its progress. Greenstock's leadership of the CTC during its initial months of operation serves as a model for more proactive Committee leadership, and the use of this function to coordinate compliance with Security Council mandates.

Implementation

The proposal to create the role of a sanctions coordinator is linked to the question of establishing a budget for sanctions implementation. Whenever the Security Council imposes sanctions it should develop a mechanism for financing necessary implementation efforts. Funding is essential for travel and administration of special sanctions committee missions. In the case of the Fowler mission, the government of Canada covered the considerable expenses involved. It is not appropriate or realistic to expect that individual member states can take on this financial responsibility. Developing nations that chair Security Council sanctions committees may not have the ready means to make such a financial commitment. A budgeting process for sanctions committees and their implementation efforts would assure that the funding is available for special missions and other coordination functions. Budgets are developed for humanitarian operations and peacekeeping missions, and the same should be true for sanctions cases. A budgeting exercise would focus greater attention on the steps necessary for effective implementation of sanctions and lend a greater sense of realism to the imposition of sanctions, thereby helping to impress targeted authorities with the seriousness of the UN effort. A budget approval process and the accompanying appeal for contributions would also vest member states more thoroughly in the sanctions undertaking.

The proposed budget for sanctions implementation should also cover the costs of expert investigative panels and humanitarian assessment missions. The Security Council has established monitoring mechanisms in most recent sanctions cases. These panels have proved to be of immense value in identifying sanctions violations and recommending means to enhance compliance. The governments of France and the United Kingdom have proposed the creation of an independent sanctions expert unit as a regular feature of Security Council policy making. Security Council members have debated the proposal, but as of this writing no action has been taken to create such a unit. Whether such a unit is established permanently, or on an ad hoc basis for specific cases, the presence of an independent monitoring mechanism is invaluable for strengthening the implementation of sanctions. Such monitoring mechanisms would work in conjunction with a sanctions coordinator to enhance compliance. The Security Council has also ordered humanitarian assessments in recent cases, to anticipate and prevent potential humanitarian problems. Such humanitarian assessments also would be conducted in coordination with the mission of a sanctions coordinator and would be financed through the same budgeting process.

Options for structuring the role of sanctions coordinator

Three options are available for structuring the functions of a sanctions coordinator. One possibility would be to expand dramatically the formal roles and responsibilities of the relevant sanctions committee chair and vice chair. The sanctions committee chair and vice chair could cooperate to share the necessary tasks of sanctions management. One would continue to convene the relevant committee to oversee the administrative aspects of monitoring member state compliance and humanitarian concerns. The other could assume a wider "in the field" role following the model of the Fowler mission. The vice chair might assume the role of convening the sanctions committee in New York and would work through the committee to oversee the various components of the implementation effort, including special missions, monitoring mechanisms, and humanitarian assessments. The chair would take on the more visible public role of engaging with states and other players in affected regions, identifying special assistance needs, and recommending any necessary adjustments in Security Council policy.

With this option, the sanctions committee chair and vice chair would assume greater responsibilities. They would need, in addition to an approved budget, assured access to administrative and professional staff assistance to carry out their expanded duties. They would also need access to specialized experts, either through an existing monitoring mechanism or on a special contract basis. As noted, the experience of the Counter-Terrorism Committee, where the chair and vice chairs assumed significant leadership responsibilities, could be a model for this approach. Coordination and lines of responsibility between the sanctions committee leadership and the Secretariat staff would need to be strengthened and clarified.

Another option is for the Security Council to appoint a senior diplomatic official to assist the sanctions committee in implementation efforts. The experience of SRSGs would be relevant here. In this approach, the coordinator would be a special representative selected by the Security Council to work closely with the sanctions committee chair. The coordinator would report to the Council through the sanctions committee chair. Each sanctions case would have its own sanctions coordinator. Such a structure would permit the selection of an individual with knowledge and experience in the region where the sanctions are imposed, or someone with specific expertise in the functional areas relevant to a particular case, for example international finance.

A third option is to establish a senior position within the Security Council division of the Department of Political Affairs of the UN Secretariat. In this approach, coordinator duties would be institutionally connected to the current Secretariat staff that assists the sanctions committees. A senior official would be vested with responsibility to coordinate all sanctions cases. Those most likely to be candidates for such a position are former diplomats or senior executives within the Secretariat who are experienced in the workings of sanctions committees or who have served as members of expert monitoring panels. The proposed position would expand upon the duties currently performed by the chief of the sanctions branch within the Secretariat. The sanctions branch has a small professional staff, which assists the various sanctions committees and monitoring panels. The new position would build upon and expand these duties and add the functions of public diplomacy, special assistance, and policy guidance. Additional staffing and expert assistance would be needed to carry out these enlarged responsibilities.

In all three options, the proposed sanctions coordinator would function in support of existing sanctions committees and would seek to strengthen the ability of the Security Council to encourage greater member state compliance. Whichever structural option is chosen, it is clear that a sanctions coordinator would warrant a small staff and a budget for travel and communications. For the first and second options, sanctions coordination costs would be folded into the budgeting process established when sanctions are imposed and a sanctions committee is created. In the third option, the coordinator's office would become part of the regular budget of the Department of Political Affairs within the UN Secretariat.

Since every new sanctions case of recent years has had some form of time limitation placed on it by the Council, the term of service of the sanctions coordinator would be delimited by the mandate in the relevant Security Council resolution. As it considers the potential benefits of a sanctions coordinator, the Security Council may wish to experiment by appointing a sanctions coordinator in a case. The experience from a test case could then be utilized to evaluate the utility of a more permanent institutionalized position of sanctions coordinator.

Whichever approach is taken – expanding the authority of sanctions committee chairs, appointing a special representative, or creating a new position within the Secretariat – a greater commitment to sanctions coordination is crucial to enhancing the effectiveness of Security Council policy. Many of the recent cases of sanctions – from Iraq, to Yugoslavia, to Angola – would have benefited from greater international coordination efforts. Leadership is vital to the success of political action, whether that action takes diplomatic, military, or economic form. A sanctions coordinator could help to provide that leadership on the economic front, and enhance the prospects for effective implementation.

Notes

1. See our discussion of recent innovations in sanctions policy in D. Cortright and G. A. Lopez, "Reform or Retreat? The Future of UN Sanctions Policy," chapter 11 in *Sanctions and the Search for Security: Challenges to UN Action* (Boulder, CO: Lynne Rienner, 2002).
2. United Nations Security Council, *Letter Dated 4 June 1999 from the Chairman of the Security Council Committee Established Pursuant to Resolution 864 (1993) Concerning the Situation in Angola Addressed to the President of the Security Council*, S/1999/644, New York, 4 June 1999; and United Nations Security Council, *Letter Dated 28 July 1999 from the Chairman of the Security Council Committee Established Pursuant to Resolution 864 (1993) Concerning the Situation in Angola Addressed to the President of the Security Council*, S/1999/829, New York, 28 July 1999.
3. United Nations Security Council, *Report of the Panel of Experts on Violations of Security Council Sanctions Against UNITA*, S/2000/203, New York, 10 March 2000; *Interim Report of the Monitoring Mechanism on Angola Sanctions Established by the Security Council in Resolution 1295 (2000) of April 2000*, S/2000/1026, New York, 25 October 2000; *Final Report of the Monitoring Mechanism on Angola Sanctions*, S/2000/1225, New York, 21 December 2000; *Addendum to the Final Report of the Monitoring Mechanism on Sanctions Against UNITA*, S/2001/363, New York, 11 April 2001; *Supplementary Report of the Monitoring Mechanism on Sanctions Against UNITA*, S/2001/966, New York, 12 October 2001; *Additional Report of the Monitoring Mechanism on Sanctions Against UNITA*, S/2002/486, New York, 26 April 2002; *Additional Report of the Monitoring Mechanism on Sanctions Against UNITA*, S/2002/1119, New York, 16 October 2002.
4. The recommendations listed here are drawn from FAFO (Norwegian) Institute for Applied Social Science, *Command from the Saddle: Managing United Nations Peacebuilding Missions*, 1999. Available online at FAFO <http://www.fafo.no/pub/rapp/266/sdrag.htm> (30 September 2003).

6

INTERNATIONAL ARMAMENT EMBARGOES AND THE NEED FOR END-USE DOCUMENTS

Björn Hagelin

The Charter of the United Nations empowers the Security Council to take various measures in order to exert influence on states and actors and thus safeguard international peace and security. As a rule, when peace is threatened the Security Council first tries to use non-military sanctions, such as arms embargoes or breaking off economic, diplomatic and other relations. The Council's demands may be presented in the form of binding decisions, resolutions or recommendations. It is therefore essential that sanctions are effective, humane and targeted.

One particular aspect of the Stockholm Process on the implementation of targeted sanctions is how to make arms embargoes more efficient.[1] This chapter discusses the use and effectiveness of national so called end-use certificates for conventional arms transfers. It is suggested that in order to strengthen the effectiveness of end-use controls in connection with mandatory United Nations Security Council (UNSC) arms embargoes, international end-use documents should become standard procedure.

No distinction is made in this chapter between major conventional weapons, small arms or light weapons. They are here regarded as equally important for efficient controls and should be treated together. This is so even if the actual measures to control the transfer of these different types of weapons as well as their direct importance for a particular conflict may vary.

The recommendations are formulated on the assumptions that UN member governments want to make arms embargoes efficient and, therefore, are willing when asked to support international armament controls including arms embargoes more strongly than they support the transfer of goods and other ingredients used in support of world armaments.

National end-use certificates and international arms embargoes

An end-use certificate is a trade security control document. It is used by supplier governments for (certain) arms and other transfers to (certain) recipients. They generally verify, by signatures from the supplying and recipient companies and/or governments, the final destination of the transfer (end-user). The document in most cases assures that further transfer without the approval of the original supplier government is unlawful.

End-use certificates are used under normal circumstances, i.e. when there are no sanctions involved. Although the EU in accordance with its Code of Conduct has stipulated arms export coordination rules, and while the Wassenaar Arrangement in December 1999 issued an 'indicative list' of end-use assurances (Box 6.1), the actual content and implementation of national end-use certificates are according to the national arms export control laws or guidelines. This means that there is neither an internationally agreed format for or content of an end-use certificate, nor internationally agreed implementation rules. To establish an international end-use document as well as implementation rules, and to make them directly relevant for a particular sanction mechanism, are necessary steps for making arms embargoes more effective.

Mandatory (binding) UNSC arms embargoes imply that no or only defined categories of arms (the term 'arms' is used here for simplicity but the coverage of an international end-use document will be discussed below) are allowed to be transferred from the member states to the defined recipient (target). In other words, no end-use certificate will be issued for the embargoed arms by those governments that adhere to the embargo.

So why discuss end-use certificates in relation to international arms embargoes? The reason is that such embargoes are not theoretical. They are (real) political decisions limited by what governments regard as real security considerations for themselves as well as for friends and allies. The actual outcome is therefore that arms embargoes are not always complete in their coverage. The language may be unclear or imprecise as the result of tradeoffs between agreeing on an embargo or no embargo at all. The end result or aim of the embargo may be defined in more or less clear terms and the means to reach it left to be nationally defined and implemented. This might lead to difficult national decisions of implementation as well as for decisions about when the embargo is not complied with. This may be especially so if there are grey zones with regard to potential military use of civilian items. Then there are also illegal transfers to be considered.

From this follows a number of important conclusions. First, national end-use certificates are not sufficient for making UNSC arms embargoes more effective. Instead, second, an international end-use document, defining the same rules for every state, should be produced. Third, it must cover all those goods, services and other activities that are defined as relevant for achieving the purpose of the arms embargo. Fourth, the aims of the arms embargo, the terminology used, as well as

Box 6.1 List of end-use assurances

A non-binding list of end-use assurances to be used by Participating States at their discretion agreed at the Wassenaar Plenary, 1–3 December 1999

1   Parties involved in the transaction
1.1   Exporter's full name and address;
1.2   Intermediate consignee's(s') full name and address (if applicable);
1.3   Final consignee's(s')[a] full name and address;
1.4   End-user's full name and address (if different from the final consignee);

2   Goods
2.1   A detailed description of the goods which discloses their true identity;
2.2   Include quantities and values;

3   End-use
3.1   Describe the specific end-use of the goods;
3.2   Provide assurances that the goods will not be used other than for stated purposes; and/or
3.3   Provide an undertaking that the goods will be used for civil end-uses; and/or
3.4   End-user certification that the goods will not be used for chemical, biological or nuclear weapons, or for missiles capable of delivering such weapons;

4   Location
4.1   Provide certification that the goods will be installed at the premises of the end-user or will be used only by the end-user;
4.2   The final consignee/end-user agrees to allow on-site verification;

5   Re-export/diversion
5.1   The final consignee's/end-user's undertaking not to trans-ship or re-export the goods covered by the End-use Certificate/Statement; and/or
5.2   No re-exports without approval from the government of the original exporting country; and/or
5.3   The final consignee's/end-user's assurance that any re-exports will be done under the authority of the final consignee's/end-user's export licensing authorities;
5.4   The final consignee's/end-user's undertaking not to divert the goods covered by the End-use Certificate/Statement to another destination or location in the importing country;

6   Delivery verification
6.1   Provide a commitment by the final consignee to provide the exporter or the exporting government with proof of importation, upon request (e.g. provide a Delivery Verification Certificate (DV));

> 7 Documentation
> 7.1 Signature, name and title of final consignee's/end-user's representative;
> 7.2 Signature and end-use certification by the final consignee's/end-user's government or other authority as to the authenticity of the primary details provided in the document;
> 7.3 If issued by government authority, a unique identifying Certificate/Statement number;
> 7.4 Original End-user Certificate/Statement or legally certified copies.
>
> *Source*: http://www.usun-vienna.usia.co.at/wassenaar/ public00e.html
>
> *Note*
> a Meaning the last destination of the export (goods) known to the exporter.

the means to reach the aims must be clear and unambiguous. This is not only important for the implementation of the embargo but also in order to decide when the arms embargo has not been complied with. Fifth, the punishment for not complying with the embargo should be explicit and severe.

It is clear from the above that the effectiveness of an international end-use document is not only dependent upon what is stated in the document as such; it is directly related to how it is implemented by governments. In order to decide if governments adhere to an arms embargo or not, embargoes must be constantly monitored while in force.

More efficient arms embargoes should be possible if certain conditions are fulfilled. Some of those conditions have been mentioned above and will be further elaborated below. They may be summarized in five necessary conditions:

1 The formulation and implementation of end-use certificates that are today more or less left to individual government decisions must become an internationally coordinated undertaking directly related to a particular UNSC arms embargo decision.
2 The relationship between the explicit aims of the arms embargo and the implementation of the international end-use document must be made into a control system that permits 'real-time inter-action' between the UNSC, national export control authorities and people in the field.
3 'Real-time inter-action' requires that the national implementations of the international end-use document are internationally coordinated and monitored.
4 Such a control system puts more responsibility and demands on, as well as requires more resources to be allocated for implementation to, for instance, the UN Secretariat or to member states.
5 Governments must in their national policies strongly tip the balance in favour of international armament controls including arms embargoes in relation to the perceived need for national arms transfers.

EMBARGOES AND END-USE DOCUMENTS

The following discussion is based on an assumption that there is such a will, or that it can be developed. Political, financial, personnel and other factors or considerations that could restrain and limit the realization of effective international arms embargoes are therefore not considered here.

This chapter will discuss international end-use documents in support of effective international arms embargoes from a 'holistic' perspective as shown in Figure 6.1. Below, the different aspects of this international control system will be discussed. The main conclusions are summarized as recommendations at the end, where the tentative content of an international end-use document is also exemplified.

Some clarifications

What should be controlled?

There are two basic ways to define a 'military' good, and both have their benefits and drawbacks. First, the *construction* of military equipment. The most obvious example is a military weapon or other piece of equipment that has characteristics not found in civilian arms, vehicles, etc. In most cases military goods are clearly

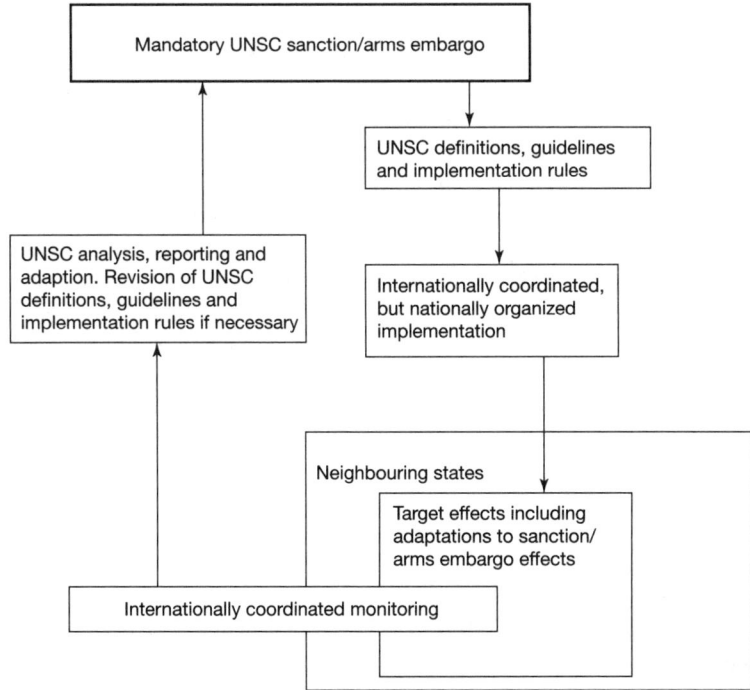

Figure 6.1 A holistic approach to end-use controls in support of international arms embargoes

distinguished from civilian goods. But it has become more and more common among defence companies and military establishments to make use of civilian society in a variety of ways. The reasons are financial as well as technological. The standard example is in the field of electronics where civilian developments have been fast and approach military functional and technological requirements. The result has been products that can fulfil military demands at a lower price than for specifically developed military goods.

To use a distinction only based on a military construction is therefore no longer meaningful. The *use* is the focus of the second type of definition. In fact, this is the core function in the end-*use* document. With regard to UNSC embargoes relevant users could include organizations that use or support the use of force or repression (such as military establishments and armed forces, i.e. also certain governments); paramilitary, police and private security organizations; and the producers of the means of force or repression (industrial and other research and manufacturing undertakings). Any of these, but not limited to these, could be the 'target' of an arms embargo.

But military establishments use everything from paperclips to space observation and navigation systems. Distinctions have to be made in order to define relevant aspects of use, for instance categories such as goods (equipment), installations and/or skills (services and know-how). These categories cover relevant civilian (dual-use) items, manufacture, science and technology (research and development), training – all of them possible loopholes in a narrowly defined arms embargo. An international end-use document should cover all of these categories and permit the specification within each category of particular goods, installations and/or skills to be embargoed. An UNSC embargo should, in order to reflect this wider ambition, not be called an arms embargo but an *armament* embargo.

It is not always possible for policy- or lawmakers to be imaginative or far-sighted enough, especially in times of rapid technological change and imaginative targets. It may therefore be desirable to be able to control the transfer of goods, installations and/or skills that have not been specifically referred to in the decision if UNSC members become aware that they are or could be used in a way contrary to the objectives of an armament embargo. Such a control may be achieved in two ways. First, the real-time inter-action system suggested here permits the UNSC to be informed about attempts to circumvent the embargo. The UNSC can therefore reformulate an embargo decision while it is in force, thereby 'plugging' such loopholes.

Second, the embargo decision may include a 'catch-all' principle. This principle would here mean an obligation on an exporter to request a national end-use certificate for a particular good, installation and/or skill if its military use is possible even if that is not mentioned in the UNSC decision. The way in which this principle is formulated in laws and regulations and then implemented through national export control systems has been a subject for much controversy during the 1990s. Criticisms include that the principle is unfair and should not be written into law, or that the principle is unenforceable in law. The principle is, nevertheless, already written into the national laws of a significant number of states and does fulfil an important purpose.[2]

However, the catch-all method puts much responsibility on the supplier and could result in unintended illegal transfers. The proposed real-time inter-action system should, in fact, be sufficient. These two approaches should not be considered as either-or, but the use of a catch-all principle in national export decisions should be complementary to the proposed real-time inter-action system.

What is a transfer?

By a transfer is here meant:

- The movement of goods, installations and/or skills that actually do or might assist the target to acquire or produce a controlled good, installation and/or skill.
- The movement could involve, for example, a final product (good) including weapons (as new, second-hand or surplus); technology to build installations or equipment through documentation and blueprints; a licence agreement and/or services and other forms of assistance; person-to-person interactions such as science and technology training and/or higher or specialized education including direct military, paramilitary or police training.

It is irrelevant for the definition of a transfer if it is paid for or not. A transfer could be:

- directly from country A to the target (in) country B;
- from country A to target (in) country B *via* a third (or more) 'agent' (be it a government, organization or individual);
- take place inside country A to a person or other recipient representing the target (in) country B; or
- take place in country B by a representative of (the supplier in) country A.

Even countries that are presented as self-sufficient with regard to (certain) military equipment often depend upon transfers from foreign countries of goods, installations and/or skills because it is cost-effective or because they lack specific competences.[3] This is straightforward and easy to understand when it involves a lack of capacity to produce certain types of military equipment. It is equally easy to disregard transfers involving goods, installations or skills not directly recognized as military. In some cases experts are needed in order to define the possible or potential military use.

Project Hindsight, published in 1969, investigated the kind of science and technology utilized by the United States in 20 weapon systems. It concluded that publication was the dominant mode for the transfer of scientific (basic science) information while informal, person-to-person contacts were most important for the transfer of technology information. Already in 1946 the quality of personnel was called 'the most important single factor in scientific and technical work'. More than thirty years later it was again emphasized by the then Director of Strategic Technology and Munitions Control at the US Department of Defense that the key to effective (military or defence) use of foreign science and technology is the amount and nature of person-to-person exchanges.[4]

Oxfam in December 1998 published a commissioned report about loopholes in the UK export control system.[5] It identified brokering and licence manufacture abroad as two major loopholes for evading UK arms export restrictions. The fact that these loopholes were identified in the UK is important for several reasons. The UK government has defined an 'ethical foreign policy' that includes arms transfers. That policy is especially important for a country such as the UK since it is one of the largest arms exporters in Europe with close transatlantic links. Both these loopholes are covered in the system proposed here.

Problems involved in foreign licence manufacture have been known for a long time. It is not only that foreign manufacturers learn technologies and manufacturing skills that may over time be used to develop and manufacture indigenous military equipment. Arms suppliers have also, as a competitive tool, offered foreign licence manufacturers the right to re-transfer manufactured equipment.[6] Re-transfer markets so decided are often limited to regional markets where the original supplier is not present with that particular type of equipment. Such offers may be ways to circumvent national export controls. If such regional markets include or are neighbouring embargoed targets, there may be increased risk of such equipment reaching that target. This points to the need for effective monitoring of an armament embargo.

Similar possibilities may exist in international cooperation for the development and manufacture of military equipment, especially if the participating countries have very different national export policies. Generally, nations cooperate in order to arm rather than to disarm or to control the conventional armaments of others.[7] Military production capacities are over time spread to more nations through the permission to license manufacture foreign equipment. Subsystems are becoming interchangeable in many weapon systems and can thus use such systems from different suppliers. Moreover, as a result of increasing international cooperation and the creation of large multinational and private arms producers, international trade is in some cases not only transnational but intra-company transfers with much reduced transparency.

The six countries that signed the Framework Agreement Concerning Measures to Facilitate the Restructuring and Operation of the European Defense Industry in 2000 – France, Germany, Italy, Spain, Sweden and the UK – account for about 90 per cent of the EU's total transfers (among themselves as well as with other countries) of major conventional weapons. Military transfers between companies in these countries are basically free for cooperative weapon projects and are likely to increase as the national defence industrial base is reduced in many of these countries. If and how such transfers may become transparent for the public as well as for parliamentary control is not yet clear.[8]

Depending on which country is studied, different types of loopholes exist since laws and regulations differ among nations. It is therefore important that, as a minimum, international control mechanisms that have for a long time been used to control and limit the spread of weapons of mass destruction and missile technology are employed also for conventional weapons in general as well as specified in international end-use documents.

An international end-use document

Oxfam's December 1998 report identified a third major loophole, namely the national end-use certificates themselves. The existence of end-use certificates does not prevent the transfer of controlled goods to unauthorized targets. One problem is that it is easy to get a (false) national end-use certificate. It has been well known for a long time that end-use certificates are systematically forged. In 1984 British press and Danish TV described how Soviet weapons during the late 1970s were sold to South Africa via Bulgaria. The end-use certificate stated that the weapons were destined to Nigeria. The Danish programme showed that it was not difficult – although expensive – to get a false end-use certificate.[9] The Oxfam report also gives more recent examples. Moreover, in preparing the report Oxfam managed within a matter of days, and with only one phone call to a contact in a foreign government, to receive an end-use certificate on official headed paper complete with a *bona fide* signature and a government stamp from the 'importing' defence ministry.

Governments, agencies and persons involved in the legal transfer of goods, installations and/or skills must be able to trust the authenticity of the necessary documentation. Some nations have taken special measures in order to complicate the falsification of end-use certificates, and this procedure has to become widespread. The creation of an international end-use document to be used in UNSC armament embargoes would be a further step in that direction.

International coordination of monitoring

A major problem in the implementation of export controls is how to know what happens outside the exporting state. The use of national end-use certificates is clearly not fail-safe. Initial knowledge about cases of alleged illegal arms transfers from Sweden during the 1980s came from foreign sources and was not the result of Swedish 'checks and balances'. Oxfam's 1998 report identified the problem as the virtual lack of arms transfers monitoring during shipment, delivery or subsequent use. It found that a cargo of military equipment could be shipped from one EU country and be flown out of another with virtually no control and no knowledge of its eventual destination.

A recent study of lessons from international arms embargoes found that they have been frequently imposed but seldom enforced – with the noted exception of Iraq. Some explanations are that stand-alone UN arms embargoes in Africa were imposed primarily as symbolic gestures, and that the existence of arms smuggling networks result in illicit trafficking in nearly all cases of UN arms embargoes. The study concludes:[10]

> The ineffectiveness of arms embargoes stems not from shortcomings of the instrument itself, we believe, but from flawed enforcement and inadequate implementation.

The control problem in Europe mentioned by Oxfam might have been reduced since then as a result of better EU coordination. The EU Code of Conduct illustrates that coordination among states can be achieved. But it also points at a regional arms export control problem that is likely to be more difficult in other parts of the world where arms export control policies are less developed and transparent and where acquisitions from abroad are more important than indigenous production.

It was a major breakthrough in international arms control when the Soviet Union and the United States accepted on-site inspections to avoid violations of control/disarmament agreements related to weapons of mass destruction. It is necessary for effective conventional armament embargoes that they are monitored by internationally coordinated activities involving representatives of the states taking part in the embargo. Such monitoring needs at a minimum to include on-site target inspection. However, such monitoring may find that the target has indeed received embargoed goods, installations or skills. In order to prevent that from happening, monitoring should preferably also take place inside neighbouring countries. Such monitoring needs to involve a variety of agencies/organizations and individuals in order to be effective.

By way of conclusion

Recommendations

The recommendations formulated here are directly related to the steps in Figure 6.1. They are of three kinds:

1 those that refer to the content and coverage of an international end-use document (IED);
2 those that refer to the implementation of the IED and internationally coordinated monitoring; and (if applicable)
3 the implementation of national end-use certificates for related but not embargoed goods, installations and/or skills.

Some recommendations support and strengthen conclusions formulated in the previous steps of the international process dealing with targeted sanctions:

1 IEDs should be prepared by/under the auspices of the UNSC for every mandatory UNSC armament embargo.

2. An IED should be issued to and be used by all participating states and their representatives when a mandatory UNSC armament embargo has been decided. It replaces national end-use certificates with regard to the defined target(s).
3. Information about every IED issued under a particular armament embargo should be stored electronically in a classified UNSC database that can be securely retrieved only by authorized individuals from any part of the world at any time by computer or phone.
4. The IED should cover all relevant categories and possible types of transfer that will or could help the target to acquire embargoed goods, installations and/or skills.
5. The coverage of and formulations in the IED should be revised as soon as possible after the UNSC receives reliable information about or has reason to believe that the embargo does not have the specified effects on the target(s).
6. A military and technology experts group should be established by/under the UNSC to prepare the IEDs and advise the UNSC on any relevant matter.
7. The UNSC expert group should be financed from the normal UN budget but also by direct contributions from member states' arms export promotion/marketing budgets. For each UNSC armament embargo, 20 per cent of a member state's public and private export promotion/marketing budgets should be paid directly to the expert group.
8. A mimeographed IED should be attached to each UNSC armament embargo decision. If an embargo decision is changed, a copy of the latest produced IED should be made available.

Producing an international end-use document

The Wassenaar list (Box 6.1) has here been revised to illustrate a tentative IED (Box 6.2). Although the IED should be self-explanatory, a few particular aspects may be worth emphasizing.

It has in the past been suggested to use part of the income from national arms exports for arms export control purposes. That contains an inbuilt dilemma in that the result that you want to achieve is financed from the activities that you want to reduce.

Recommendation 6 gets around that dilemma. Complying with that recommendation will show the willingness of member states to support armament embargoes more strongly than they support transfers of arms and other ingredients used in support of world armaments. This was mentioned above as one necessary condition for successful UNSC armaments embargoes. Thus, according to this recommendation, when there are five UNSC armament embargoes in force at the same time there will be no government or arms exporting company funds left for export promotion/marketing in any participating state. It follows that all UN members will have to make these budgets transparent.

Box 6.2 Example of an end-use document

A tentative international end-use document

1 The purpose(s) of the armaments embargo
In accordance with UNSC decision.. (explanation)

2 Target(s)
2.1 (Part of) Government...................... (specify) in country...................... (specify)
2.2 Company/-ies........................... (specify) in country........................... (specify)
2.3 Installation.............................. (specify) in country.............................. (specify)
2.4 S&T/R&D organization.................... (specify) in country...................... (specify)
2.5 Educational/training institute................. (specify) in country................. (specify)
2.6 .... (such as middlemen, agents, etc.; specify)
2.7 Organization(s)/institution(s) using force or repression: (specify)

3 Embargoed categories
3.1 Goods: types (military/civilian main systems, sub-systems, components, spare parts, etc.): (detailed description)
3.2 Installations: types (military/civilian): (detailed description)
3.3 Skills: types (military/civilian): (detailed description)
3.4 Other transfers that may aid the target to acquire embargoed goods, installations and/or skills: (detailed description)

4 Embargoed categories and forms of transfer
Each box to be detailed

	Goods	*Installations*	*Skills*	*Other*
Directly to target (in) country B				
To target *via* 'agent'				
Activities inside country A				
Activities inside country B [1]				
As result of *international cooperation* [1]				
As result of *multinational company* [1]				

(1) Each participating state shall file with the UNSC a list of all relevant undertakings with the target(s) in these categories.

5   Not embargoed but related categories (If applicable)
This IED does not involve a total embargo of all goods, installations, skills and/or other to.............. (target(s)) to prevent continued armament. The following goods, installations, skills and/or....... (specify) critical to the above armament embargo may be transferred to the (target(s) when accompanied by valid national end-use certificates.

Critical categories and forms of transfer

	Goods	*Installations*	*Skills*	*Other*
Directly to target (in) country B				
To target *via* 'agent'				
Inside country A				
Inside country B				
Result of *international cooperation*				
Result of *multinational company*				

If a government permit transfers as specified above, the national end-use certificate should include

- *all the necessary documentations;*
- *information about partners involved, end-use, location, re-export/diversion and delivery assurances;*
- *this IED reference number; and*
- *an Armament Control Statement.*

In case weapons and other military goods with identification markings are included among such transfers those markings should be noted on the national end-use certificate(s).

A copy of national end-use certificates involving any of the above shall immediately be sent to the UNSC and information about the above be stored in and be retrievable from a secure UNSC database.

6   Parties previously involved in illegal transfers to target(s)
See Appendix for list.

7   On-site inspections
The government in country........... (specify target country or country where target is located) agrees to an unspecified number of but pre-notified on-site inspections by UNSC appointed individuals to verify compliance with the armament embargo.

8   Monitors
(Specify number of monitors in each box. The aim should be to have 1–5 monitors in each relevant country)

	In target country	In neighbouring countries
Monitors from country A		
Monitors from country B		
Monitors from country C		
Monitors from country D		

See UNSC database for detailed information.

9   Revisions made in original armament embargo

9.1   Original decision:..................

9.2   1st revision:................................... Nature of change(s):...................................

9.3   2nd revision:.................................. Nature of change(s):...................................

9.4   ....

9.5   Further explanations:..

10   Punishment
If proved in legal procedures that a participating government, organization, company or individual has *deliberately and wilfully* not complied with the conditions of the armament embargo and this IED it will be sentenced to..

If proved in accordance with normal legal procedures that a participating government, organization, company or individual has *unintentionally* not complied with the conditions of the armament embargo and this IED it will be sentenced to....................

11   Signatures
Government representative:..

Specific target representative(s) (if applicable):..

Other (if applicable):..

This IED has been produced in xxx originals.

IED sequential number yyy (non-detectable by unauthorized individual).

Point 4 in the tentative IED (Box 6.2) is an attempt to be all-inclusive when defining categories and the basic forms of transfer. However, the content of each box must be defined in detail by the proposed expert group for each particular armament embargo and target(s).

The reason for demanding national lists of relevant undertakings with the target(s) in the specified forms of transfer is, first, that these forms are particularly untransparent. Second, such lists will support the monitoring process by making monitors aware of existing relations that could be used for illegal transfers. Third, it may assist the UNSC expert group in revising the embargo/IED.

It was suggested above that an UNSC armament embargo might not include all categories necessary in order to be 100 per cent effective. This leaves certain categories that may be legally transferred to the target(s) even under a mandatory UNSC armament embargo. The IED should specify and thereby inform the participating states of those categories that may – although permitted – be most critical for armament activities by the target(s). By so doing, the aspiration is to convince many, if not all, participating states to voluntary prevent also these categories from being transferred (point 5 in the tentative IED).

If, however, states decide to permit such transfers, such a decision should be accompanied by an 'Armament Control Statement'. In that statement the supplier government should explicitly and clearly declare how the transfer benefits the recipient as well as the supplier, and how that transfer could influence the UNSC armament embargo and armament controls more generally. A copy of that statement, as well as all national end-use certificates prepared for that target, should immediately be sent to the UNSC expert group and be included in the UNSC IED database.

Points 6–9 in the tentative IED relate to the inspection and monitoring of the implementation of the embargo. The acceptance by the target government (or government of country in which target is located) of specified pre-notified on-site inspections should be sought. If such acceptance is not given, sanctions against that government may be considered. The UNSC can appoint any person to participate in such on-site inspection teams. It is likely to include members of the UNSC expert group, as well as individuals from Interpol and other experts and specialists. Such inspections may include visits to the specific target(s)/end user(s) as specified in the IED and national end-use certificates as well as other pre-notified sites; land, sea and air entry/exit points; shipping agents; customs authorities, etc.

Even without the consent to such on-site inspections, internationally coordinated monitoring should be organized with representatives from participating nations on the ground. This could involve embassies, companies, NGOs, etc. in the target country and neighbouring countries. The IED should include a table listing the number of appointed monitors in the target country itself and in neighbouring countries. More detailed information, including names and contact information, should be included in a classified database similar to the IED database.

Every monitor should have access to the IED and monitors' databases in order to be able to detect forgeries and to contact other monitors. The monitors are not allowed to perform illegal activities but would function as 'intelligence networks' by making use of all means at their disposal to monitor the target's(s') compliance with the armament embargo. Such monitoring should also be supported by a listing of parties that are known to have been involved in illegal transfers to the target(s). Such a list (point 6), with relevant tracing information, should be appended to the IED.

Reliable information that suggests that the embargo has been circumvented by fraud and illegal acts – for instance that the target has acquired embargoed categories, that non-embargoed categories have been transferred without proper documentation or been used contrary to end-use assurances – should immediately be reported to the UNSC expert group and to the respective supplier government when it relates to non-embargoed categories. The expert group may perform or direct further investigations and propose to the UNSC about punishment as well as a revision of the embargo decision (point 9).

An IED should explicitly specify what kind of punishment will follow from deliberate as well as unintentional breaches of the armament embargo/ IED. It is important that the punishment is severe enough to function primarily as a deterrent. Should that fail the punishment should be higher than the anticipated gains from not complying with the embargo.

At the bottom of each IED should be mentioned how many original IEDs have been produced as well as a hidden individual sequential number of that particular IED. Every government, organization and individual that receives an IED will also receive an individual IED sequential number. This hidden number may be produced as a watermark or in another form that is difficult to forge. This means that there will be no 'copies' of an IED – all IEDs are originals with an individual sequential number. This permits for on-site inspectors, monitors and others to immediately check any IED against information retrieved from the UNSC database. Any IED not complying with the information in the database is, by definition, a forgery.

Notes

1 P. Wallensteen, C. Staibano, M. Eriksson, *Making Targeted Sanctions Effective: Guidelines for the Implementation of UN Policy Options* (Stockholm: Elanders Gotab, 2003), pp. 70–72 and 104–110.
2 Find more information at the SIPRI web page: http://projects.sipri.se/expcon/expcon.htm
3 For two examples, see B. Hagelin, *One for All or All for One? A Study of Pentagon Tapping of Foreign Science and Technology.* Report No. 42. Uppsala: Uppsala University, 1997; B. Hagelin, 'Sweden's Search for Military Technology', in M. Brzoska and P. Lock (eds) *Restructuring of Arms Production in Western Europe* (Oxford: Oxford University Press/SIPRI, 1992).
4 Hagelin, 1997, p. 39.
5 *Out of Control: The Loopholes in UK Controls on the Arms Trade* (Oxford: Oxfam, 1999).
6 B. Hagelin, *Kulorna rullar* (Stockholm: Ordfront, 1985), p. 158.
7 B. Hagelin, 'International Cooperation in Conventional Weapons Acquisition: A

Threat to Armaments Control?', *Bulletin of Peace Proposals*, Vol. 9, No. 2, 1978, pp. 144–155.
8 B. Hagelin, P. D. Wezeman, S. T. Wezeman and N. Chipperfield, 'Transfers of Major Conventional Weapons', in *SIPRI Yearbook 2001. Armaments, Disarmament and International Security* (Oxford: Oxford University Press, 2001), p. 350.
9 Hagelin, 1985, pp. 157–158.
10 D. Cortright and G. A. Lopez (eds) *Smart Sanctions: Targeting Economic Statecraft* (Lanham, MD: Rowman & Littlefield, 2002), p. 14. Several of the chapters give examples of failed and ineffective UN arms embargoes.

Part III

NEW ACTORS
Empowering organizations

7

THE EU AS A NEW ACTOR ON THE SANCTIONS SCENE

Anthonius W. de Vries and Hadewych Hazelzet*

Since the 1990s, the European Union (EU) has become a new actor in the field of sanctions.[1] This is apparent in the fact that sanctions legislation is nowadays largely enacted at the EU rather than the Member States' level. Also, over the past decade or so, have seen that the EU develop a somewhat distinct approach towards sanctions.

If there is any European sanctions policy, it would be a preference to use positive rather than negative measures, or carrots over sticks. This might be explained by a genuine belief that such instruments are more effective to further respect for international law and human rights, and by the lessons learned from the sanctions against Iraq and, to a lesser extend, Haiti. The truth of the matter is, however, that it is also much easier and less costly for the various Member States to agree on positive rather than negative measures. That way the political risk to disappoint those constituents at home that would carry the costs of sanctions is minimal, whereas the economic costs of, for instance, using development assistance to promote foreign policy goals are evenly shared.

Despite its increasing significance and ambitions to act as a credible player in world affairs, for the moment, the EU does not have many foreign policy instruments at its disposal other than economic ones. The European Security and Defense Policy (ESDP) is still in its infancy. Nevertheless, many players within the EU have not been too keen to use sanctions as an instrument of foreign policy. In fact, in typical EU jargon, EU insiders prefer to speak of "restrictive measures" rather than sanctions. Such measures tend to be used on the one hand as instruments to react to violations of international law or violations of human rights, the rule of law and democratic principles, and on the other hand as instruments promoting respect for these rights and principles. Besides issuing public declarations and carrying out confidential "démarches," the EU has developed a variety of instruments "between words and wars."

Legislation needed for implementing UN Security Council sanctions is nowadays passed at the level of the EU. This chapter focuses on describing the role of the EU in respect of sanctions imposed by the United Nations Security Council and those imposed by the EU. Starting with a brief overview of the EU sanctions "decade," we will analyze the four essential elements identified by the Stockholm Process as necessary for an effective use of sanctions as an instrument of foreign policy: legislation, enforcement, monitoring and planning.[2] We will conclude with a discussion of the future role of the EU. In our view, the EU may turn out to be an increasingly effective actor in the field of sanctions, but to realize that potential it would have to address a number of shortcomings, in particular with regard to planning, monitoring and enforcement. Encouraging steps in this regard are the recently ongoing revision of EU sanctions policy, the European Security Strategy of 2003, the process of enlargement and, finally, the implications of the European Convention once adopted.

Legislation

UN Security Council sanctions

The appearance of the EU as a new actor on the sanctions scene has much to do with the implementation legislation that most sanctions resolutions of the UN Security Council require. An important reason for Member States to accept or even to press for EU sanctions legislation is the fact that such legislation minimizes the risk of different interpretations given to UN Security Council resolutions by Member States. Such differences could lead to serious distortions of competition in a market without internal borders.[3] Another reason was and still is the fact that EU legislation on average can be adopted much quicker than national legislation.

Decisions taken by the UN Security Council under Chapter VII of the UN Charter (sanctions) are not directly applicable and binding decisions within the EU or any of its Member States. There is therefore a need for legislation to provide the legal basis for the required actions by governments, their agencies and services, citizens, companies or other entities. This legislation differs depending on the type of sanction.

Member States of the EU already have national legislation in place which enables them to control most of their external trade in arms. Therefore, the implementation of arms embargoes of the UN Security Council does not require new legislation by the Member States or the EU. The existing legislation forms the legal basis for the necessary administrative directives/instructions to the relevant state agencies and services. Normally this implies instructions to refuse the export licenses that are required for any export of arms. Recent arms embargo decisions of the UN Security Council extend their scope to the provision of services to the military or for military activities. Because not all Member States have legislation in place to deal with this prohibition, these activities are being regulated through EU legislation.

Only few Member States have legislation in place in respect of arms brokering. In those cases, the legislation is limited to arms brokering within the territorial jurisdiction of the Member State. Certain sanctions legislation of the EU however also extends to brokering for the provision of goods or services outside the territory of the EU.[4]

For a long time Member States based the implementation of UN Security Council embargoes in respect of trade in dual-use goods on national legislation. Since the European Court of Justice has decided that those goods fall under the exclusive competence of the EU, these types of embargoes are henceforth implemented on the basis of Council Regulation (EC) No 1334/2000.

For the implementation of travel restrictions, all Member States have national legislation in place that allows them to instruct border authorities to prohibit the entry into or exit from their territories of persons. Of course, travel bans for citizens of a country are more easily implemented if there is a visa requirement for all citizens of that country. The introduction of a general visa obligation, that is the establishing of the list of countries whose citizens have to ask for a visa to enter the territory of the EU, is done at the level of the EU. Sport bans or cultural embargoes will require in most cases specific legislation by the EU Member States, because the EU does not have the relevant competencies in these fields.

With respect to trade and financial sanctions there exists a rather peculiar situation. Already at the creation of the European Community in 1956 the Member States transferred to a large extent their competence in respect of international trade to that body. Therefore, Member States can no longer adopt national legislation on international trade that deviates from the legislation adopted within the framework of the EU. But also from the start Member States agreed that this transfer of competencies in the field of trade should not apply to the implementation of UN Security Council sanctions.[5] Given the very few (non-arms) trade sanctions imposed by the UN Security Council, this exception was hardly invoked. Nowadays Member States refrain from creating national legislation for implementing trade sanctions.[6]

As of 1994 the same applies regarding financial sanctions insofar as they concern international payments and international movement of capital and investments. Hence, for trade and financial sanctions the general rule is that legislation is adopted at the level of the EU. In most cases this legislation is specifically geared to the particular sanctions regime, avoiding any unnecessary infringement of the trade and capital movement liberalization that characterizes generally the EU's trade and financial relations with third countries.

Although the EU has no exclusive competence in respect of trade in certain types of services, the flight bans imposed by the UN Security Council have all been implemented on the basis of EU legislation.

To sum up: with regard to arms embargoes and travel restrictions, it is mainly the existing legislation of Member States which creates the legal bases for the implementation of UN Security Council sanctions. Notably since 1990 EU legislation has become the main basis for the implementation of sanctions in respect of finance, payments, investments, trade in goods and/or services.

Autonomous EU sanctions

The UN Security Council can take sanctions under Chapter VII of the UN Charter in cases of a breach of the peace or a threat of such a breach. It can not take sanctions with a view to protect labor rights, democracy, and the rule of law or good governance by the authorities of a country. But the member states of the United Nations can do so, insofar as they are not prevented by international obligations under international law (such as those contained in the agreements concluded within the framework of the World Trade Organization).

Autonomous EU sanctions have a relatively young history.[7] Before 1990 it was the Member States of the EU that took, individually or collectively, sanctions against certain countries without a prior UN Security Council decision. Some sanctions concerned the protection of their territorial integrity. But there has been a steady growth in sanctions with a view to protect human rights, democracy, labor conditions or more generally good governance in third countries. Most of these sanctions are now being taken at the level of the EU.[8] In terms of the legal basis for such sanctions, there exists a large overlap with the legal basis for the implementation of UN Security Council sanctions. However, in most cases the trigger for activating the use of the existing legal basis or of an ad hoc one is not formed by a decision of the UN Security Council but by the adoption by the Council of the EU of a Common Position or Joint Action specifying the sanctions to be taken, against whom, and for how long.[9]

Nowadays a Member State of the EU can hardly impose unilateral sanctions towards third countries. The Treaty of Nice provides that Member States will not "impede, or otherwise undermine" the Common Foreign and Security Policy (CFSP) of the Union, and will support it "actively and unreservedly in a spirit of loyalty and mutual solidarity." On the other hand, the requirement of unanimity gives each Member State tremendous influence over whether or not sanctions are imposed, and if so, what type and against whom.

Whereas European sanctions *sensu stricto* have a young history, the EU developed a substantial and wide-reaching policy of development cooperation fairly early on in its history. Cooperation is most extensively developed with former colonies of Member States, over whom the EU has traditionally had an important economic and political leverage. The ways in which this leverage was brought to bear, have however not always been explicitly institutionalized to the extent that they are today.[10] Therefore, in addition to the sanctions the EU takes autonomously on the basis of Common Positions or Joint Actions and their implementation of national or EU legislation, there exists a range of other legal instruments that allows the EU to take sanctions.[11] These take the form of Council and Commission Regulations and decisions which implement the provisions of international agreements that the EU has concluded with third countries, that allow the EU to take appropriate measures such as the full or partial suspension or even termination of the agreements in case the "essential elements" clauses concerning respect for democracy, human rights, rule of law, and good governance are not respected.

In most cases, the EU only decides on imposing restrictive measures after an intensive consultation procedure with the third countries concerned. Such a consultation procedure is followed even in the case of an intended withdrawal of trade benefits under the Generalized Scheme of Tariff Preferences (GSP), which is *sensu stricto*, a unilateral instrument. Such withdrawals can take place in cases of serious disrespect or violations of international obligations concerning labor standards.

Enforcement

An effective sanctions regime requires legislation that spells out the obligations for governmental authorities at several levels of responsibility, as well as for others, be it citizens, legal persons such as companies, or other entities. Equally important is the enforcement of that legislation. An important element of an effective enforcement is legislation that allows the imposition of penalties on those who violate a sanctions regime. Until now EU legislation only obliges Member States to pass legislation on the penalties, and for the penalties to be effective, dissuasive and proportionate. [12]

Some Member States have passed such legislation on a permanent basis, but most of them have to pass legislation specifically related to the EU sanctions legislation concerned. Experience has shown that the adoption of such legislation sometimes takes a very long time. This clearly has an impact on the effectiveness of sanctions. Given the absence of internal borders within the EU for trade, capital and payments flows, the strength of the EU sanctions is determined by the weakest link in the chain of Member States.

Even with legislation on penalties in place, enforcement requires appropriate checking of compliance. Such checks are relatively easy to perform in cases of arms embargoes and visa bans because arms exporters or applicants for visas have to provide the competent authorities with prior information on intended exports or entries whether a sanctions regime is in place or not. When trade in goods and services, and movements of capital or payments are not subject to border controls or other checks, the imposition of an embargo will require special and additional resources to be dedicated to the control of compliance with the sanctions.

In theory, as a sanctions regime becomes more comprehensive in nature (for instance, prohibiting all trade with and all capital movements to a country), the less cumbersome the enforcement will be for the competent authorities. When a sanctions regime becomes more targeted, however, the control will be more demanding in terms of resources by the competent authorities.[13]

Little is known about how the competent authorities in the EU Member States have coped with the additional tasks required by sanctions regimes. The general impression is that the enforcement is simply a task added to existing tasks, which therefore has to compete with other priorities of the services or agencies concerned (such as prevention of drugs imports/exports, money laundering and tax evasion). The budget of the EU does not contain standing provisions for sanctions implementation or assistance. Similarly, Member States do not budget *ex ante* sanctions enforcement.

A few examples exist where specific resources were dedicated to the enforcement of sanctions at the EU level or by Member States. The most notable example is the contribution of the European Commission to the Sanctions Assistance Missions during the UN Security Council sanctions against the Federal Republic of Yugoslavia (Serbia and Montenegro) during the years 1991–95. Major contributions thereto were also made by a number of Member States. The overall lead for the Sanctions Assistance Missions lay however with the Organization for Security and Economic Co-operation in Europe (OSCE). Furthermore, it was within the framework of the North Atlantic Treaty Organization (NATO) that a fleet composed of vessels of several NATO Member States operated in the Adriatic Sea to enforce those sanctions.

While an active enforcement role by the competent authorities, agencies and services in the EU may be hampered by insufficient resources, this situation is partly compensated for by a strong willingness of a large part of the business community to cooperate with the authorities to effectively enforce the sanctions. This is notably the case for the banking and financial services industry within the EU. An active and productive discussion between the European Commission and the banking and financial services industry has been brought into existence since 1996. Whereas the motivation of the private sector for the willingness to cooperate may lie primarily in the wish to avoid damage to its reputation (when caught in sanctions busting), the cooperation is very helpful. Through this cooperation the designing of targeted financial sanctions, the drafting of the appropriate legislation and the introduction of more sophisticated control mechanisms (such as dedicated hardware and software for detecting accounts and tracking payments) have been greatly improved.

The EU is currently revising its overall sanctions strategy, and acknowledges that enforcement is key to any effective sanctions regime.

Monitoring

The UN Security Council now recognizes that proper monitoring is an essential element of any sanctions regime it establishes. Expert Panels and Monitoring Mechanisms have been created for investigating compliance with sanctions regimes by the UN member states.

Within the EU the issue of proper monitoring is also recognized. Explicit reporting requirements are a standard element of the sanctions legislation of the EU. The EU's Code of Conduct on arms exports contains a strong monitoring mechanism. The diplomatic representatives of the EU and its Member States in the countries where sanctions targets are established tend to report regularly on the effectiveness of the sanctions, including their effects on non-targeted persons.

In the case of the EU's sanctions against Yugoslavia, a sanctions management committee was established which consisted of technical experts from Member

States, that advised the Commission on implementing legislation or decisions to be taken by the Commission. At the same time, the committee allowed for an exchange of experiences and resolving problems posed by that specific sanctions regime. In this case, monitoring showed that the initial targeted sanctions were circumvented easily by the targets, which led to a reinforcement of the sanctions. This cycle was repeated several times. Monitoring also allowed for creating exceptions, such as the supply of heating oil to certain cities that were governed by the opposition at the time.

The experience of the EU in monitoring the effectiveness of sanctions and in taking corrective action is not yet fully appreciated by the UN Security Council.[14] This is probably largely due to the fact that within the EU the division of tasks involved in the implementation of sanctions regimes is rather complicated, as shown above. Furthermore, even when most of the implementing legislation is done at the level of the EU, its Member States still prefer to report thereon in their individual capacity as UN Member States. Another reason why the EU is only slowly becoming recognized as an actor in the field of sanctions is its status as observer in the UN, which is comparable to that of other international organizations. The EU is however a rather *sui generis* type of international organization. The country holding the Presidency of the EU does speak on behalf of the Union in the UN.

The European Commission can play an effective role in the monitoring of the implementation of sanctions. For most of the EU legislation the Commission can hold Member States accountable for the proper and timely implementation of the legislation or other legal acts and activities taken there under. Whereas the UN Security Council monitoring system has to rely on peer pressure in cases of violation of sanctions, the European Commission can take Member States to the European Court of Justice for not enforcing the implementing EU legislation. Continued violation of its obligations under the EU legislation can also lead to penalties imposed on the Member State concerned. However, where sanctions are implemented on a national basis monitoring mechanisms are less clear. This is the case for UN Security Council sanctions as well as autonomous sanctions of the EU.

Planning or pre-assessment

The Stockholm Report states that "a reasonable pre-assessment of the feasibility of targeted sanctions and their likely implications is critical for the implementation of sanctions."[15] According to that report, sanctions planning should at least include the identification of:

- the problem or type of problem to be solved (usually an armed conflict or serious violations of human rights);
- the main responsible persons, institutions or other entities;
- the means and methods used by those persons, institutions or entities;

- the leverage of third parties on those parties (including the possibilities to avoid, circumvent or neutralize sanctions);
- the cost of sanctions to the sender;
- the relation with other means to solve the problem (parallel or consecutive);
- ways and means to adjust to the effects (positive or negative) of the applied sanctions;
- possible effects on non-targeted parties.

So far the role of the EU in the planning or pre-assessment of UN Security Council sanctions has been minimal. Yet, in respect of EU sanctions, serious efforts have been undertaken to improve planning or pre-assessment of sanctions.

If sanctions are being considered, one of the first items that is researched by the European Commission is the compatibility with the legal obligations of the EU.[16] The many multilateral and bilateral agreements, to which the EU is a party, restrict in many cases the possibilities to impose sanctions. Country desks within the services of the Commission, together with other units responsible for trade or financial relations with third countries, are usually able to identify the main economic and financial links between the EU and the third country concerned. Such mainly macro-level data are of course only of limited value for determining the most appropriate targeted sanctions. To a certain extent, reports by Heads of delegations of the Member States and of the European Commission in the third country concerned have shown to be useful in identifying the main responsible actors and for determining the vulnerability to sanctions by those actors. It has been more difficult to determine the various manners in which targets can circumvent the intended sanctions.

Information based on intelligence sources has so far played a modest role at the EU level. Most information is still obtained from open sources. Theoretically the planning phase could be a rather politically neutral exercise: a menu of options, where possible indicating expected costs and benefits and probabilities of success and failure for each type of sanction.

In reality, the process of presenting a menu of measures is a little bit murkier. In fact the planning phase is prone to becoming an imbroglio of quite diverse opinions on the effectiveness of sanctions in general as well as of conflicting interests in the potential target country. For instance, a factor limiting the efforts for adequate planning is the view that sanctions are more a means to signal disapproval of certain situations or behavior than a credible instrument to change those situations or behavior. Quite clearly, signaling requires a considerably smaller effort of planning than sanctions that really bite. Another factor is that sanctions as discussed in this book are an instrument of foreign policy, but mostly entail measures in fields for which Ministers of Foreign Affairs have little influence or no primary competence.

Furthermore, sanctions are meant to restrict relations between parties, while the general thrust of policies covering international trade, finance and traveling is the liberalization of those relations. Any serious planning of sanctions requires the cooperation of fellow Ministers and their ministries and departments with often different agendas. They are therefore not naturally inclined to actively engage in the planning of restrictive measures. On top of all these factors that play an important role at state level, the EU, like the UN Security Council, has to deal with the fact that its Member States have different levels and types of relations with the targeted parties.[17]

EU sanctions in the near future

The future of European sanctions depends at least on two aspects. First, what (compromise) perspective would EU Member States reach on sanctions as an effective foreign policy instrument, and under what conditions would they agree to impose them? Second, how will the EU's institutional capacity develop, and what impact would that have on the imposition and implementation of sanctions?

The foregoing sections have shown that the EU is to a certain extent already capable of ensuring an effective use of sanctions. The implementing legislation can deal effectively, rapidly and with the necessary precision for almost all types of sanctions. This applies to UN Security Council sanctions as well as autonomous sanctions. Over the past ten to fifteen years, the EU has remarkably enhanced the coordination and therefore credibility of its Common Foreign and Security Policy, of which sanctions have been an important tool. The lessons learned from the sanctions decade are starting to pay off: quality, coherence and consistency of EU legislation in this area has increased; experience with dozens of sanctions regimes in the 1990s has facilitated cooperation with the UN and major allies in many areas, such as identifying individual and group targets of sanctions and targeting sanctions in a smarter manner to those responsible for violations on international law and human rights. The EU has also shown it is able to use its diplomatic representations for the purposes of monitoring as well as planning of sanctions, in particular in identifying the targets.

The foregoing sections have also shown that there is still considerable scope for improving and strengthening the capacity of the EU in respect of the four elements, in particular planning, monitoring and enforcement. Sanctions legislation should not remain a dead letter. In terms of enforcement of sanctions regimes, the EU and its Member States still need to set up an effective monitoring system and install penalties for those who bust sanctions. Some Member States have taken the lead by passing permanent legislation. It is furthermore not excluded that the European Court of Justice would recognize the competence of the EU itself to pass the required penalties legislation. Timely and watertight implementation is key for sanctions to be effective. Questions regarding the effects and effectiveness of sanctions will need to be addressed, but should not be seen independently of their poor implementation because of lack of resources and political will in the past.

Both the content of the EU's foreign policy and its institutional capacity are currently undergoing a transition. The diverse reactions of EU Member States and their constituents to the war against Iraq prompted the development of an EU security strategy and a revision of its CFSP/ESDP. First, the EU is currently reviewing ways towards a more effective sanctions policy, looking both at strategic considerations and at issues of implementation. Effective cooperation with main partners, such as the USA, should be an essential element, especially in terms of enforcement. Also, EU's trade and development cooperation with third countries should be part of the strategy, in particular the application of human rights clauses in such agreements. Finally, the strategy would need to analyze lessons learned from the numerous sanctions cases in the 1990s and address the role of Member States and the European Commission in effective enforcement. The adoption of an EU Sanctions Strategy will certainly not be an easy task. The 15 existing Member States often found it extremely difficult to arrive on a common position on this instrument; it may be even more difficult to arrive at a consensus among 25 Member States.

Second, in December 2003, the European Council adopted the European Security Strategy. This strategy states *inter alia* that conditionality and targeted trade measures form an important feature of EU policy, which should be further reinforced. The strategy also recognizes the importance of export control of dual-use goods for the prevention of proliferation of weapons of mass destruction. It states furthermore that countries that "have placed themselves outside the bounds of international society" should "understand that there is a price to be paid, including in their relationship with the EU." The future will show what this means in practice.

The development of the EU security strategy coincided with the process of enlargement that was already well under way. As of 1 May 2004, the EU consists of 25 Member States. It is widely recognized that its current Treaty provisions will no longer be workable, especially the frequent requirement of unanimity in decision making. Therefore, a process was set in motion to revise and simplify the Treaty. The Convention, the body tasked to prepare an EU constitution under the chairmanship of Mr Giscard d'Estaing, presented its proposals in June 2003. Amongst others, it is proposed to give the EU one legal personality and get rid of the three pillar structure, to enhance possibilities for majority voting and to appoint a Union Minister for Foreign Affairs. The Council of the EU is still discussing the proposals, following lack of agreement on a number of issues at the European Council in December 2003.

The proposal made with regard to sanctions might survive the current negotiations without major difficulties, since it would merely simplify and codify current practice. The decision whether or not to react would still be taken under the relevant provisions of the CFSP, while the type of measure would be subject to qualified majority voting. Any such decisions would be taken on the basis of a joint proposal from a future European Minister of Foreign Affairs and the Commission. The European Parliament would be informed of such measures. In view of the increasing use of financial sanctions directed against individuals and groups (and not states) it is important to note that the same procedure would be valid for deciding on the imposition of restrictive measures against persons, groups or non-state actors.

However, simplified legal provisions do not guarantee smoothened decision making, nor an effective and credible common foreign policy. Underlying divisions in terms of perspectives and interests will remain and political determination and vision are needed to act together on the international stage. Alignments will surely change within the EU depending on the issues at stake, and blocking minorities will still be easily formed, thereby potentially impeding any progress or change. The new Member States with their own place in history and geopolitical allegiances will no doubt influence the content and strategic focus of EU foreign policy. Becoming the guardians of the enhanced borders of the EU, the new Member States will have to play a crucial role in the effective implementation of any future sanctions regime. Enforced by a Union of 25, European sanctions will bite much more than sanctions imposed by the current 15. Monitoring their effective implementation will be a major task, and will require increased resources.

The future of EU sanctions depends on the future of EU foreign policy. A matured EU will have more foreign policy instruments at its disposal, including military action. Whereas the threat and imposition of sanctions used to be the strongest possible reaction of the EU to misbehaving dictators, the building up of EU military capacities will also increase the credibility and sophistication of EU foreign policy. When choosing something between words and wars, sanctions have thus recently acquired a new place amongst the foreign policy options. The more the EU engages itself in defining its role in military matters, the more it may become interested in finding alternatives for the use of force.

The future European Minister of Foreign Affairs may be capable of giving a more strategic and coherent direction to EU foreign policy, depending on her or his personal capacities as much as her or his formal powers. A clearer chain of command and increased and more effective coordination between the various institutions, as well as between national policies and better use of diplomatic and material resources and intelligence services, should result in the EU being the determined and credible actor on the world stage that it aspires to be.

The potential weight of the EU as an international actor is enormous. Its foreign policy toolkit is about to change, regarding both the type and scope of instruments at its disposal. The realization of its potential will however depend on the EU's institutional and political capacity to speak and act with 25 or more Member States. If accompanied by proper political and institutional backup, sanctions may continue to form a viable option. But no matter how successful the institutional and strategic transformation of the European enterprise, it is more than likely that the EU will continue to tend to prefer positive measures to negative ones.

Notes

* The views expressed by the authors in this chapter are personal and do not bind the institutions for which they work in any way.

1 From a legal point of view the EU was created by the Treaty on the EU (TEU), also called the Treaty of Maastricht that was signed in 1992 and entered into force at the end of that year, and partly, inter alia in respect of financial sanctions, on 1 January 1993. For reasons of space the term EU will be used anachronistically for the European Communities already existing before the TEU.
2 See the Stockholm Report, P. Wallensteen, C. Staibano and M. Eriksson (eds) *Making Targeted Sanctions Effective: Guidelines for the Implementation of UN Policy Options*, Department of Peace and Conflict Research, Uppsala University (Stockholm: Elanders Gotab, 2003).
3 The different interpretations that Member States gave to the financial sanctions vis-à-vis Iraq contained in UN Security Council resolution 661 are a good example of this risk.
4 Common Position 2003/468/CFSP requires that all Member States regulate arms brokering, even when taking place outside their territorial jurisdiction.
5 This exception only applies to those Member States that were already member states of the United Nations before becoming Member States of the EU. Therefore the exception does not apply to Germany, nor will it apply to the three Baltic States that will become Member States in 2004.
6 In fact all Member States, except the United Kingdom, have refrained from invoking this exception and thereby from introducing national legislation for the implementation of UN Security Council trade or financial sanctions. We will refrain from discussing the legality of parallel national and EU legislation here.
7 For a comprehensive overview and analysis of all types of EU sanctions legislation and their application from 1989–2001, see H. Hazelzet, "Carrots or Sticks? EU and US reactions to human rights violations (1989–2000)," PhD dissertation (European University Institute, San Domenico di Fiesole, Italy, 2001).
8 See the example of Serbia-Montenegro discussed in A. de Vries, "European Union Sanctions against the Federal Republic of Yugoslavia from 1998 to 2000: A Special Exercise in Targeting", in D. Cortright and G. A. Lopez (eds) *Smart Sanctions: Targeting Economic Statecraft* (Lanham, MD: Rowman & Littlefield, 2002).
9 The Treaties concerning the EU require that the Council of the EU also adopts a Common Position or Joint Action before specific Community legislation can be passed by the (same) Council for the implementation of UN Security Council sanctions. But whereas a Common Position or Joint Action creates an obligation for the EU Member States to implement the Common Position or Joint Action which would otherwise not exist, the Common Positions or Joint Actions adopted within the framework of UN Security Council sanctions are de facto redundant because the obligation to take sanctions follows already from the UN Security Council decision under Chapter VII of the Charter. For reasons which fall outside the scope of this chapter, efforts during the conception of the new European Constitution to remedy this redundancy failed.
10 For a history of the Lomé Conventions and the Cotonou Agreement see K. Arts, "Integrating human rights into development co-operation: The case of the Lomé Convention," PhD thesis (Vrije Universiteit Amsterdam, 2000) and B. Martenczuk, "From Lomé to Cotonou: The ACP–E.C. Partnership Agreement in a Legal Perspective," *European Foreign Affairs Review*, Vol. 5, No. 4, Winter 2000, pp. 461–487. For the application of the human rights clause see Hazelzet, 2001.
11 See Hazelzet, 2001. For more on autonomous trade measures, see also B. Brandtner and A. Rosas, "Trade Preferences and Human Rights," in Alston Philip (ed.) *The EU and Human Rights* (Oxford: Oxford University Press, 2000) and B. Brandtner and A. Rosas, "Human Rights and the External Relations of the E.C.: An Analysis of Doctrine and Practice," *European Journal of International Law* (EJIL) (1998), pp. 468–490.

12 A legal battle is still ongoing between Member States and the European Commission, supported in this by the European Parliament, on the competence of the EU to determine the character of the penalties (notably their penal character) in cases of violation of EU legislation.
13 If diesel engines can be used by the targeted persons/groups for military services, but they are also needed for electricity generators used by hospitals in the targets' country, reliable information has to be obtained prior to export; similarly, for instance, how can it be prevented that correspondent bank accounts are not used for payments to targeted persons?
14 The monitoring mechanism on the sanctions against the Taliban initially assumed that the EU Schengen Information System was the only mechanism by which visa bans were implemented within the EU. The expert panels on the trade embargoes on rough diamonds sold by the UNITA or the Sierra Leone rebels overlooked the fact that additional compliance measures by one EU Member State could simply be undermined by the absence of internal market controls. The existence of the internal market and relevance of effective controls at the external borders of all EU Member States was recognized by the Kimberley Process on the certification of the international trade in rough diamonds.
15 Cf. section 271 of the Stockholm Report (2003).
16 A good example is the reversal of the decision to take sanctions against Haiti, after it became clear that the intended sanctions would violate the obligations of the EC under the Lomé Convention (currently the Cotonou Agreement).
17 Hazelzet, 2001, shows that the level of economic importance of the target country overall does not impede the EU from imposing sanctions. Nevertheless, if one compares sanctions towards former colonies, and looks at the attitude of individual Member States, it is clear that certain former colonial powers tend to try and shield their former protectorate from sanctions, whereas others take a more open attitude towards the use of this instrument in pushing for regime change (pp. 169, 200–201, 205–211).

8

EU SANCTIONS

Three cases of targeted sanctions*

Mikael Eriksson

European Union sanctions

This chapter presents some general proposals for enhancing the capacity of the EU to implement targeted sanctions. These proposals are based on a review of sanctions imposed by the European Union (EU) on Belarus, Burma (Myanmar) and Zimbabwe. This review centers on the effects of EU imposed sanctions in the three separate cases, and also explains why and under what circumstances these targeted sanctions were imposed.

While comprehensive sanctions have been used for several decades in forms of blockades and embargoes, the new type of targeted sanctions has only been developed during the past ten years. Thus, this chapter builds on the experiences and reports developed by the Bonn–Berlin, Interlaken and the Stockholm processes.

Targeted sanctions are here seen as a political measure that includes economic initiatives in which a "sender" takes an explicit action against a particular "recipient" in an effort to make the latter comply with international norms, standards and practices. One of the objectives of such sanctions is to target the leaders of a country, and thus avoid affecting the general population. There are many types of targeted sanctions commonly used today: aviation bans, financial sanctions and arms embargoes to mention some. A targeted sanction is – at least in theory – designed to isolate certain entities such as companies, rebel groups or criminal networks from access to needed resources. Primarily, the targeted sanctions are directed at individuals, both privately and in their official capacity. To be able to implement these sanctions measures, precise and accurate information is required, which today is not always available. This chapter analyzes experiences from the EU's use of sanctions.

While the EU and the UN have similarities in their capabilities to implement sanctions, there are fundamental differences in terms of why sanctions are imposed. The UN is a global organization with global interests. It imposes sanctions on the basis of its Charter, and often monitors them via the Security Council sanctions committees. The EU, on the other hand, is a regional organization with mainly regional interests. It imposes sanctions to promote respect for human rights and democratic principles of governance and adopts policies on the basis of the general objectives of the Common Foreign and Security Policy (CFSP).[1] The EU has a consensus decision-making process for sanctions.[2] There are different procedures for different types of sanctions: economic and financial sanctions fall under community law,[3] while travel sanctions and diplomatic sanctions are decided on the member state level. For sanctions that need to be regulated by community law, the European Commission has to propose the necessary measures, which are then adopted by the Council of the European Union.[4] The European governments within the EU are bound by UN sanctions resolutions, but there are also situations where the EU has acted outside this framework, as is the case, for instance, of Belarus, Burma (Myanmar), China, Indonesia and Zimbabwe.[5]

Why then look at the EU in the first place? There are two main reasons. First of all, general insights on conditions for successful sanctions could be gained from the way targeted sanctions have been imposed, administered and monitored. The manner in which the EU does this is different from how the UN carries out sanctions. Second, the observed direct and indirect effects could increase our knowledge on how sanctions work in practice. To know how EU sanctions work can benefit the UN in its planning.

This chapter presents three cases of sanctions imposed by the EU: Belarus, Burma and Zimbabwe. They are different in terms of political contexts and economic prerequisites, which might affect the outcome in terms of implementation. They share one common denominator: strong authoritarian leaders governed in all the countries at the time when targeted sanctions were considered.

In dealing with these EU cases, questions raised in the Stockholm Report will be kept in mind. Key questions are: what were the goals of the sanctions? How were these sanctions monitored and implemented? How did those targeted by the sanctions perceive their situation? Were there known cases of evasion and circumvention?

Three cases

Belarus

Introducing targeted sanctions

After the collapse of the Soviet Union in 1991, the European Union established normal diplomatic contacts with Belarus. However, during the first few years of the state-building process, the European governments followed with great concern how Belarus entered a political path that diverged from the democratic future they had expected. In 1996, acting President Lukashenko decided to change the constitution by concentrating powers around himself and by extending his term in office. This act made several European governments realize that a pessimistic analysis of Belarus was effectively confirmed. As such the European Council, in an act to show dissatisfaction, suspended its diplomatic relationship. High-level contacts with Belarus would only go via the EU Presidency or the EU Troika (in effect, this was a ban on high-level bilateral contacts).

To continue following Belarus's political and democratic path, the Organization for Security and Cooperation in Europe (OSCE) concluded a Memorandum of Understanding (MoU) with Belarus, creating an OSCE-led Advisory Monitoring Group (AMG) in 1997. The AMG repeatedly reported deteriorating democratic conditions. These were confirmed in particular in the parliamentary elections of 2000 and in the presidential elections of 2001. AMG concluded that the elections were not fair. Owing to the AMG being critical of the political situation in the country, the relationship between President Lukashenko's administration and the AMG changed for the worse. The government of Belarus concluded that the AMG went beyond the original mandate and purpose, as agreed in the MoU.[6] Hence, the Belarus government tried to obstruct AMG operations, by restricting or refusing to grant accreditation to members of the group. As a result, the cooperation between the AMG and the Belarus government came to a point where it could no longer work. In October 2002, the last remaining foreign staff left the office.

On November 19, 2002, fourteen of the fifteen EU governments decided to impose targeted sanctions on senior members of the Belarus government in reaction to the *de facto* discontinuation of AMG. Portugal objected to the sanctions as it was concerned over the impact they would have on the upcoming high-level summit. In the first round of targeted sanctions, the EU imposed travel restrictions on President Lukashenko and seven other members of the Belarus government and key members of the Presidential administration. The sanctions meant that those placed on the sanctions list were not allowed to enter into fourteen EU countries. Furthermore, the EU position included additional targeted, restrictive measures, at a later date, if the situation did not improve. It was also underlined that the measures were designed not to harm the ordinary citizens of Belarus.[7] On December 31, 2002 the AMG mission was closed, but an OSCE office was allowed to open in Minsk on the following day. As the OSCE office in Minsk was established, the conclusion was that the government of Belarus was cooperating and should therefore be rewarded. In light of the positive steps taken by the Belarus government to ensure a good working climate, the targeted sanctions against Lukashenko and the other individuals placed on the list were lifted on April 14, 2003.[8]

Experiences of targeted sanctions

It seems important, based on the experience recounted, that the goals of the sanctions are clear and that the sender makes sure that action is not removed until the conditions are fully meet. In Belarus, the short-term goal was to enhance democratic structures and to reinstate OSCE monitoring capacities. Although the OSCE mission was allowed to function, the overall democratic situation did not improve. In the long run, therefore, the credibility of the sender may have been tarnished, as the EU had not achieved what it initially asked for. Thus, properly assessing the target is important to be able to stipulate achievable goals.

Moreover, it is necessary to make sure that there is unity among those actors deciding to implement sanctions. A united attitude is likely to increase the credibility of the seriousness of the policy, signalling this both to the recipient as well as to the domestic actors of the sender and to the rest of the region. As seen, one EU member state abstained for its own political purposes.

Placing targeted sanctions on the leadership may at least have sent some signals. Imposing travel restrictions is often an effective tool to isolate officials and political representatives. In the case of Belarus, however, this may not have been so effective. Lukashenko, for instance, had no real reason for traveling to Europe, but was unhindered from going to other states, notably Russia. This suggests that cooperation with neighboring countries is important for effective targeted sanctions. A closer working relationship with neighboring states or organizations is more likely to increase political pressure.

Burma (Myanmar)

Introducing targeted sanctions

The political situation in Burma/Myanmar has been unstable and insecure for at least half a century, with military regimes succeeding one another. Few steps have been taken to solve the complex political situation, which concerns many interests including democratic movements, opposition parties, ethnic groups and armed rebels. This has been a reason for concern in the international community.

On September 18, 1988, the State Law and Order Restoration Council (SLORC), was placed on suspension by international institutions and the donor community. The EU, for its part, ended all its non-humanitarian and development projects with Burma.[9] The rationale for introducing such disincentives was to promote democracy.

Citing the handling of the May 27, 1990 election, the EU noted the Burmese government's lack of adherence to the democratic will of the people. As a result, an informal decision on the removal of military staff from Myanmar's diplomatic missions in all member states was adopted. At the same time, the EU withdrew all military attachés from member states' missions in Burma/Myanmar. The decision was made to promote progress of democracy and the release of political prisoners. Connected to this informal but explicit act, EU member states later decided to impose an embargo on arms and military related equipment.[10] The ambition was also to press the Burmese military regime to accept the 1990 elections result, and to end violations of human rights.

The political situation had further deteriorated by 1996 and the European Council reiterated its concern for the lack of democratization and the government's continued violation of human rights. In October, the European countries introduced a visa ban on senior members of the SLORC and their families and other senior military and security officers.[11] High-level governmental visits to Burma/Myanmar were also suspended. The European governments demanded the immediate and unconditional release of political prisoners, and called for a continued dialogue with pro-democratic groups to reach national reconciliation.

On March 24, 1997, as a result of international and European labor unions' reports on the massive use of forced labor in Burma, the EU removed Burma/Myanmar from its Generalized System of Preferences (GSP).[12] This was an action not traditionally included in the targeted sanctions toolbox. It meant that Burma/Myanmar was not granted special tariff reductions for goods exported to the EU or benefit from duty and quota-free access to the EU market for exports as one of the Least Developed Nations (LDCs). The EU made clear that these measures would be lifted if the use of forced labor ceased. In 1997, possibly as a concession to international pressure, the SLORC changed its approach and the name was changed to the State Peace and Development Council (SPDC).

In 1997 Burma became a member of the ASEAN (Association of South East Asian Nations). While the EU had acted on a sanctions strategy providing for a change of government policy, ASEAN acted more on a long-term "carrot" approach with the hope that cooperation within the organization would stimulate a change. A problem with this particular strategy was that the ASEAN charter stipulated a policy of "non-interference" in internal affairs of member states.[13] On the contrary, Burma's membership was, by many, seen as a way of giving the regime international legitimacy.

In 2000, after an EU troika had visited Burma/Myanmar, sanctions were strengthened as there was little sign of democratic progress. In April 26, 2000, the EU imposed a ban on the supply of equipment that might be used for internal repression or terrorism. This Common Position also published a list of persons covered by the visa ban and whose funds were frozen. The list included members of the SPDC and others, described as persons that formulated, implemented or benefited from the policies that "impede Burma's transition to democracy." The regulation was approved on May 22, 2000, and entered into force on May 24. This was part of increased international attention to the situation in Burma/Myanmar. For instance, in April 2000, the United Nations Secretary General appointed Tan Sri Razali Ismail as the Special Envoy for Burma. The purpose of the EU actions was the same as before: for the regime to end violations of human rights and take steps towards democracy and national reconciliation.[14]

Since October 2000, the EU has continuously extended the sanctions already in place.[15] However, the EU also made it possible to permit Burmese officials to attend United Nations meetings and conferences held within EU territory. For instance, this allowed the Burmese foreign minister to attend an EU–ASEAN meeting in 2002.

At this time, the EU has sent four official-level EU troika missions to Rangoon, the latest one in September 2002,[16] to explain the EU position and to encourage reconciliation between the SPDC, the National League for Democracy (NLD) and ethnic minority groups.

On April 28, 2003 the EU agreed on a new Common Position, which was an update of the 1996 version. This new Common Position called for further use of sanctions, as well as for a broader inclusion of people to be placed on the sanctions list. This was an overt threat and meant that broader targeted sanctions would be enforced not later than October 29, 2003, if there was no progress towards democracy and national reconciliation. However, as the situation deteriorated in Burma/Myanmar, especially with the imprisonment of Aung San Suu Kyi in May 2003, and more harassment of the NLD, the Council decided on June 20 to immediately impose the new measures.[17] The sanctions were updated on December 22, 2003, and therefore were not softened by the reshuffle of the government of Burma/Myanmar. The EU measures called for a process leading to national reconciliation, and for support of the UN Special Envoy Razali Ismail. The acceding countries to the EU also aligned themselves to this updated sanctions policy. The EU Common Position on Burma/Myanmar was extended in April 2004.

Experiences of targeted sanctions

Targeted sanctions on Burma/Myanmar have been imposed gradually over a long time period. There are different schools of thought on how sanctions should be used, with some arguing that centralized authoritarian regimes are best dealt with in an immediate and comprehensive manner.[18] The EU sanctions approach has been to be more targeted and this has continued, with a certain element of escalation over the years. As could be expected, the sanctions have been dismissed by representatives of the regime. For instance, the Burmese ambassador to London once said "we are not worried about US and European sanctions, as trade with India, China and Thailand is already good."[19]

Obviously, little change has hitherto been witnessed but this is not to say that the measures are without impact. Rather, one can see a pattern of the regime trying to adapt its policies when new measures are introduced. Thus, there is sensitivity to the actions of the international community. However, impact may have been greater if there had been a special political relationship between the EU and Burma/Myanmar, apart from the economic ties. It underlines the importance of providing credible reasons for imposing sanctions. For instance, UN sanctions on Burma/Myanmar would have had a higher legitimacy and the North–South divide would not come to play a role in the sanctions issue.

Second, there are practical monitoring problems. It is difficult for EU countries to monitor the possibility of joint ventures of European and Myanmar/Burmese companies working on the Burmese market. To effectively enforce targeted sanctions the EU needs monitoring on the ground.[20] By reducing its presence in the country the EU might run the risk of loosing capacities, which may affect the credibility of the sanctions.

Third, a problem with the EU's sanctions policy on Burma/Myanmar is that it is not specific enough. It needs to be more concrete in terms of what it wants the Burmese officials to do for it to remove the sanctions. [21] This would make compliance easier and it would be easier for the EU to measure if the government is taking sincere steps of compliance.[22] The EU should clearly set standards on how it perceives important issues such as the Bangkok forum, the ongoing National Convention efforts, the forthcoming chairing of the ASEAN, the Financial Action Task Force (FATF) program on Burma/Myanmar.

Fourth, another area which needs to be strengthened is the listing of individuals exposed to the sanctions. Fundamentally, the list needs to be improved as the information on the targeted individuals is poor and unclear. Also, the list itself is not easily located. In order for funds to be frozen and official representatives to be prevented from traveling to European countries, the list needs to have more personal details, such as date of birth, account numbers, aliases, passport number, addresses, career history, etc. This problem, however, partly stems from the fact that member states do not share necessary information among themselves or with the Commission. Additionally, it could be useful to clarify the motives for why a specific official member is placed on the list and what that person is to do to be removed. There are not only State Peace and Development Council members on the list, but also former members of the SLORC, regional commanders, former high-ranking military staffs, individuals related to tourism authorities, former members of the government, intelligence, and members of the Office of Strategic Studies. The extent to which and how much all these persons contribute to the present state of affairs in the country is not obvious. Clearly, their significance must vary.

Fifth, as we observed in the case of Belarus, the reaction of key neighbors is important. In this case, it means countries in the region, such as China, India, Indonesia, Japan, Malaysia and Thailand. Cooperation with countries outside the European space is obviously a necessity for effective targeted sanctions. In this way there would be more information available which could decrease the likelihood of the target circumventing the EU sanctions. Likewise, the sanctions might be more effective if cooperation with regional organizations were initiated, notably ASEAN.[23]

Sixth, the four visits of the EU troikas on fact-finding missions were probably strategic moves to show that the EU was seriously monitoring the political and economic situation. At the same time they provided an opportunity for the Burmese government to explain its position. A pilot study on Burma/Myanmar recommended that the EU create a special office for an EU envoy to coordinate its activities.[24]

Finally, domestic support for sanctions on Burma/Myanmar seems strong among the opposition groups. This is important as the Burmese government has tried to mobilize popular sentiments against EU actions by raising issues of "national pride and survival."[25] Domestic support could increase the legitimacy and efficacy of sanctions.

Zimbabwe

Introducing targeted sanctions

The Mugabe government took over power at the internationally recognized independence of the country in 1980. Robert Mugabe was seen as one of the liberation heros, and little attention was paid to the domestic affairs of the country. However, by the late 1990s concern started to arise. An opposition party, Movement for Democratic Change (MDC), was formed and the political tension in the country increased. As part of the upcoming elections for President, the regime began to stimulate forceful occupations of land owned by remaining white settlers. The land issue as well as the democracy issue gave rise to international concern. A dialogue to provide for a democratic process was initiated between the EU and Zimbabwe in February 2001.[26] The dialogue was based on a consultation framework with the EU in accordance with Article 96 in the Cotonou Agreement, and was to focus on priority issues, such as ending the political violence, having the EU monitor the elections, allowing for the protection of the media, enhancing the independence of the legal system, and ending illegal occupation of land.[27] However, the results of the dialogue were poor. On election day in March 2002, the record of human rights abuses was long, and the international community had to react. In fact, the election in Zimbabwe stirred up feelings among many countries, both in the region and outside.[28] Several countries supported the outcome of the election result while others opposed it. This division was particularly noticeable in the Southern African Development Community (SADC) and in the Commonwealth.[29]

Before election day, the EU took a binding, unified decision on the political situation in Zimbabwe. It presented a set of conditions that had to be met by Zimbabwe if the elections were to meet legitimate democratic standards. Unless the Zimbabwean government, formed by the Zimbabwe African National Union–Patriotic Front (ZANU–PF), responded positively to these demands, targeted sanctions would be imposed. First of all, the EU wanted the government of Zimbabwe to accept an EU election observation mission and to agree not to prevent the mission from operating effectively. Second, the government of Zimbabwe was not to prevent the international media from having free access to cover the election. If there was a continuing deterioration on the ground, in terms of a worsening of the human rights' situation or attacks on the opposition, sanctions were to be imposed. Sanctions were also to be introduced if the elections were not determined as being "free and fair."[30] These conditions were not met, and so the EU on February 18, 2002 imposed targeted sanctions on 20 high-ranking individuals.

The EU measures were intended to affect the listed individuals in economic terms:

> Funds, financial assets or economic resources of the persons listed in the Annex, who are engaged in activities that seriously undermine democracy,

respect for human rights and the rule of law in Zimbabwe, will be frozen ... [and that] ... no funds, financial assets or economic resources will be made available directly or indirectly to the persons referred to.[31]

However, after the EU gave its first warning, there was a period during which the targets could rearrange their financial positions.[32] One report demonstrates that top officials and army generals were sending money to safe havens in Europe and depositing cash in US banks.[33] Another source concludes that as much as £10 million was deposited in banks in the Far East (e.g. Malaysia). It also claims that before the end of January the US government noticed that Zimbabwe's ruling elite was sending wealth abroad, well ahead of the Presidential election.[34] The time it took between the threat of imposing financial sanctions and the adoption of sanctions may explain why only a limited amount of funds has been frozen by EU member states (another reason could be that the targeted individuals have built family trusts that are out of the reach of sanctions).[35] In early 2004, it was reported that 29 bank accounts in the UK worth £513,000 had been frozen since sanctions were introduced, and that another US$50,000 had been frozen in Ireland.[36]

The EU also introduced travel restrictions on the individuals placed on the list. This meant visa bans and bans against transiting via EU territory. However, a targeted individual could be exempted if the journey was motivated by humanitarian reasons, religious matters, or for the sake of participating in meetings arranged by international institutions or meetings on the situation in Zimbabwe.[37]

Although targeted sanctions were enforced, senior members of the Zimbabwean government were able in some instances to travel to, or via, EU countries. For example, Mr Mugabe himself traveled to the UN in May 2002, on a flight that went via Paris with a Libyan airplane; in June 2002 he visited Rome to attend the World Food Summit.[38] In another instance, however, one clear attempt of circumvention was discovered. The cabinet minister Joshua Malinga was detained in London in July 2002 on his way to New York and was placed on a plane back to Zimbabwe.[39] Besides exercising economic pressure and implementing travel bans on the elite, the EU Council took further measures. This included an arms embargo on all types of supply or sale of arms and related material to Zimbabwe. Since then there has been at least one report citing allegations of circumvention.[40] The EU also withdrew US$110 million in development aid for the 2002–7 period, but would continue to channel humanitarian aid.[41]

In July 2002, the EU concluded that political violence in Zimbabwe was continuing without any positive signs, and introduced a new list of targeted individuals. Besides members of the military, parliament, police, prison and state security, a family member, Robert Mugabe's spouse, was added to the sanctions list. It also included persons in the political bureau of ZANU–PF. In this second step of sanctions, 24 persons were added to the list of targeted individuals making a total of 52 individuals. At the same time, the EU strengthened its efforts to directly support the population, mainly through non-governmental organizations working on HIV/Aids and democracy issues.

In a third step, the EU added seven new government members to its list, thus covering all members of the incumbent government. One reason was that Mugabe rearranged his government in August 2003. In mid February 2004, the EU extended its sanctions against Zimbabwe for a third year. In the latest round the list was extended to cover 95 Zimbabwean officials (several governors were included). The EU also renewed its embargo on supplies of arms and military equipment.[42]

In spite of these measures, and accompanying activities from the United States and Commonwealth countries, the Mugabe regime remained in power in Zimbabwe.

Experiences of targeted sanctions

The sanctions on Zimbabwe have received considerable coverage in the media and the debate on how to implement them has been intense. There are a number of incidents that illustrates the complexities of these sanctions, carried out by a regional actor. It is of interest to review some of these, as the debate and the decisions taken have impacted on the credibility of these particular sanctions as well as on the sanctions instrument as such.

The difficulties in upholding the travel sanctions have been those most discussed. For instance, in August 2002 Zimbabwe's Head of the Police, Augustine Chihuri, was granted a visa to attend an Interpol conference in Lyon.[43] In September 2002, the Zimbabwean Minister of Trade was given a visa to enter Belgium for a week to attend an ACP (Africa–Caribbean–Pacific forum) EU meeting.[44] The November 7–8, 2002 meeting of the EU–SADC was moved to Maputo, Mozambique, from Copenhagen, Denmark. The change of venue was caused by hints that several delegates would boycott the meeting in Copenhagen if the EU stood by its decision not to allow Zimbabwe's Foreign Minister to attend.[45] Furthermore, the EU debated for a long time whether to allow Minister of State Enterprises and Parastatals, Paul Mangwana and Deputy Minister of Finance and Economic Development Christopher Kuruneri to attend the November 25–28, 2002 EU–ACP Fifth Parliamentary Assembly Session in Brussels. Two officials were finally allowed to travel to Belgium, despite the travel restrictions that applied to them.[46] However, lawmakers from the ACP countries boycotted the meeting when they found out that the delegates from Zimbabwe were not allowed to enter the building where the meeting was held.[47] A most important EU debate was whether or not to invite Robert Mugabe to Paris at the invitation of the French President Jacques Chirac. Mugabe was eventually welcomed to Paris. France had asked its EU partners to grant a temporary exemption from the ban to allow Mugabe to attend the Franco-African meeting on February 19–21, 2003. France did so by invoking a clause in the EU sanctions allowing for an exemption from the travel ban on the grounds of seeking a "political dialogue" for promoting democracy and the rule of law. Many objected that there was no need for entering into such a dialogue with Zimbabwe.

Mugabe also traveled to non-European countries, particularly as part of his "look east" policy.[48] On these travels he tried to open new business links to ease

Zimbabwe's isolation. Mugabe and his entourage are known to have traveled to Thailand, Malaysia and Singapore. In Malaysia, Mugabe attended the Thirteenth Conference of the Non-Aligned Movement, which adopted a resolution calling for the end of sanctions. In all, 59 world leaders attended this meeting. Mugabe also went to Khartoum, Sudan for a summit of the Common Market for East and Southern Africa (COMESA) in March 2003. There he seems to have convinced the leaders to call for the removal of the Commonwealth sanctions on Zimbabwe.[49]

These experiences can be interpreted in different ways. One is to say that they may undermine the credibility of the sanctions, as some evasion is possible. On the other hand, it shows that traveling is obviously important to the leader in Zimbabwe. His difficulty in getting to Europe, which after all is a most significant trading partner, affects his legitimacy as well.

The introduction of targeted sanctions against Zimbabwe under the Common Foreign and Security Policy framework on March 9–11, 2002 marks the EU's political standpoint. This continues to be a problem for ZANU–PF. As of today, however, the sanctions have not had the effect of altering the behavior of the Zimbabwean government. As the fine-tuning of the sanctions instrument continues, the EU has to decide whether the intention of sanctions is to be symbolic or to de facto hit the targeted individuals. If one chooses the latter, there is an absence of political will that needs to be addressed. In the present situation there is no strong sanctions enforcement infrastructure.

In general, there seems to be a discrepancy between what was regarded as "symbolic sanctions" stated in EU policy papers, and the actual enforcement of the sanctions. First, there is a clear gap in the coordination between regional and international entities (states and organizations) capable of monitoring or implementing sanctions, such as the EU, the Commonwealth, the SADC, the USA, etc. In particular, a closer coordination between the EU, the US and the UK would have been necessary.[50] If the USA had introduced sanctions earlier, instead of several months after the EU, it would not have allowed for a crucial time-gap in which the targets could move their financial assets. The US approach is different in another respect as well, as it has not announced publicly who is on the restriction list.[51] Also, the EU did not try hard enough to establish cooperation with the countries in the region so that the sanctions, when introduced, could have been implemented more effectively.

Second, there have been no official explanations for why specific persons have been placed on the list. As we saw in the case of Burma, the lists did not include specific information on the individual, other than birth dates and names of the targeted subjects. More information would be needed in order for the individuals to be identified by financial operators, media, travel companies, etc.[52]

Third, the EU introduced an instrument not only to block money at the present time, but also a requirement to trace earlier transactions. This is likely to increase pressure on the target. However, foreign envoys were reported to have carried out financial transactions for individuals targeted by sanctions, by use of diplomatic bags, and it seems that EU diplomats were aware of such transactions.[53]

Fourth, sanctions on Zimbabwe have received considerable media attention. This, in turn, has led the authorities in Zimbabwe to counteract with propaganda (i.e. that the sanctions are intended for new neo-colonial purposes). In fact both sides have been effectively engaged in trying to convey their messages. The EU has tried to portray the sanctions as being aimed at the accountable leadership and not the general population; the government of Mugabe has tried to see them as a racial tool used by "white" Europeans. The government has turned to the domestic as well as regional and global audiences. An important lesson is to make sure that a sender of sanctions keeps an upper hand in explaining the reasons for the sanctions. Particularly important is that the sanctions are aimed against government representatives, and not against the general public.[54]

General conclusions from the three cases

Imposing targeted sanctions is a difficult and cumbersome affair, both in political and economic terms. It is difficult to assess the impact EU sanctions have had on targeted leaders and host countries. The EU experiences in trying to enforce different types of targeted sanctions over the past few years give rise to some general observations on how to improve sanctions.

The sanctions against Burma have been in place for the longest period of time. Unfortunately, little has really changed in the country, the political landscape remains largely the same. The duration of sanctions against Belarus was the shortest, and yet the most "effective" in terms of compliance. However, Belarus still had an authoritarian regime at the time when the targeted sanctions were withdrawn. The sanctions implemented against Zimbabwe are still rather new and ongoing, thus making them too early to evaluate at this stage. At the time of writing, however, Mugabe still remains in power. Hence, no sanctions have been working effectively in any of the three countries. They all continue to have strong authoritarian regimes with no intention to progress in a democratic direction. Below follow ten general conclusions and practical suggestions for improving the use of targeted sanctions. Although based on EU cases, these suggestions may be of value for UN targeted sanctions. In fact, many of them underline the conclusions in the Stockholm Report.

1   As the general situation has not improved in any of the three cases (none has reached the goal of introducing democracy at a substantial level) a conclusion can be made that before future sanctions programs are implemented, the sender should consider ways to assess and evaluate its policies in advance so that the goals are achievable. A good way would be to present clear and concrete sub-goals, which will make it easier for the sender as well as for the recipient to deal with the sanctions. Unless the goals are clear, senders risk losing credibility. This will also set a threshold for future sanctions. An assessment should also be made afterwards to examine what impact the sanctions have caused.

2 While the UN imposes sanctions only on situations that are perceived as threats to international peace and security, the EU has introduced sanctions in situations where there is a lack of or declining democratic progress. The UN could draw some experiences from this. Also, in its sanctions uses, the goals could be to further democratic progress, which means being involved in internal situations before they deteriorate on a political level.
3 The chain of implementation often misses vital enforcing and monitoring components. This may make targeted sanctions more politically important as symbolic acts than as effective and concrete tools. For instance, information sharing should be developed throughout the process of implementing sanctions. There is a need for increased coordination both within and outside the region of the target. The sender should also consider how much one can allow the sanctions to cost.
4 The international responses to targeted sanctions tend to divide nations between those in favor of and those against the measures. One reason is a state's own interest in the country exposed to sanctions. While some countries may agree with the policy of sanctions in particular situations, they may not like them for more practical reasons, as the implementation of sanctions can affect them economically and politically. As it is up to each country to decide whether or not it is in its own interest to support the sanctions policy, when imposed by the EU, different levels of support are to be expected. For instance, to make sanctions effective, the sender has to assist neighboring states with their sanctions infrastructure.[55] If necessary support is not given, the sanctions are more likely to fail.
5 The three sanctions cases highlight the role of information. It is important that the sender works closely with media, in such a way that both the targets and the domestic audiences can have a balanced picture of the significance of the sanctions. Furthermore, to effectively keep sanctions in place a continued dialogue is needed between the sender and the receiver. This dialogue is useful for both parties to find out where the other party stands. It should be the sender that sets the frame and the conditions for this talk. For instance, in the case of the introvert government of Burma, the EU has taken the initiative by sending a troika on several occasions. In the case of Zimbabwe, however, this extrovert government wasted no opportunity to show that there is a split among the senders. Hence, the EU should be careful in allowing itself to be drawn into an untimely dialogue. As there are effective sanctions in place, such a decision should not be devalued by several exemptions made on basis of national, rather than the collective, interest.
6 An important observation is that there is a problem in using exemptions in sanctions programs. There are reasons, for instance, for allowing targeted entities to enter dialogue, there could also be humanitarian reasons, but evaluations must be made carefully. The sender needs to understand the impact of granting exemptions as they may damage the credibility of the sanctions.

7 A regional organization, such as the EU, using sanctions, is limited in its global reach. In contrast, international actors, such as the UN, have worldwide mandate. Thus, effective implementation strategies must include an increased investment in cooperation between regional organizations and the UN. It is also important to coordinate and settle political difference both among the sender countries as well as with and within the region surrounding the target. In the case of Zimbabwe, regional organizations were involved in the sanctions but were not coordinated and lacked fundamental infrastructure, which affected the whole sanctions policy. Also, in the case of Burma, regional cooperation was lacking.

8 The background motivations for placing individuals on lists should be made available; this probably increases the credibility of the policy as it becomes more transparent. In terms of listing individuals, efforts must be placed on clarity issues. Efforts must be made to ensure that complete lists are available to the implementers. Also, by providing background documents describing the purposes of the sanctions, as well as the procedure underlying the choice of sanctions, the general public could easier identify themselves with the sanctions. This could greatly increase, although not necessarily guarantee, the effectiveness of the sanctions within the receiver state, on the sender state and in the international arena.

9 Goals that are set up in the various sanctions programs are often very abstract. Hence, before implementing sanctions, it is important to assess the target in order to draw up concrete and achievable goals. An assessment should be based on realistic conditions upon which the sanctions could build. It should contain clear goals, clear ideas on how to effectively monitor sanctions, how the sender could help and supply other states in sustaining the sanctions, etc. The assessment should be made so that the stated objectives are achieved in the best possible way. By doing this, the sender minimizes the risk of not achieving what was intended, which in turn increases the legitimacy of the sanctions. Unless sanctions are made concrete, senders may not fully implement them and this will help the receiver to circumvent the sanctions. With clear goals, clear monitoring standards follow. None of the reviewed sanctions cases seemed to have clear monitoring instruments.

10 EU procedures for bringing about a sanctions program could be seen as politically and legally very complex. This creates problems in several areas: quick decisions may be hindered, difficulties in division of responsibility, different management of sanctions cases, difficulties in explaining to an audience why the sanctions were enforced and how they work. By creating a simpler sanctions infrastructure within the EU's decision-making branches, sanctions policies would be more accurate and monitored in the long run. In concrete terms, this means that there should be a sanctions unit, which on a daily basis informs key agencies, organizations, banks, airports, etc. on both an EU and a national level, on the latest developments – in terms of changing positions, changing regulations, changing legislation – relating to the target.

The EU sanctions unit should therefore have the capacity to keep the sanctions debate alive in each member state. Contact nodes across societal sectors on national levels should be maintained and activated. Currently there is a debate within the Council on how to improve the sanctions infrastructure. This is very much welcomed. The problem, however, seems to be the very different views of the individual member states on how to use and implement targeted sanctions. Although the Commission often puts forward reasonable proposals, the end result always emerges from a final compromise of different member states. With the incorporation of the "new" Europe into the EU, the decision-making process might be even more complex.

Notes

* This chapter has benefited from material collected by Jacob Risberg and Tomas Nordberg. The responsibility for this chapter, however, rests solely with the author. The present chapter is a revised version of a longer paper. The revision has been done by the editors.
1 That is to safeguard common values; to strengthen the security of the union in all ways; to develop and consolidate democracy and the rule of law, and the respect for human rights and fundamental freedoms. In many cases, however, sanctions come as a direct result of UN decisions. Daniel Bethlehem describes this as the *regional interface*. For a detailed judicial clarification on the complex legal procedure on which a sanction is anchored, see: "Regional interface between Security Council decisions and member states implementation: the Example of the European Union," in V. Gowlland-Debbas (ed.) *United Nations Sanctions and International Law* (The Graduate Institute of International Studies, The Hague: Kluwer Law International, 2001).
2 Unanimity is required for a CFSP Common position.
3 The 1957 Treaty Establishing the European Community (Treaty of Rome).
4 See also articles 60 and 301 of the EC Treaty.
5 I. Anthony, "Sanctions Applied by the European Union and the United Nations," in *SIPRI Yearbook, 2002: Armaments, Disarmament and International Security*, Stockholm International Peace Research Institute (Oxford: Oxford University Press, 2002).
6 Apparently the invitation of opposition politicians by the AMG disturbed the Belarus government.
7 Council of the European Union document no. 14075 2002, Brussels, November 12, 2002.
8 Council of the European Union document no. 8220 2003 (Presse 105), Luxembourg, April 14, 2003.
9 Throughout this text the EU is used as a concept, although the organization underwent important changes also in name. For more on the ending of projects see also Institute of International Economics, "Myanmar", http://www.iie.com, May 13, 2002.
10 Confirmed in a Declaration by the General Affairs Council on July 29, 1991. See also Council of EU Common Position no. 635, 1996, Common Foreign and Security Policy.
11 For a specification of the European Council's particular concerns, see the Council's Common Position on Myanmar no. 635, 1996, Common Foreign and Security Policy.
12 European Council Regulation (EC), no. 552, 1997, March 24, 1997, and OJ L085, March 27, 1997.
13 Zaw Oo and Kai Grieg, "Carrots and Sticks for Democratisation in Burma," p. 107, in

H. Stokke and A. Tostensen (eds) *Human Rights in Development: Global Perspectives and Local Issues* (The Hague: Kluwer Law International, 1999).

14 Council of the EU Common Position no. 346, 2000, Common Foreign and Security Policy.

15 The EU extended the Common Position of October 28, 1996 for the fourth time by six months. The extension was made until April 2001. On October 29, the EU extended its sanctions on Burma until April 29, 2002, see Council Common Position on Myanmar (Burma) no. 757, 2001, Common Foreign and Security Policy.

16 At least at the time of writing this chapter.

17 European Council. Council Decision on April 28, 2003: CFSP 297, and Council Decision on June 20, 2003: CFSP 461. As a result of the May incident, the US, as part of its Burma Freedom and Democracy Act of July 2003, introduced bilateral targeted sanctions. In particular the US sanctions involved targeting individuals and economic entities benefiting from the Burma/Myanmar government. The textile industry was especially hit by this measure. See: US Department of the Treasury, Office of Foreign Assets Control "Burma," An Overview of the Burmese Sanctions Regulations Title 31 part 537 of the US code of Federal Regulations, July 29, 2003.

18 For more on sanctions tactics see C. de Jonge Oudraat, "UN Sanctions Regimes and Violent Conflict," in C. A. Crocker, F. O. Hampson and P. Aall (eds.) *Turbulent Peace: the Challenges of Managing International Conflict* (Washington, DC: United States Institute of Peace, 2001).

19 Kyaw Win, Burmese ambassador to London. In *BBC News*, "Do Sanctions against Burma Work?" BBC Internet edition, June 20, 2003.

20 Although the EU has no formal judicial instrument to do this.

21 Some good examples exist, such as the specific call for dialogue between the government and the democratic opposition and the release of Aung San Suu Kyi.

22 Zaw Oo and Kai Grieg, 1999, pp. 132–133.

23 According to Zaw Oo and Kai Grieg, ASEAN's efforts to promote political change in Burma has been weak. ASEAN has not discussed root causes of the current situation. Zaw Oo and Kai Grieg, 1999, p. 131.

24 The pilot study by the Department of Peace and Conflict Research at Uppsala University, Sweden, suggested that the EU could promote the idea of a EU Special Envoy to better coordinate the Burma/Myanmar issue (see www.smartsanctions.se); P. Wallensteen, C. Staibano and M. Eriksson, *Routes to Democracy in Burma/Myanmar: The Uppsala Pilot Study on Dialogue and International Strategies* (Uppsala: Universitetstryckeriet, 2004).

25 Zaw Oo and Kai Grieg, 1999, p. 117.

26 European Commission, "Message from the European Commission on initiating consultations with Zimbabwe according to article 96 in the Cotonou Agreement", COM (2001), 623 (Brussels, October 26, 2001).

27 Ibid., p. 3. These issues were based on the partnership agreement that was signed in Cotonou on June 23, 2000, which among other things deals with the respect of human rights, democratic principles and an independent legal system.

28 The *Africa Confidential* writes that the presidential vote "has become an election lesson about Africa's future," and that "Zimbabwe is a painful symbol of thwarted political ambition and dashed hopes for development. Across the continent, Africans identify with the demand for land right although they question Mugabe's arbitrary tactics. Equally they question the enthusiasm the West shows for sanction against the Mugabe regime compared to its reluctance to sanction South Africa's apartheid regime" (*Africa Confidential*, p. 3, March 8, 2002).

29 In fact the whole regional dimension and the Commonwealth division is worth its own discussion but will be left out in this chapter.

30 European Council. European Council Decision, "Council Common Position of 18 February 2002 Concerning Restrictive Measures Against Zimbabwe," no. 145, 2002, Common Foreign and Security Policy, in *Official Journal of the European Communities*. Brussels, February 18, 2002.
31 Ibid.
32 From as early as April 2001 there was an open debate on what action the EU had done to identify overseas assets held by Mugabe, i.e. under what legal jurisdiction sanctions could be introduced (i.e. under Article 8 of the Cotonou Agreement), and also under what conditions the sanctions could be introduced (for instance, the EU Commission publicly shared the views expressed by the MDC leader on how to enforce sanctions), *Official Journal of the European Communities,* December, 2001.
33 *Sunday Times*, "Probe into Highlife of Mugabes's Elite," February 3, 2002, and *BBC News*, "Zimbabwe Leaders Face Financial Probe," January, 23, 2002. Articles to be found at: http://www.globalpolicy.org/nations/corrupt/2002/0123zimb.htm
34 *Africa Research Bulletin*, Political, Social and Cultural Series. Vol. 39, No. 1, January, 2002, p. 14719.
35 *Sunday Times*, "Smart Sanctions will Hurt but Don't Expect to Recover Riches," February 3, 2002.
36 *Zimbabwe Independent*, January 4, 2004.
37 This clause was something the French government evoked when inviting Mugabe to Paris in 2003. See also, European Council. Legal acts and other instruments. The Council's Common Position on Restrictive Measures Against Zimbabwe, DG E IX, 15951/02.
38 *Africa Research Bulletin*, No. 6, June, 2002, p. 14906.
39 *BBC News*, "Fury as Zimbabwe Official Held," July 27, 2002.
40 The UK seemed to have some problem sustaining its sanctions. For instance, a UN panel of experts report on DRC mentioned that deals were made on defense equipment between UK businesses and Zimbabwe. Allegedly, a white Zimbabwean in Britain tried to force business deals with Zimbabwe, which included spare parts for military purposes; for more on this see: *The Guardian,* November 8, 2002, and *The Herald,* November 11, 2002.
41 *Keesings Contemporary Archives*, "Imposition of EU Sanctions." Online edition: http://www.keesings.com (February, 2002).
42 European Council. European Council Position, "Council Common Position of 18 February 2002, Renewing Restrictive Measures Against Zimbabwe," Common Foreign and Security Policy, in *Official Journal of the European Communities*. Brussels, February, 2002). In early March 2004, the US government renewed for a second year an executive order that freezes the assets of Mugabe and officials who undermine Zimbabwe's democratic process or institutions. The motive for signing the order was that the government of Zimbabwe posed an extraordinary threat to the foreign policy of the United States. When the first round of US sanctions was adopted a time gap from the EU's implementation left space for sanctions evasion. See US Executive Order "Zimbabwe: Blocking Property of Persons Undermining Democratic Processes of Institutions in Zimbabwe," issued on March 7, 2003, by US Department of Treasury, Office of Foreign Assets Control.
43 van Orden, "EU Travel Ban Review: MEP Letter to Jack Straw et al. European Parliament," January 23, 2003. For more on this see also the International Crisis Group, *Zimbabwe: Danger and Opportunity*. Africa Report, No. 60, March 10, p. 13 (Brussels: ICG, 2003).
44 *Daily Telegraph*, "Features: Letters to the Editor: EU Sanctions on Zimbabwe should Bite," October 8, 2002.
45 Ibid., "EU Talks Moved so Zimbabwe Can Attend," October 24, 2002.

46 The Belgium government apparently received no objections when asking all the other EU governments whether to invite the Zimbabwe officials.
47 *Zimbabwe Independent*, "EU Plans Direct Intervention in Zimbabwe," November 15, 2002, and *Reuters,* "Zimbabwe Claims Victory after EU Talks Boycotted," November 26, 2002.
48 Meaning an interest in Asia, rather than in Western countries.
49 For several months after the EU sanctions had been imposed, the Commonwealth discussed how it would deal with Zimbabwe. Having suspended Zimbabwe from the Commonwealth for a period of one year after the 2002 elections, the Commonwealth troika, which includes Australia, South Africa and Nigeria, had then to decide how to deal with Zimbabwe in the future. On the one hand, Australia and New Zealand wanted the organization to take a harder stance against Zimbabwe. On the other hand, Nigeria and South Africa continued to oppose the renewal of sanctions, which were scheduled to be renewed on March 19, 2003. Both Nigeria and South Africa wanted to continue to deal with Zimbabwe in a manner of constructive engagement. In retrospect, it seems that South Africa's policy of "quiet neutral diplomacy" has gradually shifted to be more open and supportive of Zimbabwe. The policy of the Commonwealth undermined the credibility of the sanctions imposed by the EU.
50 The UK is mentioned separately from the EU in this context as it has a particular political relationship with Zimbabwe, although it takes part in the EU decision-making process.
51 See US Department of the Treasury Office of Foreign Assets Control: "Blocking property of persons undermining democratic processes or institutions in Zimbabwe," information taken from
http://www.treas.gov/offices/eotffc/ofac/sanctions/t11zimb.pdf
52 Although there are grounds for being critical, the introduction of targeted sanctions on individuals may be having an effect. Several sources have reported that some cabinet ministers have children in foreign schools, and some sources claim that top ZANU–PF members struck by sanctions are experiencing problems in this regards (*Financial Gazette* "Chefs Wipe Out Forex," July 25, 2002).
53 *Financial Gazette*, "Zim Chefs Use Diplomats to Bust Sanctions", August 8, 2002. The article cites Western diplomats in Harare as a source.
54 In September 2003, the EU issued an important statement in which it made clear at whom the targeted sanctions were aimed and for what reasons. The statement underlined that the EU continued cooperating with the people of Zimbabwe, while at the same time keeping a strong watch on their leaders. See "Position of the European Union on Sanctions Against Zimbabwe," Embassy of Italy, Harare.
55 Support is crucial and important in this context, and, for instance, is recognized in the work of the UN Counter-Terrorism Committee.

9

AFRICAN SANCTIONS
The case of Burundi*

Lennart Wohlgemuth

Since the coup in October 1993, in which the first democratically elected president was assassinated, Burundi has been in a severe crisis. This is the latest in a cycle of conflicts over the past forty years. The international community has aimed at preventing the escalation of the conflict and at contributing to a process for sustainable peace in the country. This case study presents and discusses the sanctions, which were imposed on Burundi between 31 July 1996 and 23 January 1999.

These sanctions began as a total economic blockade. Over time, however, humanitarian concerns expressed primarily by UN organizations and NGOs led to a gradual relaxation in the sanctions regime. At the same time, profiteering, intensive cross-border smuggling and organized sanction-busting by air, diluted the sanctions' impact.

A special feature of these sanctions was that they were initiated and maintained by the neighbouring countries in the region and only later were supported by the Organization of African Unity (OAU) and the UN. It was perhaps one of the first major efforts to genuinely introduce an 'African solution to an African problem'. Interestingly, at the same time as this expression was hailed by the international community it was also criticized by many of its actors who had difficulties in yielding the initiative to neighbouring countries. In spite of many problems, the sanctions had a major effect both economically and politically and could as far as sanctions go – indiscriminate instruments as they are – be seen as a successful intervention.

Civil strife and peace in Burundi

The Great Lakes region, encompassing Burundi, the Democratic Republic of Congo (DRC) and Rwanda, has met with an increasing amount of conflict and violence in the past decade. The genocide in Rwanda, the war in DRC and the continuous conflict in Burundi are cases in point. The overriding problem was that all conflicts in the region were intertwined and none of them could be solved without major improvements in the rest of the region. Thus, the regional perspective must be kept in mind.

Although Burundi had gone through a number of problems in the 1980s, it was seen as a rather successful country – although not doing as well as Rwanda appeared to be doing at that time. With the fall of the Berlin Wall and the following worldwide democratization process, Burundi was seen as one of the best examples of democratic development in Africa.

Elections took place in June 1993 and were declared fair and successful by the international community observing the event. However, to the surprise of many – including President Buyoya, a Tutsi who called the elections – the electorate voted in accordance with its ethnic allegiance. The party representing the Hutu majority – Front pour la democratie au Burundi (Frodebu) – took 71 per cent of all votes and in the election for President, the Frodebu leader Ndadaye received almost as large a portion of the votes. Buyoya accepted defeat and Ndadaye took over the presidency. For the first time in the modern age Hutus received recognition and gained responsibility for the country. This meant that the Hutu self-respect grew enormously – a very important fact in order to understand what happened thereafter.

Democracy was never allowed to gain a foothold. Some Tutsi leaders, particularly within the army and the legal and other professions, did not accept the new situation. As soon as the Tutsis felt threatened – as they did when more and more Hutus were introduced to government jobs – trouble started, leading in October 1993 to the assassination of President Ndadaye together with a number of the most prominent Frodebu leaders. The Frodebu party maintained control over the government, however. Over the next three years, the country experienced 'a creeping coup', as Professor Filip Reyntjens puts it,[1] eroding the power of the elected government and increasing the influence of mainly Tutsi extremists. In July 1996, after the death of Ndadaye's successor in a plane crash and the killing of tens of thousands on both sides, Buyoya was returned to power through a military coup. The Parliament was suspended. The international community encountered serious problems in how it should handle a government coming to power through a military coup, and thereby ending a democratic system and a democratic government elected only a few years earlier, when, at the same time, the majority of international actors were alarmed over the political chaos just before the military coup and considered that an alternative to Buyoya might have resulted in increased oppression of the majority.

While a majority among the major powers gave Buyoya 'the benefit of the doubt', the neighbouring states took clear positions against the military coup. With the support of the OAU they imposed sanctions against Burundi and demanded the re-establishment of the pre-coup parliament; free political activities and negotiations between the different partners. Former President Julius Nyerere of Tanzania was appointed as the mediator between the combating groups within and outside Burundi. Thus, a strategy of regional sanctions and regional peace talks was initiated, two parts of an unusual policy formulated to solve an African problem by African means.

International interest in the Burundi peace efforts

After the 'attempted coup' in October 1993, the international community followed the development of the crisis in Burundi with great concern. Particularly after the genocide in Rwanda in April 1994, and the resulting self-criticism among international organizations and the major powers, this led to a number of initiatives, which all aimed at preventing the escalation of the conflict in Burundi. The United Nations and OAU appointed special representatives to Burundi. A number of international organizations, bilateral donors and NGOs sent missions and observers to assess the situation and give suggestions as to what they should do in order to alleviate the crisis. International awareness can, therefore, be clearly established and there was no doubt that there was a willingness to contribute to de-escalation of the crisis.

However, most actors lacked previous experience in preventive diplomacy and, thus, did not have a strategy on how to act. During this time of confusion, the UN Secretary General's Special Representative for Burundi (SRSG), Mr Ould Abdallah, made a unique and important contribution, particularly in preventing escalation and in conflict management. As far as his mandate allowed, he assisted in the coordination of outside interventions and in the assignment of specific roles to the different actors on the scene. The UN and OAU continued to have a high-level representation in Burundi with the aim of preventing the crisis from worsening.

The regional implications of internal conflicts became more and more serious and obvious. A civil war in one country will immediately affect its neighbours. In this case, the vast numbers of refugees that poured out of Rwanda into neighbouring states, and the economic, social and political effects they brought about, made the neighbouring states even more concerned about the continuing upheavals in Burundi. As the internal crisis in Burundi developed, they decided jointly to intervene in an effort to defuse the conflict. The heads of state of the region first met under the auspices of the Carter Center, which arranged two meetings on Burundi in November 1995 and February 1996. Later on the region took its own initiative. At the first of their joint meetings in Mwanza in early 1996, the former President of Tanzania, Julius Nyerere, was appointed by the regional states as peace negotiator, an agreement endorsed by OAU. Following the military coup in July 1996, the efforts were intensified and regional sanctions were imposed on Burundi in an effort to push Burundi to reinstate democracy. Nyerere, at that time, was trying hard to reach a sustainable peace, but in spite of the strong pressure exerted by the neighbours, very little was achieved. Regional pressures on Burundi have been applied ever since the effects of the coup in 1993 became visible. There are few other national conflicts in Africa where so many states have been so insistently involved and so active in promoting peace and democracy in a neighbouring state. It has, however, also to be clearly recognized that these states all had their own specific interests and agendas.

Many of the major powers, such as the United States, France and Belgium (the latter, for historical reasons), have intervened and been active on the international scene as regards the conflict in Burundi, but done surprisingly little on the ground in Burundi itself. In fact, most of them withdrew their aid and military assistance as a consequence of the attempted coup in October 1993. Of the European countries, Belgium, France and Germany (until December 1999) retained embassies in Bujumbura. However, both the United States and Europe,[2] in addition to their resident ambassadors, have appointed special envoys for Burundi. Interestingly, while the other European countries slowed down or completely halted their direct assistance to Burundi, Sweden and Norway became more active. A number of NGOs also entered the Burundi scene in attempts to contribute to the peace process.[3]

The sanctions and the peace process from 1996 to 1999

The initial phase of sanctions (July 1996–May 1997)

The military coup d'état took place in Bujumbura on 25 July 1996, putting Buyoya back as President and thereby wiping out the achievements and gains of democracy reached since 1993.

The regional heads of state (RHoS) – the leaders from Tanzania, Uganda, Kenya, Rwanda, Ethiopia, Zaire and Cameroon (as chair of the OAU), OAU Secretary General, Salim Salim, and the mediator Julius Nyerere – reacted swiftly and strongly on the coup and the back-tracking of democracy. In a meeting in Arusha, Tanzania, on 31 July – that is only one week after the coup – they decided to put 'maximum pressure on the regime of Burundi, including the imposition of total economic sanctions'. The sanctions were to be maintained until political parties were again allowed to operate, the Parliament had been reinstated and negotiations with the armed rebels had started. This was the first time that African countries imposed sanctions on another African country in matters that concerned internal affairs. The summit itself did not establish a mechanism or a common framework through which this would be done. It was up to the individual countries to do so. The formal decisions were taken in official country declarations concerning the imposition of sanctions on 2 August in Tanzania, 5 August in Kenya, 7 August in Ethiopia and Uganda, 9 August in Rwanda and Zaire and 16 August in Zambia.[4] The sanctions were specified as 'comprehensive' exempting 'only human medicines and emergency basic food aid to Rwandese refugees'. A travel ban against 'all members of the Buyoya regime' was imposed. An exemption for emergency food aid to displaced populations was denied.[5]

A Regional Sanctions Coordinating Committee (RSCC) was created on 16 August by the foreign ministers of the region. It was under the chair of the Tanzanian High Commissioner to Kenya and its task was to harmonize, monitor and coordinate the activities of the national sanctions committees. The sanctions were immediately supported by the OAU. Its Mechanism for Conflict Prevention on 5 August issued a Communiqué on Burundi that 'fully supported the conclusions of the Second Arusha Regional Summit'.[6] Also the OAU, despite not mentioning sanctions, was generally understood to be wholly supportive of the embargo. Both the chair and the secretary-general were present at the 31 July Arusha meeting when sanctions were announced. Only those countries participating in the Arusha agreement were specifically bound by the terms of the sanctions. Nonetheless, most African countries, in spite of some reluctance, abided by their terms.[7]

The UN Security Council pronounced an initial position on 30 August, when it condemned 'the overthrow of the legitimate government and constitutional order in Burundi'. It further expressed 'its strong support for the efforts of the regional leaders, including their meeting in Arusha on 31 July, 1996, of the OAU and of former President Nyerere, to assist Burundi to overcome peacefully the grave crisis'. The resolution contains no direct reference to economic sanctions imposed by the governments involved. It does, however, set a deadline of 31 October, before which unconditional negotiations between all political parties and fractions must begin – or the UN will consider 'the imposition of measures . . . [including] . . . a ban on the sale or supply of arms . . . and measures targeted against the leader of the regime and all factions'.[8] The UN, in other words, issued a threat of joining the sanctions policy of the regional states, to which it never reverted again.

While the neighbouring countries took their decisions alone and without any pressures from outside, by supporting the regional 'efforts', the Security Council members appeared to lend their weight to the sanctions initiative without shouldering any legal, political or humanitarian responsibilities. The sanctions came into effect immediately and the last international flight arrived in and left Bujumbura on 13 August. As the neighbouring states control the main trade routes to landlocked Burundi, they made it difficult for countries not supporting the sanctions to trade with that country. The reactions from the new government of Burundi on the sanctions came quickly. To show good faith, political parties were unbanned and the immediate restoration of the 'Assemblée Nationale' (Parliament) was announced on 12 September.

In spite of this development, the reaction from the major European countries was not very positive as they had already begun to question the sanctions. For instance, Belgium backed Buyoya and stated on 18 September that sanctions were premature.

The sanctions created serious problems for humanitarian agencies operating in Burundi. The initial near-total lack of exemptions of the sanctions placed many UN and NGO programmes in difficulties and made them complain vociferously.[9]

RHoS met again, this time in Kigali, Rwanda, on 25 September, and concluded that the Buyoya regime had not fulfilled the conditions set for the sanctions to be removed. No extension of exemptions was therefore allowed. Buyoya was invited to the next RHoS meeting, although not as head of state but merely as a faction leader. Buyoya insisted, however, that he would only go to such a meeting, again to be held in Arusha, as head of state. Thus, the third regional summit on Burundi went ahead on 10 October without him. At this meeting, no further concessions were made, and the sanctions were maintained. A deadline of 31 October was imposed on the regime to begin negotiations with the leaders of the Hutu militias.

US Secretary of State for foreign affairs, Warren Christopher, came to Arusha to visit, the regional summit. After having lectured the leaders present on the need for African solutions to African problems, he argued that they should change their Burundi policy and relax sanctions. The French government shared that opinion.[10]

At the meeting of the RSCC on 24 October, humanitarian exemptions were extended to include food, bean seeds, water purification agents, blankets, plastic sheeting, jerrycans and buckets, cooking utensils, sanitary facilities and mats.[11]

At the end of October the sanctions, which in early August seemed to be hitting hard, were slowly starting to lose their bite. There were reports on increased smuggling through porous borders on all sides of Burundi. Professional sanction-busters arrived immediately after the introduction of the sanctions and they were observed as guests in major hotels of Bujumbura. At the airport, large transport aeroplanes were coming in day and night. However, as imports (oil and other products) and exports (coffee) by air are not a cost effective way of trading the import prices were rising considerably. Apart from the decline in export revenue, Burundi also lost most of its official development assistance, which stood at some US$250 million annually before the 1993 crisis. The World Bank announced in October 1996 its suspension of nearly all support to Burundi. Foreign currency reserves, already low before the coup and the sanctions, were rapidly depleted. The impact of these revenue losses made it increasingly difficult for the government to finance its ongoing social programmes and to pay the salaries of civil servants.[12]

In late 1996, it became obvious that in spite of the sanction-busting sanctions were still hitting hard. This can be seen by the fact that they were beginning to be used as a scapegoat domestically. Shortages of goods and other problems that had occurred even before the sanctions were imposed, were now said to be caused by the sanctions. Although at higher prices, most commodities, necessary as well as luxury, were available in the shops. Higher salaries did not compensate higher prices and the government blamed all hardship on sanctions. An indicator of the effect of the sanctions was the increasing difference between the official and parallel exchange rates (Table 9.1).

The government began to take every opportunity to denounce the sanctions, and not without success. A meeting of central African states, convened in Brazzaville, on 2 December, ended with a resolution condemning sanctions. Following this, air flights were resumed between Brazzaville and Bujumbura. After visiting Burundi

Table 9.1 Exchange rates in central Bujumbura

	July 1996	7 Feb. 1997	% change
Bufr: $1 official	317	333	+ 5.0
Bufr: $1 parallel	350	495	+41.4

Source: FAO quoted in EIU 1997: 1.

in January 1997, a group of German parliamentarians found that the sanctions mainly affected the poorer strata of the society and therefore called for them to be lifted.

The Burundi leader Buyoya revealed, initially to the fourth meeting of the RhoS on Burundi on 16 April 1997 and then publicly to the Burundian nation on 13 May, that his government had been conducting secret talks with the Conseil national pour la defense de la democratie (CNDD), the political wing of the militia that had fought the Burundian Army since 1994. The announcements were not a complete surprise, as the CNDD had acknowledged the talks sometime before, although Buyoya had always denied them. The talks had taken place under the auspices of the Saint Egidio religious community in Rome, with the then Cabinet Minister of Energy and Mines, Bernard Barandereka, leading the government delegation, and the former provincial governor, Leonce Ndarubagiye, heading the CNDD delegation.[13]

Buyoya paved the way for this admission in Burundi by politically neutralizing the most militant Tutsi opponents beforehand, including former president, Jean-Baptiste Bagaza, who headed the Parti pour le redressement national (Parena). Bagaza's house was searched and large quantities of arms were said to have been found. He was subsequently put under house arrest. Bagaza was known to enjoy considerable support among Bujumbura's by now exclusively Tutsi university student body. At least 400 students took part in the protest against the talks, despite explicit warnings not to do so, and troops were deployed to prevent more students joining in. On 20 May some 23 trade unions also condemned the talks and issued a joint call for resistance against giving in to 'Hutu domination'.[14]

Buyoya's news to the regional leaders about his government's talks with CNDD helped them decide, during their meeting on 16 April, to ease the sanctions imposed on Burundi. This was to the consternation of the CNDD, who wished to see continued external pressure put on the government. Additionally, for the first time, the regional leaders invited Mr Buyoya to the meeting and did him the political favour of referring to him as 'president'. As Buyoya had not yet told the Burundian people about the talks with CNDD, the regional leaders were unable to refer to them in their final communiqué. Nonetheless, the easing of sanctions was in part their reward to Buyoya for complying with one of their key demands. The official position after the meeting was that food products, agricultural inputs, educational and construction materials and medicines might all pass freely into Burundi, and that other imports needed to be negotiated only with the regional country of origin or transit, and not with the regional sanctions committee in Nairobi. Burundians were allowed to travel outside Burundi, although according to some interpretations, notably in Rwanda, they might have more trouble getting back in. Fuel imports were still subject to sanctions, as were all of Burundi's exports, most notably tea and coffee. The Rwandan government was critical of the easing of sanctions due to a conflict over export of coffee from Burundi. As a result, it kept its border controls tight and refused any planes to and from Burundi permission to cross its airspace.

The easing of sanctions in mid-April had a speedy effect in bringing down prices, but made less of a difference with regard to the availability of imported goods since most had entered the country anyway, albeit at a price, since December. Commercial flights to and from Bujumbura took time to resume, but the unofficial cargo flights that had been running before the easing of sanctions continued to operate and new ones were set up.

International reactions in the second year of sanctions (second half of 1997)

Talks between Burundi's warring factions and some of its political parties were supposed to have begun in Arusha (Tanzania) on 25 August 1997 but were indefinitely postponed. The Burundian government justified its withdrawal by citing the decision of regional heads of state to maintain sanctions against Burundi and the allegedly aggressive posture Tanzania was taking towards Burundi at that time.[15]

Although the situation in Bujumbura was tense and radical Tutsi opposition against the talks strong, Buyoya maintained until the very last moment that he and his government would participate. On the morning of 22 August the government delegation cancelled its participation referring to security reasons. From interviews carried out at that time in Bujumbura, it became clear that the main reason behind the cancellation was serious threats from powerful Tutsi extremists opposing the dialogue. The government subsequently paid a high price for the failure to participate in Arusha. Its image suffered badly internationally and its credibility concerning willingness to negotiate received a blow. It also certainly delayed the lifting/suspension of the sanctions.

In an effort to prepare the ground for negotiations, a conference on 'Building the Future of Burundi', sponsored by the UN Educational, Scientific and Cultural Organization[16] was organized on 26–29 September in Paris. The conference had been discussed and prepared for several months within the UN system. When the Foreign Minister, Luc Rukingama, in late May had presented the idea of all-party talks to be held under the auspices of UNESCO in Geneva, the proposal had, however, been rejected by the political wing of the mainly Hutu militia, the CNDD, which, at that time, perceiving the initiative as coming from the government, would have rather revived the pending bilateral discussions with the government.

Despite being presented by UNESCO as exploratory and explicitly not as negotiations, the conference was taken seriously by the Burundian government, which showed up in force. That is also how it was seen by the CNDD, which judged it worthwhile to attend. The dominant Frodebu faction led by Jean Minani, however, boycotted the conference. Delegates affirmed the need for a democratic constitution and seemed to express support for the notion that group rights should be protected. That was an encouraging sign for the Burundian government, since this was a minimum condition for genocide-fearing Tutsis but unacceptable to ethnic supremacists among Hutus, who always insisted on majority democracy, with rights afforded to people as individuals only.

Delegates also agreed to continue the UNESCO process. Organizers were at pains to point out that the conference was not intended to detract from the Arusha process, but a number of international participants were so dissatisfied with the way the negotiations were organized, and with the Arusha and the sanctions stalemate, that they pronounced an interest in continuing to look for alternatives.[17]

On 10 November 1997, the critique against the sanctions received further support. The finance and economic ministers of the Common Market for Eastern and Southern Africa (COMESA) called for sanctions against Burundi to be lifted. The statement expressed concern about the adverse effects on Burundi, and, tellingly, its COMESA partners, also noting that Burundi continued to trade with non-COMESA countries, and that the sanctions should be lifted as soon as possible. It is to be noted that out of the 20 members of COMESA, five, i.e. all but Tanzania and Cameroon (who are not members of COMESA), took part in the original decision to impose the sanctions. The next day, the UN's human rights special rapporteur on Burundi urged the easing of sanctions as soon as the government showed a tangible commitment to peace and national reconciliation. The special rapporteur, Paulo Sergio Pinheiro, called for the continuation of an arms embargo on Burundi, which, he said, should be directed at both government and rebel forces. The Burundian government strongly reacted to any suggestions that the sanctions should only be partly lifted, but privately must have been pleased with the events.[18]

Although fuel was still on the regional sanctions list, it came down further in price over the fourth quarter (1997) to about Bufr 350 per litre ($1 per litre). This was double the July 1996 cost of Bufr 165 per litre, but considerably less than at the peak of sanctions, when fuel cost Bufr 1,000 per litre in some Burundian towns. Contributing to the fall in price was Kenya's unilateral decision to exempt fuel from its sanctions and increased commercial activity at Lake Tanganyika's Congolese ports. This is where Burundi was procuring increasing amounts of fuel and also a whole range of other goods.

DR Congo was never part of the regional sanctions regime against Burundi, but it was only on 30 October 1997 that DRC and Burundi officially revived economic contact. The level of unofficial trade was already considerable so that the only noticeable change was the reopening of telephone links between Bujumbura and Kinshasa.

Regarding the humanitarian effects of the sanctions, two major studies were conducted during 1997. The first, which summarized the situation up to April 1997, by Hoskins and Nutts, reported humanitarian suffering to an extent that they ask whether 'there is a threshold of human suffering . . . beyond which sanctions should no longer be imposed'.[19] The second – a UN review – was based on a mission by two DHA (Department of Humanitarian Affairs) officials to the region in October. It concluded that while sanctions had not been formally lifted, they no longer caused serious humanitarian distress among civilian populations or serious logistical impediments to aid operations.[20] By the time of the later report many humanitarian essentials had been exempted by the RSCC, although governments varied in the extent to which they controlled shipments that crossed their borders into Burundi.

By the end of 1997 the sanctions, although clearly relaxed, were still maintained. To meet the demands set by the RHoS in Arusha on 31 July 1996, Buyoya had unbanned political parties and restored the 'Assemblée Nationale' (Parliament) on 12 September 1996. He had also held, with Nyerere's tacit support, secret talks with CNDD in Rome from October 1996 to March 1997. After the disclosure of the talks in May 1997, they were not resumed. Given the strong radical Tutsi opposition, especially in the capital Bujumbura, against any form of dialogue with 'the genociders', Buyoya played for time, hoping to be able to tame the opposition as time passed.[21]

Nyerere appreciated the efforts to get negotiations with CNDD started and agreed to considerable exemptions from the sanctions in April 1997. He therefore prepared for a follow-up of the Rome talks with a more inclusive participation to begin in Arusha on 25 August. This was not possible, giving instead a role for UNESCO in confidence building. At the same time, the sanctions were gradually relaxed to avoid unacceptable humanitarian consequences and in the face of increasing reluctance among African states to pursue this policy. The effect may, however, have been to make the sanctions somewhat more targeted on the regime itself.

The Partnership Agreement and the ending of sanctions (1998–1999)

In early 1998, observers believed it could not be long until the RHoS officially abandoned sanctions. None of them, except the President of Tanzania Mkapa, expressed much enthusiasm for sanctions any longer. The Burundian government had proved that it could and would keep its military campaign at previous levels. Economic operators had demonstrated they could always get essential commodities in and out of the country. It therefore became harder and harder to justify the added burden sanctions placed on the poor majority of Burundians, who were already enduring a particularly vicious civil war. There were calls to lift sanctions from various bodies, not only from the COMESA but also from the Francophone summit, which met in Hanoi in November, and the Eritrean government. Even Mr Pinheiro called for their review but also for a more focused sanctions regime. There was talk about a new summit on sanctions in January, but no meeting materialized.[22]

The RHoS met in Kampala, Uganda, on 21 February 1998, to discuss Burundi and the sanctions imposed against it by the region. It was reported that the foreign ministers meeting beforehand had decided to end the sanctions but were, it seems, overruled.[23] Heads of state were divided on the issue, and well-placed sources alleged that the final communiqué was released only after those opposing the maintenance of sanctions had gone home. However, the communiqué reported unanimity over the decision to maintain sanctions.

The Burundian government was unceasing in its denunciations of the sanctions, which it blamed on the Tanzanian and Ugandan governments, and found more and more people listening and intervening in the discussions. Sanctions subsequently attracted better-known critics, among them President Jacques Chirac of France and the Pope, who received visits in early March (1998) from Buyoya and the EU Great Lakes representative, Aldo Ajello. In addition, the Brussels-based think tank, International Crisis Group, published a report that was strongly critical of the embargo, emphasizing that 'the embargo hit the wrong people and aggravated general poverty, and thus actually adding to the conflict rather than deflecting it. The embargo also supported certain people in Burundi in enriching themselves through sanction busting. It further marginalised moderate elements and thus strengthened resistance to negotiations.'[24]

Despite the contention over the peace process and sanctions, some of the tension between Burundi and Tanzania eased during the second quarter of 1998, with fewer border incidents and less inflammatory rhetoric coming from each government. The UN High Commission for Refugees (UNHCR), Burundian and Tanzanian government technical teams held tripartite talks on 12 March in Mwanza. On 23 March, Tanzanian police arrested 30 Burundians for alleged military training in the Kigoma refugee camp and removed them to another area.

A report released in April 1998 by the IMF entitled 'Burundi: Recent Economic Developments' had comprehensive analysis of the economic downturn in Burundi since 1993. According to figures in the report, Burundi experienced real GDP growth at market prices in 1997 for the first time since 1992. It showed real growth to have been 4.4 per cent, compared to the negative growth of 8.4 per cent recorded in 1996.[25]

After some time of secret dialogue, a major breakthrough in the negotiations between President Pierre Buyoya and the leading Hutu organization Frodebu took place in April 1998, which later resulted in the formation of a new multiparty government, with two vice-presidents, an enlarged Parliament and a constitutionally endorsed president – Buyoya. This developed into an internal settlement of the political impasse created by the coup in 1996, known as the Partnership Agreement. Following this breakthrough, a series of events unfolded rapidly. The government and Frodebu finalized the arrangements in mid-May, and then took time to explain the agreements to a variety of interested parties. For instance, a Frodebu delegation travelled to Kenya and Tanzania to explain and gain support for what they had agreed with Frodebuists living in exile, and Frodebu's Speaker of the Parliament held talks with senior government officials in Kenya, Tanzania and Uganda.

In late May the Minister of Defence held consultations with senior officers in the Burundian Army and by 2 June the Cabinet felt ready to approve the draft laws that would enact the agreement. The Parliament then approved the Transitional Constitution on 4 June, though not without considerable debate from uneasy Frodebu delegates. On 6 June, Mr Buyoya and the Speaker of the Parliament signed agreements to cement their new partnership and the Transitional Constitution was then promulgated by Presidential decree. Mr Buyoya was legally sworn in as president on 11 June and later that day appointed his two vice-presidents, one from the Hutu-dominated party – Frodebu – and one from the Tutsi dominated – Uprona. The following day Buyoya swore in his new Cabinet, picked following the suggestions of his vice-presidents, and on 19 June, Buyoya appointed members to the Constitutional court. The new assembly members were not appointed until 16 July, and included, as expected, members of small political parties and hand-picked (and generally pro-Buyoya) 'civil society representatives' as well as Frodebu's replacements for those of its parliamentarians still in exile.[26] This now meant that Burundi had an internally legitimate government.

The external dimension was important, however. Frodebu's exiled president, Jean Minani, denounced the power-sharing agreements when they were first announced and condemned the Parliament's passing of the Transitional Constitution on legal grounds. However, just before the first round of the external peace process in Arusha on 17 June, Mr Minani said that he had changed his mind. The way in which he did so was an indication to most observers that Mr Minani was forced to accept the new arrangements in Burundi in order to retain his influence in the internal wing of Frodebu.

At the same time as events unfolded inside the country, the external peace process was revived in Arusha. As we saw, this process, mediated by the former Tanzanian president, Julius Nyerere, was in serious trouble during 1997 and the first part of 1998. The Burundian government was openly suspicious of Mr Nyerere's neutrality. However, Mr Nyerere persisted in his efforts, and succeeded in bringing the government to a new round of talks in Arusha. These began on 16 June, despite the refusal of regional heads of state to accede to the Burundian government's demand that they end sanctions before talks began. Getting the other parties to the June talks was easier, as Uprona's pro-Buyoya faction was perfectly willing to attend and Frodebu had long been committed to the process. Burundi's minor political parties saw the talks as an occasion to raise their profile. The CNDD, whose militia were losing ground against the Burundian Army, which they had been fighting since 1994, now identified the Arusha talks as its most realistic path to power.

A serious problem, however, emerged with the split in the CNDD in June 1998,[27] which saw the military leadership distance itself from the CNDD president, Leonard Nyangoma, and announce a breakaway faction called Conseil national pour la defense de la democratie–Forces de la defense de la democratie (CNDD–FDD). Mr Nyerere decided to stick with Mr Nyangoma as the CNDD's representative, and Mr Nyangoma duly signed up to the impressive agreement entered into by all participating groups on 21 June to 'suspend hostilities' before 20 July, the date of the following round of talks. However, the new group CNDD–FDD instantly distanced itself from the agreement, saying it was not represented in Arusha. This was quickly followed by a statement from Burundi's Minister for the Peace Process, Ambroise Niyonsaba, who said that the suspension did not apply to the Armed Forces, as they had a constitutional obligation to keep the peace.

The decision by the main protagonists of the armed struggle in Burundi that the suspension of hostilities did not apply to them did surprisingly little to dampen the enthusiasm of most observers. However, the Tanzanian President, Benjamin Mkapa, said just before the June talks that sanctions would remain in place until 'a comprehensive peace agreement has been concluded'. This was rather different from the original two conditions set by the RHoS – that constitutional rule should return to Burundi and unconditional negotiations should be entered into – both of which had now been met.

The Arusha talks commenced on 21 July and ended on 30 July. The first few days were taken up with arguments over the agenda and the rules of procedure. Much of the rest of the time was taken up with long-winded presentations from each delegation on the causes of the Burundian conflict. The government delegation also pushed hard for sanctions to be included as a topic for discussion, and generally made it clear that as long as sanctions were in place the delegation would remain at the talks but would seek to ensure that little was achieved. The CNDD–FDD reiterated its view that Mr Nyangoma did not represent its fighters, with Mr Nyangoma attempting unsuccessfully to play down the split as a 'minor crisis'. Palipehutu (another Hutu party with its own fighters) spokesmen in Burundi also denounced their delegation and said that their fighters were not bound by the agreements. Connected to these developments was another upsurge of violence in late July, with incidents reported in Burundi at Kayanza, Bubanza, Cibitoke, Bururi and Muramvya.

The talks concluded with a commitment from everyone to return to Arusha in October. The EU and the Belgian, British and US governments all hinted that sanctions should be ended to improve the prospects for achievements at the next round. Since the negotiation process needed funding, their views carried weight, though the regional heads of state were determined not to be dictated to.[28]

The all-party talks began in Arusha on 13 October. However, not much was expected from these talks as Frodebu certainly was less interested in them since it had won power. Second, the CNDD and the FDD, the main militia fighting the Burundian security forces, remained deeply split. It became more and more evident that only one CNDD faction was represented in Arusha and the other, which exercised most control over the FDD on the ground, remained excluded.

The Burundian government pursued its argument that it would ensure that little progress would take place in Arusha for as long as the embargo against Burundi remained in place. Between June and October the RSCC stubbornly ignored the growing number of international calls for sanctions to be lifted and the embargo remained in place. Furthermore, at the beginning of the October round of the Arusha talks, Nyerere's team confirmed that sanctions were not on the agenda for discussion. However, Nyerere subsequently said that if he found that the Burundian government was 'serious about progress' at the Arusha talks, he would pass this information on to the RSCC, claiming that sanctions could then be lifted 'within a week'.[29]

Burundi's donors had never been happy with sanctions, but nonetheless suspended most of their assistance for fear of being seen to be undermining 'African solutions for African problems'. However, by November 1998 most donors did not see the rationale for sanctions any more, and made plans to resume cooperation with Burundi under the guise of 'enlarged humanitarian assistance' whether sanctions were lifted or not. Nyerere met EU development ministers in connection with a Council meeting on 29 November in Brussels, when they relayed this position to him. Donors were actually paying for the Arusha peace talks Nyerere was leading. Most of the donors were dissatisfied with the way the talks were being conducted on a political, managerial and financial level but had nonetheless continued to disburse funds and to affirm their commitment to the talks in public. However, that position could not have survived a public split between the donors and Nyerere on the sanctions issue.

On 23 January 1999 the meeting of the RHoS announced, on the recommendation of Nyerere, the suspension of economic sanctions against Burundi. The communiqué, issued by the seventh heads of state meeting since Pierre Buyoya seized power in 1996, asserted that the decision had been taken because of the progress that had been made towards a negotiated settlement to the Burundian conflict at multiparty talks in Arusha, Tanzania.

The Burundi sanctions: conclusions

What makes the sanctions against Burundi so special is that they were initiated and maintained by the neighbouring countries in the region. They were decided upon by the heads of state in the neighbouring countries shortly after the July 1996 military coup ended the first period of efforts to establish democratic rule – as fragile as it was – in the history of Burundi. The OAU only gave its support after the decision was taken and the UN reluctantly did so after some time. The international community, including the major powers and some important NGOs active in the region, never really gave sanctions their blessing and at times criticized the actions taken by the regional states. Earlier experiences of sanctions in Africa had been against Rhodesia, South Africa and the Portuguese colonies and were part and parcel of the decolonization process of Africa. What is special and new with the sanctions against Burundi is that they are supposed to defend values such as democracy, peace and security, thereby expressing issues that are integrated in the new constitution of the African Union.

Why did the neighbouring states act so swiftly and so decisively?

This is a very difficult question to answer in view of so many other cases more violent than this one, where inaction by neighbours is the rule. The major reason to my mind is the aftermath of the genocide in Rwanda. Following the passivity of all parties as regards Rwanda, Burundi came into the limelight as a potential new candidate for genocide. When trouble started in 1993 – and in particular after the genocide took place in Rwanda in April 1994 – the international community kept a watchful eye on the developments in Burundi and many actors who had never before been active in Burundi became involved. So did even the neighbouring countries, which between 1993 and 1996 followed the developments closely and even appointed a mediator from their midst, Julius Nyerere, in early 1996 to help find solutions to the imminent problems in the country.

A second reason – and one that should not be underestimated – is the symbolic character the non-violent and smooth democratic process in Burundi had in the region. In spite of all its problems in the past, Burundi had chosen a democratic path with support, it seemed, of most of its population. This was a case where Africa could solve its problems by democratic means and not only as in Rwanda by force and disaster.

A third reason was that at this very moment it had become fashionable to implement African solutions to African problems. The superpowers and the UN had shown limited ability to help in solving crises in Africa (Somalia, Rwanda) and at this time withdrew and emphasized that they were ready to support African solutions, something that led among other things to strengthening of the crisis prevention unit in the OAU.

A fourth reason stems from the major involvements and efforts made by the neighbours in the peace process before the coup. Stung by what seemed like a betrayal of their mediation efforts, neighbouring countries were swift to declare their opposition to Major Buyoya's regime. The regional leaders, including Nyerere, thus, in all likelihood, felt personally offended and betrayed by the coup.

A fifth reason was to establish a precedent against military coups in the region. The Kenyan regime, democratic on the surface but authoritarian and repressive in reality, had experienced attempted coups in the past and had all reason to fear new attempts. The Ugandan regime, itself having come to power by military means, wished to encourage a break in that tradition. Tanzania had not experienced military intervention in politics since 1964, but had an obvious need to reinforce its image as democratically reliable, especially since it had only held its first democratic and multiparty election in October 1995.

A final reason could be the fact that there are not so many other peaceful instruments available to enforce a solution on a country that does not behave according to accepted norms. The neighbouring countries are here trying to find an alternative to military intervention and create a new African experience.

What did the neighbouring countries hope to achieve?

At the outset the neighbouring states made it very clear that they wanted to see a political solution in Burundi, reviving the democratic process from 1993, before they suspended the sanctions. It is interesting to note that they upheld this strict stance for all the two and a half years the sanctions were maintained and even added new demands on Burundi as the original ones were fulfilled. What is also interesting is that they did not budge in spite of strong and increasing pressure from most of the international community, from other African states, from the superpowers such as the US and EU (Harold Volpe and Aldo Ajello the special representatives), from UN agencies such as the UN's human rights special rapporteur on Burundi, from NGOs such as the International Crisis Group and in the end also from some of the original backers of the sanctions in the region. The most engaged countries all through the period were Tanzania and Uganda.

What is most intriguing is the stance of some actors in appraising the policy of African solutions to African problems on the one hand and interfering in the policy decisions taken by the African neighbours on the other hand in the same speech, as was the case with the US Secretary of State in Arusha 1996 (as outlined in the section on the initial phase of sanctions). What is most noticeable in this regard is the constant criticism of the mediator who was appointed by the neighbours, and later was also sanctioned by both the OAU and the UN. He was blamed for many of the decisions by the heads of state in the region that were not approved by the outside representatives of the different actors in the region.

Did the sanctions have any effect and if so was it the one hoped for originally?

As can be seen from the chronology, the sanctions had an immediate and strong effect on the availability and prices of goods and services in Burundi. Export goods became difficult to sell and expensive to trade and import goods became scarce and costly. Through efficient sanction-busting, trade picked up again and most goods could be traded but the prices stayed very high. Furthermore, Burundi became a very isolated country mainly due to the air traffic boycott. The effect on the economy was severe, resulting in a marked decline. A reason why the effects were so immediate and noticeable was that the neighbours were responsible both for the decisions on the sanctions and for their implementation. The very countries that were supposed to enforce the sanctions owned the project.

As in most similar cases, the effects were mainly felt by the poor. As can be seen from the account, humanitarian assistance had serious difficulties in reaching the needy. This was also discussed at length by the enforcement bodies and over time restrictions on import of emergency relief were eased. The serious effects on the poor were also the reason for the interventions from many of the different actors referred to above. However, over time the sanction regime had been so diluted by all the exceptions added to it to deal with the humanitarian consequences that it had become very different from what it originally was supposed to be.

As regards the political effects of the sanctions, one can only speculate. The author is, however, of the opinion that Buyoya was forced and/or helped to act politically by the consistent and unwavering stance of the neighbours. He did whatever he could to put pressure on the neighbours to waive the sanctions. This was done through trying to convince the international community of his willingness to implement the necessary reforms and pointing at the suffering of the majority of the Burundian population. He hoped that this would indirectly lead to pressure on the neighbouring states. He did implement an internal process leading to the Partnership Agreement between the de facto government and the democratically elected Parliament in June 1998, he started secret talks with CNDD as early as November 1996 and he finally took part in the Arusha talks as an active participant in the second half of 1998. It is doubtful that he would have done so without the strong pressure that came from the sanctions. The counter-pressure on him from the more extreme forces within his minority group was formidable – and often fuelled by the attitudes of the neighbours – and he was close to being ousted a number of times during this process. It seems that the strong and consistent pressure from the neighbouring states was an efficient means to keep him performing in the way he did.

There are also other views on the political effects of the sanctions. One view is that the sanctions were generally badly conceived and badly implemented and rather delayed and prevented the smooth development of the peace process. The sanctions gave support to the groups applying counter-pressure on Buyoya. Some made huge profits out of sanction-busting, and had good reason to see to it that the sanctions remained in force. This may have led them to intensify their resistance to negotiations with the armed opposition.

It has also been proposed that while the sanctions, at least initially, probably had a positive impact on the process, the failure to lift the sanctions immediately after the conclusion of the so-called Partnership (between the government and Frodebu) in June 1998 was a major mistake. When the sanctions were finally suspended more than six months later and after tremendous pressure from the international community, especially from Western countries, they were lifted for the wrong reasons. The way the sanctions ended only cemented the unfortunate perception that African politics is perpetually directed by European donors.[30]

In conclusion, it should be emphasized that the sanctions introduced and maintained by the neighbouring states were a unique undertaking, they worked rather well both in their immediate objective on trade and prices in isolating Burundi and politically in enforcing political reform. As with most sanctions, they hit the poorest most and probably had lasting negative effects on the economy – as stated above, comprehensive sanctions are a very indiscriminate instrument. They were also not always very well implemented. What, however, should be noticed in particular are the reactions from most outside actors, on the one hand emphasizing the policy of African solutions to African problems and African ownership, and on the other to a large extent counterbalancing this by critique both of the actions by the regional heads of state and regional bodies and in particular the appointed mediator. Mediation only works when outsiders do not interfere and give alternative options to the warring sides. What is surprising is that the regional heads of states withstood all pressure and interference and upheld their policies until they themselves were convinced that the time was ripe for the dismantling of the sanctions.

Notes

* Thomas Ridæus of the Nordic Africa Institute has contributed substantially to the background research of this chapter.
1. F. Reyntjens, *Small States in an Unstable Region: Rwanda and Burundi, 1999–2000* (Uppsala: NAI, 2000).
2. EU, Declaration by the Presidency on Behalf of the EU, Dublin/Brussels, August 19, 1996.
3. L. Wohlgemuth, *NGOs and Conflict Prevention in Burundi: A Case Study* (Uppsala: NAI, 2000).
4. E. Hoskins and S. Nutt, *The Humanitarian Impacts of Economic Sanctions on Burundi*, Occasional Paper, 29, 1997, Thomas J. Watson Jr Institute for International Studies.
5. Joint Communiqué of the Second Arusha Regional Summit on Burundi, Arusha, Tanzania, July 31, 1996.
6. Organization for African Unity, 'Communniqué on Burundi', Addis Ababa, August 5, 1996.
7. Hoskins and Nutt, 1997.
8. UN Security Council Resolution 1072, August 30 1996.
9. Hoskins and Nutt, 1997.
10. The Economist Intelligence Unit (EIU) Country Report, Uganda, Rwanda, Burundi 1996:3–1999:1, 1996:4, p. 36.
11. Report of the Third Regional Sanctions Coordinating Committee meeting, October 24, 1996.
12. Hoskins and Nutt, 1997.
13. International Crisis Group (ICG) Africa Report, No. 1, April 28, 1998.
14. IRIN News, Weekly Reports 1996–2002, UN Office for the Coordination of Humanitarian Affairs 2002, http://www.irinnews.org
15. EIU, 1997:3, p. 32.
16. UNESCO, Press Release, No. 97–160, September 28, 1997.
17. EIU, 1997:4, p. 37 and UNESCO, 1997.
18. IRIN.
19. Hoskins and Nutt, 1997.
20. UN, Department of Humanitarian Affairs, 'DHA Report on Regional Sanctions against Burundi', New York: DHA, December 1997.
21. ICG, 1998.
22. ICG, 1998 and IRIN.
23. EIU, 1998:2, p. 40.
24. EIU, ICG, 1998.
25. International Monetary Fund, 'Burundi: Recent Economic Developments', 1998.
26. ICG, 1998 and IRIN.
27. International Crisis Group, Africa Briefing 6/8, 2002.
28. ICG, 2002 and IRIN.
29. ICG, 2002 and IRIN.
30. Gregory Mthembu-Salter, *An Assessment of Sanctions against Burundi* (London: Action Aid, 1999).

10

IMPLEMENTING TARGETED SANCTIONS

The role of international agencies and regional organizations

David Cortright, Linda Gerber and George A. Lopez

Because the Security Council and the UN Secretariat lack the institutional capacity to ensure full compliance with sanctions by nation-states, UN sanctions implementation often depends on the cooperation of relevant specialized international agencies and regional organizations. This is increasingly the case as sanctions become more specialized in type, and more precisely targeted in their "smart" form. While considerable policy research has focused on the challenges of gaining member state support and cooperation in sanctions implementation, much less attention has been devoted to understanding the role of international and regional organizations.[1] This chapter offers some observations and insights into the role of various international bodies, from the global to the regional level, in the implementation of UN sanctions.[2]

International agencies and organizations

As various chapters in this volume document, Security Council sanctions policy has shifted dramatically from the use of general trade sanctions to the application of more targeted and selective sanctions in the form of arms embargoes, travel sanctions, financial sanctions, and commodity boycotts. As a result, international organizations that deal with arms control, travel and transportation, finance, and commodities have become more relevant to the implementation of UN sanctions. Indeed, the involvement of specialized agencies has become crucial to the possibility of sanctions success. Both UN specialized agencies and different, functional intergovernmental organizations (IGOs) have played varied roles in sanctions monitoring, implementation, and compliance.[3]

International Atomic Energy Agency

The International Atomic Energy Agency (IAEA) is the UN agency responsible for safeguarding nuclear facilities from the diversion of fissile materials for nuclear weapons purposes. The two sanctions cases in which the IAEA played a role are Iraq and Libya. In the former, the agency was tasked with the mission of disarming Iraq's nuclear capabilities under Security Council Resolution 687 (1991). In the latter, the IAEA has become the primary guarantor of an important component of the changed policy and behavior of the Libyan government in 2003, which led to the lifting of sanctions imposed in SCRs 748 (1992) and 883 (1993). We will discuss only the Iraq case here.

The Agency's role in the implementation of arms inspections, which were bolstered by sanctions against Iraq, was at the heart of the impasse between the Council and the government of Saddam Hussein. This continuing crisis ultimately ended in a US-led military intervention in March 2003. To insure Iraqi compliance with SCR 687, IAEA Action Teams mounted an unprecedented program of intrusive monitoring in which the UN Special Commission (UNSCOM) 1991–98, and the UN Monitoring, Verification and Inspection Commission (UNMOVIC), November 2002–March 2003, each operating under Security Council authority, also cooperated with and provided support for the IAEA mission in Iraq.

In nearly eight years of operation, UNSCOM identified and dismantled nearly all of Iraq's vast store of prohibited weapons. In its brief four-month effort UNMOVIC thoroughly monitored and confirmed the depleted state of Iraq's capabilities. During the 1990s UNSCOM and the IAEA conducted hundreds of inspection missions, surveying more than 1,000 potential and actual weapons sites and documentation centers. In the process, they systematically uncovered and eliminated Iraq's nuclear weapons program and destroyed most of its chemical, biological, and ballistic missile systems. The British government reported in its September 2002 dossier on Iraqi weapons that "UNSCOM and the IAEA Action Team have valuable records of achievement in discovering and exposing Iraq's biological weapons programme and destroying very large quantities of chemical weapons stocks and missiles as well as the infrastructure for Iraq's nuclear weapons programme."[4]

IAEA inspectors found an extensive and alarming nuclear program when they entered the country in 1991, and they systematically eliminated all weapons-related activity. Inspectors destroyed all known facilities relating to the nuclear weapons program and verifiably accounted for the entire inventory of nuclear fuel.[5] In 1998, the IAEA and UNSCOM concluded that "there are no indications that any weapon-useable nuclear material remains in Iraq" and no "evidence in Iraq of prohibited materials, equipment or activities."[6]

The IAEA resumed inspections in late November 2002 and in the four months before war began conducted 237 inspections at 148 sites. IAEA Director General Mohamed El Baradei reported to the Security Council in March 2003 that inspectors found "no indication of resumed nuclear activities . . . nor any indication of nuclear-related prohibited activities at any inspected sites." The IAEA report observed that, "During the past four years, at the majority of Iraqi sites, industrial capacity has deteriorated substantially." In addition, the inspectors examined documents related to alleged Iraqi attempts to import uranium from Niger and found them to be "not authentic." The UN officials saw "no indication that Iraq has attempted to import uranium since 1990." Responding to claims about the import of specialized aluminum tubes, the inspectors reported "no indication that Iraq has attempted to import aluminum tubes for use in centrifuge enrichment."[7]

The IAEA inspection system proved to be far more successful than was generally recognized before the war.[8] As Hans Blix wrote in his book, "the UN and the world had succeeded in disarming Iraq without knowing it."[9] Moreover, the dynamic interactive support between the economic sanctions imposed by the Council and the inspections it mandated are clear: if Iraq wanted sanctions lifted, it had to cooperate in full with the inspections process. Sanctions provided the clout behind the inspections; the inspections served as the leverage on Iraq which wanted the sanctions to end.

Wassenaar Arrangement

The Wassenaar Arrangement (WA) was established in July 1996 by representatives of 33 states. Much like trading arrangements, such as the General Agreement for Tariffs and Trade (GATT), the WA is less of a standing organization than a set of rules for arms control and monitoring. Most of the major arms exporting states participate in the Arrangement, including the United States, Russia, and major western European countries. The member states have agreed upon common lists of munitions and dual-use goods and technologies. Members are expected to share information on exports of weapons and "sensitive" dual-use goods to non-Wassenaar countries. Two separate control lists are maintained: a munitions list, and a list of dual-use goods and technology. The goal of the Arrangement is to promote transparency and greater responsibility with regard to transfers of items on these lists.[10]

Currently, neither the mission nor the usual operational concerns of the WA includes the enforcement of UN arms embargoes, but its efforts to prevent destabilizing arms build-ups fits with the purpose of most UN arms embargoes. However, members of the Council have increasingly relied on some of the technical terms and definitions of the WA when drafting arms embargo resolutions. These definitions and listings find their way into the language of Security Council arms embargo resolutions and their technical appendices.

The WA terms and classifications played a critical role in the development of the Security Council's short-lived "smart sanctions" reformulation of the Iraqi sanctions. As the Council sought new ways to induce Iraqi compliance with SCR 1284 (1999) and obtain a cooperative re-entry of inspectors in exchange for a loosening of the control of non-military goods under the sanctions, Russia and the USA engaged in an extended negotiation about what kinds of materials and goods would be contraband. They essentially refined the WA list and institutionalized it as a "Goods Review List" in what became SCR 1409 (2002).[11]

This recent history of interaction and shared experiences has led some analysts to recommend a more formal linkage, suggesting that Wassenaar Arrangement definitions and terms be adopted as the formal basis for identifying the military goods and dual-use technologies subject to UN sanctions. Germany has encouraged the use of the Wassenaar Arrangement as a common basis for defining the scope of both European Union and United Nations arms embargoes.[12]

Interpol

One of the most important international organizations for the implementation of Security Council sanctions is Interpol. With a mission of enhancing and facilitating cross-border police cooperation in criminal prosecutions, Interpol is potentially a crucial player in the enforcement of UN sanctions. Interpol specializes in investigating and prosecuting such crimes as weapons smuggling, trafficking in human beings, money laundering, and support for terrorism. The work of Interpol is thus of direct relevance to the implementation of all forms of targeted sanctions, including arms, travel, financial, and commodity sanctions.

With a membership of 179 countries, Interpol is one of the largest international organizations in the world, second to the United Nations itself. Interpol deals with international crime, not national crime. It cooperates with police agencies in multiple countries and helps to coordinate criminal investigations and prosecutions. Every member country has an Interpol office called a national central bureau, which is staffed by its own police officers. This bureau is the contact point for cooperation with other governments and helps to provide or receive assistance in criminal investigation and prosecution. Interpol maintains a database with photos or fingerprints of missing individuals and criminal suspects wanted in international investigations.

UN officials regularly interact with Interpol in the implementation of sanctions. To date sanctions-related cooperation with Interpol has involved three different levels of organization: the sanctions committees and their chairs, the UN Secretariat staff, and the expert panels. The Angola Sanctions Committee under the chair of Canadian ambassador Robert Fowler made a special point of seeking Interpol support for the enforcement of sanctions against UNITA. The Angola Monitoring Mechanism continued and deepened these contacts. Investigators with the Monitoring Mechanism met with Interpol officials and developed specific plans for enhanced criminal investigation and prosecution of violators of UN sanctions. The Interpol subregional office in Harare was designated as a center for the exchange of intelligence information in the subregion.[13]

The Angola Monitoring Mechanism sought the assistance of Interpol primarily to uncover and prosecute violations of the arms embargo and diamond sanctions against UNITA. The monitoring team conducted a detailed investigation into diamond smuggling from UNITA-controlled regions and sought the support of Interpol in following up this information. The Monitoring Mechanism also cooperated with Interpol in conducting background checks on arms dealers and arms brokering companies involved in possible illegal shipments to UNITA. UN investigators were briefed on Interpol's Weapons and Explosive Tracking System (IWETS), a new effort to improve databases on the delivery of arms and explosives.[14] The UN also cooperated with Interpol in the Sierra Leone, Liberia, and Afghanistan cases.

Cooperation between the United Nations and Interpol has increased after September 11 and the adoption of SCR 1373 on counter-terrorism. But the transition to interactions that are part of a systematic and continuing exchange of information from what has been essentially an ad hoc relationship has not been easy. Establishing more formalized and regular cooperation between the United Nations and Interpol would strengthen cooperation and improve sanctions implementation in the post September 11 era. Moreover, several UN Expert Panel reports recommended that formal and regularized links be established between the UN Security Council and Interpol to strengthen sanctions monitoring and enforcement.[15] Greater clarity in defining and deepening the liaison between the Security Council and Interpol would improve sanctions implementation.

International Civil Aviation Organization and the International Air Transport Association

To assist in the enforcement of arms embargoes and travel sanctions, UN officials have enlisted the assistance of the International Civil Aviation Organization (ICAO) and the International Air Transport Association (IATA). The ICAO was founded in 1947 to improve the techniques of international air navigation. It consists of 185 member states and organizations and has an extensive organizational network including regional offices. The IATA was founded in 1919 to promote cooperation and establish common standards among airline companies. With regional offices around the world, the IATA seeks to harmonize air traffic management and enhance airline safety and security. Officials of the UN Secretariat and members of expert panels have frequently interacted with the ICAO and the IATA regarding the implementation of specific Security Council sanctions.

In the case of Sierra Leone, the Panel of Experts report found that air transportation played a central role in the illegal shipment of military supplies to the Revolutionary United Front rebels.[16] The Panel recommended that Liberian-registered planes be required to file new registration documents with the ICAO. It urged that Liberian aircraft involved in illegal arms shipments be grounded, and that the ICAO be asked to help enforce this recommendation.[17] The Liberia Panel of Experts also urged that Liberian aircraft be registered with the ICAO. Members of the Liberia Panel met with ICAO officials in Montreal to discuss endemic problems with illegally registered Liberian aircraft. The Panel recommended more vigorous ICAO efforts to educate its members on illegal plane registrations and to upgrade its registration lists and website. Overall, the Liberian Panel of Experts reported receiving helpful assistance and cooperation from the ICAO.[18] The Afghanistan Sanctions Committee also worked closely with the ICAO and IATA, first in enforcing the aviation ban on Taliban-controlled Afghanistan and subsequently in banning the travel of designated Al-Qaida and Taliban leaders.

More consistent and regularized interactions between the United Nations and the ICAO and IATA would improve the implementation of Security Council sanctions. To date these interactions have been irregular, and at times the results have been uncertain. Partly this reflects the hesitancy of the ICAO and IATA to take actions that will have the effect of restricting international aviation. Since the mission of both organizations is to support and encourage air transportation, the enforcement of sanctions presents an inherent dilemma. A concerted effort is needed to address the commercial concerns of the air transportation sector while simultaneously carrying out the mandate of Security Council sanctions that restrict the travel of designated individuals and prohibit specified forms of air transport.

World Customs Organization

Founded in 1952 with a mission to enhance the effectiveness and efficiency of customs administration, the World Customs Organization (WCO) now has 159 members. Among the services provided by the WCO is a Customs Enforcement Network, which provides an accessible database that can be used to facilitate communication and cooperation among customs enforcement officials in member states. Because of its central role in managing customs administration, the WCO can play a critical role in enforcing arms embargoes, travel sanctions, and commodity embargoes. Sanctions implementation often depends on the effectiveness and professionalism of customs officials in states that are principal trading partners of a targeted regime. WCO efforts to improve the administration of customs can enhance the overall effectiveness of UN sanctions implementation.

UN officials have had some limited interaction with the WCO on sanctions implementation issues. The Sierra Leone Panel of Experts noted the potential importance of the WCO in monitoring aircraft flights from Liberia. The Panel urged the WCO to recommend ways of improving monitoring and detection mechanisms to prevent illegal arms imports and diamond exports. The WCO designed a standardized single document that could harmonize cargo inspection at ports, border crossings, and airports.[19] Neither the UN Secretariat nor the Sierra Leone Sanctions Committee followed up these developments. Nor have UN officials taken further steps to cooperate with the WCO in upgrading customs administration and harmonizing cargo inspection systems in ways that would assist in the implementation of Security Council sanctions.

International Maritime Organization

Maritime shipping accounts for the largest volume of international trade and is vital to the implementation of UN sanctions. The International Maritime

Organization (IMO) is the specialized UN agency responsible for enhancing international cooperation on technical matters affecting commercial shipping. The IMO has 157 members and assists member states in improving port control and cargo inspection systems. It enables governments to obtain the technical expertise necessary to maintain effective cargo processing and monitoring systems.

There is little indication of UN officials seeking the cooperation of the IMO in sanctions implementation. The only reference to the IMO in recent UN sanctions-related documents came in the report of the Liberia Panel of Experts. The Panel requested and received assistance from IMO in the investigation of sanctions violations.[20] No further record is available of interactions between UN officials and the IMO in support of sanctions implementation.

World Diamond Council and the Diamond High Council

With the imposition of diamond embargoes against UNITA in Angola, the Revolutionary United Front in Sierra Leone and the Taylor government in Liberia, the Security Council placed great emphasis on commodity sanctions as a means of exerting targeted pressure on rebel groups defying UN mandates. These sanctions have attempted to prevent the import of conflict diamonds, which are defined as "diamonds that originate from areas controlled by forces or factions opposed to legitimate and internationally recognized governments."[21] Sanctions committee representatives, UN Secretariat staff, and expert panels have interacted frequently with diamond industry representatives and specialized intergovernmental agencies to assure compliance with Security Council diamond embargoes.

Diamond industry representatives have taken the initiative to cooperate with the United Nations and nongovernmental organizations in assuring sanctions compliance. The diamond industry has been far more proactive in cooperating with UN sanctions than other industry groups. Diamond traders have taken this initiative because of the unique vulnerability of their industry to the possibility of a consumer backlash. A concerted human rights campaign to boycott conflict diamonds could have a devastating impact on the industry. Diamond companies and trading associations have sought to keep their industry clean by screening out conflict diamonds and by supporting technical initiatives to track diamonds. In this instance, the commercial interest of the industry and the human rights interests of the international community have coincided to generate a concerted effort to prevent the marketing of conflict diamonds.

In July 2000, the World Federation of Diamond Bourses and the International Diamond Manufacturing Association founded the World Diamond Council (WDC). The mission of the WDC was the development, implementation, and oversight of a tracking system to prevent the export and import of conflict diamonds. The WDC developed technical proposals in this regard for consideration by the United Nations and various national governments and intergovernmental agencies. The WDC has offered extensive cooperation to UN sanctions committees, the UN Secretariat staff, and expert panels in the implementation of sanctions.

Even before the founding of the WDC, the Diamond High Council (DHC), the official representative of the Belgian diamond industry, participated in hearings in New York in 1999 in connection with the diamond embargo against the RUF in Sierra Leone. The DHC assisted the government of Sierra Leone in establishing a certificate of origin system for diamonds. The DHC also offered assistance to Liberia in producing a certificate of origin system, and aided in the implementation of sanctions against UNITA in Angola.[22]

When armed conflict diminished in Sierra Leone and Angola, interest in the conflict diamond issue waned. It would be important for UN officials, national governments, and human rights organizations to continue cooperating with the diamond industry to develop a workable global system of diamond certification to prevent the marketing of conflict diamonds. Such a system would help to ensure more effective implementation of future diamond sanctions and could serve as a conflict prevention measure.

Regional organizations

In addition to engaging with intergovernmental specialized agencies, UN officials have also cooperated frequently with regional organizations. In geographic areas where UN sanctions are imposed, the relevant regional security organization has usually cooperated with the Security Council in the monitoring and enforcement of sanctions. The cooperation of these regional organizations is extremely important to the effectiveness of sanctions. The regional organizations usually include the neighboring states and principal trading partners of a targeted regime, which makes their participation and support vital. The regional organizations may deploy security forces and monitoring teams that play a direct role in the investigation and interdiction of prohibited activities. Regional organizations also have experience in political and diplomatic relations with a targeted regime and can play a positive role in the political bargaining process that often accompanies the imposition of sanctions. For all of these reasons, regional organizations play a decisive role in assuring sanctions implementation.

European Union

The European Union was deeply involved in efforts to implement Security Council sanctions against the former republic of Yugoslavia during the years 1991–95. European countries had a direct interest in the political dynamics associated with the breakup of the former Yugoslavia and the subsequent armed conflicts in Croatia and Bosnia. When the Security Council imposed an arms embargo in 1991 (Resolution 713) and general trade sanctions in 1992 (Resolution 757), the emerging institutions of the European community contributed significantly to the monitoring and enforcement of these measures. A network of sanctions assistance missions (SAMs) was organized by the Conference for Security and Cooperation in Europe (CSCE) and the European Community (EC). The SAMs system represented a significant innovation in the implementation of Security Council sanctions and stands today as the most important example of regional organization support for the implementation of UN sanctions.

Soon after the adoption of Resolution 757 (1992), the CSCE and the EC formed a sanctions liaison group to provide technical assistance for sanctions implementation in the countries bordering Yugoslavia. Out of these efforts the first SAMs were formed in Bulgaria, Hungary, Romania, Albania, Croatia, and the former Yugoslav Republic of Macedonia. The EC established a sanctions assistance missions communications center (SAMCOMM) in Brussels and established the position of sanctions coordinator to manage this network of missions. These sanctions assistance efforts were reinforced by direct security contributions from the Western European Union (WEU) and the North Atlantic Treaty Organization (NATO). The WEU established a Danube Patrol Mission to inspect riparian traffic, while NATO created a combined naval task force in the Adriatic to check vessels entering or leaving the port of Bar. The contributions of these European institutions made the Yugoslavia sanctions among the most effectively implemented in history.[23]

With the adoption of the Common Foreign and Security Policy following the 1992 Maastricht Treaty, the European Union developed its own unique and rather highly evolved system for imposing economic sanctions. EU sanctions have been applied for the purposes of preventing conflict, promoting human rights and democracy, and supporting UN sanctions. The most important of these cases involved targeted sanctions applied against Yugoslavia in 1998–2000.[24] The European Union is also a principal partner with the UN in implementing Security Council sanctions. The sanctions office of the European Commission is in regular communication with the UN Secretariat and has participated in international symposia to improve the implementation of UN sanctions.

Economic Community of West African States

Founded in 1975 to promote economic integration and development in the West African region, ECOWAS coordinates the activities of its 15 member countries in a broad range of economic and other activities, including regional security. Three of the most prominent cases of Security Council sanctions – Sierra Leone, Liberia, and Angola – involved African regimes, with two of these cases affecting the West African region directly. As a result, ECOWAS and its military arm, the Economic Community of West African States Military Observer Group (ECOMOG), were intimately involved in efforts to implement UN sanctions. The Security Council followed the lead of ECOWAS in its decision to impose sanctions against Sierra Leone (Resolution 1132, 1997). It also cooperated with ECOWAS in imposing an arms embargo (Resolution 788, 1992) and more extensive targeted sanctions (Resolution 1343, 2001) against Liberia. ECOWAS was involved as well in the sanctions against UNITA in Angola because of allegations that ECOWAS member states provided support to the UNITA movement in violation of Security Council sanctions.

Security Council Resolution 1132 (1997) called for ECOWAS to report regularly to the Security Council Sanctions Committee on implementation efforts. ECOWAS established a group of five that had primary responsibility for obtaining information on sanctions implementation, approving requests for humanitarian exemptions, and reporting on sanctions violations. The UN Sanctions Committee sent reminders to ECOWAS requesting regular reports, but it received very little information in return. The chair of the Sierra Leone Sanctions Committee met with ECOWAS officials and leaders of West African states to encourage greater cooperation in sanctions enforcement.

Despite the attempts of the UN Sanctions Committee to encourage compliance, ECOWAS and its member states were unable to devote much effort to sanctions implementation. ECOWAS has been hampered by political divisions among its member states, by political turmoil and armed conflict within the region, and by a lack of resources. In one of the most impoverished regions of the world, with both Sierra Leone and Liberia ravaged by war, the means for enforcing sanctions simply did not exist. Nigeria and its ECOWAS partners devoted their energies to military intervention and peacekeeping and had few resources available for sanctions enforcement. ECOWAS nations lacked sufficient naval vessels to monitor and interdict illegal shipments into the ports of Sierra Leone and Liberia.

In October 1998, ECOWAS established a general moratorium on the import, export, or manufacture of light weapons in West Africa. The Liberia Panel of Experts recommended that this moratorium be broadened to include an information exchange mechanism on weapons procurement among member states.[25] The Sierra Leone Panel of Experts made a similar recommendation and encouraged international support for ECOWAS's Program for Coordination and Assistance for Security and Development (PCASED).[26] The Angola Monitoring Mechanism also encouraged support for the ECOWAS arms moratorium and interacted with ECOWAS officials to ensure more effective implementation of the travel sanctions and other Security Council measures imposed against UNITA in Angola.

UN officials have made concerted efforts to cooperate with ECOWAS to enhance sanctions implementation, but these efforts have been hampered by limitations within ECOWAS itself and by the lack of a sustained and coordinated liaison effort at the UN. The problems within ECOWAS are the result not only of the political and military conflicts within the region but the lack of resources necessary for sanctions implementation. The West African region in general and ECOWAS in particular are in need of massive assistance from more developed nations. Some donors link economic development support to progress toward good governance, which includes the strengthening of regional institutions designed to enhance security and cooperation. At the United Nations, a more coordinated and sustained effort is needed to maintain regular liaison with ECOWAS and other regional and intergovernmental organizations to ensure more effective international cooperation in sanctions implementation.[27]

Southern African Development Community

As the United Nations took steps to increase sanctions pressure against UNITA in the late 1990s, the role of the Southern African Development Community (SADC) in monitoring and enforcing these measures became increasingly important. SADC member countries, led by South Africa, have recognized that armed conflict and the weapons trafficking that goes with it are harmful to economic development and cooperation. In September 1994, SADC and the European Union formed working groups to reduce the flow of weapons exports to southern Africa and to exert greater control over the arms trade in the region. When the Security Council imposed travel sanctions against UNITA in 1997 (Resolution 1127) and added a diamond embargo and financial assets freeze in 1998 (Resolution 1173), SADC initiated efforts to monitor and interdict illegal flights into UNITA-controlled territory. The goal of these efforts was to prevent illegal trafficking in arms and diamonds. SADC became involved in efforts to monitor the delivery of petroleum fuels into Angola. SADC also approved a project to establish mobile radar systems to monitor air traffic in the region.

The Angola Sanctions Committee and the Angola Monitoring Mechanism interacted frequently with SADC in ensuring the proper monitoring and enforcement of sanctions. Canadian ambassador Robert Fowler met with SADC officials during his 1999 mission to the region. Fowler recommended that the ICAO and IATA provide support to governments in the region in the development of more effective aircraft radar and monitoring systems. He also encouraged international support to South Africa and other governments in the region to monitor and establish a database on the sale of petroleum products. The Angola Monitoring Mechanism followed up many of Fowler's recommendations and maintained close contact with SADC on sanctions implementation issues. When the Security Council created the Monitoring Mechanism (Resolution 1295, 2000), it specifically asked SADC to take measures to strengthen air traffic control, prevent the diversion of petroleum supplies to UNITA, and halt diamond smuggling in the region.[28] The Monitoring Mechanism reported that SADC was cooperating with the diamond industry in creating a certificate of origin system and attempting to prevent diamond smuggling. It also commended SADC for developing a sound regional policy to control weapons sales and prevent illegal arms trafficking.[29]

Organization of American States

The sanctions experience of the Organization of American States (OAS) with United Nations mandated sanctions came in a relatively unique situation in the 1990s: the UN sanctions were meant to bolster the pre-existing sanctions imposed by a regional actor. The UN actions of 1993–94 were also an extension of its own substantial commitment to democratic governance, as the UN had invested a great deal of its resources and prestige in the first democratic elections in Haiti in 200 years when it established and monitored the procedures which resulted in the elections of Jean-Bertrand Aristide in December 1990. But in May 1991, a military coup and subsequent military repression prompted an OAS trade and arms embargo in October.

In many ways, the case of Haitian sanctions is a complex one, involving the big power politics of the US on the Security Council and its traditional sphere of influence, as well as illustrating the relationship between sanctions imposition and the Council's concern about other issues such as peacekeeping and protecting human rights and refugees.[30] To buttress the OAS effort in light of the unwillingness of the military government of Raul Cedras to restore Aristide, the US imposed a strict freeze on the financial assets of the ruling junta and denied them travel visas in June 1993. This was followed quickly by UN Security Council Resolution 841 (June, 1993) which placed a fuel and arms embargo on the nation and established a Sanctions Committee to manage the UN actions.

The following fifteen months involved overlapping efforts, on and off again sanctions based on the military's backsliding on prior agreements, and ultimately a US-brokered agreement for Cedras's group to leave the nation just as US troops were arriving to remove Cedras in September 1994. The lesson of the Haitian case parallels that of the cases of Liberia and Sierra Leone: when regional organizations take the lead in imposing sanctions, they often need the substantial resources and political clout of the UN Security Council to develop effective monitoring and enforcement mechanisms.

League of Arab States

Founded in 1945 to promote economic development and defense and security cooperation among Arab states, the Arab League played an important role in the Security Council sanctions imposed against Libya in 1992 (Resolution 748) and 1993 (Resolution 883). The League was also intimately involved in the UN sanctions against Iraq. League member states were deeply concerned about the severe humanitarian consequences of sanctions in Iraq, and member countries took the lead in urging the lifting of civilian trade sanctions against Iraq. The Arab League also supported the call for diplomatic efforts to mediate the dispute between Iraq and the Security Council.

While some members of the League were skeptical of UN sanctions against Libya, participating states generally complied with the ban on flights to Iraq. The greatest contribution of the League was in finding a diplomatic solution to the impasse. In September 1997, the Arab League began to take steps to relax enforcement of the air embargo, in the hopes that this would spur a negotiated settlement. These efforts, and the announcement by the Organization of African Unity in June 1998 that it would openly defy the flight ban, spurred US and British leaders to negotiate a settlement of the dispute, and led to the suspension of sanctions.[31]

Toward a more intense future

As a number of analysts have documented, the competence and capacity of the UN Secretariat and the Security Council in both the peacekeeping area and in the formulation and implementation of sanctions, have been hallmarks of institutional learning of the past decade.[32] As this chapter has shown, a remarkable mix of international and regional organizations have contributed both positively and problematically to the sanctions process. One of the most unprecedented of these organizational dynamics was spawned by Security Council Resolution 1373 (September 2001), which created and defined the work of the UN's Counter-Terrorism Committee (CTC). As the UN's institutional and policy response to the challenge of Al-Qaida terrorism and the events of September 11, the CTC monitored and certified that UN member states were complying with a variety of international conventions which renounce and control terrorism. In addition, the CTC assessed how well states had done in locking down terrorist financial assets and in denying designated individuals and organizations the right of travel within their borders. Thus, while not a sanctions resolution per se, Resolution 1373 mandated that member states employ smart sanctions – in the form of financial and travel controls – against a designated list of individuals and organizations. And the CTC, an arm of the Council, was the organizational structure in which this occurred.

The Security Council developed specific policy recommendations for the future of the CTC as it implemented Resolution 1535 (March 2004), whose aim is to "revitalize" the Committee by mandating the creation of a 30-person Counter-Terrorism Executive Directorate (CTED). Indications are that the CTED will expand the work of the CTC in some particular functions: enhancing regional coordination, providing technical assistance to states needing help in developing the capacity to implement counter-terrorism mandates, linking technical assistance to long-term development aid, and strengthening specific measures to suppress terrorist financing and coordinate international law enforcement efforts. That some see the emergence of a CTED as an appendage as significant to the Security Council as the IAEA has been brings our own argument full circle regarding the importance of supportive organizations for sanctions implementation.

Notes

1 One outstanding exception to this generalization is the recent study of European Union sanctions and incentives policies by Hadewych Hazelzet; see Hadewych Hazelzet, "Carrots or Sticks? EU and US Reactions to Human Rights Violations (1989–2000)," PhD thesis (European University Institute, Department of Social and Political Science, Florence, 2001).

2 Of particular interest in the analysis of the effectiveness of UN Security Council Resolutions and their implementation is the increase in scholarly and policy assessment of the interface between the UN and other organizations – both regional and international – in peacekeeping operations. See C. L. Sriram and K. Wermester (eds) *From Promise to Practice: Strengthening UN Capacities for the Prevention of Violent*

Conflict (Boulder, CO: Lynne Rienner, 2003) and M. Pugh and W. P. Singh Sidhu (eds) *The United Nations and Regional Security* (Boulder, CO: Lynne Rienner, 2003).

3   As the importance and utility of IGOs have risen, so too has that of international nongovernmental organizations (NGOs), most notably in the commodities arena, and in the form of NGOs with a mandate to report controversy and influence global public opinion on various issues from arms embargoes to the character of a new ruling coalition in a war-torn nation. For further discussion and examples of this see D. Cortright and G. A. Lopez, *Sanctions and the Search for Security* (Boulder, CO: Lynne Rienner, 2002), pp. 172–175;190–195; 203–213.

4   British Government, Joint Intelligence Committee, *Iraq's Weapons of Mass Destruction: The Assessment of the British Government* (London: British Government, September 2002), p. 39, <http://www.number-10.gov.uk/files/pdf/iraqdossier.pdf> (accessed 5 February 2004).

5   United Nations Security Council, International Atomic Energy Agency, *Fourth Consolidated Report of the Director General of the International Atomic Energy Agency Under Paragraph of the Security Council Resolution 1051 (1996)*, S/1997 /779, New York, 6 October 1997, para. 72.

6   United Nations Security Council, *Emergency Session of the United Nations Special Commission Established Under Paragraph 9(b)(i) of Security Council Resolution 687 (1991)*, S/1997/922, New York, 24 November 1997, para. 5.

7   Mohamed El Baradei, International Atomic Energy Agency, "The Status of Nuclear Inspections in Iraq: An Update" (statement, UN Security Council, New York, 7 March 2003) <http://www.iraqwatch.org/un/IAEA/iaea-elbaradei-030703.htm> (accessed 12 February 2004).

8   J. Cirincione, J. Matthes, G. Perkovich with A. Orton, *WMD in Iraq: Evidence and Implications* (Washington, DC: Carnegie Endowment for International Peace, January 2004), p. 8 <http://www.ceip.org/files/pdf/Iraq3FullText.pdf> (accessed 9 February 2004).

9   H. Blix, *Disarming Iraq* (New York: Pantheon Books, 2004), p. 259.

10 Stockholm International Peace Research Institute, *SIPRI Yearbook 2002: Armaments, Disarmament and International Security* (Oxford: Oxford University Press, 2002), p. 755.

11 D. Cortright, A. Millar and G. A. Lopez, "Sanctions, Inspections and Containment: Viable Policy Options in Iraq," in Gerhard Beestermoller and David Little (eds) *Iraq: Threat and Response* (Hamburg, London: Lit Verlag, 2003), pp. 136–137.

12 M. Loy, "Proper and Prompt National Implementation of Arms Embargoes: The German Case," in M. Brzoska (ed.) *Smart Sanctions: The Next Steps* (Baden-Baden: Nomos Verlagsgesellschaft, 2001); see also the recommendations of Loretta Bondi in her chapter, "Arms Embargoes," in the same volume.

13 United Nations Security Council, *Addendum to the Final Report of the Monitoring Mechanism on Sanctions Against UNITA*, S/2001/363, New York, 18 April 2001, par. 112.

14 United Nations Security Council, *Supplementary Report of the Monitoring Mechanism on Sanctions Against UNITA*, S/2001/966, New York, 12 October 2001, par. 117–120.

15 See, for example, United Nations Security Council, *Letter Dated 28 July 1999 from the Chairman of the Security Council Committee Established Pursuant to Resolution 864 (1993) Concerning the Situation in Angola, Addressed to the President of the Security Council*, S/1999/829, New York, 28 July 1999, par. 174.

16 United Nations Security Council, *Report of the Panel of Experts Appointed Pursuant to Security Council Resolution 1306 (2000), Paragraph 19, in Relation to Sierra Leone*, S/2000/1195, New York, par. 22.

17 Ibid., par. 33 and 34.

18 United Nations Security Council, *Report of the Panel of Experts Pursuant to Security*

Council Resolution 1343 (2001), Paragraph 19, Concerning Liberia, S/2001/1015, New York, 26 October 2001, par. 6, 7, 11, 12, and 85.

19 United Nations Security Council, *Report of the Panel of Experts Appointed Pursuant to Security Council Resolution 1306 (2000), Paragraph 19, in Relation to Sierra Leone*, S/2000/1195, New York, 20 December 2000, par. 41 and 239.

20 United Nations Security Council, *Report of the Panel of Experts Appointed Pursuant to Security Council Resolution 1343 (2001), Paragraph 19, Concerning Liberia*, S/2001/1015, New York, par. 85.

21 United Nations Department of Public Information, *Conflict Diamonds: Sanctions and War*. Online. 21 March 2001. Security Council Affairs Division, Department of Political Affairs. Available: http://www.un.org/peace/africa/Diamond.html [29 June 2001].

22 United Nations Security Council, *Final Report of the Monitoring Mechanism on Angola Sanctions*, S/2000/1225, New York, 21 December 2000, par. 195.

23 United Nations Security Council, *Letter Dated 24 September 1996 from the Chairman of the Security Council Committee Established Pursuant to Resolution 724 (1991) Concerning Yugoslavia Addressed to the President of the Security Council, Report of the Copenhagen Roundtable on United Nations Sanctions in the Case of the Former Yugoslavia, Held at Copenhagen on 24 and 25 June 1996*, S/1996/776, New York, 24 September 1996, par. 17.

24 For a description and analysis of these measures, see A. W. de Vries, "E.U. Sanctions Against Yugoslavia, 1998–2000," in D. Cortright and G. A. Lopez (eds) *Smart Sanctions: Targeting Economic Statecraft* (Lanham, MD: Rowman & Littlefield, 2002), pp. 87–108.

25 *Report of the Panel of Experts Pursuant to Security Council Resolution 1343 (2001), Paragraph 19, Concerning Liberia*, S/2001/1015, New York, 26 October 2001, par. 25.

26 United Nations Security Council, *Report of the Panel of Experts Appointed Pursuant to Security Council Resolution 1306 (2000), Paragraph 19, in Relation to Sierra Leone*, S/2000/1195, New York, 20 December 2000, par. 36.

27 It is this lack of both institutional clout and commitment that has prompted some to call for more direct UN Security Council "power" in sanctions imposition and implementation, one form of which is the sanctions coordinator discussed in Chapter 5 in this volume.

28 United Nations Security Council, *Security Council Resolution 1295 (2000)*, S/RES/1295, New York, 18 April 2000.

29 United Nations Security Council, *Supplementary Report of the Monitoring Mechanism on Sanctions Against UNITA*, S/2001/966, New York, 12 October 2001, par. 108 and 253–256.

30 For a detailed account of these complexities see D. M. Malone, *Decision-Making in the UN Security Council: The Case of Haiti* (Oxford: Oxford University Press, 1998); D. Cortright and G. A. Lopez, *The Sanctions Decade: Assessing UN Strategies in the 1990s* (Boulder, CO: Lynne Rienner, 2000); and S. von Einsiedel and D. M. Malone, "Haiti," in D. M. Malone (ed.) *The UN Security Council: From the Cold War to the 21st Century* (Boulder, CO: Lynne Rienner, 2004), pp. 467–482.

31 See Cortright and Lopez, *The Sanctions Decade*, pp. 107–121.

32 D. Cortright and G. A. Lopez, "Reforming Sanctions," pp. 167–181; and S. Forman and A. Grene, "Collaborating With Regional Organizations," pp. 295–309, in David M. Malone (ed.) *The UN Security Council: From the Cold War to the 21st Century* (Boulder, CO: Lynne Rienner, 2004); S. Chesterman and B. Pouligny, "Are Sanctions Meant to Work? The Politics of Creating and Implementing Sanctions Through the United Nations," *Global Governance*, Vol. 9, No. 4 (October–December, 2003), pp. 503–518.

11

THE WORLD TRADE ORGANIZATION

Sanctions for non-compliance

Steve Charnovitz

The idea that a specialized international organization should have a compliance mechanism that would include the possibility of an economic sanction against a country judged to be in violation of international rules originated in the International Labour Organization (ILO) of 1919.[1] The ILO chose not to employ such sanctions however. Eight decades later, the notion of a judicial-like compliance system capped by the possibility of a multilaterally agreed trade sanction has flowered in only one international organization, the World Trade Organization (WTO). In some quarters, the WTO dispute system is perceived as a paragon of enforceability. Envy of the WTO armamentarium has led champions of various causes to try getting the WTO to deploy its compliance system in support of non-trade values.

The most noteworthy feature of the WTO judicial system is that the member governments have agreed to compulsory jurisdiction. The WTO Understanding on Rules and Procedures Governing the Settlement of Disputes (known as the "DSU") provides that any member government can lodge a complaint against any other member government and secure an independent panel to consider the complaint and render a judgment. After a possible appeal to the WTO Appellate Body, a final decision is entered, and is automatically adopted by the WTO Dispute Settlement Body (DSB) which includes delegates from all member governments. The government found to be in default is then given a "reasonable period of time" to come into compliance, after which the complaining government(s) may seek authority to "suspend concessions or other obligations."[2] For shorthand, I have called that authority a "SCOO."[3] A SCOO enables the suspension of any concession or any obligation on a prospective (rather than retroactive) basis.

A scholarly debate is ongoing as to whether the SCOO is more properly viewed as an offensive act of sanctioning, or as a defensive act of rebalancing trade concessions. In fact, both features are present. The SCOO in the WTO reflects the traditional remedy of "Termination or suspension of the operation of a treaty as a consequence of its breach," as provided in the Vienna Convention on the Law of Treaties.[4] In other words, the victim country counteracts the breach by suspending some of its obligations to the breaching countries. But viewing the SCOO merely as defensive misses the important evolution of WTO practice that recognizes the SCOO as a purposive act designed to change behavior in the defendant country.[5] Because the SCOO is authorized to induce compliance, the SCOO is being used as instrumentally as any trade sanction could be. The fact that the obligation to comply persists notwithstanding the SCOO reinforces this conclusion. Having appreciated this new reality, the WTO Secretariat now routinely designates SCOO actions as "sanctions."[6] Indeed, in a recent report, the Secretariat suggests that the lack of retroactivity in WTO remedies affords the possibility that governments "could go *unpunished* for acting inconsistently with their obligations, at least for the duration of the dispute."[7]

This chapter considers three questions about WTO trade sanctions: first, are WTO sanctions effective? Second, are they well targeted against the individuals who are causing WTO rules to be violated? Third, is the use of sanctions by the WTO transferable to other international organizations?

Effectiveness of WTO trade sanctions

So far, only three SCOOs have been imposed – two by the United States against the European Communities (the *Bananas* and *Meat Hormones* cases), and one by Canada against the Community[8] (*Meat Hormones*). In all three instances, the sender government imposed a 100 percent *ad valorem* tariff on certain imports from the Community. None of the three episodes induced near-term compliance. The sanctions in the *Meat Hormones* dispute are still being imposed. The *Bananas* sanctions were removed as part of a settlement in which the Community will comply by 2006.

The inutility of WTO sanctions – in the only two disputes where they were used – seems to belie the mythology of a powerful WTO enforcement system with "teeth." Evaluating the effectiveness of a sanction mechanism is a complex endeavor, however, because of the counterfactual. Perhaps the prospect of a sanction is so effective a deterrent that the sanction itself rarely needs to be employed.

Here is the WTO record:[9] as of 1 August 2003, 69 disputes have been fully adjudicated in the WTO.[10] Of those, a violation was found in 59 cases (86 percent). In some instances, these violations were corrected. In others, the disputing parties settled, perhaps with less than full compliance. In many others, the complaining government continues to wait for compliance. In 11 of the 59 findings of violation (19 percent), the complaining government filed a follow-up (DSU Article 21.5) complaint that the defendant government did not comply during the prescribed period.[11] Of those 11 complaints, non-compliance was found in 9 (82 percent). Out of those 9 cases, the complaining parties have sought authority to SCOO in 4 (44 percent), but may do so in others in the future.[12] Seven authorizations to SCOO have been granted to governments in 5 separate disputes, and this authority has been used three times.[13] Of the 7 instances in which authority to SCOO has been granted, none have ended with a determination of full compliance. Looking at the data another way, of the 59 cases where violations were originally found, the SCOO has been used in only 2 (twice in Meat *Hormones* and once in *Bananas*).

Based on these data, diverging conclusions are possible about the effectiveness of WTO dispute settlement, and about the utility of the SCOO. One conclusion might be that the SCOO plays only a marginal role, and its threatened use does not seem to induce compliance. A quite different conclusion is that the SCOO might work better if it were used more often. Another is that the overall compliance picture would be a lot worse without the SCOO. Eventually, analysts will perform sophisticated tests on these data and draw quantitative conclusions. The problem facing such studies is obtaining measurements of the degree of compliance in each dispute.

The most interesting result may be that the SCOO was not used in 57 percent of the cases in which it was authorized, and no sanction has been imposed since 1999. Governments are manifesting a queasiness about using trade sanctions, perhaps because they are harmful to the sending nation, or perhaps because their use seems to contradict the purpose of the WTO. Advocates of using trade sanctions to settle intergovernmental disputes are probably disappointed with this trend.

Targetability of WTO trade sanctions

Targeting trade sanctions is not easy. Ideally they would be targeted against the perpetrators of policies that contradict the basic tenets of the international community. In the WTO context, this ideal raises a threshold question. Do WTO rules reflect such basic tenets? In general, WTO disputes are not about accepting the WTO rule; they are about the interpretation of an often ambiguous rule. After a claim has been adjudicated, a losing government does have an obligation to comply, but compliance will often take time as governments work through parliamentary processes to refit underlying policy into the four corners of WTO rules. Is a delay in coming into compliance with the rules of antidumping[14] really comparable to the violations of international law that draw sanctions by the UN Security Council? If not, then the idea of targeted WTO sanctions may not make much sense.

Suppose the WTO champion disagrees, and says that violating the antidumping rules may not be as bad as attacking a trading partner, but is still sufficiently serious that it warrants trade sanctions. This view would imply a targeting strategy that goes after the elites in the scofflaw country refusing to change its antidumping law. So elected officials, trade bureaucrats, and parliamentarians would be the most appropriate targets. The sending country could also target the private actors who sought the import protection in the first place, and who now may be lobbying to resist compliance with WTO rules.

Yet it is one thing to target dictators, warlords, rebels, etc., and quite another to target individuals in a democratic polity who are playing their roles of representative, administrator, judge, or just plain rent-seeker. Would it be proper for the WTO to approve a proposed SCOO that targets the major employer in the constituency of the chair of the responsible parliamentary committee? That is a hard question, and one just beginning to be asked.

Under WTO rules, the Dispute Settlement Body cannot second-guess the hit list of products imported from the scofflaw country that the complaining government proposes to sanction. Thus, the sending government *can* aim to target the chair's district. So far, such tailored trade sanctions have not been employed, but they have been discussed.

In the three actual SCOOs, Canada and the United States used discriminatory, prohibitive tariffs, yet as noted above, a SCOO can assume other forms also. For example, in a dispute regarding the WTO's intellectual property rules, a complaining government could ask the WTO to authorize the abrogation of specific copyrights or trademarks. The guiding principle for the WTO seems to be "eye for eye, tooth for tooth."

Given the integration of modern economies, any SCOO is likely to cause collateral economic damage, and hurt innocent victims, such as workers, suppliers, and consumers. That is, unless one takes the view that every denizen in the European Communities is complicit when the European Commission does not comply with the WTO's *Hormones* decision. When innocent bystanders are receiving the same penalty as the intended victims, the sanctions employed can hardly be labeled "smart."

Another problem with WTO sanctions is that smaller countries would have a hard time using sanctions against bigger countries. Such asymmetries of economic power are common of course, but they cut deeper in the WTO than in, say, the Security Council. If the Security Council agrees to a trade sanction, then all UN member countries ought to take part, and together they have economic power. But in the WTO, the only country that can impose the sanction is one lodging the dispute (and any co-complainants).

Transferability to other international organizations

The WTO is popularly credited with having dispute settlement with "teeth," and as a result, sanction-envy is commonly heard in international policy discourse. Commentators often suggest that the WTO dispute settlement system would be a good model for other treaties and international organizations. Leaving aside the doubts we have already considered as to whether WTO sanctions even work, could they be grafted on to other organizations?

Almost all of the features in the DSU that are valuable could be replicated in other treaties. The compulsory jurisdiction, the rapid timetable for decisions, the possibility of appeal, and the compliance review process are all features that ought to be copied.[15] The trade sanctions, too, are capable of being copied, and would probably be more morally justifiable in other regimes, especially those with weightier community value than exist in the trading system. Afterall, the only current use of trade sanctions in the WTO is the *Hormones* case where the complaint is that exporters in Canada and the United States cannot ship meat produced with hormones to Europe. Even the most stolid supporters of treaty enforceability may be uneasy with the *Hormones* case as the archetype for when sanctions should be used.

Copying WTO-style enforcement into other organizations runs into a legal problem however. Implementing a trade sanction outside the WTO can violate WTO rules. The trade discrimination inherent in a WTO-approved sanction would violate WTO rules if done unilaterally,[16] yet avoids the violation because the DSU provides for multilateral enforcement of WTO obligations.[17] No similar dispensation exists for a noncompliance procedure in other specialized international organizations or treaties. The only trade sanction external to the WTO that is specifically permitted by WTO rules is an interruption of economic relations authorized by the UN Security Council.[18]

Whether some of the public policy exceptions in WTO rules could be used to justify trade sanctions imposed by other treaties or organizations has been a topic of international law research for several years.[19] No consensus is in sight. Any effort to follow the WTO's practice in another organization would surely meet the objection that such mimesis is illegal under WTO rules.

Notes

1 Treaty of Versailles, 28 June 1919, art. 414, available at http://www.lib.byu.edu/~rdh/wwi/versailles.html
2 See WTO Understanding on Rules and Procedures Governing the Settlement of Disputes (DSU), esp. arts. 21.3, 22.6.
3 "The WTO's Problematic 'Last Resort' Against Noncompliance," *Aussenwirtschaft. Swiss Review of International Economic Relations*, December 2002, pp. 409, 412, available at http://www.geocities.com/charnovitz
4 Vienna Convention on the Law of Treaties, 23 May 1969, 1155 UNTS 331, art. 60.
5 "Rethinking WTO Trade Sanctions," *American Journal of International Law*, Vol. 95, 2001, pp. 792, 803–805, available at http://www.asil.org/ajil/v95792.pdf
6 For example, see WTO, *WTO Policy Issues for Parliamentarians,* May 2001, p. 7, stating that:

> The long-term outcome of the dispute settlement process must be complete restoration of full compliance with WTO rules. However, if a country fails to implement a WTO ruling there are two temporary measures which can be taken. Either the offending member can offer "compensation" for the harm done to the trade interests of another member or the DSB can authorize a level of retaliatory sanctions.

7 WTO, World Trade Report 2003, p. 177, available at http://www.wto.org/english/res_e/booksp_e/anrep_e/world_trade_report_2003_e.pdf. See also DSU arts. 22–23.
8 The EU within the WTO is officially known as the European Communities; it is shortened here to the Community to conform to current usage.
9 Tabulations by the author.

10 This number does not include DSU Article 21.5 compliance panel reports and one case that was refiled after a procedural rejection. Parallel cases processed concurrently are counted as one.
11 This number does not include settled cases, unadopted Article 21.5 decisions, or complaints that were refiled after a procedural rejection.
12 Cases where the determination of the SCOO level has been halted for negotiations are not counted.
13 The 7 authorizations include 4 cases that had DSU Article 21.5 compliance decisions (Ecuador v. EC *Bananas*, Brazil *Aircraft*, US *Foreign Sales Corporations*, and Canada *Aircraft*), plus three cases that did not (US v. EC *Bananas*, US v. EC *Hormones*, and Canada v. EC *Hormones*).
14 The rules of antidumping prescribe when a government can impose tariffs on imported products that are priced low for export according to the WTO's parameters.
15 See J. Lacarte-Muró and P. Gappah, "Developing Countries and the WTO Legal and Dispute Settlement System: A View from the Bench," *Journal of International Economic Law*, Vol. 3, 2000, pp. 395, 401 (suggesting that the dispute settlement mechanism of the WTO is a significant achievement in the global impetus towards peace and prosperity).
16 Trade sanctions require discrimination, and discrimination against particular countries is prohibited by Article I of the General Agreement on Tariffs and Trade (GATT), Article II of the General Agreement on Trade in Services (GATS), and Article 4 of the Agreement on Trade-Related Aspects of Intellectual Property Rights (TRIPS). Whether any of these rules can be trumped by various exceptions in WTO law continues to be a topic of debate.
17 WTO, World Trade Report 2003, p. 173. See also DSU arts. 22–23.
18 GATT art. XXI(c), GATS art. XIV *bis* 1(c), TRIPS art. 73(c).
19 See, e.g., S. H. Cleveland, "Human Rights Sanctions and the World Trade Organisation," in F. Francioni (ed.) *Environment, Human Rights, and International Trade* (Oxford: Hart, 2001), pp. 199–261.

Part IV

NEW TARGETING
Enhancing legality and effectiveness

12

THE COUNTER-TERRORISM COMMITTEE

Its relevance for implementing targeted sanctions

*Curtis A. Ward**

The need for state capacity

This chapter, in examining the relevance of the Security Council Counter-Terrorism Committee's capacity building program for implementing targeted sanctions, begins with the widely accepted premise that targeted sanctions are more difficult to implement than general economic sanctions. This is compounded by the fact that most States lacked legal and executive capacity to implement them. Reference here is made specifically to implementation of targeted financial sanctions, arms embargoes, travel and aviation bans, and sanctions against illegal trade in precious metals and commodities. Each of these targeted sanctions requires a precise legal framework and effective executive machinery to implement, and hence a State's legal and executive capacity has a direct bearing on whether the targeted measures can be effectively and successfully implemented. This is particularly true of the disproportionate responsibility of front-line neighboring States to the target of the sanctions, or of States that have a close relationship to the target and therefore are required to carry out more vigilant and effective sanctions enforcement action. This invariably has a direct correlation to the effectiveness of targeted sanctions.

Recognizing that many States lacked the legal and administrative capacity to implement targeted sanctions, the Stockholm Process,[1] *inter alia*, undertook an examination of targeted sanctions to determine what was required of States to fulfill their obligation under the Charter of the United Nations to implement Security Council decisions.[2] States are obliged to give effect to decisions taken by the Security Council for the maintenance of international peace and security, particularly those decisions taken under Chapter VII of the Charter, as are sanctions measures.[3]

State capacity and targeted sanctions

In addressing the capacity required by States to implement targeted sanctions, it is essential to examine the State's capacity as it relates to specific types of targeted sanctions. This examination will focus primarily on three types of targeted sanctions – financial sanctions, arms embargoes, and travel bans – to illustrate the capacity in a State's executive machinery that is required for effective implementation of each of the designated sanctions. Others have examined issues surrounding implementation of targeted sanctions and have concluded that, as a prerequisite, generally, all States must have in place the required legal framework to implement UN Security Council decisions.[4] That is, enabling legislation which empowers the State to adopt implementing legislation and regulations to give effect to the decisions taken by the Security Council.[5] All States should also have penal laws to enforce compliance with sanctions orders issued under authority of these enabling laws and regulations, including punishment that is commensurate with the nature of the prohibited offence. It is also important that sanctions violations are criminalized in domestic laws in order to facilitate cooperation, including mutual legal assistance in criminal proceedings brought against sanctions violations in another jurisdiction.

The following discussion of specific types of targeted sanctions and the capacity required by each State to implement each type of sanction aims at demonstrating the importance of the legal framework and executive machinery required in each case. Most importantly, it will also serve to relate the capacity needs of States to implement targeted sanctions with the capacity-building process being employed by the Security Council Counter-Terrorism Committee (known by its acronym "CTC") to help States implement Resolution 1373 (2001).[6] The analysis will show that there is a correlation between the work being carried out by the Counter-Terrorism Committee in its capacity-building program, and the relevance of this program to the capacity to implement the measures imposed by targeted sanctions.

Financial sanctions

Of the targeted measures, financial sanctions and arms embargoes are the two most frequently employed sanctions by the UN Security Council. They are usually imposed in conjunction with other measures such as travel bans and, in relevant circumstances, restrictions on the trade in precious materials and commodities. The sanctions measures imposed on Jonas Savimbi's União Nacional para a Independência Total de Angola (UNITA),[7] the Government of Liberia and Charles Taylor and other senior members of the former Liberian government,[8] and the former Afghanistan Taliban regime, Usama bin Laden and Al-Qaida[9] are prime examples of the combined use of these sanctions measures.

In the case of financial sanctions,[10] the requirements are, *inter alia*, that each State identifies and freezes suspicious or identified assets found within its jurisdiction belonging to the targeted State, group or individual, or it requires the State to act upon receipt of notification from a Security Council sanction committee identifying assets of the target. The requisite action would include freezing the assets found within its jurisdiction belonging to, or associated with, individuals on lists issued by Security Council sanctions committees.[11] In order to carry out this obligation, each State must have an authority that is empowered by domestic law to act upon the freezing request or upon identification of the targeted assets. Immediate action is necessary, as the freezing authority must be able to act without delay to prevent the assets from moving out of the State's jurisdiction to escape the sanction. This is of particular importance as financial assets can easily move from the reach of one jurisdiction to another in a matter of seconds. The domestic laws of a State must, in general, empower a minister of government, central bank official, a financial intelligence unit (FIU), an equivalent authority, or some combination of these to act expeditiously on these matters.

It is also important to underscore that in a situation where a State lacks the investigative capacity of an FIU with well-trained personnel having access to computerization and relevant database, it would be a severe handicap to that State's ability to carry out its responsibilities. It also requires that each State has appropriate banking and financial laws and regulations which would compel financial institutions to respond to an order from the freezing authority, and that would also preclude bank secrecy laws from impeding the investigation of suspicious assets and carrying out of the freezing order.

Arms embargoes

As to arms embargoes, a State requires adequately trained and equipped customs officers; secured air, land and sea port facilities, as appropriate; personnel trained in detection techniques to be able to recognize fraudulent shipping and customs documents and contraband; and the ability to exchange information with other States electronically in real time. This type of capacity also extends to border controls and security. Many States lack adequately staffed and equipped border posts, customs and entry points; they lack physical facilities that are secure, and staffed by adequately trained personnel for examination of people and goods entering and leaving their territory. They generally lack adequate communication and security screening equipments. This lack of capacity varies from country to country, from region to region, and between countries in each region.

To illustrate further the problem as it exists in a real practical situation, and to facilitate this discussion, a cursory look at the Southern African Development Community (SADC) sub-region serves as a good example of a sub-region where many of these problems exist. Not all of the countries in the SADC sub-region have the requisite capacity to implement targeted sanctions. While some countries in the region possess varying levels of the requisite capacity, there is an overall lack of capacity to deal with the movement of people, goods and services. There is a lack of border controls and security, including controls over migration flow throughout the region, and in particular the movement of targeted individuals in essentially an open border region. The flow of people, goods and services throughout the region and the links to transnational crimes, in particular the smuggling of illegal firearms and illicit trade in precious materials, pose significant challenges. Many of these States are challenged by these deficiencies in their capacities at land border checkpoints, including the lack of infrastructure, fences, buildings, trained personnel, document fraud detection capabilities, profiling capacity, and identification of contraband. The differences in law enforcement and judicial capacities in neighboring countries in the sub-region in areas of investigation and evidence gathering exacerbates the situation thereby adversely affecting mutual legal assistance in criminal matters and other areas of judicial cooperation, including exchange of information on targeted individuals.

Many of the problems that are found in some of the countries in the SADC sub-region have adverse implications for implementing targeted sanctions throughout the sub-region as a whole, and remedying these deficiencies therefore requires national as well as regional capacity-building solutions. A significant number of these problems, however, are not unique to the SADC sub-region and are found to exist in other regions and sub-regions as well. This problem is particularly acute where countries with different capacity levels share common borders, and the problem is even more acute and has a multiplier effect where borders exist with more than one neighboring country. Further to the north of the SADC region, Kenya serves as a good example to demonstrate the degree of difficulty faced by a country with several contiguous States. Located in Eastern Africa, Kenya's border management and control capacity is affected, and to a great extent determined by, the fact that it shares common borders with five countries – Tanzania, Uganda, Sudan, Ethiopia and Somalia – and it also has an extensive coastline on the Indian Ocean. Each of Kenya's neighbors possesses different border control capacities and poses different challenges to the region in enforcing targeted sanctions. From this perspective the degree of difficulty in implementing targeted sanctions becomes quite obvious, and requires each country to develop extraordinary capacity in order to be effective. Without a common determination among all neighboring countries to build region-wide capacity, one country's efforts at enforcing targeted sanctions could easily be subverted by the lack of capacity in others.

Travel bans

Like arms embargoes, travel bans require effective migration, customs and border management and control systems. Violators of travel bans generally use fraudulent travel documents and/or passports issued by third countries to avoid the sanctions imposed on their travel. Appropriate technology and expertise to identify fraudulent documents, specifically tailored to each country's needs, are therefore required. This would include an automated border management and control system that gives inspectors real-time information about travelers and their documents by querying and identifying unwanted or suspicious travelers before they enter the country.

Such a system should allow for authenticating travelers and their documents by querying passport and visa issuance databases. This can be carried out effectively only with the use of modern technology that would prevent documentation fraud by comparison of a travel document with a picture of the document in the database, which allows primary inspectors to identify travelers with fraudulent documents in real time. The addition of alert list monitoring in real time will facilitate the identification of people traveling under false identities, those using lost or stolen documents, or those who should be detained for other reasons, such as involvement in transnational organized crime, illicit drug trafficking, illegal arms trade, and terrorism. Many sanctions targets and violators generally fit this profile.

Specific requirements

In addition to the appropriate technology, a State must also have an effective executive machinery in place, which includes adequately trained personnel at each port of entry with real-time access to a central database containing information on the target. Each State must also be able to exchange information electronically with other States on airline and other common carrier's passenger lists and other relevant information in advance of the carrier's arrival at its destination.

As a complement to the specific requirements identified for each targeted sanction, States also need adequately trained police and law enforcement personnel with the ability to investigate violations of sanctions measures, and the capacity to prosecute or extradite sanctions violators. In many States, police personnel are poorly trained, they lack investigative techniques, forensic expertise and equipment; communication equipment; and have limited mobility. Prosecutorial staff and judicial personnel often lack training in sanctions-related enforcement.

States also require the capacity for judicial cooperation in criminal matters, which involves judges and prosecutors trained to respond to requests from other States for mutual legal assistance in investigation and prosecution of a sanction violator found within the jurisdiction of the requested State, or on activities carried out within the requested State's jurisdiction by the sanction violator. This type of cooperation generally takes place within the context of bilateral or multilateral arrangements, which must be implemented in domestic law, and could entail, *inter alia*, investigation and taking of evidence or statements from persons, summoning witnesses to provide testimony, effective service of judicial documents; executing searches and seizures of sanctioned goods, immobilization and sequestration of property, freezing of assets, financial and otherwise as required by financial sanctions; examining objects; providing originals or certified copies of relevant documents and records, including bank, financial, corporate or business records, shipping documents and end-user certificates, in particular as it applies to arms that might be diverted from legal trade in violation of arms embargoes. In situations where extradition is requested, the double criminality principle must be satisfied, and sanctions violations must therefore be prohibited acts in the penal codes of all States.

Implementing targeted sanctions necessarily relies on national, regional and international systems allowing for data exchange, border enhancement and migration management and control. Strengthening national systems to be able to feed into international efforts and networks will be key to a proactive and sustainable strategy. It is also important that capacity be seen in a regional context, particularly as neighboring States have important complementary roles in enforcing targeted sanctions.

Capacity for implementation

From the examples cited and discussed above, it is clear that the capacity required, or lack thereof, can have significant effect on a State's ability to effectively implement targeted sanctions. The difficulties inherent in implementing targeted sanctions and the importance for States to possess the requisite legal and executive capacity to carry out their responsibilities are clearly identified. An attempt to address these issues in the Stockholm Process led to a series of recommendations. This discussion focuses on those which are set out in Part III of the Stockholm Report.[12] These recommendations are premised on the assumption that the Security Council is committed to seeing its sanctions measures effectively implemented, and include suggestions for Security Council action, as well as necessary actions of States and the UN Secretariat to build effective capacity to enforce sanctions measures.

In order for targeted sanctions to be effective, the Security Council and all States have been urged to give serious consideration to these recommendations. In particular, the recommendations, described as: *Principles for Effective Implementation of Targeted Sanctions*[13] include a provision which recommended that the Security Council should call on all States to take the following actions: enact sanctions enabling legislation[14] to give effect to Security Council resolutions in domestic law; inform the relevant sanction committee if they lack capacity to effectively implement the sanctions measures; seek assistance where necessary to build their capacities; and encourage those States with capacity to offer assistance to others needing it. This platform for effective implementation of targeted sanctions also calls for the Security Council to facilitate the capacity-building process by creating a database, in cooperation with the UN Secretariat, of available technical assistance for capacity building.[15]

The recommendation that calls for technical assistance to build capacity to implement sanctions is important to effective implementation of targeted measures. In making this recommendation, recognition is given to the significance of the Security Council's precedent-setting decision with respect to combating terrorism.[16] The recommendation on capacity building for sanctions implementation placed obligations on those needing assistance as well as those having the capacity to provide assistance, and the Security Council through its sanction committees would have a demonstrably important role in facilitating this process. It is also important for the capacity-building process to be carried out in cooperation with the UN Secretariat, and where possible with relevant UN agencies, funds, and programs.

The Counter-Terrorism Committee (CTC)

The experience of the Counter-Terrorism Committee (CTC) serves as an example of a capacity-building program that has gained considerable support and momentum. However, while making comparisons and identifying similarities, there is an important distinction between the CTC and the Security Council sanctions committees, which should not be discounted. The political will to support Resolution 1373 has been, and continues to be, significantly greater than for sanctions measures. The CTC is not a sanctions committee and was never intended to be one. This principle has been stated repeatedly by the Chairman of the CTC, and this distinction was highlighted by the Security Council in its request to the 1267 Committee,[17] itself a sanction committee, "to cooperate with other relevant Security Council Sanctions Committees *and with the Committee established pursuant to paragraph 6 of its Resolution 1373 (2001)*".[18] Like the sanctions measures, Resolution 1373 was adopted under Chapter VII of the Charter, thereby making its provisions mandatory on all States. However, the way the CTC functions differs considerably from the sanctions committees.[19]

Unlike sanctions regimes, which generally target individuals and single States, Resolution 1373 sets out mandatory obligations on all States, requiring them to enact domestic legislation and to create executive machinery to implement the resolution. These mandatory requirements are far-reaching. It is significant, however, that the capacity to implement a number of the requirements of Resolution 1373 are similar, and in some cases identical, to the capacity required to ensure effective enforcement of targeted sanctions. It is particularly true for enforcement of targeted financial sanctions, arms embargos and travel bans.

In the case of Resolution 1373, paragraph 1(a) sets out its core mandate: all States are required to take measures to effectively prevent and suppress the financing of terrorist acts.[20] In order to do so, each State must put in place a strong legislative framework supported by institutional mechanisms having the capacity to fully implement all areas covered by the resolution. This includes the requirement that all States have appropriate mechanisms in place for the expeditious freezing of funds and assets related to terrorist activities.[21] This legal and executive capacity to combat the financing of terrorism bears strong correlation to the capacity required for implementing targeted financial sanctions. The mandatory requirements of Resolution 1373 also aim at preventing the movement of terrorists across borders through effective border controls and other measures,[22] and denial of safe haven to terrorists.[23] The legal and executive machinery to achieve this contemplates putting in place a regime that is capable of monitoring the movement of a person or persons placed on a watch list in the case of terrorism and/or subject to travel restrictions imposed by travel bans as in the case of terrorists and their supporters.

Furthermore, Resolution 1373 requires all States to prevent the movement of hazardous materials, trafficking in illicit drugs, small arms, explosives or sensitive materials.[24] This requires relevant capacities in customs and border management and control mechanisms and security measures that monitor the movement of goods across borders hence preventing surreptitious and illegal movement of arms subject to Security Council arms embargoes.

States are required, pursuant to Resolution 1373, to prohibit certain activities and to create penalties for violations in their domestic legislation, and to undertake certain other specific actions regardless of any pre-existing, current or future relationship with the target, in this case terrorists. All States are required to cooperate with other States in the exchange of information, investigation and prosecution of persons subject to these provisions. The measures and obligations set out in Resolution 1373 are permanent obligations on all States and are universal in their application. Once implemented, they become permanent tools at the State's disposal to be employed in the suppression and prevention of terrorist acts. Sanctions regimes on the other hand are temporary measures targeting States and individuals to change their behavior or to make it difficult for them to carry out certain specific proscribed activities. Once the desired outcome is achieved, the sanctions are usually removed.

Resolution 1373, in paragraph 6, established the Counter-Terrorism Committee to monitor implementation of the resolution and called on all States to report to the CTC on the measures they have taken or contemplate to give full effect to the resolution. The implementation of Resolution 1373 is aimed specifically at building each State's capacity to suppress and prevent terrorism, but, when implemented fully, it will have significant effect on a State's capacity to enforce Security Council sanctions measures. States are required to put in place legislation implementing all relevant provisions of Resolution 1373, and to have the executive machinery necessary to give effect to the legislation. As of the end of September 2003, two years after adoption of Resolution 1373,[25] a significant number of the 191 Member States of the United Nations have either adopted counter-terrorism legislation or are in the process of doing so. Many of those that are lagging behind in this process are for the most part those that are in need of legislative drafting assistance, which is being facilitated through the CTC capacity-building facilitation program.

All UN Member States have reported to the CTC with many having filed second and third supplementary reports. The CTC received 412 such reports from UN Member States within the first 24 months after it began its operations.[26] This capacity building and reporting process will continue for some time, as new legislative and executive measures become necessary to meet evolving new challenges posed by international terrorism, and the CTC continues to broaden the monitoring of how States implement their counter-terrorism laws, and how States cooperate with each other in combating international terrorism.

Undoubtedly, the requirements of Resolution 1373 are far more complex than sanctions measures, and most States lacked the requisite capacity to effectively implement them. For the vast majority of States the obligations of Resolution 1373 have been overwhelming.

The Security Council recognized that many States lacked the capacity – legislative and executive – that was required to effectively implement Resolution 1373, and that they would need assistance. Most lacked experience in combating the financing of terrorism and related areas. This included enacting new legislation supported by the establishment of a financial investigation unit; specialized training of immigration and customs officers, border control personnel, and of police and law enforcement personnel, as well as appropriate equipment to enhance the efficiency of the State's relevant executive machinery. The Security Council undertook to facilitate the provision of assistance to these countries to build their capacities to implement fully the measures required by the resolution.

Need for technical assistance

The mandate for the CTC to develop a technical assistance facilitation program was established through the adoption of Resolution 1377 (2001) on 12 November 2001, in which the Security Council, in its Ministerial Declaration, recognized that many States lacked the capacity to implement fully the measures mandated by the Resolution and invited them to seek assistance from the CTC. The Ministerial Declaration also set out its objectives for the CTC technical assistance facilitation program (CTC/tafp). The scope of the CTC/tafp was expanded and further elaborated in subsequent Statements of the President of the Council[27] and in its Ministerial Declaration of Resolution 1456 (2003).[28]

More specifically: the Security Council stated in its Ministerial Declaration of Resolution 1377 (2001) "that many States will require assistance in implementing all the requirements of Resolution 1373 (2001), and invites States to inform the Counter-Terrorism Committee of areas in which they require such support." The Council also invited the CTC

> to explore ways in which States can be assisted, and in particular to explore with international, regional and sub-regional organizations: the promotion of best-practice in the areas covered by Resolution 1373 (2001), including the preparation of model laws as appropriate; the availability of existing technical, financial, regulatory, legislative or other assistance program which might facilitate the implementation of Resolution 1373 (2001); the promotion of possible synergies between these assistance programs.

The Council also called on all States to assist each other to implement fully the Resolution.

Following on Resolution 1377, in its Statement by the President on 15 April 2002,[29] the Security Council reiterated the importance of assistance by inviting the CTC to continue "to explore ways in which States can be assisted to implement the resolution; [and] to build a dialogue with international, regional and sub-regional organizations active in the areas covered by Resolution 1373." The Council again invited the CTC to continue this process in its Statement by the President of 8 October 2002.[30]

In a further demonstration of the importance it placed on capacity building, the Security Council, in its Ministerial Declaration of Resolution 1456 (2003),[31] *inter alia*: called upon States to make full use of the sources of assistance and guidance which are now becoming available;[32] stated that the CTC must intensify its efforts to promote the implementation of the resolution in particular through the reviewing of States' reports and facilitating international assistance and cooperation;[33] stated that States should assist each other to improve their capacity to prevent and fight terrorism, and invited the CTC to step up its efforts to facilitate the provision of technical and other assistance by developing targets and priorities for global action;[34] stated that international organizations should evaluate ways in which they can enhance the effectiveness of their action against terrorism;[35] and stated further that regional and sub-regional organizations should work with the CTC and other international organizations to facilitate sharing of best practice in the fight against terrorism, and to assist their members in fulfilling their obligation to combat terrorism.[36]

Following the mandate given by Resolution 1377, the CTC appointed an Assistance Expert, effective 1 May 2002, as adviser to the Committee in the area of liaison and assistance,[37] with specific responsibility, as explained by the Chairman of the CTC, "to take overall charge of assistance and liaise with Member States and international organizations."[38] The CTC established a technical assistance team (TAT) to carry out the program. The TAT was tasked with an assistance action plan having a number of specific objectives. These included: facilitating self-help by making information on standards, best practice and sources of available assistance by establishing a Directory of Assistance and Guidance on the CTC's website;[39] encouraging donors to respond to assistance needs identified as a priority for each State; working through regional and sectoral organizations to tackle regional/sectoral shortcomings; and encouraging capacity strengthening of regional organizations to respond to the identified needs of their member States.

In promoting the CTC/tafp, that is, to help each State to develop a platform of legislative and executive capacity to implement fully Resolution 1373, the TAT, on a continuing basis, *inter alia*, engaged in the following activities:

(a) bilateral consultations with each State needing assistance, advising each State on the importance of evaluating the gaps in its capacity and related assistance needs; advising each State on the availability and sources of assistance in the context of the priorities set by the CTC; and providing guidance to States on how to request and access assistance;
(b) discussions and correspondence with assistance providers (and potential assistance providers) – States, organizations and institutions – in order to

explain the CTC/tafp; to identify for them the areas of need for each State, to facilitate the provision of assistance and targeting of priorities;

(c) encouraged development of new assistance programs, as appropriate, by donor States, organizations and institutions to meet the needs identified and to fill gaps in the assistance program;

(d) maintained the CTC Directory of Assistance and Guidance on the CTC's website, including by seeking information on updates of original offers of assistance and on new offers for inclusion in the Directory;

(e) attended conferences, seminars and other forums, hosted by international, regional and sub-regional organizations, and encouraged organizations to develop programs of assistance for their members within their respective mandates and competences;

(f) served as a focal point for coordination of counter-terrorism assistance programs in order to help donors avoid duplication and overlap in providing assistance, and encouraged assistance providers to inform the CTC of the results of their programs; and followed up on assistance programs for desired outcomes;

(g) engaged in efforts aimed at building political will among States to fully implement the resolution.

While the CTC's assistance program facilitates assistance to those needing it, the CTC itself does not provide assistance directly to States. The requests for assistance received by the CTC are included on an Assistance Matrix, which is frequently updated and circulated to assistance providers and potential assistance providers (currently circulated to designated persons in 18 donor States and 20 organizations) for their use in targeting assistance to those who need assistance, and in areas where assistance is most needed. The Assistance Matrix helps to guide providers in avoiding overlap and duplication in assistance programs. It also serves to guide the TAT in identifying gaps in the assistance program, that is, underserved areas, or areas not covered by existing programs, and to encourage assistance providers to address those needs. As of the end of September 2003, some 160 States were listed on the CTC Assistance Matrix as either having requested assistance directly through the CTC or receiving capacity-building assistance bilaterally from assistance providers.

The CTC's assistance facilitation program has continued to expand to cover all areas covered by Resolution 1373 in support of the original concept as laid out in its paper "Assistance: Next Steps,"[40] in which the CTC, *inter alia*, explained that,

> Assistance will be effective only if it brings about practical measures which further the implementation of Resolution 1373. For example, the production of model legislation should lead to the enactment of new laws; and training courses should lead to the adoption of new procedures. Donors should make sure that their assistance programmes give States all

the tools they need to take the necessary action.... The CTC will encourage States and organisations to design their assistance programmes accordingly. It will monitor the results achieved through its continuing correspondence with Member States.

While recognizing that all States have an obligation to implement fully all areas covered by Resolution 1373, the CTC set priorities for implementation. These included States having legislation in place covering all aspects of 1373, and a process in hand for becoming party as soon as possible to the 12 international conventions and protocols relating to terrorism; and having in place effective machinery for preventing and suppressing terrorist financing. This was to be followed by States strengthening their executive machinery to implement Resolution 1373-related legislation, including cooperation on measures to deal with links between terrorism and other threats to security: arms trafficking, drugs trafficking, organized crime, money laundering and illegal movement of nuclear, biological and chemical weapons.

In summary, the CTC's assistance facilitation program has provided assistance to States by: facilitating self-help, by making information available through its assistance Directory on the CTC's website; encouraging assistance providers to respond to the needs identified as a priority for each State; working through international, regional and specialized organizations to tackle regional and specialized shortcomings; and encouraging capacity strengthening of international and regional organizations to respond to the identified needs of States.

The type of assistance provided in the early stages of the program followed the priorities set by the CTC, which was in legislative drafting in the first stage, while many States were receiving simultaneously training and other institutional capacity-building assistance in banking and finance; police and law enforcement; customs, immigration, and border management and control; and prosecutorial and judicial cooperation.

CTC and targeted sanctions

The areas in which capacity building is being carried out by the CTC as required by Resolution 1373 bears striking similarity to those discussed above and identified as needed for the effective implementation of targeted sanctions. Whether the objective is to help States implement Resolution 1373 or to enforce sanctions measures, the capacity-building process undertaken by the CTC pursuant to resolutions 1373 and 1377 serves both purposes. The CTC capacity-building program to combat terrorism, while intended to deal specifically with prevention and suppression of terrorism, augurs well for the future effectiveness of targeted sanctions as well, particularly financial sanctions, arms embargoes and travel bans. In the long run, as all States fully implement Resolution 1373, as they are required to do, and achieve the objectives set for them, they will possess the requisite capacity to implement targeted sanctions.

Capacity building, whether to implement Resolution 1373 or targeted sanctions, should not be viewed as a quick-fix process. Some States will reach an acceptable level of compliance within a reasonable short period of time, particularly with respect to the legislative framework. The speed at which this is achieved will depend primarily on resources available to each State, whether on the State's own resources or through the CTC assistance facilitation program, and on constraints posed by differences in administrative practices, legal systems, and delays inherent in some parliamentary procedures. Beyond adoption of legislation, capacity building of executive machinery will be a long-term process for most States, primarily because of the enormous gaps existing in their capacities to implement UN Security Council mandated measures. The commitment to capacity building therefore will have to be maintained over an extended period by the Security Council, whether through the CTC or through its future sanctions regimes, in order to create the global capacity necessary for effective implementation of targeted sanctions.

Notes

* This chapter is written in the author's private capacity and his association with the UN and the Stockholm Process is for identification purposes only.
1. For the full report on the outcome of the Stockholm Process on the Implementation of Targeted Sanctions, see P. Wallensteen, C. Staibano and M. Eriksson (eds) *Making Targeted Sanctions Effective: Guidelines for the Implementation of UN Policy Options*, Department of Peace and Conflict Research, Uppsala University (Stockholm: Elanders Gotab, 2003). Hereinafter referred to as "the Stockholm Report."
2. Article 25 of the United Nations Charter, "The Member States of the United Nations agree to accept and carry out the decisions of the Security Council in accordance with the present Charter."
3. Under Article 41 of the UN Charter, "The Security Council may decide what measures not involving the use of armed force are to be employed to give effect to its decisions, and it may call upon the Members of the United Nations to apply such measures."
4. See, for example, discussions in the Interlaken Report, T.J. Biersteker, S.E. Eckert, A. Halegua, N. Reid and P. Romaniuk, *Targeted Financial Sanctions: A Manual for Design and Implementation – Contributions from the Interlaken Process*, the Swiss Confederation in cooperation with the United Nations Secretariat and the Watson Institute for International Studies, Brown University (Providence, RI: Watson Institute for International Studies, 2001); and the Bonn–Berlin Report, M. Brzoska (ed.) *Design and Implementation of Arms Embargoes and Travel and Aviation and Related Sanctions: Result of the Bonn–Berlin Process*, Bonn International Center for Conversion, German Foreign Office, and United Nations Secretariat (Bonn: BICC, 2001).
5. For a full discussion of the issue of a Model Law meeting this requirement, see the Stockholm Report, pp. 81–89.
6. The Counter-Terrorism Committee was established by paragraph 6 of Resolution 1373 (2001), S/RES/1373 (2001) of 28 September 2001.
7. UNITA sanctions imposed by S/RES/864 (1993), S/RES/1127 (1997), S/RES/1173 (1998) and S/RES/1176 (1998).
8. Liberia sanctions imposed by S/RES/1343 (2001).
9. Taliban, Usama bin Laden and Al-Qaida sanctions imposed by S/RES/1267 (1999), S/RES/1333 (2000), S/RES/1390 (2002) and S/RES/1455 (2003).
10. For a discussion on financial sanctions, see the Interlaken Report.

11 For example, the list prepared by the 1267 Committee.
12 The Stockholm Report, p. 66: "Supporting Member State Capacity to Implement Targeted Sanctions."
13 The Stockholm Report, p. 66.
14 The Stockholm Process examined the model laws developed in the Interlaken and Bonn–Berlin processes and recommended a consolidated draft Model Law for States to use as a guide in drafting appropriate legislation. See pp. 81–89 of the Stockholm Report.
15 Ibid., p. 67.
16 Security Council Resolution 1377 (2001) of 12 November 2001, S/RES/1377 (2001).
17 1267 Committee is the Security Council Committee established pursuant to paragraph 6 of Resolution 1267 (1999).
18 S/RES/1390 (2002), Resolution 1390 (2002) of 16 January 2002, italics added for emphasis.
19 For discussions on the role of the CTC, see E. Rosand, "Security Council Resolution 1373, the Counter-Terrorism Committee, and the Fight Against Terrorism," *American Journal of International Law*, Vol. 97, No. 2, p. 333 (2003); and C. A. Ward, "Building Capacity to Combat International Terrorism: The Role of the UN Security Council," *Journal of Conflict and Security Law*, Vol. 8, No. 2, pp. 289–305 (2003).
20 Paragraph 1(a) of Resolution 1373 (2001) of 28 September 2001.
21 Paragraph 1(c) of Resolution 1373.
22 Paragraph 2(g) of Resolution 1373.
23 Paragraph 2(c) of Resolution 1373.
24 Paragraph 3(a) of resolution 1373.
25 Resolution 1373 was adopted on 28 September 2001.
26 The CTC held its first meeting on 4 October 2001, and after two years, had received First Reports from all 191 Member States, Second Reports from 150, and Third Reports from 71 States. As of 30 April 2004, a total of 507 reports had been received, including 48 States having filed follow-up Fourth Reports.
27 Statements by the President of the Security Council, 15 April 2002, S/PRST/2002/10 and 8 October 2002, S/PRST/2002/26.
28 Security Council Resolution 1456 (2003) of 20 January 2003, S/RES/1456 (2003).
29 Statement by the President of the Security Council, 15 April 2002, S/PRST/2002/10.
30 Statement by the President of the Security Council, 8 October 2002, S/PRST/2002/26.
31 Security Council Resolution 1456 (2003) of 20 January 2003, S/RES/1456 (2003).
32 Paragraph 2(a) of Resolution 1456.
33 Paragraph 4 of Resolution 1456.
34 Paragraph 5 of Resolution 1456.
35 Paragraph 7 of Resolution 1456.
36 Paragraph 8 of Resolution 1456.
37 Provisional summary record of the Twenty-eighth meeting of the CTC, 23 April 2002, S/AC.40/SR.28, p. 5, para. 30.
38 Provisional summary record of the Twenty-seventh meeting of the CTC, 9 April 2002, S/AC.40/SR.27, p. 4, para. 32.
39 The CTC provides a comprehensive directory of assistance and guidance on its website: http://www.un.org/sc/ctc
40 Document of the CTC, "Assistance: Next Steps," agreed following meeting of CTC on 21 October 2002. As of the end of April 2004, there were 53 States that had received general counter-terrorism (CT) legislative drafting assistance; 59 in combating the financing of terrorism (CFT) legislative drafting assistance; 71 training in CFT; 98 in customs and border control; 50 in immigration control; and 115 in CT and police and law enforcement work.

13

PROTECTING LEGAL RIGHTS
On the (in)security of targeted sanctions

Iain Cameron

The purpose of the present chapter is to examine the problems involved in the lack of legal safeguards applicable to the process of adopting and implementing UN Security Council targeted sanctions and to suggest solutions. I will not look at the EU and unilateral sanctions programs, such as the US programs, even though these can also be problematic from the perspective of legal guarantees.[1] These sanctions systems have some common features with the UN sanctions system. However, they involve certain special problems of their own, e.g. the complications caused for understanding and reforming EU sanctions, and EU implementation of UN sanctions, caused by shared EC/member state competence, and the pillar structure of the EU, and problems of compatibility of sanctions with the World Trade Organization (WTO) regime. I refer to the EU and US sanction systems insofar as this contributes to understanding the UN sanction system and possible improvements which might be made in the UN system.[2]

General (economic) sanctions obviously affect the lives of a large number of people – many more people than targeted sanctions. The human rights of civilian populations in states subjected to economic embargoes, particularly Iraq, has been the subject of some discussion.[3] However, the issue of whether legal safeguards, including human rights standards, apply, or should apply, to targeted UN sanctions has arisen only relatively recently. The issue was raised in the Interlaken and Bonn–Berlin processes, but at the time, there were few concrete cases to inform the discussion.

The present chapter is not intended to be the last word on the matter, but to stimulate discussion on finding solutions to the problems identified. This discussion is likely to continue for some time. The present chapter has grown out of a report on the subject that I wrote for the Swedish Foreign Office at the time the Swedish government was hosting the Stockholm process.[4] However, the views expressed herein do not represent the policy of the Swedish government, or any other government. An amended and updated version of this report has also been published as an academic study.[5] The present volume is not directed primarily at lawyers, so I have tried to "delegalize" my argument as much as possible. However, the arguments as to whether, how and why human rights bind the Security Council, and if so, what can be done about it, are complicated and highly technical. The risk is plain that the present chapter contains rather too much legal material and thinking for non-lawyers, and not enough for lawyers.

What are Security Council targeted sanctions and how do they work?

I will not devote space to introducing the basis for, and UN Security Council experience with, sanctions generally – issues which are dealt with in detail by other chapters in the present volume.[6] Basically, under Article 24(1) UN Charter, the Security Council has the primary responsibility for the maintenance of international peace and security. After a determination under Article 39 that a situation constitutes a threat to or breach of the peace, the Security Council can order states to undertake sanctions against the entity responsible for the threat or breach. The sanctions are then implemented at the national level, by all states, or they should be so implemented,[7] as all states have an obligation under international law to comply with Security Council Chapter VII resolutions. One can distinguish between a general trade or economic embargo directed against a particular entity, and a range of lesser "targeted" measures, such as the freezing of financial assets; the suspension of credits and aid; the denial and limitation of access to foreign financial markets; trade embargoes on arms and luxury goods; flight bans and the denial of international travel, visas and educational opportunities. When sanctions are targeted on individuals, this is primarily done by means of a "blacklist." The Security Council adopts a resolution and delegates to a Sanctions Committee, consisting of all the members of the Security Council, the task of drawing up a list of blacklisted persons. The main regimes of interest as far as targeting named individuals are concerned are the Angola, Liberia, Sierra Leone and Afghanistan/Al-Qaida sanctions. In the present chapter, I concentrate on the last of these, Afghanistan/Al-Qaida, for reasons explained below, although I am aware that this regime varies from the other three.

Security Council targeted sanctions began with the UNITA sanctions in 1997 and 1998.[8] These sanctions have now been ended but at their height 157 individuals were subjected to assets freezing and travel bans.[9] The latest Sierra Leone list contains 48 individuals subject to travel bans.[10] The "secondary" travel ban sanctions imposed on Liberia as a result of its lack of cooperation in regard to the Sierra Leone sanctions now encompass 144 individuals.[11] The Sierra Leone and Liberia sanctions have given rise to complaints and discussions in the relevant Security Council sanctions committees regarding the basis for adding particular people to the blacklists.[12]

However, the issue of legal safeguards arose to greater prominence in European states as a result of the Taliban/Al-Qaida financial sanctions, for the simple reason that these sanctions affected European nationals. On 15 October 1999 and 19 December 2000, the Security Council, by means of Resolutions 1267 and

1333 respectively, brought in sanctions against the Taliban regime in Afghanistan. Resolution 1267, *inter alia*, ordered states to freeze funds controlled directly or indirectly by the Taliban. Resolution 1333, *inter alia*, ordered states to freeze funds controlled directly or indirectly by Usama Bin Laden and individuals associated with him. As of 8 August 2003, there were 152 individuals and one entity on the Taliban list and 102 individuals and 98 entities on the Al-Qaida list.[13] The bulk of money seized/frozen under UN Resolutions 1290 and 1333 is Taliban money (particularly the Afghan central bank's assets, later unfrozen). Following the defeat by the Northern Alliance, assisted by US forces, of the Taliban, the Security Council adopted Resolution 1390 of 16 January 2002.[14] This resolution renewed the Taliban/Al-Qaida blacklists, extending even travel and arms embargo sanctions to the listed persons.

Resolutions 1333 and 1390 do not involve a much larger circle of people than the Sierra Leone/Liberia resolutions. However, Resolution 1390 is "open-ended" and so involves a qualitative difference in that there is no connection between the targeted group/individuals and any territory or state. Although the Security Council has previously adopted resolutions directed against non-state entities (particularly the UNITA resolutions), Resolution 1390 is the first, and only so far, example of a sanctions resolution without a territorial connection.[15] In Resolution 1455, of 17 January 2003, the Security Council reiterated states' obligations to comply with the earlier resolutions and required the submission of updated implementation reports within 90 days.

It can also be noted here that in the wake of the terrorist attacks of 11 September the Security Council adopted a further Resolution, 1373, of 28 September. This Resolution imposes obligations on all states *inter alia* to criminalize acts of financing of international terrorism, and to freeze and seize funds used for terrorism. It amounts, in effect, to an obligation to implement the operative provisions of the Convention on the Financing of International Terrorism.[16] This Resolution contains no time limit. There is a reporting obligation, and a monitoring committee (the Counter-Terrorism Committee, CTC) was established with competence *inter alia* to review the reports submitted. But no blacklists are attached to the Resolution.[17]

The blacklist obviously involves identifying targets. As the UN Secretariat, which assists the sanctions committees, lacks both capacity and expertise in identifying persons supporting, or otherwise influential in relation to, a targeted government, the information on which names are produced comes from other sources. These sources are: first, those member states which have both an interest in the matter, and sufficient diplomatic and intelligence gathering capacity; second, expert panels established by sanctions committees to monitor the implementation of sanctions; and third, public sources. It is not always clear which states have proposed which individuals for blacklisting. It is reasonable to assume that those states with economic and historical (former colonial) interests in particular target states have taken the lead in blacklisting. The main source of the names in UNITA travel and financial sanctions was apparently the Angolan government. The sources for the Liberia and Sierra Leone names appear to have varied, with certain states, e.g. the US, the UK and France, suggesting some names, and other names coming from the expert panels' reports on implementation. The main (or exclusive?) source of the names on the Afghanistan/Al-Qaida lists has been the US.

Experience from US blacklisting (which has been going on for some time) indicates that the formal basis is often a public source, company registers, newspaper reports, etc. Banking suspicious and unusual transaction reports can also be a source as regards people suspected of money laundering.[18] However, secret intelligence material or confidential material such as embassy reports can lie behind the formal source, either as leads in looking into the person in the first place, or as confirming the public reports. As regards terrorist suspects, secret intelligence material can be assumed almost invariably to lie behind the listing. It is clear, at any rate, that the identifier information on the Resolution 1267/1390 list is too limited to have come from bank reporting duties regarding suspicious transactions. As far as I am aware, on the occasions in which a sanctions committee member has asked a designating state for the basis for a particular blacklisting to be disclosed, and this basis is intelligence or diplomatic material, the reply has been given that the information comes from a reliable source, but that national security considerations rule out disclosing it. Occasionally, information might be given on a bilateral basis where the designating state trusts the requesting state to maintain the confidentiality of the information.

This is also an appropriate place to mention that there are differences between governmental and anti-terrorist sanctions as regards what change in policy is sought. One can, of course, argue that the purpose of some sanctions is not, realistically, behavioral modification, and the termination of the threat against international peace and security, but making a political statement.[19] Or that the real motive, and this applies to all the sanctions lists, is punishment. Anti-terrorist sanctions are unlikely to end before the targeted group is destroyed. Finally, there can be obvious differences in the time frame between terrorist and government measures. Where the root causes of conflict persist, then the war against terrorism risks being a "forever war."

Legal problems with the targeted sanctions regimes

There are two basic legal difficulties involved in accepting the present targeted sanctions regimes. They are interrelated. Much can be written about them, but reasons of space rule out doing more than simply sketching them out. There are naturally arguments which can be made for maintaining the present system, or making only minor improvements in it, but I will not deal with them here.[20]

The first problem relates to *accountability*. In any legal system, even the international legal system, a body exercising power should bear the responsibility for the exercise of this power. However, the sanctions committees can be, and have been, put in the position of simply "rubber stamping" individual states' own blacklists, in particular the US anti-terrorist blacklists. The speed of the procedure

– notification to the Security Council members and, occasionally, to the state of nationality, 48 hours before the sanctions are adopted – may well be necessary to retain the element of surprise, but it means that there is very little time for any other state to check if they have any intelligence on the people proposed. If several people are proposed at the same time, which is usually the case, then even states with major intelligence resources have only very limited possibilities for checking the proposed lists against their files. Moreover, the consensus nature of the procedure in sanctions committees means that, once a name is on a list, any Security Council member can block its removal. The sanctions committees have rarely, or ever, evaluated the "evidence" that the named person is engaged in activities involving a threat to international peace and security. Indeed these activities are never defined, and so there are no criteria to measure the "evidence" against, even if it is submitted to the sanctions committee. When the name comes from a state, the sanctions committees are more or less in a position of having to trust it. Once the blacklist has been approved, there is no (or little, see below) basis for challenging it at the national level. The UN has immunity from suit before national courts. Power is thus being exercised without mechanisms for ensuring legal responsibility on either the national or international level.

The second difficulty is that *procedural and substantive rights* which individuals possess under national and international law are not being respected. UN sanctions are an interstate mechanism of pressure that is now being used against individuals in their capacity as members of governments, terrorist organizations, etc. Now, from one perspective, it might seem to be typical European liberalism (and lawyerism) to be making a fuss about the human rights of tyrants and terrorists. But being a terrorist suspect or a member of a dictatorial government (or a member of his/her family) does not mean that one is divested of one's human rights. The results of an order freezing assets (and, to a lesser extent, imposing travel restrictions) are severe for the individuals affected, and their families (although, on a scale, as admittedly very much worse abuses of human rights are being justified in the name of anti-terrorist measures in the world today). While the interests at stake in bringing to an end conflicts as bloody as the Angola, Liberian and Sierra Leone civil wars, and stopping the Al-Qaida network, are obviously vitally important, this does not mean that we are free totally to ignore the concerned individuals' rights. But nor does the existence of these rights mean that we are blocked from ever taking effective action against people suspected of threatening international peace and security – simply that we must take these rights into account in devising and implementing targeted sanctions.

The rights involved depend upon the type of sanctions (financial, travel, arms embargo). In all cases, it tends to be what are known as "civil and political rights" which are affected. Air travel bans interfere primarily with freedom of movement (although there can be secondary effects on private and family life, and even on the right to life, e.g. where a targeted person needs foreign medical care). Financial sanctions interfere with a person's private and family life, and his or her property rights. Arms embargoes can interfere with the seller's rights to dispose of his or her property as well as the buyer's property rights, when weapons paid for already are not permitted to be transferred. In all three cases, travel, financial and arms sanctions, an interference which cannot be appealed to a tribunal may violate the right of access to court as well as the right to effective remedies. In all three cases, particularly travel and financial sanctions, there may be an interference with the right to reputation. Certainly, being put on the list (either travel sanctions or financial sanctions) now involves a social stigma, particularly damaging for businessmen who live on their reputation/cash flow.[21]

Now, it can be argued that the UN Security Council is not bound by human rights at all. After all, it has, and must have, very wide discretion, in determining threats to international peace and security, and this power of determination cannot be delegated.[22] But this is not the issue: the issue is whether having made such a determination, the Security Council is bound by any legal norms in exercising coercive measures as a consequence of the determination.[23] Like every other organ of an international organization, the Security Council is bound by its mandate, and by general international law. The arguments in relation to this point have been set out well several times and I will not rehearse them here.[24] Simply put, the approach that nothing should stand in the way of the maintenance of international peace and security is untenable. It is bizarre that arguments are even being made that the Security Council is not bound by the standards the UN organization has been lecturing states about for fifty years.

Still, it is important to know how legally binding human rights bind the Security Council. There are three different ways in which rights can affect UN targeted sanctions. First, paradoxical as it might seem to a non-lawyer, the UN has not ratified, indeed cannot ratify, the principal UN treaty most at issue, the International Covenant on Civil and Political Rights (ICCPR).[25] Thus, legally speaking, the Security Council, as an organ of the UN, is only bound by those rights which have passed into general or "customary" international law, and those rights which can be seen as authoritative interpretations of the human rights obligations in the UN Charter (particularly, in Articles 1, 55 and 56), which circumscribe the powers of the Security Council. Here, one looks in particular to a General Assembly resolution, the Universal Declaration on Human Rights (UDHR), which is undoubtedly an authoritative interpretation of the UN Charter and is seen as customary international law (even though, in many states, it is often more honored in the breach).[26] But the UDHR standards are vague, and there is no international institution with the power to make interpretations of it which are binding on states. What about the ICCPR? Arguably, the core contents of the ICCPR are authoritative interpretations of the UN Charter and are in effect binding on the Security Council as such, but this is naturally open to debate. Moreover, the international body which is entrusted with interpreting the ICCPR, the Human Rights Committee, is not explicitly given the power to take decisions binding on state parties (and *ipso facto*, the Security Council) – unlike the European Court of Human Rights (ECtHR), and the equivalent body for the Organization of American States (OAS), the American Court of Human Rights. So, in short, relatively little concrete assistance can be derived from the UDHR or core content of the ICCPR as binding the Security Council directly.

Second, the states which are members of the Security Council can, if they have ratified human rights treaties, be bound by these treaties even when acting together collectively within the Security Council in adopting sanctions, although there are naturally conceptual problems in adapting for an international organization taking decisions on security issues a treaty designed for states in full control over territory. And third, all states acting in implementation of Security Council sanctions remain bound by whatever human rights obligations they may have undertaken, either constitutionally or by means of universal or regional treaties.[27] Thus, even if the targeted individuals are resident in, or operating out of, a state which has not ratified (i.e. accepted as binding) human rights treaties, where measures are taken against them they may still have human rights by virtue of the fact that the state in which sanctions are implemented is bound by such treaties.

The second and third means by which human rights can affect Security Council sanctions presuppose that states' competence to delegate power to the Security Council is not unlimited. Constitutionally speaking (and, as noted below, from the perspective of the ECtHR) it is not possible for states to avoid constitutional/ international human rights obligations by creating an international body and delegating to it the power to do something they are unable to do by themselves. From the perspective of constitutional law, the authority to enter into a treaty, including the UN Charter, comes from constitutional law.[28] States acting together jointly in the Security Council thus continue to bear any responsibility they might have under constitutional or international human rights norms when acting unilaterally. And, notwithstanding the clear international law authorities that a state cannot plead national law in avoidance of its international obligations, a final answer does not exist to the question of which system – public international law or constitutional law – is "supreme." Just as EU states have accepted the supremacy of EC law over national law in practice, states can also accept, in most matters, the supremacy of public international law. But this acceptance is based on the principle of reciprocity, and the perceived legitimacy, and need, for the system of international law as a whole. But when public international law purports to force a state to do something against its own fundamental constitutional principles, then a state's acceptance of the reasonableness of the international claim is put sorely to the test. It is an open question, when push comes to shove, which will be preferred.

But, notwithstanding all this talk about human rights, does Article 103 of the UN Charter not mean that the Security Council is free to ignore them? Article 103 provides that if a state's obligations under international law conflict with its obligations under the UN Charter, then the latter are to prevail. The typical area of application for this is where an embargo is ordered and this conflicts with a pre-existing treaty obligation to deliver, e.g. oil, or weapons or to allow transit through territory. Article 103 obviously only comes into operation when a state's obligations under other treaties conflict with its obligations under the UN Charter

– which (as already mentioned) include human rights obligations, albeit vague. More to the point, as regards obligations under regional human rights treaties, if a system of legal safeguards can be devised to reconcile regional human rights norms with targeted sanctions norms, then there *is* no conflict between these two sets of norms. The lack of accountability, and procedural safeguards built into the present UN system, is not inherent, or unavoidable. Thus, there is no logical incompatibility between the requirements of whatever human rights norms may be applicable and the UN Charter. If the Security Council and state obligation to comply with human rights is to have any significance at all, then it must mean that, where it is at all possible, the Security Council/states acting within the Security Council must design and implement sanctions so as not to violate human rights. In most conceivable cases – and all conceivable cases of targeted financial and travel sanctions I can think of – there is thus no need, or room, for applying Article 103 to avoid human rights obligations. And, in either case, I would say that it cannot be for the Security Council to determine wholly at its discretion that its sanctions regimes satisfy whatever human rights it is prepared to concede that it is bound by, and/or that no alternative methods of designing and implementing targeted sanctions exist.

Even if these concerns have not been fully articulated, a number of states, independent experts and members of the UN Secretariat have felt for some time that steps should be taken to improve legal safeguards for individuals subjected to UN targeted sanctions. For Sweden, the catalyst for activity came in November 2001 when three Swedish citizens woke up to find that their assets had been frozen as a result of EC Commission regulations, passed to implement Resolution 1267.[29] Two of the people in question, after 9 months, were removed from the list as the result of an agreement between them and the designating state (the US).[30] However, as shown below, the problem cannot, by any means, be said to have been solved. Legal proceedings were brought before the EC Court of First Instance by the three Swedes, and two other people subjected to sanctions, and these proceedings may continue.[31] It is uncertain whether these particular proceedings will ever result in a judgment on the merits. However, other cases before national and European courts will almost certainly be brought in the future, and so the potential exists for an explicit conflict between European human rights norms and Security Council targeted sanctions. This potential will increase, the more that names of European residents are added to the various sanctions lists.[32]

What specific human rights are affected?

The rights to an effective remedy, to access to court/fair trial, to reputation, to freedom of movement and to property are all contained in the UDHR (Articles 8, 10, 12, 13 and 17, respectively). The ICCPR contains the right of freedom of movement (Article 12). Article 14 sets out rights and obligations in a suit at law and Article 17 protects against interferences in a person's "privacy, honor and reputation." There is no protection of property rights as such in the ICCPR. As regards the three regional treaties setting out civil rights generally, the European

Convention on Human Rights (ECHR),[33] the American Convention on Human Rights (ACHR)[34] and the African (Banjul) Charter on Human and Peoples Rights,[35] the situation is as follows. The rights under the ECHR which are relevant are primarily: to access to court/fair trial (Article 6), to property (Article 1, Protocol 1), to private and family life (Article 8,), to freedom of movement (Article 2, Protocol 4) and to effective remedies before national bodies (Article 13). As regards the ACHR, the rights which are primarily relevant are: to access to court/fair trial (Article 8), to privacy (Article 11), to honor and reputation (Article 12), to property (Article 21), to freedom of movement (Article 22) and to effective remedies at the national level (Article 25). As regards the African Charter, the rights which are primarily relevant are: to appeal to competent national organs (Article 7), to freedom of movement (Article 12) and to property (Article 14).

All of the rights in question are relative rather than absolute rights, i.e. they can be restricted by states subject to certain conditions contained in the rights themselves.[36] It is necessary to look at the case law of the supervisory organs to determine whether a restriction is compatible with the treaty in question. I consider it is possible to make good arguments for limiting almost all of the above rights in the interests of maintaining international peace and security. However, as regards two rights, to property and to access to court, at least as these have been interpreted for European states, by the case law of the ECtHR, I consider that the present system of Security Council sanctions raises serious questions because of the absence of adequate procedural safeguards.

Why are procedural safeguards necessary? The problems of using intelligence material

As the rights in question can be balanced against other interests, it is necessary to go a bit deeper and explain why procedural safeguards are important when it comes to coercive measures which restrict rights. By designating individuals and subjecting them to coercive measures, the Security Council is now behaving as a "quasi-criminal" investigating, prosecuting and sentencing agency. It is starting to do things which were previously only done by national judges, police, prosecutors and intelligence officials. At the national level, involvement of judges in approving police or intelligence operations involving coercive means against individuals is considered an essential safeguard for individuals' rights. The interposition of a judge between the executive and the individual also provides a degree of quality control on the targeting process. In particular, as regards using intelligence material, long national experience shows that mistakes can easily be made in identifying people suspected of terrorism. Intelligence material is inherently of limited reliability.[37] Many examples from national practice show that the intelligence community often, or even invariably, errs on the side of caution in assessing threats.[38] That is its job after all. The pressure is great to get results. But, even the – by the standards of most other states – vast US intelligence community is stretched thin, with coverage often only "one analyst deep."[39] Of course, there is often no alternative but to rely on intelligence material. In countering certain forms of threats, including terrorist threats, democratic states have been forced to accept that special measures, such as opening files on suspects, initiating surveillance of suspects, or employment checks, must use intelligence material. Most of this will be derived from open source information, but informers and technical means (interception of communications, bugging, etc.) naturally form part of it. The essence of good intelligence work is putting together the "jigsaw" of material, and providing decision-makers with usable and reliable intelligence. But there is no doubt that mistakes are made in assessing threats. People are wrongly identified. People can have suspicious associates, or are in the wrong place at the wrong time, or are simply wrongly determined to be threats on the basis of inadequate or inaccurate material.

Now, the relevance of intelligence material can be expected to vary depending upon the target (government/governmental entity/terrorist group). There are "evidential" differences between, first, identifying the government, second, identifying the scope of the circle of "government" (as occurred in the Liberia/Sierra Leone sanctions) and third, identifying a terrorist group, especially a terrorist network (this being the object of Resolutions 1267, 1333 and, particularly, 1390). The members of a government are easy to identify. It is more difficult to identify people who are strongly linked to a government, or to a particular governmental activity, believed to be a threat to international peace and security. But the "core" of the target is clearly identified. And the "periphery," the business circles, will usually be acting openly, or relatively openly, because effective business usually demands that people know who is in charge of what. Even where ownership is concealed, where companies are exploiting primary resources (timber, diamonds, etc.) the chain of ownership can presumably be traced, beginning with the geographical location of the primary resource. This can also be done, although presumably with more difficulty, where the trade is in manufactured products, import–export licenses, etc. In any event, the intelligence problem is not so much identifying the periphery, but identifying the influence it has on the core, and determining whether this is sufficient to justify including given individuals on the blacklist. But even here, there is disquiet regarding the inability of the sanctions committees, and the UN Secretariat, to exercise any meaningful supervision over the basis for making such an assessment.[40]

However, the problems are greater as regards a terrorist group or, for that matter, organized criminality, which operates in secret. Certain senior members may be well known, but the rank and file will not. And where it is a terrorist network, the "nodes" may be operating in almost complete isolation from one another. There might not even be a "core." And, as the Al-Qaida network shows, there may be no connection to a single state or territory, and few, or no, goals shared by the whole network. The very idea of a network is open-ended, both in membership and goals. What is stopping adding, for instance, Chechen fighters to the Al-Qaida network?[41] And what of those who support terrorism in non-financial ways, e.g. in ideological ways?[42] With the UNITA and Sierra Leone sanctions, the focus of the sanctions was the primary resource earning export money for the targeted groups (oil, diamonds, etc.) but for a terrorist group, there may not be a primary resource linked to territory which is being exported. Or the resource may be illegal, such as narcotics. The problem, in other words, is identifying the whole group.

Property rights and the right of access to court under the ECHR as regards anti-terrorist sanctions

Although arguments can be made that the present UN sanctions regimes violate rights under the UDHR and ICCPR, I think that the main problems lie with compatibility with the ECHR (and, although I have not made a detailed study of the issue, I suspect, the ACHR), and that these problems mainly concern financial sanctions. Travel sanctions will rarely be problematic as human rights treaties tend to place relatively few limits on states' wide discretion as to which aliens they chose to admit. And the same applies for arms sanctions, as arms sales are typically subject to stringent licensing requirements and so it is difficult to speak at all of an individual international "right" to sell or receive weapons.[43] Although the points made below are directed at anti-terrorist sanctions, they can also have applicability in sanctions directed against members of target governments or quasi-governmental bodies and, particularly, against their business associates and members of their families. In this respect it should be noted that, from a rights perspective, at the national level, a coercive measure such as freezing of assets is usually directed against a suspected criminal, or his/her associates, or against the asset itself because it is "tainted" in some way by unlawfulness (e.g. it is stolen or laundered property). Where an asset belongs to a member of a suspect's family, but it is not so tainted, then coercive measures cannot usually be directed against it unless it is seen as, in practice, belonging to or used by the suspect. It is certainly not possible to punish the owner for being the family member of a criminal, however odious that criminal may be.

As regards the issue of protection of property (including business accounts, etc.), this is protected under ECHR Article 1, Protocol 1. The content of the property right is relatively weak: basically, interferences with property rights must be proportionate. Proportionality in ECtHR case law means a test of both necessity and a reasonable relationship between the measure and the aim to be achieved. If the issue is simply to balance the threat to international peace and security in the *abstract* with the infringement of property a temporary freezing entails, then the scales can invariably be assumed to come down on the side of maintaining international peace and security.[44] This is probably the most important purpose of the UN, and courts will be, and should be, cautious of going against the determination of the Security Council.

But I would argue that, as the sanction is quasi-criminal in nature, and affects drastically targeted individuals, the main issue should be one of whether there is sufficient proof of involvement in terrorism justifying the measure. This demands a specific, concrete test of proportionality.[45] This means that, at some level, national or international, there must be a judicial, or at least, quasi-judicial (i.e. objective) body capable of examining whether the specific measures directed against the specific individuals are necessary in the circumstances to advance international peace and security, and if so, whether the gain to international peace and security by freezing these particular persons' assets is proportionate to the infringement of their property rights. This does not involve questioning the determination of the Security Council that there is a threat to international peace and security: only the proportionality and necessity of the measure adopted against a particular individual.

Where does access to court come in? Property rights are "civil" rights, and as such, Article 6 ECHR guarantees access to a court to determine disputes over such rights. Now, the right of access to court is naturally not absolute: restrictions in it can be made. The ECtHR has not been willing to accept that access can be totally blocked for security reasons or that a national court is, for security reasons, not capable of determining the disputes on the merits.[46] However, the ECtHR has accepted that access to a court, exceptionally, can be blocked because a state is obliged to do so, in order to fulfill another international obligation. It is now well established that the contracting parties to the ECHR continue to bear collective responsibility under the Convention for implementing in their jurisdiction acts of international organizations.[47] The issue of responsibility should be distinguished from the issue of jurisdiction over the acts of an international organization under Article 1.[48] The European members of the Security Council, sitting in New York, are performing acts within their jurisdiction within the meaning of Article 1 and implementation of freezing measures are clearly within the jurisdiction of the executing state. The ECtHR has stressed that states cannot in general avoid their obligations under the Convention by transferring power to an international organization.[49] However, the specific question is whether a state's obligations under the UNC would justify limiting access to court, bearing in mind the fact that the UNC predates the ECHR (even if the institution of targeted sanctions naturally postdates it). As far as concerns the issue of immunity of suit of international organizations, the Court has taken the view that this immunity is an essential means of ensuring the proper functioning of such organizations, free from unilateral interference by individual governments.[50] However, the Court considered it would be incompatible with the purpose and object of the Convention if the Contracting States were absolved from their responsibility under the Convention by granting competence to an international organization in a particular field. Thus, the question became whether the individuals whose right of access to national courts was removed had available to them reasonable alternative means before an international body to protect effectively their rights under the Convention. There have been cases in which the Court has accepted a total bar on access, without alternative means of pursuing a claim, but these were where the lack of such alternative means was unavoidable.[51] In my view, the lack of safeguards built into the present UN system is not unavoidable, and so there is no reason to accept what is in effect a total bar on access to court/judicial remedies against a measure freezing all of a person's economic assets for an unlimited period of time, as well as a total bar on subsequent damages claims if the measure is ever lifted. Where there is no means whatsoever of challenging the Security Council measure before some form of independent tribunal satisfying, more or less, the standards of the ECHR, the very essence of the right of access to court is impaired.

What are the legal consequences of an incompatibility between obligations for European states under the ECHR on the one hand and the sanctions regimes on the other? It does not mean that the latter are invalid. For non-European states (assuming compatibility with customary human rights law and other regional human rights treaties which might apply), there *is* no incompatibility. On the other hand, for reasons set out already, and despite Article 103 of the UN Charter, one cannot say that for European states UN obligations in the present case have precedence over the others. Instead, for European states, the two sets of obligations must be reconciled. The logical consequence is that, until something is done about providing an equivalent level of protection, European states in the Security Council would be obliged not to accept new freezing sanctions, or renewals of old ones, where these breached their nationals' or residents' rights under the ECHR. If they do so, they are avoiding the application of Convention obligations, but not creating broadly equivalent levels of protection. The Security Council contains, at any given time, several European states, including three permanent members.

An incompatibility between European human rights law and the present sanctions regimes would obviously not prevent the Security Council from continuing with such measures against non-European nationals where these have no European connection (property, family life, etc.). But that this is hardly acceptable. Obviously, no one wins from a situation of incompatibility. It is in this light that one should see the problem, and read the following section that presents some possible solutions.

Proposals for improvements

My proposals for improvements are of a tentative nature. More work needs to be done in investigating the practicalities of each of these. One's approaches to the proposed solutions are dependent on one's view of whether or not there is a problem, and the extent of this. As soon as it is accepted that sanctions imposed by the Security Council resemble similar such sanctions imposed by national executive bodies, and that these can or do infringe individual rights, then it is necessary to speak about remedies which can be set in motion by individuals, and which lead to a binding determination of the dispute between the individual and the executive. But from the perspective of individual procedural rights, the only mechanism which has so far been created, the Resolution 1267 delisting procedure, is gravely deficient. It cannot be initiated by the individual. It relies on the right of diplomatic protection of nationals (slightly expanded to include residents). But the state(s) of nationality/residence may not be interested in intervening. I would say that whatever arguments of principle might have existed for not granting individuals a right of petition to an interstate body, the Security Council, these have disappeared when the Security Council itself is directing sanctions on individuals. And the UN Resolution 1267 procedure contains no possibility for the petitioning state to compel the production of sufficient information, or any information whatsoever, justifying the blacklisting of one of its nationals or residents. The designating state can refuse to provide any information, and continue to block the removal from the list, and the petitioning state cannot force a determination of the issue before some objective body. The right of consultation which the targeted individual's state has, is, in the circumstances, of little concrete value.[52] I can say that the reaction of Swedish procedural and criminal lawyers to the lack of procedural safeguards in the Al-Qaida sanctions was one of shocked disbelief: they saw 200 years of building up safeguards in criminal procedure at the national level being removed by what could only be described as an international law magic (black magic) wand.

If one is convinced that there is a problem, then previously politically unacceptable solutions become feasible or even desirable. I think it clear that new methods of regulating and controlling such sanctions have to be created. Still, the difficulties in persuading the US of the unacceptability of the present system should not be underestimated. From the perspective of economic warfare on terrorists the present practice of (more or less) endorsing selected parts of the US lists, giving them a universal validity, is presumably ideal. There may also be a typically legal inability to see beyond one's own familiar legal forms. Thus, American lawyers may find it difficult to grasp that while freezing measures may not infringe rights under US constitutional law, they can infringe European human rights norms. And there may be an inability to understand the fact that European solutions can be devised to protect intelligence material in judicial proceedings: it is not a question of either accepting full disclosure in a jury trial or doing nothing.

It is useful to sketch out some points which should be borne in mind in considering the following proposals. This involves a degree of recapitulation of previous comments.

First, the problem is not simply a practical one, of identifying the right people. If this were so, then improved executive procedures (particularly better mechanisms for exchange of information between friendly governments/ intelligence agencies) would ameliorate the problem. But there is a conceptual problem with the blacklisting technique as such: it is an executive mechanism infringing rights, with no judicial or quasi-judicial safeguards. Second, the human rights problems generally speaking vary in intensity depending upon type of sanctions involved (travel, financial, arms embargoes). Third, the value in practice of a review mechanism will vary according to the type of target (government, non-government). This last point must be explained. Blacklisting is in effect a statement that the blacklisted person is doing something which is damaging to international peace and security. There can be a wide variety of different ways individuals can contribute to a particular threat identified by the Security Council. In some cases, the connection between the individual's conduct and the threat is obvious, e.g. where the individual is a member of a government believed to be engaged in the supply of weapons to guerrillas, or known to be in occupation of foreign territory. But in other cases, this connection will not be obvious. Blacklisted individuals may genuinely not know what it is that they are "accused" of. If they know what it is they are accused of, they can formulate a challenge to the claim and/or the evidence for the claim. This challenge is likely to take one of the following forms:

1. I am not the person, X, who the sanctions committee wishes to blacklist. There may be a person X who is engaged in activities damaging to international peace and security, but, contrary to what the sanctions committee claims, I am not him/her. In other words, I have been wrongly identified.
2. I am the person, X, identified by the sanctions committee, but I am not responsible for, or am no longer engaged in, the activities damaging to international peace and security.
3. I am the person, X, identified by the sanctions committee, and I am engaged in activities which the Security Council considers to be damaging to international peace and security, but these activities are not, in fact, so damaging.
4. I am the person, X, identified by the sanctions committee, but I consider that the sanction is disproportionate.

These challenges involve reviewing different types of decision. For claims falling under 1, 2 and 4, providing some mechanism of legal challenge would be a big improvement from the present system of political safeguards which is woefully inadequate from a rights perspective. The first is a claim that a simple error has been made. The second and third claims allege more material errors. The fourth claim can be seen as either a claim of a material error and/or a request for some form of humanitarian exception. How meaningful it is to require some form of legal review of the claim depends upon the type of decision and the evidence that exists for the claim.

Challenges to all four of the claims can involve looking at sensitive material. The first claim (error) will usually be the simplest case, and may well be the most common. This is the sort of claim that even a political body ought to be prepared to handle, and be capable of doing so. But even here there may be cases where some sort of judicial procedure (a right to be heard, to submit information, etc.) would be desirable. And even here, albeit exceptionally, intelligence material may be relevant to show that X has been wrongly, or correctly, identified. The second type of claim will be the sort made by business executives accused of supporting targeted governments or entities, by family members of government officials or by people accused of being terrorists or of supporting terrorist groups. Ruling on this claim involves looking at the factual evidence for the accusation. This will usually be the most problematic case from the perspective of the evidence.

The third type of claim can conceivably also be made by a business executive/ suspected terrorist supporter, but is more likely to be made by a government member, or executive official. It differs in an important way from the second type of claim as it is essentially a challenge to the political determination of the Security Council that the government or entity is engaged in activities damaging to international peace and security. While conceivably the evidence for this determination can partly consist of sensitive intelligence material, it must be assumed that there will be ample evidence that a threat exists from public sources. Both the type of decision and the evidence means that providing a legal mechanism of challenge will almost invariably be of little use to the applicant in claim 3. This does not mean that there is not a duty to provide a legal mechanism: simply that it will be of very limited value.

One could then say that it must be a simple matter to provide a remedy before national courts for people making claim 3. In Europe, for example, while the ECHR requires the provision of a judicial remedy for interferences in property rights, the issue to be determined by a national court in claim 3 cases is whether the Security Council is correct that the government is involved in activities threatening international peace and security. A European court is not going to go against the Security Council's determination that something is a threat and so, providing a legal remedy will hardly sabotage the effective implementation of UN sanctions in Europe.

However, conceding the power of European courts in theory to question the determination of the Security Council necessarily involves conceding the same power to the courts of other states. In many countries of the world, including some European states, the courts are insufficiently independent from the government. Where the government in a state is indifferent to particular Security Council sanctions, or even hostile to them, then allowing the courts in these states to challenge the validity of Security Council sanctions will risk sabotaging these sanctions. If this happens in a state that has an important geographical relation to a targeted state (e.g. the main trading partner, or transit state) the sanctions may be totally undermined.

Fourth, the number of people likely to apply make claims falling under 1–4 above is likely to be limited. US experience shows that only a small number of people will go to the trouble of hiring a lawyer to secure removal from the list and these will usually be people who feel strongly that the decision is erroneous.

Fifth, one can envisage either a post hoc review procedure and/or a preventive control mechanism (i.e. a legal standard to be satisfied before measures are ordered). The former functions as a guarantee of non-abuse, the latter as a remedy. But even if a preventive measure can be devised, it alone will not meet the human rights difficulties if the measure is of very long duration. Moreover, there can be practical problems (delay, etc.) in having a preventive control mechanism. As regards travel sanctions, the need for speed is less. As regards arms embargoes, there can be situations in which it is necessary to act quickly, but these will probably be rare. As regards asset freezes, the need for speed and secrecy would seem to mitigate against a preventive control. On the other hand, one can pose the question how speedy and secret is the present procedure for asset freezing?

Circulation of lists before a decision is taken is already the customary procedure, in order to facilitate an effective freeze. And the US lists on terrorism are often published first, thus warning international terrorists. A requirement to submit a draft list would at least allow checking against whatever objective criteria might be devised (see below). Of course, there is nothing stopping both improved procedures before the imposition of the measure and post hoc procedures.

Sixth, time limits on sanctions are not a solution to the human rights difficulties. Rigid time limits are anyway unlikely to be popular, as they can undermine the effectiveness of the sanctions. As mentioned, Resolution 1390 is different from the other sanctions resolutions as it can be, in practice, of unlimited duration. As regards the other sanctions resolutions, which have to be periodically renewed, a time limit obviously means that the interference in human rights is of shorter duration. But this does not necessarily reduce the degree of infringement. Damage to protected interests can sometimes occur rapidly. This applies particularly to the right to reputation, especially for business people. However, time limits may have a role to play as regards the procedures for challenge. For example, one could also set a sliding temporal scale of justification, i.e. the longer the measure continues, the more the onus of proof shifts more and more to the state wanting to keep a name on the list.

Seventh, humanitarian exceptions, such as the exception now provided under Resolution 1267/1390, may remove some human rights problems, and will certainly ameliorate the position of individuals affected by sanctions, but will definitely not solve all the problems involved.

Eighth, there are issues of both practicality and principle in designing a body at the UN level. Logically, it is the Security Council that should require the evidence to be submitted to it, because it is the body which takes the decision (and so should have the responsibility). However, this would involve creating an "in-house" UN intelligence capacity, and many states see major problems involved in this. This is shown *inter alia* by the refusal of states to implement the Brahimi Report recommendations regarding intelligence capacity.[53] There are special problems involved in giving international bodies access to very sensitive intelligence material. There is a real risk of leakage of intelligence to hostile states, which may well be members of the Security Council. There is the cost issue and the issue of policy – many states are reluctant to do anything which can contribute to an expansion of a UN bureaucracy, which is occasionally accused, with varying degrees of justification, of lacking in expertise, impartiality, etc.

There is relatively little experience of international judicial or quasi-judicial bodies handling intelligence material. The ECtHR has seldom seen the intelligence basis for a particular challenged compulsory measure, surveillance, etc. but has tended to rule *in abstracto* on the issue on basis of the structural, mainly procedural, safeguards applicable at national law.[54] The issue of access to intelligence material arose *inter alia* for the International Court of Justice (ICJ) in the Corfu Channel Case, without being satisfactorily resolved.[55] In Prosecutor v. Blaskic,[56] the Appeal Chamber of the International Criminal Tribunal for the Former Yugoslavia

(ICTFY) refused to let state withhold information or prevent an individual from giving evidence because it would prejudice national security, where this evidence was material to the prosecution. The experience of the Blaskic case led to the adoption, for the International Criminal Court, of Article 72 of its statute, which attempts to balance the interests of justice with legitimate national security concerns. The issue has also arisen in the context of the WTO dispute settlement understanding.[57]

In any event, anything so radical as to require amendment of the UN Charter can obviously be ruled out in practice. But even changes in Security Council practice take time to negotiate, and big and small power rivalries and bureaucratic infighting can make the end result uncertain. One might end up with something worse than one began with.

Applying these points, I come up with three different types of mechanisms, although these can be combined and constructed in a variety of different ways. I deal with all of these in detail in my report to the Swedish government. All of them are accompanied by problems, political, legal and practical, and are likely to meet severe opposition from states satisfied with the present position (particularly the US). Basically, the first of these mechanisms is to require states wishing to blacklist individuals to blacklist them at the national level first, provided they have established proper criteria for listing and fair procedures at the national level whereby the material basis for blacklisting can be scrutinized by a national, independent, competent and objective body capable of ordering delisting where the criteria were not satisfied. This would involve, for example, guarantees of fair procedures, of a security screened advocate to assist, of independent and expert judges with full powers to look at the merits of the case.

This national listing, and adequate national safeguards, would be a condition of Security Council listing. A practice must follow of Security Council delisting where the national listing has been successfully challenged. The EU states have taken the first steps towards establishing criteria on 27 December 2001 in adopting two common positions and a regulation setting out basic requirements to be followed in future freezing cases.[58] Article 4 of the Common Position on the Application of Specific Measures to Combat Terrorism sets out minimum objective criteria for blacklisting, and attempts to establish a degree of "quality control." However, the criteria are not enough in my view, and no control mechanisms have been established.

If there was a genuine possibility of challenging blacklisting before the courts of the state proposing a name for a blacklist, some of the objections against the present system would disappear. However, we should be wary here. There are unfortunately many historical (and, regrettably, some present-day) examples in Europe and elsewhere, of purely formal mechanisms of challenge as far as security matters are concerned.[59] For example, a court's jurisdiction may be limited by standing requirements, or it may only be able to review the legality of the measure, and not its merits. Or the judges may have no expertise in security matters, or they may be unable in practice to look at *all* the intelligence material in question. Or there may be a tradition that the judicial branch defers to the executive in matters of foreign policy and/or national security. In such cases, a right of appeal, or review, can be useless. It can be worse than useless, as it gives the impression of just procedures, without the reality. The law serves only an ideological function, as a smokescreen. This is my view of the present state of US law, at least as regards challenges by aliens without a "substantial connection" to the US, sufficient to allow them to mount a constitutional (as opposed to administrative law) challenge.[60]

This option would entail some form of scrutiny at the Security Council level (or an expert body appointed by it) for checking if the courts in the state in question really were not only capable of providing a remedy on paper, but expert enough, and willing enough, to do so. It would not necessarily involve giving it any power to look at actual cases, simply at the powers of the courts, the procedures and the "legal culture." Even this is likely to be much too controversial for many states, as it would create an "A" and "B" league of states: those with satisfactory human rights safeguards which could propose blacklists, and those which could not.

The second type of mechanism is to create an international review body. Many of the difficulties associated with an international judicial body disappear if one uses *arbitration*. Such a body could be organized in the following way. All members of the Security Council propose a member. The integrity of these judges would be vital, because the targeted individuals and their home states would have to trust them. The arbitral body could sit in panels of three members. Targeted individuals could request their cases to be heard and propose a panel to hear the evidence. The state proposing the blacklist would also have to propose a panel. Failure to do so within a given period of time would mean removal of the blacklisted person from the list. Both the individual and the proposing state would have a veto on the composition of the panel, but pending agreement on the composition, the individual would remain on the blacklist. In practice this would mean that the panel would consist of a judge from the state proposing the blacklist (A), and two judges from two other states which A trusts. There would have to be mechanisms designed to ensure as fair a procedure as possible. An arbitral body would be cost-effective, as it would have no standing secretariat at all. And the risk of leakage of intelligence material would be very small.

Of course, the procedure would not be ideal from anyone's perspective. The state proposing the blacklisting would have to accept that two foreign judges saw very sensitive intelligence material. And the blacklisted individual may well not consider that he or she has had a fair hearing before three judges one of whom comes from the blacklisting state and (probably) two from allied, or at least, friendly, states. It would seem sensible to have only one such arbitral body for all the targeted sanctions committees, rather than several. To fully satisfy the human rights objections, the decision of the arbitral body would have to be binding on the sanctions committee, but as this is formally speaking a separate (and subordinate) entity from the Security Council itself, this would not mean that the authority of the Security Council as such is undermined.

This proposal has definite advantages, *inter alia* making explicit the individual nature of the rights, and procedural safeguards. But there are bound to be problems in practice in getting states to agree on an advisory body in the Security Council which does not include them. Although I think that the argument is incorrect, for political reasons some states are likely to be adamant that an arbitral body would hinder the Security Council in its task of maintaining international peace and security and it is presumably unthinkable for the US to reveal intelligence material to an international arbitral body. On the other hand, where intelligence material does not lie behind the evidence, then there would be no problem in having an arbitral body.

The third mechanism is to abandon the present system of UN targeted sanctions as far as these concern individuals not belonging to governments/governmental entities and return to unilateral national sanctions, enforced among like-minded states by means of mutual recognition of judicial decisions. This would have major advantages from the perspective of legal safeguards, but there would be obvious disadvantages, in particular, sanctions would no longer have a universal applicability. Some states would fail to take measures against people who were identified, either through inefficiency or because they disagree with the policy.

On the other hand, as far as terrorist supporters, particularly financiers, are concerned, one can question what is the point in practice of the Security Council continuing to list them directly. Those states which faithfully implement UN targeted sanctions have already implemented, or are in the process of implementing, UN Resolution 1373, which contains a general obligation to freeze terrorist assets to suppress the material supporting of terrorism and to prevent the financing of terrorism. When such implementing national legislation is in place, the listing of terrorist/terrorist financier suspects can be handled on a bilateral basis, with the state, or states, possessing information indicating that a given person is involved in terrorist financing transferring this information to the state where the person and/or his/her assets are situated, which can then take the measures in accordance with national law and practice. This already works well as regards money laundering.

Moreover, as regards US–European cooperation, with the adoption of the EU Framework Decision on Freezing of Assets, the US could choose to act through one state, which then can issue an order which will be implemented in all the other EU states.[61] This system ought to be acceptable to European human rights law. As regards states which do not want to cooperate with the listing for political or other reasons, it is true that they can sabotage the freezing, by, e.g. setting a spuriously high national standard which allows them to demand more, and more secret, information from the designating state, information which the designating state is unwilling to give. But, in practice, one is not in a worse position than before, when the UN Security Council listed the names directly. As the reports of the Monitoring Group established under UN Resolutions 1267/1390 clearly show, non-cooperating states have anyway found ways of evading the obligation to freeze assets, which in any event only works when there is enthusiastic, and speedy, implementation of sanctions. It would naturally be desirable to seize all the assets of a terrorist network such as Al-Qaida, but if this is unrealistic, it might be better to content oneself with first having effective controls over the major financial markets, i.e. the EU (and Switzerland), Japan and the US/Canada and second, trying to prevent or at least make more difficult, terrorist operations in those states which the particular terrorist network is most opposed to. In the case of Al-Qaida, which the Security Council has been most concerned with, it is the US and its close European allies. Carrying out major terrorist operations in the US and European states will mean transfer of assets to the target state – at which point they can be frozen. So worldwide measures, while desirable, may not be strictly necessary.

Concluding remarks

I consider that the adoption by European states in the Security Council of certain targeted sanctions programs, and the implementation of these programs in European states, gives rise to several possible violations of the ECHR. Of course, confirming a definite violation means waiting for a judgment from the ECJ or ECtHR. Predicting the outcome of a case before any court is risky, especially as regards an implicit right (access to court) and, moreover, in a politically charged issue such as the present one. And, obviously, a case has to get to one or other of these courts in the first place.[62] Nonetheless, at the end of the day, the issue is not so much what the ECJ, or ECtHR, will do, but the legal sensibilities of the states party to the ECHR. This Convention, like the similar regional conventions for Latin America and Africa, constitutes the minimum shared standard of rights for the region. It is a symbol of what the states in question regard as acceptable. The states most likely to experience difficulties with the lack of legal safeguards in the present system are democratic states which respect human rights, and which faithfully attempt to implement UN sanctions, and do so with a large measure of effectiveness. These states are the mainstay of whatever effectiveness targeted sanctions might have. In this respect, the goals of legitimacy and effectiveness are not opposed to each other, but co-dependent. The implementation of UN Security Council sanctions is a delicate business. If states are not wholehearted in their implementation, if the customs authorities, the export control agencies, the financial inspection units, and financial police are less than enthusiastic, then the sanctions are very easily undermined. It is in this sense that possible conflicts with the ECHR should be understood. And it is in this sense that reform is needed.

Notes

1 For EU sanctions, see E. Paasivirta and A. Rosas, "Sanctions, Countermeasures and Related Action in the External Affairs of the EU," in E. Cannizzaro (ed.) *The European Union as an Actor in International Relations* (The Hague: Kluwer, 2001) and chapters 7 and 8 in the present volume. For criticism of these sanctions from a legal rights perspective, see T. Andersson, I. Cameron and K. Nordback, "EU Blacklisting: The Renaissance of Imperial Power, but on a Global Scale," *European Business Law*

Review, 14, 2 (2003), pp. 111–141 and I. Cameron, "EU Anti-Terrorist Blacklisting and Human Rights," *Human Rights Law Review*, 4 (2004). For analysis and criticism of the US sanctions programs, see P. Fitzgerald, "'If Property Rights Were Treated Like Human Rights, They Could Never Get Away with This': Blacklisting and due process in U.S. economic sanctions programs," *Hastings Law Journal*, 51 (1999), pp. 73–169; P. Fitzgerald, "Drug Kingpins and Blacklists: Compliance Issues with US Economic Sanctions," pt 1, *Journal of Money Laundering Control*, 4 (2000), pp. 360–381, pt 2 and 3, *Journal of Money Laundering Control*, 5 (2001), pp. 66–86, 162–182 and "Judicial Review Commission on Foreign Assets Control," Final Report to Congress (January 2001), http://www.law.stetson.edu

2 The UN anti-terrorist sanction regime can naturally also be seen in a wider context of national, regional and global action against terrorism following the September 11 attacks.

3 See e.g. R. Normand, "A Human Rights Assessment of Sanctions: The Case of Iraq, 1990–1997," in W. J. M. van Genugten and G. A. de Groot (eds) *United Nations Sanctions: Effectiveness and Effects, Especially in the Field of Human Rights. A Multidisciplinary Approach* (Antwerp: Intersentia, 1999) and M. Bossuyt, Working paper on the adverse consequences of economic sanctions on the enjoyment of human rights, Commission on human rights, Sub-Commission on the Promotion and Protection of Human Rights, Fifty-second session E/CN.4/Sub.2/2000/33 (21 June 2000).

4 I. Cameron, *Targeted Sanctions and Legal Safeguards*, Report to the Swedish Foreign Office (October 2002), http://www.jur.uu.se/sii/html.index. Certain governments, particularly the US, were very negative about the issue of legal safeguards being discussed during the Stockholm process. However, it inevitably arose several times during the discussions. See e.g. the 17–18 June 2002 meeting of the SPITS Working Group on Strengthening the Role of the UN in Implementing Targeted Sanctions (http://www.smartsanctions.se). See also P. Wallensteen, C. Staibano and M. Eriksson (eds) *Making Targeted Sanctions Effective: Guidelines for the Implementation of UN Policy Options*, Department of Peace and Conflict Research, Uppsala University (Stockholm: Elanders Gotab, 2003), p. 97.

5 I. Cameron, "UN Targeted Sanctions, Legal Guarantees and the European Convention on Human Rights," *Nordic Journal of International Law*, 73 (2003). As regards methods used, in addition to the usual legal-academic analysis of literature, case law, official reports, etc., I have interviewed a number of people involved in the implementation of UN sanctions at the national and international level. An early draft of the report was discussed at a seminar in Stockholm in April 2002, which was arranged by the Swedish Foreign Office. I am grateful to all the participants in this seminar for valuable comments. I would especially like to thank Peter Wallensteen, Peter Fitzgerald, Martin Björklund, Torbjörn Andersson, Daniel Nord and Fredrik Stenhammar.

6 Useful analyses and overviews can also be found in M. P. Doxey, *International Sanctions in Contemporary Perspective*, 2nd edition (New York: St Martins Press, 1996), D. Cortright and G. A. Lopez, *The Sanctions Decade: Assessing UN Strategies in the 1990s* (Boulder, CO: Lynne Rienner, 2000), P. Wallensteen, *A Century of Economic Sanctions: A Field Revisited*, Uppsala Peace Research Papers No. 1, Department of Peace and Conflict Research, Uppsala University, (Uppsala: Universitetstryckeriet, 2000) and F. Stenhammar, "UN Smart Sanctions in Political Reality and International Law," in D. Amneus, D. and K. Svanberg, *International Law and Security: New Trends and Phenomena* (Stockholm: Norstedts, 2003).

7 The problems of implementation at the national level were the main subject of discussion at the Stockholm process and are well set out in the present volume.

8 S/RES/1127 (1997) imposed travel sanctions on UNITA leaders and their immediate

family members. S/RES/1173 and S/RES/1176 (1998) imposed financial sanctions on UNITA members.
9 See Press Release SC/7162. Two people and their families were later removed from the list, see Press Release SC/7322. The travel sanctions were suspended on 17 May 2002 by S/RES/1412 and all the sanctions lifted and the Sanctions Committee dissolved on 12 December 2002 by S/RES/1448.
10 See the revised list under S/RES/1171 (1998), at http://www.un.org/Docs/sc/committees/SierraLeone/1171_list.htm. So far, nine people have been removed from this list (last consolidation, 30 May 2003).
11 See the revised list under S/RES/1343 (2001), at http://www.un.org/Docs/sc/committees/Liberia2/1343_list.htm (last consolidation, 30 May 2003).
12 See e.g. the replies drafted by the Liberia Sanctions Committee to queries posed by Gambia and Lebanon, S/AC.39/2002/Note 8 and the Annual Report of the Sierra Leone Sanctions Committee, S/2002/470, p. 35.
13 See the list at http://www.un.org/Docs/sc/committees/1267/pdflist.pdf (last consolidation, 25 June 2003).
14 There is only one sanctions committee for the three resolutions. There is also a monitoring group, which was appointed by S/RES/1363 (2001). Its mandate was extended for a further year by S/RES/1390 (hereinafter the "1267/1390 Monitoring Group").
15 The US move towards less geographically oriented sanctions came as far back as 1995, with the first blacklist of "specially designated terrorists" suspected of hindering the Middle East peace process, Fitzgerald, 1999, p. 90.
16 1999, text at http://www.untreaty.un.org/English/Terrorism.asp
17 Although the EU has implemented S/RES/1373 by means, *inter alia*, of blacklists. For a discussion see Cameron, 2004.
18 For a general discussion of the apparatus of countermeasures against money laundering, see W. C. Gilmore, *Dirty Money: The Evolution of Money Laundering Countermeasures*, 2nd edition (Strasbourg: Council of Europe Publishing, 1999) and Fitzgerald, 2000 and 2001.
19 See e.g. Fitzgerald, 1999.
20 See Cameron, 2002, pp. 13–16.
21 The 1267/1390 Monitoring Group states that "individuals designated on the list must be terrorists or terrorist suspects," Third Report, op. cit. para. 53.
22 K. Sarooshi, *The United Nations and the Development of Collective Security. The Delegation by the UN Security Council of its Chapter VII Powers* (Oxford: Clarendon Press, 1999), p. 33.
23 A. Reinisch, "Developing Human Rights and Humanitarian Law Accountability for the Imposition of Economic Sanctions," *American Journal of International Law* 95 (2001), p. 856. J. Dugard, 'Judicial Review of Sanctions United Nations Sanctions and International Law', in V. Gowlland-Debbas, M. Garcia Rubio and H. Hadj-Sahraoui (eds) *United Nations Sanctions and International Law* (The Hague: Kluwer, 2001), p. 88.
24 See Reinisch, 2001, D. Schweigman, *The Authority of the Security Council under Chapter VII of the UN Charter: Legal Limits and the Role of the ICJ* (The Hague: Kluwer, 2001). See further Judge Weeramantry's dissenting opinion in the Case Concerning Questions of Interpretation and Application of the 1971 Montreal Convention Arising from the Aerial Incident at Lockerbie (Libya v. UK, US), Preliminary Objections, ICJ, 27 February 1998, available at http://www.icj-cij.org (Lockerbie Case), Judge Fitzmaurice's dissenting opinion in the Namibia Advisory Opinion, ICJ Rep. 1971, para. 116, Judge Eli Lauterpacht, separate opinion in the

Application of the Genocide Convention Case (Provisional Measures), ICJ Rep. 1993, p. 440 and the judgment of the appeals chamber of the ICTFY in the Tadic case, 2 October 1995, IT-94-1-AR72. See also Dugard, 2001, pp. 86, 90.

25 999 UNTS 71 (1966). At the time of writing there are 148 states party to this treaty, including four permanent members of the Security Council (and the other permanent member is a signatory).

26 UN Doc. A/811, 1948. The customary law nature of the UDHR was stressed by the Vienna Declaration of the World Conference on Human Rights, 1993, endorsed by the General Assembly in Res. 48/121 (1993).

27 In particular, it should be noted that almost all European states are parties to the ECHR, including three permanent members of the Security Council, and most states in the OAS are party to the ACHR (although the US is not).

28 See, as regards the US, e.g. Reid v. Covert, 354 US 1, 77 (1957), Diggs v. Schultz, 470 F. 2d 461, 466–67, (DC Cir. 1976). As regards a European perspective, see the famous cases of Wünche Handelsgesellschaft (re) ("Solange II") and Brunner v. European Union Treaty, from the German Constitutional Court, regarding the transfer of legislative powers to the EU (reported in English in 1987 CMLR 225 and 1994 1 CMLR 57).

29 In March 2001, S/RES/1267 (1999) and S/RES/1333 (2000) and the Common Positions implementing the resolutions, 1999/727/CFSP (15 November 1999), 2001/56/CFSP (22 January 2001) and 2001/154/CFSP (26 February 2001), were followed by Council Regulation 467/2001/EC. This was implemented by *inter alia* Commission regulation 2199/2001 (12 November). In May 2002 these regulations were replaced by Council Regulation 881/2002 which has since been amended many times by Commission regulations. For a description and analysis of the case, see Andersson *et al.*, 2003 and P. Cramér, "Recent Swedish Experience of Targeted UN Sanctions: The Erosion of Trust in the Security Council," in E. De Wet and A. Nollenkamper (eds) *Review of the Security Council by Member States* (Amsterdam/ Oxford/New York: Intersentia, 2003), pp. 85–106.

30 SC/7490, 27 August 2002.

31 See Case T-306/01, Abdirisak Aden and others v. EU Council and EC Commission, Case T-315/01, Yassin Abdullah Khadi v. Council and Commission, Case T-318/01, Omar Mohammed Othman v. Council and Commission.

32 Between 22 August and 17 December 2002, 16 individuals and 22 entities were added to the list. The Third Report of the 1267/1390 Monitoring Group (op. cit.) contains a list (annex II) consisting of 97 people which the Group regards as terrorist suspects and which it wants states to list. New lists against new countries (Congo-Kinshasa) have been proposed (although not yet acted upon). See S/2002/1146.

33 ETS No. 5 (1950).

34 9 ILM 672 (1970).

35 21 ILM 59 (1982).

36 In the case of the UDHR, there are general "accommodation" clauses, Articles 29 and 30, which allow restrictions to be made in all the rights set out in the UDHR. I will not deal here with the issue of "derogation," i.e. temporary suspension of the rights. Suffice it to say that I consider that the derogation clauses in the ICCPR (Article 4), ECHR (Article 15) and ACHR (Article 27) – the Banjul Charter has no such clause – cannot be invoked successfully to justify the present system.

37 For a discussion, see e.g. I. Cameron, *National Security and the European Convention on Human Rights*, (Iustus: Kluwer, 2000), pp. 170–183. A graphic recent example of this is the controversy in the UK and the US surrounding the alleged proof that Iraq had active weapons of mass destruction programs, which was a large part of the reasons for the US/UK invasion of Iraq in March 2003.

38 It is also naturally capable of misusing its powers. There are very numerous instances of this. For a recent example from the US, concerning judicial criticism of FBI abuse of the Foreign Intelligence Surveillance Act for the purpose of gathering material for criminal prosecutions, see *New York Times*, 26 August 2002.
39 R. K. Betts, "Fixing Intelligence," *Foreign Affairs*, 81, 1 (2002), p. 48.
40 See above, note 12.
41 The 1267/1390 Monitoring Group cited 'massive' (50 state) support for the listing of Jemaah Islamiyah, the group believed to be involved in the Bali terrorist bombing, Third Report, 17 December 2002, S/2002/1338, para. 18.
42 It can be noted here that the Bonn–Berlin process regarded 'ideological support' as possibly sufficient grounds for being included in the circle of targets. See M. Björklund, "EU: n Pakotepolitiikka," *Erik Castrén Insitute Research Reports*, 11/2002 (Helsinki, 2002), p. 87.
43 Although such a right might exist at national law, e.g. Article II of the Amendments to the US Constitution (mad though it might appear to most Europeans, and, for that matter, many Americans).
44 This was the approach of the European Court of Justice (ECJ) in Case C-84/95, Bosphorus Hava Yollari ve Ticaret AS v. Minister for Transport, Energy and Communications, Ireland and the Attorney General, [1996] ECR 3953. For a discussion of the case, see I. Canor, "'Can Two Walk Together, Except They Be Agreed?' The Relationship between International Law and European Law: The Incorporation of United Nations Sanctions against Yugoslavia into European Community Law through the Perspective of the European Court of Justice," *Common Market LR*, 35 (1998), pp. 137–187.
45 One can add that in *Bosphurus Airways*, what was at issue were general sanctions, issued against an abstractly defined class of people. In this case, the direct addressees of the Commission regulations are the named individuals. So arguably it is not actually *possible* to engage in an abstract test of proportionality, measuring the abstract advantages for international peace and security against the abstract disadvantages for a class of applicants.
46 See, in particular, Tinnelly and McElduff v. UK, 10 July 1998 which involved UK blocking of access to Northern Ireland tribunals by means of executive certificates in disputes concerning failure to obtain a public procurement contract. The context was terrorist violence and information allegedly behind the certificate (if it existed at all) was presumably intelligence material (informers testimony, electronic surveillance, etc.). The Court stated that "The right guaranteed under Article 6(1) of the Convention to submit a dispute to a court or tribunal in order to have a determination on questions of both fact and law cannot be displaced by the ipse dixit of the executive" (at para. 77, referring to Chahal v. UK, 15 November 1996, at para. 131). See also Devenney v. UK, No. 24265/94, 19 March 2002 and Beaumartin v. France, 24 November 1994, A/296-B.
47 See, in particular, Mathews v. UK, 18 February 1999 (responsibility for EU norms), Naletilic v. Croatia, No. 51891/99, 4 May 2000 (responsibility for transfer of suspect to ICTFY), T. I. v. UK, No. 43844/98, 7 March 2000 (continued state responsibility for removal of refugee notwithstanding obligations under the Dublin Convention) and the Beer and Regan and Waite and Kennedy cases (see below, note 50). The Human Rights Committee may consider actions of international organizations exercising public power in a state party to be outside the jurisdiction. See H. v. d. P. v. Netherlands, 217/1986, views of 8 April 1987 at para. 3.2. On the other hand, it may be simply that it accepts that immunity of suit of international organizations is a legitimate reason for restricting access to court.
48 See, in particular, Bankovic *et al.* v. Belgium, the Czech Republic, Denmark, France,

Germany, Greece, Hungary, Iceland, Italy, Luxembourg, the Netherlands, Norway, Poland, Portugal, Spain, Turkey and the UK, No. 52207/99, 12 December 2001. For commentary on the case, see M. Happold and V. Bankovic, "Belgium and the Territorial Scope of the ECHR," *Human Rights Law Review*, 3 (2003), pp. 77–90.

49 See Mathews v. UK, op. cit. at paras 32 and 34 "The Convention does not exclude the transfer of competences to international organizations provided that Convention rights continue to be 'secured.' Member States' responsibility therefore continues even after such a transfer . . . the suggestion that the United Kingdom may not have effective control over the state of affairs complained of cannot affect the position."

50 Waite and Kennedy v. Germany and Beer and Regan v. Germany, 18 February 1999.

51 Prince Hans-Adam II of Liechtenstein v. Germany No. 42527/98, 12 July 2001. Al-Adsani v. UK, and McElhinney v. Ireland, respectively, No. 35763/97, and No. 31253/96, 21 November 2001. See also A v. UK, No. 35373/97, 17 December 2002, confirming that absolute parliamentary immunity does not breach Article 6.

52 The Resolutions 1333/1390 Monitoring Group notes the disquiet expressed by certain states regarding the lack of criteria for inclusion on and removal from the list. They also note the reluctance of states to add further names to the list (paras 26–31). However, they do not really draw the causal connection. Nor do they make any recommendations as regards human rights.

53 UN Secretary-General Report of the Panel on UN Peace Operations, UN Doc. A/55/305, 21 August 2000 (Brahimi Report). The Final Report from the Stockholm process makes extensive recommendations on enhancing UN secretariat capacity, Wallensteen *et. al.*, 2003, pp. 48–53.

54 See, in general, Cameron, 2000.

55 Corfu Channel Case, Merits (UK v. Albania), ICJ Rep. 1949, p. 4.

56 Judgment on the Request of the Republic of Croatia for Review of the Decision of the Trial Chamber of 18 July 1997, Case No. IT-95-14-AR108bis (Appeals Chamber) 29 October 1997.

57 See e.g. D. Akande and S. Williams, "International Adjudication On National Security Issues: What Role For The WTO?," *Virginia Journal of International Law*, 43 (2003), pp. 365–402.

58 Common Position on Combating Terrorism, 2001/930/CFSP, Common Position on the Application of Specific Measures to Combat Terrorism 2001/931/CFSP, Council Regulation 2580/2001 on specific restrictive measures directed against certain persons and entities with a view to combating terrorism.

59 For an examination of these issues from the perspective of the ECHR, see Cameron, 2000, pp. 157–161, and *passim.*

60 This was more or less also the conclusion of the Judicial Review Commission 2001, pp. 113–116.

61 Proposal for a Framework Decision (FD) on the execution in the EU of orders freezing assets or evidence, OJ C 75, 07/03/2001 pp. 3–8. The FD is expected to be adopted later in 2003. Article 11 provides that challenge to an order would only be before the courts of the issuing state.

62 It should be noted, however, that at least one action claiming damages has been brought regarding the *EU* anti-terrorist blacklisting (Council Decision 2002/334 of 2 May 2002) and the further implementing decision of 17 June 2002 blacklisting the PKK organization. See Osman Ocalan on behalf of Kurdistan Workers Party (PKK) and Serif Vanly on behalf of Kurdistan National Congress v. Council, Case T-229/02. Applications have been made to the ECtHR regarding EU Common Position 2001/930/CFSP on terrorism, Segi and others and Gestoras Pro-Amnistia and others v. 15 States of the EU, Nos 6422/02 and 9916/02, 23 May 2002. This was declared inadmissible on the basis that the applicants were not "victims" of the common position.

14

EXAMINING TARGETED SANCTIONS

Are travel bans effective?

Erica Cosgrove

Travel bans restrict or ban entirely travel outside of their home countries of certain individuals or classes of individuals. Some individuals are named for inclusion on lists of those banned from traveling because of their involvement in or support for regimes which are themselves the targets of broader sanctions efforts by the international community acting through the United Nations or bilaterally.

This chapter identifies ten cases of multilaterally imposed international travel bans, although there certainly may be other cases that are not covered here. The UN first imposed an international travel ban in 1968. In their 2002 study of sanctions, Cortright and Lopez identify eight cases in which travel bans have been used in the recent period, from 1990 to 2001. Since that time, the European Union and the United States have also imposed a travel ban on officials from Robert Mugabe's regime in Zimbabwe. Travel bans are rarely used on their own, but rather are one part of a sanctions episode against a target regime or entity. Each of the cases considered here involved the denial of travel of designated individuals or officials from states or non-state entities that were the subjects of broader sanctions by the international community.

Scholars who study sanctions, such as George Lopez and David Cortright, have made general claims about travel bans that relate to the reasons for their use, such as: travel sanctions have become a favored tool of Security Council policy because their scope is much more limited than that of general trade sanctions, with their attendant humanitarian costs.[1] Thus travel bans are perceived to imply lower humanitarian costs than other types of sanctions, such as broad trade embargoes.

These authors also note some interesting patterns in the use of travel bans. Travel bans of the sort considered here (which they call "visa bans") are often used in conjunction with another form of targeted sanction, the freezing of assets of certain regimes, individuals and non-state entities. This was true in the cases of sanctions against UNITA in Angola and in measures imposed by the European Union against certain Serbian government leaders.[2]

The research on this topic has been limited and suffers from two general shortcomings. First, it has not moved beyond the level of the international system or the UN, but rather has focused on the international organization itself, addressing such questions as why it uses this form of sanctions and how it fails to enforce these measures. Second, the research has only considered the general effects of such sanctions, rather than whether and how these measures affect individuals. Given that the causal chain in such sanctions seems intended to run from individuals who are the targets, to their governments or leaders, and ultimately result in changes in behavior, it is necessary to examine the effects of travel bans on individuals and how this does or does not contribute to policy or behavioral changes sought by the international community.

In spite of the fact that such sanctions have been used by the international community at least ten times since 1968, with a dramatic increase in their use in the 1990s, very little is known about whether and how they impact the individuals and groups of people who are subject to them. The aim of this study is to answer questions about their political, psychological, economic and humanitarian impact and to attempt to tease out their effects, if any, on changing the behavior of those who are subject to them. Since such measures are enacted as part of a set of measures aimed at changing the behavior of target regimes, non-state entities and individuals, it is this latter point that requires careful study.

This study analyzes travel bans as a form of targeted sanction. It addresses questions that have been raised about the efficacy of sanctions by examining travel sanctions in general, as well as the specific case of travel bans against individuals in Liberia imposed by Resolution 1343 in 2001. Through interviews with UN and other officials familiar with the sanctions, as well as with individuals who have been subject to travel bans, we aim to better understand the impact of travel sanctions on individuals, and how this relates to their efficacy. We also consider the many challenges that have arisen with respect to the use of this particular type of targeted sanction.

History and development of travel bans

An international travel ban was first used by the UN in 1968, when the Security Council imposed its first ever set of sanctions under Chapter VII of the UN Charter in response to a threat to international peace and security. It enacted a range of import and export sanctions against Southern Rhodesia to pressure the white supremacist regime of Ian Smith to move towards independence for the country that would be based on full democracy and equality for all citizens. In Resolution 253 of May 1968, the Security Council expanded an existing set of mainly commodity sanctions against the country to include a ban on flights to or from Rhodesia and a travel ban on people traveling with Rhodesian passports.[3]

A travel ban was not used by the UN again until after the end of the Cold War, during the so-called "Sanctions Decade" of the 1990s. In 1992, the Security Council imposed a travel ban as part of a broader set of sanctions against Libya in response to its support for international terrorism and its refusal to extradite leading suspects in the Lockerbie bombing for trial. Resolution 748 of March 1992 banned travel of designated officials from Libya. This travel ban was linked to a set of "diplomatic sanctions" in a section of the resolution that called for the reduction of diplomatic staff from Libya. The ban on travel was not only linked to this provision but also to the category of people from Libya who themselves had been accused by a state or states of involvement in terrorist activity. As compared to later travel bans, this one was somewhat vague about who it would apply to and what states would be expected to do with respect to preventing the entry of these people into their territories. The wording of the resolution imposing the travel ban is as follows:

> all states shall take all appropriate steps to deny entry to or expel Libyan nationals who have been denied entry to or expelled from other States because of their involvement in terrorist activities. [4]

Two years later, in May 1994, the UN banned the travel of designated members of the military junta in Haiti and their families and supporters in Resolution 917. In this case, the Security Council was somewhat more clear about the nature and extent of this travel ban. It identified three major classes of people who were to be banned from travel and it placed the responsibility for maintaining a list of who was to be banned on the Sanctions Committee for Haiti. States and regional organizations were required to identify the individuals who would be included on the travel ban list. In its operative paragraph, the resolution called on states to prevent the entry into their territories of the following groups of people:

(a) Of all officers of the Haitian military, including the police, and their immediate families;
(b) Of the major participants in the coup d'état of 1991 and in the illegal governments since the coup d'état, and their immediate families;
(c) Of those employed by or acting on behalf of the Haitian military, and their immediate families, unless their entry has been approved, for purposes consistent with the present resolution and other relevant resolutions, by the Committee established by resolution 841 (1993), and requests the Committee to maintain an updated list, based on information provided by States and regional organizations, of the persons falling within this paragraph.[5]

The pace of the Council's use of travel bans and other targeted sanctions increased considerably beginning in the mid-1990s. In the final six months of 1997, three new travel bans were initiated or threatened, including in Angola, Sierra Leone and Iraq. Several new developments and practices with respect to the use of travel bans occurred in this period, including their use against a non-state entity in the case of Angola, and their use as a targeted threat aimed at gaining rapid compliance with specific areas of a resolution that was being flouted in the case of Iraq with respect to its standoff with UN weapons inspectors.

In August 1997, the Council imposed a travel ban on the main rebel movement that was fighting government forces in Angola. The UN sought to increase pressure on the National Union for the Total Independence of Angola (UNITA) by adding a flight and travel ban to an existing arms embargo and a ban on sales of petroleum products. The new measures banned unauthorized flights into UNITA territory and international travel by senior officials of UNITA and of adult members of their immediate families. The ban included an exemption for travel by those officials necessary for the full functioning of the Government of Unity and National Reconciliation, the National Assembly, or the Joint Commission.[6] In addition, the travel ban directed states to cancel visas for members of UNITA. It instructed states to take all necessary measures:

> To suspend or cancel all travel documents, visas or residence permits issued to senior UNITA officials and adult members of their immediate families[7]

Further, the sanctions required states to close all offices of UNITA in their territories, a measure closely related to the travel and visa bans. To implement the travel ban and related measures, the Security Council Committee for Angola was charged with drawing up guidelines for the implementation of these sanctions, and designating officials and adult members of their immediate families whose entry or transit was to be prevented and whose travel documents, visas or residence permits were to be suspended or cancelled.

In October 1997, the UN imposed sanctions against Sierra Leone which included travel restrictions on members of the military junta and their families.[8] We will return to this case in more detail when considering the effects of travel bans on specific individuals.

The third travel ban of 1997 was to be directed at Iraq. However, in this case the UN merely *threatened* to impose targeted travel sanctions on certain Iraqi officials in response to Iraq's interference in and obstruction of UN-mandated weapons inspections. These sanctions, contained in Resolution 1137 of November 1997, would have denied travel by designated Iraqi officials who were identified as being involved in obstructing the work of UN weapons inspectors there. However, these sanctions were never actually imposed.

These threatened sanctions are of interest because they were an attempt by the UN to follow up on an earlier threat related to Iraq's actions with regard to weapons inspections. The inspections themselves were the most important part of the much broader set of comprehensive UN sanctions imposed on Iraq in 1991 following its invasion of Kuwait, and modified following the conclusion of the UN coalition's war against Iraq that ousted it from Kuwait. The threatened travel ban was actually meant to compel Iraq to fulfill its obligations under earlier, and more important, Security Council resolutions dealing with the end of the conflict and Iraq's ongoing responsibilities for ridding itself of weapons of mass destruction.

There are three interesting features of this travel ban that are worth noting, despite the later decision of the Council not to impose it. First, it was an attempt to use targeted sanctions (i.e. a travel ban) as a means of enforcing compliance with the terms of a broader UN sanctions effort.[9] Second, the ban itself was threatened in a series of highly detailed Security Council resolutions censuring Iraq for specific objectionable behavior related to its obstruction of the weapons inspectors. The repeated threat to impose these sanctions, coupled with harsh language condemning Iraq's behavior, clearly seemed designed to operate as a threat rather than through the actual deprivations that might be suffered by Iraqi officials if such a travel ban were imposed. Third, the sanctions as laid out in the resolutions were highly specific and were intended to last only as long as it took for the Executive Chairman of the Special Commission to report to the Council that Iraq had begun allowing the Special Commission inspection teams full access to any and all areas, facilities, equipment, records and means of transportation that they wished to inspect in accordance with the mandate of the Special Commission. Taken together, these features, as well as the later abandonment of the travel ban against Iraqi officials, mark some significant departures from earlier practice in the design of travel bans as a form of targeted sanction. Notably, these threatened sanctions were designed to be far more targeted to specific individuals and of a short duration to quickly change very specific behaviors.

Since 1999, the US and the EU have imposed their own travel bans against regimes and their supporters in instances where the UN has not acted, or where a conflict or crisis does not seem to pose a threat to international peace and security thereby triggering UN Security Council involvement. The first non-UN travel ban of this period was a joint effort of the European Union and the United States. Although not part of any UN sanctions regime, the measure may have been designed to reinforce an existing flight ban against the former Yugoslavia, which the UN had imposed in May of 1992. In 1999, the EU and the US imposed their own travel ban on designated officials in relation to the Kosovo crisis.

The second of these cases is the ongoing travel ban against Robert Mugabe's regime in Zimbabwe. Initially imposed by the EU, the United States later added its own travel ban. The two actors have taken slightly different approaches to their travel bans. The EU has listed those senior Zimbabwean officials who are forbidden to travel to Europe, while the US has only indicated that senior officials from Zimbabwe are not permitted to travel to the US, without issuing a list of specific names or government positions. In an interview with a US diplomat working on Zimbabwe at the State Department, this policy was described as one that had not been planned to work in this way. Rather, the US government found that by not issuing a list of names or positions specifying who was banned from travel, the existence of a somewhat vague travel ban had prompted considerable fear amongst those in government in Zimbabwe. As a result, applications for visas to travel to the United States had markedly decreased due to the belief by many in the country that they would be banned from traveling under the measure.[10]

In 1999, the UN also banned flights by the Afghan government, the Taliban. A year later, the UN sought to strengthen these measures by denying overflight, landing, or takeoff privileges to any aircraft if it had taken off from or intended to land in territory controlled by the Taliban. In the same Resolution, 1333, the Council banned travel of all deputy ministers and higher ranking officials of the Taliban. The ban included exemptions for travel that was humanitarian, religious or undertaken for the purposes of peace negotiations.

The other case of a travel ban that will be studied in detail in this chapter is Liberia. Briefly, the travel ban was imposed in March 2001 and prohibited the travel of designated officials associated with armed rebel groups, their family members and their representatives.

The travel bans in Liberia and Sierra Leone will be considered in greater detail in the following section and in the case studies that follow.

Background on conflicts and sanctions in cases studied: Liberia and Sierra Leone

The conflicts in several West African countries in the Mano River Union area, including Sierra Leone, Liberia and Guinea, are interrelated in important ways. The international community's response to these crises – particularly its sanctions, peacekeeping, and conflict resolution efforts – eventually began to reflect the interrelated nature of these conflicts. Armed conflict in Sierra Leone began with a coup that ousted the Kabbah government in May 1997. The coup was backed by one of the main rebel groups, known as the Revolutionary United Front (RUF). The main fighting occurred between the RUF and the elected government of Ahmed Tejan Kabbah. A peace agreement was negotiated between the parties in 1999, but the RUF violated the ceasefire in that agreement and continued to fight. In 2000, another cease-fire was reached, but fighting from the country had already spread to both Guinea and Liberia. The international community feared the violence would spread to Côte d'Ivoire, Guinea-Bissau and Senegal.

In 1997, in its multifaceted effort to end the conflict in Sierra Leone, the United Nations, at the request of the Economic Community of West African States (ECOWAS), imposed targeted sanctions on both the RUF and on the Liberian government of Charles Taylor for its involvement in supporting and financing the group. Resolution 1132 (1997) imposed travel restrictions on members of the military junta and their families. A year later, the Council passed another resolution that maintained the travel ban on former members of the junta and the RUF, while lifting the sanctions on the now restored Kabbah government in Sierra Leone.

The RUF continued to engage in violence in Sierra Leone, which prompted the Council to impose an embargo on all diamonds originating in Sierra Leone due to their role in funding the conflict. At the same time, the UN created a Panel of Experts to report on violations of the sanctions regime. The panel made a number of recommendations for enhancing enforcement of the sanctions. One of these recommendations was to impose separate, but related, sanctions against the government of Liberia to pressure it to curtail its support for the RUF. The Council acted on this recommendation on 7 March 2001, when it passed Resolution 1343 (2001) which demanded that the government of Liberia end its support for the RUF in Sierra Leone and imposed a range of targeted sanctions against Charles Taylor's government. The resolution banned the import of rough diamonds from Liberia and imposed a travel ban on senior government officials and the armed forces.

The operative paragraphs regarding the ban on the import of diamonds from Liberia and the travel ban were contained in paragraphs 6 and 7 of the resolution. Paragraph 7 is as follows:

> Decides also that all States shall take the necessary measure to prevent the entry into or transit through their territories of senior members of the Government of Liberia and its armed forces and their spouses and any other individuals providing financial and military support to armed rebel groups in countries neighboring Liberia, in particular the RUF in Sierra Leone, as designated by the Committee established by paragraph 14 below.[11]

These sanctions were delayed from coming into force for two months after the passage of the resolution to allow the Government of Liberia to comply with the demands of the Security Council. It did not, and the sanctions came into force on 7 May 2001.

The Liberia travel ban

Exemptions

The resolution also specified certain exemptions from the travel ban. The first was that no state should be obliged to refuse entry into its territory of its own nationals. The second was to allow representatives of the government of Liberia to travel abroad for meetings at international and regional organizations and to participate in peace conferences. Specifically the exemptions stated:

> nothing in this paragraph shall impede the transit of representatives of the Government of Liberia to United Nations headquarters to conduct United Nations business or the participation of the Government of Liberia in the official meetings of the Mano River Union, ECOWAS and the Organization of African Unity.[12]

List of people included on the travel ban

In June 2001, the Security Council Sanctions Committee on Liberia issued a list of persons affected by Resolution 1343, as called for in that resolution. The list included some 138 individuals, including both Cabinet-level and other senior officials in the Liberian government, spouses and ex-spouses, international arms dealers, and foreign advisors to the regime. The list has been updated several times since.[13]

Implementation and enforcement of the Liberia travel ban

There are severe limitations to the current mechanisms for implementation and enforcement of travel bans. These are reviewed and analyzed extensively in two international reports, the Report of the Bonn–Berlin Process *Design and Implementation of Arms Embargoes and Travel and Aviation Related Sanctions* (2001) and the Report of the Stockholm Process *Making Targeted Sanctions Effective. Guidelines for the Implementation of UN Policy Options* (2003).[14]

The impact of the Liberian travel ban on individuals, which is discussed in the next section's case studies, must also be understood in the context of widespread evasion of the ban and a pattern of extremely lax enforcement by states in the region and beyond. For example, in February 2002, a delegation of RUF officials was reported by Sierra Leone's Attorney General, Solomon Berewa, to have dodged the police in Freetown to travel to Nigeria in spite of the travel ban. The same report noted that an official list of those people barred by the UN travel ban from traveling outside Sierra Leone had been sent to immigration authorities and the police at Lungi International Airport.[15]

The continuation of the Liberia sanctions after the conflict in Sierra Leone had ended has also been suggested as a factor contributing to a lack of focus in their application and to increasing violations of them, given that many observers believed it was misguided to continue them after Sierra Leone had transitioned to peace. In April 2003, the Panel of Experts issued a report commenting on the Liberia sanctions. In the section entitled "Observations and Recommendations," the panel noted that although violence continued in the region and that many states and regional actors were involved, strictly speaking, the original rationale for maintaining the travel ban on Liberian officials "is no longer applicable."[16] This finding was clearly made in light of the fact that the conflict in Sierra Leone itself – which provided the original rationale for sanctions against Liberia – was finished. It must be remembered that the demands that the Security Council made of Liberia in Resolution 1343 (2001) were intended to lead to the consolidation of the peace process in Sierra Leone and to further progress in the peace process in the Mano River Union area. That resolution demanded that Liberia take three steps regarding the RUF, which included the following:

(a) Expel all RUF members from Liberia and prohibit all RUF activities on its territory.
(b) Cease all financial aid and military support to the RUF.
(c) Freeze funds or financial resources that either benefit the RUF or are controlled by the RUF.

Yet in spite of the fact that these demands appeared to have either been met by Liberia or simply overtaken by events on the ground in Sierra Leone, the Security Council has repeatedly voted to continue to apply the sanctions against Liberia.

In 2003, the panel charged with monitoring the sanctions against Liberia noted that it "continued to collect evidence of widespread non-compliance with the travel ban." These violations occurred in several different ways. At the level of the president himself, he repeatedly resorted to making unauthorized stops on flights he was on, such as in January 2003 when he directed the plane he was traveling on to stop in Libya. Taylor's spokesman described the stop as merely a "technical refueling stop," however press reports from Libya cited it as a major diplomatic meeting, with a large delegation of Libyan officials sent to meet him.

Violations of the travel bans also resulted from the failure of states in the region and beyond to ensure that their immigration and customs officials were aware of the travel bans and were enforcing them. For other Liberian officials, violating the travel ban was as simple as traveling through countries such as Ghana that failed to enforce the ban, or to travel under an assumed name, or to travel on passports they possessed due to their holding dual nationality.[17] These types of violations are not unique to the Liberia case, but are an inherent challenge to the successful implementation of any travel ban.

Impact of the Liberia travel ban: a mixed record

Some experts in the West Africa region believe that travel sanctions as currently used by the UN do create a stigma for those individuals who are on travel ban lists, and they also cite circumstances in which leaders and senior officials were prevented from traveling because of enforcement of the travel ban. However, they also cite many instances of evasion and violations of the travel bans as well, suggesting a mixed record. One UN official working on Liberia commented that sanctions and the travel ban in particular, as well as attacks on Liberian government forces by rebels there, together put pressure on Taylor's regime.

The same official also commented that members of the Liberian government of Charles Taylor were very uncomfortable with the travel ban list because it prevented them from attending meetings that were not convened under the auspices of the UN, ECOWAS, or the Mano River Union. In terms of the impact of the travel ban on the most senior ruling elites, such as then-President of Liberia Charles Taylor, the UN official mentioned that the President himself was prevented from attending a meeting in Paris concerning the situation in Côte d'Ivoire while under the travel ban. President Taylor reportedly sent a list to the UN of Liberian officials who would like to attend the meeting, and the UN then handpicked from that list who would be permitted to travel to France for the meeting.[18]

Unintended consequences

Interestingly, in the Liberia case, the travel ban appears to have had a unique and potentially positive unintended impact: it saved the Liberian government hundreds of thousands of dollars. Although no one knows for certain what the regime did with the roughly US$300,000 it is reported to have saved in travel expenses due to the sanctions, there is the possibility that developing countries under travel bans will not only reduce spending on travel but will use those funds to provide urgently needed services or programs to their populations.

Case studies

The two individuals who were interviewed for the case studies in this chapter were both listed on the original UN Sanctions Committee travel ban list. They were Omrie Golley, whose name is included on the list with no identifying information such as position, title, nationality, date of birth or passport number and Francis M. Carbah, the former Minister of Transport of the government of Liberia and former economic advisor to President Taylor.[19]

In terms of the methods used in this research, I sought out individuals who had been listed on any recent UN travel ban list who were willing to discuss the experience generally and how it affected them specifically. This presented a number of logistical challenges, as many individuals on the travel bans list are now deceased or remain in conflict zones to which it was not possible for me to travel; many others were difficult to locate. However, two individuals did agree to extensive interviews. Interviews were conducted by telephone and in person, and took the form of a semi-structured, open-ended questionnaire. This research was conducted from May to July 2003. The case studies were also informed by media sources discussing the travel bans, and the individuals involved, as well as by other interviews with UN and Member State officials with knowledge of the region and of the travel bans.

The main questions I was trying to answer in these interviews were: How do international travel bans affect the individuals who are subject to them? Do they actually affect the travel patterns of individuals? What are their psychological impacts on these individuals? How do people respond when they are put on travel ban lists? Do they pressure members of governments, rebel movements and other people and groups to change the behavior that is deemed objectionable to the international community? Do the travel bans have any unintended consequences? Do these measures have humanitarian consequences for the individuals subject to them or for their families?

In terms of general themes addressed in the case studies, there are four that are particularly important: political context, psychological impact, behavioral change and unintended/humanitarian consequences. Each of these themes is explored in the case studies and their relative importance and the findings about each theme are treated in the conclusions.

One of the most important themes is the political context in which individuals were included on the travel ban list. It appears that the level of "politicization" of the individual – meaning how closely involved in regional or domestic politics of his country each was – is partly responsible for important differences in how each person reacted to being on the travel ban list, as well as to how the list affected their behavior.

The theme of psychological impacts of travel bans on individuals is closely related to the broader theme of behavioral change. The objective here is to learn how the subjects of the ban felt about being included on the ban and to attempt to determine whether or not this resulted in changes in their behavior in line with the expectations and demands of the international community (e.g. a reduction in their support for the targeted regime). This is an extremely difficult area about which to draw firm conclusions, but the individuals interviewed for this study were forthcoming about their feelings in relation to the travel ban, and tentative conclusions can be made about the extent to which these feelings contributed to behavioral change or the lack of it.

The last main area addressed in the case studies is related to the possible humanitarian impact of travel bans, and any "unintended consequences" of these measures for individuals and their families. In the years since targeted sanctions have been used by the United Nations as an alternative to the comprehensive economic and trade sanctions imposed earlier, as against Iraq in 1990, some debate has arisen regarding the humanitarian impact of all sanctions, including targeted measures. Although they are clearly designed to avoid depriving civilians and innocent people in target countries of food, medicine and economic opportunities, some analysts argue that even targeted sanctions can have dangerous humanitarian impacts.[20] Questions were therefore asked regarding the humanitarian impact of targeted travel bans. Do they have financial or other consequences for individuals of which the international community may be unaware? Did they affect the families of those who were listed, or pose any danger to these individuals?

Case 1: Omrie Golley and the Liberia travel ban

Omrie Golley was described in a February 2002 article in *The Independent* (London) as "a London lawyer of Sierra Leonean parentage with a practice in Kensington High Street."[21] He also worked as the legal representative and spokesperson of the RUF from December 1998 to January 1999. In June 2001, his name was included on the first travel ban list issued by the Liberia Sanctions Committee. He was involved in negotiations for the peace process in Sierra Leone, although he claims that at the time that he was engaged in this work, he had already resigned from the RUF and only participated in the peace process at the request of the UN Special Representative to Sierra Leone and ECOWAS. BBC reports confirm that Mr Golley was Chairman of the Revolutionary United Front Political and Peace Council, a group that was formed in early 2001 to negotiate with the Sierra Leone government and to help implement the disarmament process in areas under rebel control.[22] Other media reports also indicate that "diplomats, human rights workers and government figures in Freetown agree that Mr. Golley has played a crucial role in the recent peace process, which has seen the RUF disarm and transform itself into a political party." The Attorney General of Sierra Leone Solomon Berewa stated, "He has been very positive in the achievement of peace."[23] Golley announced his resignation and the dissolution of the Political and Peace Council on 21 March 2002.

Mr Golley's reaction to being placed on the travel ban list was affected by several factors. First, he claims only to have discovered that he was on the list as a result of "surfing the Internet," where he looked at the Liberia travel ban list on the UN's website. He describes discovering that he was on the list as both "extremely funny and almost tragic for me." Second, he was upset by the lack of an explanation or clear delineation of criteria for including individuals on the list. Third, he was frustrated by the lack of a formal mechanism by which he could appeal his inclusion on the list.

In terms of the political impact of being placed on the list, Golley felt it was illogical for him to be included on that list given his work in encouraging the peace process in Sierra Leone. He also believed that he was put on the list for political and personal reasons. A report in the *The Independent* noted that the UN Security Council imposed the travel ban on Mr Golley and 25 other RUF figures for alleged involvement in smuggling "blood diamonds" from Sierra Leone into Liberia.[24] Mr Golley has denied these charges, both in media interviews and in personal interviews with this author. Others have told him privately that it was the government of the UK that put him on the list, and he felt that this was likely a result of the British government's displeasure with him because of his opposition to the British approach to resolving the crisis in Sierra Leone with military force.

Psychological impact

Golley described the situation regarding his being on the travel ban list as distressing, embarrassing and personally "tragic." Part of his distress was linked to the publication of the travel ban list on the Internet, which was then published on the Sierra Leone web, as well as in newspapers in London and elsewhere. He felt that there is a stigma attached to being on the list and repeatedly referred to this in interviews with this author. In an article by *Concord Times*, he stated that "It is a matter of pride. If I had not been involved in the peace process, my name would not have been on the list."[25]

In interviews, Golley also described the fear he experienced when traveling. As he put it, "I was always embarrassed in queues when traveling, even with a waiver from the Security Council. I was afraid they would pass my passport in a computer, and they would decide to take me in a room somewhere and I would be chained."

The travel ban appears to have impacted Mr Golley's travel patterns only slightly. In July 2001, a little more than a month after the travel ban list was first announced, *Concord Times* reported that Mr Golley was leaving Sierra Leone because a UN travel ban waiver on which he was traveling expired. In this report, it was suggested that Mr Golley might never return to Sierra Leone unless the UN took his name off the travel ban list.[26] As it turned out, however, the travel ban did not have such drastic consequences for Mr Golley's travel patterns.

There appear to have been several other factors at play that mitigated the impact of the travel ban on Mr Golley. First, he felt that as a dual citizen of Britain and Sierra Leone, he was not as hampered by the travel ban as he would have been had he held citizenship from only one country. As he put it, he was "saved by a couple of clauses" in Security Council Resolution 1343, particularly the one in the section imposing the ban that reads, "nothing in this paragraph shall oblige a State to refuse entry into its territory to its own nationals."[27] Golley said that "the Sierra Leone government was not too bothered by letting me travel from Sierra Leone." He believes that he was allowed to enter and exit Sierra Leone in spite of the travel ban for two reasons. First, because "they appreciate my role in the peace process," and second, "because they know I'm not going to open my mouth to criticize the government."

Mr Golley was also permitted to travel under waivers granted by the Liberia Sanctions Committee. The resolution imposing the travel ban contains a humanitarian exemption, which states that the ban "shall not apply where the Committee established by paragraph 14 below [the Sanctions Committee for Liberia] determines that such travel is justified on the grounds of humanitarian need, including religious obligation, or where the Committee concludes that exemption would otherwise promote Liberian compliance with the demands of the Council, or assist in the peaceful resolution of the conflict in the subregion."[28] Because Mr Golley has a wife and son who live in Croatia, he applied several times to the Security Council for approval to travel there, which he describes as "a laborious process." This approval was granted and he was permitted to travel there, although it is uncertain on what grounds.

Unintended consequences and lasting impacts of travel ban

Although Golley's name was removed from the travel ban list on 9 July 2002, there continue to be some repercussions of having been on the list. The first of these is the uncertainty about unilateral travel restrictions that may remain in place in certain states. Golley believes that United States law continues to prohibit him from traveling to that country because the RUF was considered "a terrorist organization."

Under the USA-Patriot Act of 2001, the Secretary of State, in consultation with the Attorney General of the United States, is authorized to designate terrorist organizations for immigration purposes. This authority is known as the "Terrorist Exclusion List (TEL)" authority. A TEL designation allows the US government to exclude aliens associated with entities on the list from entering the United States.[29] Whether or not this is the case, Mr Golley claims that he is too scared to apply for a visa to travel to the US "I am afraid of repercussions, for example of getting a big stamp in my passport saying that I was refused entry to the US." As with the UN travel ban, Golley expresses frustration at not knowing if there is a process or how to inquire about having his name removed from an American travel ban list.

With respect to the financial impact of his being on the travel ban, Mr Golley estimates the cost at roughly US$1.5 million. He attributes the losses to lost revenues and legal fees that he had to forgo because of damage to his reputation from being listed on the UN travel ban. This alleged effect of the travel ban can not be independently confirmed, and is only an estimate of lost income due to the sanctions.

In Mr Golley's case, the ban appears to have affected him in ways that should be better understood by those analyzing sanctions and by those imposing them. He clearly believes there were psychological impacts of the ban on him in terms of stigma, shame and fear, and he cites significant monetary damages as well. In terms of behavioral or policy changes, he does not attribute any changes in his allegiances to the RUF or his political views and affiliations as resulting from the pressure he came under due to sanctions. Rather the ban seems to have been more of an inconvenience to Mr Golley, and one that he was able to tolerate fairly well.

Case 2: Francis M. Carbah and the Liberia travel ban

Francis M. Carbah is the former Minister of Transport in Liberia and former Chair of the Council of Economic Advisors. He was appointed to the Council of Economic Advisors by President Taylor in 1997 and eventually became the Chair.[30]

Mr Carbah speculated that his appointment as Minister of Transport was a political response by President Taylor to the type of economic reforms, particularly policy reforms in the area of privatization, that the Council was considering at the time, and that the appointment was deliberately made to reduce his involvement in economic policy matters.

Mr Carbah discovered that he was on the travel ban list because the decision of the UN Security Council on Liberia was made available to Liberia's Minister of Foreign Affairs, with whom Carbah served on a government committee. It was also published in a local newspaper. In general, Mr Carbah's reaction to being placed on the travel ban list should be understood in light of the following: he felt that he was not politically or personally close to the president, and that President Taylor may have disapproved of the types of policy recommendations and projects in which Mr Carbah was involved.

Psychological impact

When Carbah saw his name on the list, he felt that it was simply an effort by the UN to target the Liberian government as a whole and explained that he "saw it as a punishment of the government, and being part of the government I could not see myself as being exempted." He went on to say that:

perhaps they [the UN] were not in a position to determine exactly who was important and who wasn't. So they had to target the senior officials of the government. I didn't take it as a personal penalty for what I did. It was targeting the government for that. I think they tried to target other individuals who were not senior officials of the government, but who probably would need to be engaged in facilitating some of the illicit operations that were the target, including some private ministries people and some who were some lower ranking officials in government.

Mr Carbah recalled feeling confident that "if there were any attempts to separate good people and bad people, I'm very certain that I would not have been on the list. So, I didn't think it was anything that was targeting me. I would never consider it that way. So I never really bothered to investigate why things were the way they were."

Regarding the scope of who was and was not included on the travel ban list, Mr Carbah also felt that the inclusion of spouses of government officials on the travel ban list was a decision taken for the same reason.[31] He said, "I thought that this was the general extension of the purpose – you who serve in the government shall feel the impact of the action against the government. That's what I thought it was."

In his position as Minister of Transport, Mr Carbah had very little need to travel outside the country. He reports having traveled twice in this position: to a regional aviation conference in Conakry, Ghana, and on a study tour to Senegal to observe differences in regional transportation. This seems to have contributed to his relative lack of concern about being included on the list, given that it neither hampered his work nor personal travel schedule.

Behavior change: sanctions and Mr Carbah's resignation from President Taylor's Cabinet

The travel ban itself did not operate as intended by the international community with respect to Mr Carbah. It did not pressure him to reconsider his support for the Taylor regime or to cease traveling for the purposes of facilitating the objectionable actions of the Liberian government, which in this case was deemed by the UN to be its support for the RUF in Sierra Leone. However, Mr Carbah recounts that there were revelations that came to light about President Taylor as a result of investigations into the UN's targeted sanctions against Sierra Leone and Liberia that marked a "turning point" for him in deciding to resign from the Cabinet. These developments are described below.

During his tenure in the ministry, some controversial developments involving sanctions in the region and the actions of the Liberian government came to Mr Carbah's attention. Liberian aviation operators had long been suspected by international observers of exporting illicit materials into conflicts around the world. Liberia is a "flag of convenience" for both ships and airplanes, and it has a reputation for lax regulation and monitoring of maritime and air shipping into and out of the country.[32] Mr Carbah explained that Liberia had a number of small commercial air cargo service companies that were active in many countries. As Minister of Transport, Carbah wanted to address the complex issue of Liberia's troubled aviation registry and safety problems with aircraft registered there, as well as with Liberian aircraft operating abroad. In order to do so, he sought President Taylor's approval to travel to Brussels to meet with other transportation officials about safety problems related to Liberian aircraft that were based in Europe, but Taylor never responded to his request to attend the meeting so his travel plans were canceled. He also sought permission to attend an aviation meeting in Washington, DC but again did not receive a response from the president. Mr Carbah said he "knew that President Taylor did not want him to leave." To some extent, it appears that Mr Carbah may have been under a Liberian-imposed travel ban, at the direction of President Taylor.

Mr Carbah also felt that it was part of his duties as Minister of Transport to reorganize Liberia's aircraft registry in order to address concerns about safety and to improve monitoring and regulation of what was widely believed to be a dubious business that facilitated arms trafficking in the region. Mr Carbah said that in spite of his position in the Cabinet, he was unaware that the Liberian government had contracted with the accused arms dealer, Sanjivan Ruprah, to reorganize Liberia's aircraft registry. The Liberian government's contract with Ruprah had been signed by the minister who preceded him in office.

At roughly the same time, the Sierra Leone Panel of Experts investigating sanctions violations in the Sierra Leone sanctions regime issued a report that named Sanjivan Ruprah as an arms dealer with extensive involvement in the conflicts in the region.[33] After reading this report, Mr Carbah said that he decided that he could not reform the aviation registry in his country since that task had been assigned to Mr Ruprah, a known arms dealer.[34] As a result, he decided to simply close the controversial Liberian aircraft registry and conduct his own investigation into the system. After closing the registry, Mr Carbah said that small aircraft owners in Liberia were "banging on his door to be allowed to operate their aircraft." He cited the need to address their concerns as one of the reasons why he could not resign his position as Minister of Transport immediately, which he wanted to do as a result of his dismay over his government's involvement with Mr Ruprah and its support for the RUF.

Mr Carbah's decision to leave the Liberian government was clearly only partly attributable to the UN's sanctions efforts in the region. He also cites the lack of resources and the lack of systems to measure outcomes of government spending as one of his early frustrations with President Taylor's government. According to him, the "turning point" in his decision to resign from Cabinet came when he read the Panel of Experts report on the Sierra Leone sanctions and began to understand why there was so little money for programs in Liberia: in his view, it was all going to support the RUF. He also had a meeting with President Taylor during this period in which it became clear to him that government spending was going for things that the president did not want people to know about. Thus, there were a range of factors that led to his decision to resign from government and leave the country.

Resignation from the Cabinet and asylum in Canada

Although he did not often need to travel to perform his official duties as Minister of Transport in Liberia, Mr Carbah did eventually seek to travel one last time: in order to flee Liberia and claim asylum in Canada. It was not the travel ban that made it so difficult for him to leave the country, but rather a whole series of events that Mr Carbah described as interference from Mr Taylor to prevent his leaving.

The travel ban and the other targeted sanctions imposed on Liberia required Mr Carbah to be more strategic about how he would leave the country and resign his post. He had to press the Liberian government to allow him to travel to an ICAO Ministerial meeting in Montreal in September 2002. As he recounted the sequence of events, President Taylor approved his attendance at the meeting but delayed formalizing the approval until 5:30 p.m. on the Friday before the meeting was to begin the following Tuesday.

In December 2001, Mrs Carbah and the couple's two sons left the country. Their daughter left shortly after Christmas. On 1 October 2002 Mr Carbah left Liberia under the pretense of attending the ICAO meeting in Montreal, but with the intention that he would not return. In January 2003, he wrote and faxed a letter of resignation to the government of Liberia.[35]

Unintended consequences

Mr Carbah raised the issue of an unintended consequence or potential pitfalls of travel bans as a form of targeted sanction. Given the highly repressive and personally vindictive nature of President Taylor's regime in Liberia, he speculated that there may have been certain benefits to being included on the travel ban list, including the fact that anyone excluded from the list might be suspected of being disloyal to the regime or collaborating with the international community:

> I also thought that it brought a lot of blessings to me to have been included, otherwise I may have been taken for somebody who is in the government, and is not *part* of the government and probably accused of providing information that probably led to this kind of situation.

Three ministers in Liberia's Cabinet – the Minister of Health, the Minister of Education and the Minister of Agriculture – were excluded from the travel ban list issued by the UN. However, Mr Carbah speculated that this was done because of the nature of their portfolios and not for more individualistic, political reasons having to do with the nature of their ties to the Taylor regime. In other words, it did not appear to him that they were excluded from the list by the UN because they were deemed to be individuals who did not support President Taylor.

Regarding other unintended consequences (and possible humanitarian impacts of sanctions), Carbah believed that governments such as Taylor's regime in Liberia used sanctions as excuses for their continued bad behavior. As an example, he cited the fact that the Liberian government was eight months in arrears with respect to paying the salaries of civil servants in Liberia when he left the country. At the time that sanctions were imposed, they were four months in arrears. He believed that sanctions exacerbated the situation and provided an excuse for the government's nonpayment of civil servant's salaries.

Problems or challenges of travel bans

One of the problems Mr Carbah discussed with travel bans is related to the nature of the regime against which they were imposed. The research on sanctions also suggests that it is extremely difficult to use them effectively against authoritarian regimes, which tend to have tight control over potential opposition to their rule. Not surprisingly, in Liberia the travel ban and other sanctions did not appear to inspire any kind of concerted political opposition to President Taylor within Liberia because of the fact that when the sanctions were imposed, the civil war in Liberia was already underway and, according to Mr Carbah, "the government was set to accuse anyone as being part of the insurgents. I think that this was the reason why political parties, they didn't make this a major issue." He also explained that "the opposition parties had already been literally silenced by the vendetta that Mr Taylor engaged in against his former rivals during the conflict. As you know, he tried to kill many of them."

In discussing his general views on sanctions, rather than the specific impact of the travel ban on him, Mr Carbah stated that "Sanctions create hope, anxiety and fear." He believed that sanctions create hope for victims of regimes like Mr Taylor's because in imposing sanctions the UN sent a signal to people that it had decided to get involved in the situation there. He also expressed his belief that they create anxiety for those who do not know exactly what the impacts of sanctions will be, and that they create fear for those who are beneficiaries of the system.

Mr Carbah felt that sanctions failed to impact the government in Liberia, which was the true target, and that they correspondingly failed to improve the lives of the government's victims. He also cited his belief that travel bans in particular do not work, especially against the people they should affect. He attributed this to the power of the government to issue travel documents with false names, and the fact that without photo identification included in the travel ban lists, individuals on the list were able to travel under assumed names. He expressed his certainty that those who President Taylor wanted to be allowed to travel continued to do so despite the travel ban.

Conclusions

The two case studies considered here suggest sharp differences in the impact or potential impact of travel bans depending on the political context, and on the specific role of the individuals subject to them in the domestic and regional politics of the situation. Omrie Golley appears to have been more politically active and more politically oriented than Francis Carbah, and the travel ban affected him differently as a result. He felt that he was included on the list for political reasons rather than valid substantive ones, and he repeatedly sought to be removed from the list and questioned governments involved regarding why he was included. Being on the travel ban had the potential to greatly impact Mr Golley's travel, work and personal life since he was traveling frequently to the region and had a business as well as a family in a third country. However, the impact of the ban was limited by some of the exemptions included in the Security Council resolution, which permitted Mr Golley to travel with some regularity.

Regarding the psychological impact of the ban, Mr Golley reported far more negative feelings and suffering greater anxiety as a result of the ban. He also reported long-term impacts related to his ability to travel to the United States and the financial impact of the sanctions on him.

The case of Mr Carbah is quite different in that he felt he was not included on the ban because of an attempt to target him specifically. Rather his description of events reveals that he felt the ban was not intended to affect him personally and that, basically, it did not. The psychological impact of the ban on him was minimal to non-existent, given that he felt he was simply included on it because he was a Cabinet official in Taylor's regime. He appears not to have suffered any anxiety or personal losses as a result, in large part due to the fact that he describes himself as having been an increasingly reluctant participant in the Liberian government due to his mounting concern and frustration over its alleged role in supporting the RUF at the expense of the Liberian people and given its shady dealings with Sanjivan Ruprah, the arms dealer. Given that he was trying to leave the country and ultimately did so to seek asylum abroad, Mr Carbah appears to have been in a position where the travel ban was the least of worries; rather he had to contend with the difficulties of plotting his escape from a highly authoritarian regime, which presented far greater challenges to him personally.

It is interesting to note, however, the ways in which travel bans are part of broader sanctions efforts and the consequences that may result from synergies between different types of targeted sanctions and even from reports about sanctions. In terms of encouraging officials who are part of a target regime to withdraw their support for their governments, Mr Carbah's story suggests that the Panel of Experts report on Sierra Leone, and what it revealed publicly about the nature of the Taylor regime in Liberia, had a far greater impact in cementing his desire to quit the government and flee the country.

While it is impossible to generalize about travel sanctions on the basis of a limited set of case studies, they can be instructive in highlighting additional considerations for those studying and using travel bans in the policy world. These cases suggest the following:

- Travel bans are more likely to impact individuals who need to travel to carry out their work, and not all members of government or senior officials are in this position.
- Psychological impacts of travel bans vary widely and in part may depend on whether individuals feel "singled out" for inclusion on the ban, or whether they see themselves as natural targets based on their official positions or group affiliations.
- Individuals on travel ban lists may feel political pressure to limit or end their support for the target governments or entities, not only because of the travel ban but because of additional pressures or suspicions of them on the part of their superiors in target regimes.
- Individuals subject to travel bans uniformly report feeling a sense of injustice at the lack of transparency in the process by which they become listed and in the difficulty in appealing their inclusion on lists.[36]
- Travel bans have the potential to impose severe economic harm on individuals included on the lists whose professional reputation suffers from the stigma of being listed, even if lax enforcement or exemptions permit them to continue to travel. This is more likely to be the case if the individual is employed in the private sector or in another field where one's clientele expects or demands a good reputation (e.g. lawyer, accountant, business consultant, etc.).
- Even when individuals are removed from UN travel ban lists, they may not feel free to travel and may continue to be subject to unilateral or regional travel bans.

These findings should be added to more general conclusions about travel bans reached by other experts who have studied multiple sanctions episodes, as well as those who were deeply involved with the Liberia sanctions.

In conclusion, travel bans are best viewed as part of broader sanctions efforts, and more research should be done on how they do or do not support other forms of targeted sanctions to create meaningful impacts that translate into political change. Travel bans require careful consideration of local and regional political developments and much more stringent monitoring and enforcement. They have the potential to have very different impacts on individuals, but we can tentatively conclude that there is a stigma associated with them. The desired causal links between the stigma and practical inconveniences of being on a travel ban and the removal of support for objectionable governments sought by the UN when it imposes travel bans is also unclear, and more research is needed to learn more about these issues.

We do not have sufficient information yet to draw conclusions about the humanitarian impact of travel bans. Given that the UN includes specific exemptions to them to allow individuals to apply to the relevant UN sanctions committees for travel ban waivers to travel for a variety of purposes, the risk that an individual could not travel for a humanitarian purpose such as seeking medical treatment abroad or visiting family abroad is minimized. There is evidence of other potential humanitarian impacts that should be further explored, such as the risk to certain individuals working for authoritarian regimes of *not* being included on a travel ban list, due to suspicions on the part of leaders in those countries that these individuals are disloyal or are collaborating with the international community.

Notes

1 D. Cortright and G. A. Lopez, *Sanctions and the Search for Security* (Boulder, CO: Lynne Rienner, 2002), p. 133.
2 Cortright and Lopez, 2002, p. 136.
3 The travel ban included an exemption for exceptional humanitarian circumstances, which would become a *de facto* norm for the UN and others when using this type of sanction. S/RES/253 (1968), 29 May 1968, paras. 5, 6.
4 S/RES/917, Para. 6(c).
5 Para. 3 (a, b, c).
6 Para. 4a.
7 Para. 4b.
8 S/RES/1132.
9 S/RES/687 of 1991, which was the ceasefire resolution ending the war against Iraq and requiring it to disarm.
10 Personal interview with State Department official, January 2003.
11 S/RES/1343 (2001), 7 March 2001.
12 Ibid.
13 Names were added to the list on 31 October 2002; other names were deleted on several occasions and the list was updated on 19 December 2001, 11 March 2002, 9 July 2002, 4 September 2002, 31 October 2002 and 6 June 2003.
14 Reports available at http://www.smartsanctions.de and http://www.smartsanctions.se
15 Panafrican News Agency (PANA) Daily Newswire, 14 February 2002.
16 S/2003/498, para. 9.
17 S/2003/498, Report of the Expert Panel on Liberia Sanctions, 24 April 2003, paras. 165–169.
18 Interview with author.
19 The case studies are based on interviews with the author, and are published with the approval of the individuals concerned.
20 See discussion and analysis in the Report of the Stockholm Process on the Implementation of Targeted Sanctions (2003), available at http://www.smartsanctions.se.
21 D. Walsh and R. Verkaik, "British Lawyer Insists Brutal Reputation of Sierra Leone's Rebel Front is Unfair," *The Independent*, 9 February 2002, p. 15.
22 BBC Monitoring International Reports, "Sierra Leone: Revolutionary United Front Peace Council Dissolved," 21 March 2002.
23 Walsh and Verkaik, 9 February 2002.
24 Walsh and Verkaik, 9 February 2002.
25 "Travel Ban: RUF Political and Peace Council Chairman Forced to Return to London," *Concord Times*, 26 July 2001. Accessed via Africa News.
26 Ibid.
27 S/RES/1343 (2001), para. 7a.
28 S/RES/1343 (2001), para. 7a.
29 The ramifications of this designation are that individuals providing support to or

associated with TEL-designated organizations may be found "inadmissible" to the US (i.e. such aliens may be prevented from entering the US). Although this particular travel ban appears to be unrelated to the UN travel ban in which Golley was included, and later removed, there may be links between the two. For instance, the US government may use names and designations from the UN list to inform its listing or decision-making regarding foreign individuals who are prohibited from traveling to the US under the TEL list.

30 The Council of Economic Advisors was not a legislated body in Liberia but rather a body created by President Taylor to advise him on economic matters. As such, it was not a body that was reserved for those who were politically close to President Taylor. Mr Carbah was not a member of the president's political party.

31 Although Mr Carbah's spouse was not listed, the spouses of other Cabinet members were. President Taylor's wives and ex-wives were included on the travel ban list.

32 S/2000/1195 (2000) Report of the Panel of Experts for Sierra Leone.

33 S/2000/1195 (2000) Report of the Panel of Experts for Sierra Leone.

34 Mr Carbah also explained that he contacted the International Civil Aircraft Organization (ICAO) to ask for assistance in reorganizing civil aviation in Liberia, and ICAO agreed to help Liberia reform its registry.

35 Mr Carbah sought to be removed from the travel ban after traveling to Montreal and seeking asylum in Canada. He believed that having resigned from Taylor's government, he should be removed from the list.

36 This point is drawn from interviews with UN officials involved in sanctions, as well as from interviews with individuals on the travel ban lists.

15

POSITIVE SANCTIONS

On the potential of rewards and target differentiation

Peter Wallensteen

The utility of sanctions

In the span of international measures for peace and security, ranging from words to wars, sanctions have been placed in the middle. The range of actions that writers and observers often use emphasizes negative actions. The focus is on measures that introduce more and more 'pain' on the recipient side. This is how actors are expected to change behavior. It also has the advantage to the sender of the actions to observe that 'their' pain is worse than 'ours'. Punishment, however limited and ineffective, is handed down on a target that has acted wrongfully. Early in sanctions studies it was noticed that sanctions serves to solve internal political dilemmas on the sender side,[1] no matter what their effects may have been on the recipient. Increasing uses of such sanctions during the 1990s have, however, resulted in a debate over repeated failures to bring about desired changes. The targeted countries and their regimes have too often appeared skillful in avoiding the negative effects that sanctions produce. The anger of the population has been directed against the external sanctions, rather than against the internal functions of the government. Regimes have even been able to turn the 'pain' to their advantage: humanitarian hardship has been due to the sanctions, rather than the government itself. The targeting of sanctions is the most reasonable way, so far developed, to avoid this development. In this book that has been a continuous theme.

However, the span of action may not only contain negative, disruptive and deprival measures. There is also in the vocabulary of sociology and psychology the reverse: positive sanctions. These are measures that promise or actually deliver valuables to the targeted actor, in the hope of seeing changed behavior or as a reward for actually having changed behavior. That is a strategy that receives less attention. It is not unknown, however, as much international development assistance is of this nature. Donors view their action as ways of stimulating the development of countries on terms that meet the interest of both sides, donors as well as recipients. There is a tendency, particularly among major powers, to distribute aid according to strategic and foreign policy considerations. In doing so, they are rewarding preferred behavior. For many years, Israel and Egypt have been major recipients of US assistance, so as to cement the peace between the two countries as well as secure their cooperation in other situations.

During the Cold War this was also a pattern among other donors, notably the Soviet Union (with allied regimes in Afghanistan, Cuba, Ethiopia and Vietnam being major targets) as well as the United States.[2] In this way, assistance could strengthen already existing ties, but in addition, indicate a price for non-compliance: aid could be reduced. Flows of assistance could be turned into negative sanctions. Support systems served as a web in which actors became entangled. Linkages amounting to a political dependency on external forces and outside control could develop.

In the form of 'conditionality' this was turned into a formalized and explicit policy by the international donor community. An example is the World Bank: in order to get loans countries have had to commit themselves to carrying out certain changes within a prescribed period of time. The countries had an incentive to make changes, but that would also give the donor influence over 'domestic' policies. The conditionality may be tied, for instance, to the introduction of new legislation on land reform, women's rights, democratization, and market liberalization. The use of conditionality for the latter purposes, in conjunction with 'structural adjustment' of national economics, have given it a bad name in parts of the world and among non-governmental organizations.

Furthermore, the record of actually achieving changes has not been striking.[3] As it may result in the one-sided opening up of economies for international penetration it means a long-term strengthening of global inequalities, it has been argued. It could correctly be pointed out that carrying out similar measures for the agricultural and textile markets of rich countries may be more effective in stimulating investment and reducing inequality between North and South. The creation of such general incentives has not been a priority by major trading partners, notably the USA and the EU. Such incentives have been used, however, for more specific concerns (e.g. political support in critical situations) or to achieve specific concessions. In other words, the use of incentives and positive sanctions is not uncommon; it is only in the field of peace and security that it has been less attended to.

This neglect can be further demonstrated by the fact that the UN Charter alludes to sanctions in the negative form. Thus, in the writings of international law, 'sanctions' are almost entirely understood as negative instruments, a form of disruption of goods and services that are of value to the recipient side. However, the Charter could not be read to exclude positive measures.[4] Instruments that could be of use, notably development assistance, are normally not treated in the security context. For instance, it is not part of the agenda of the UN Security Council, but belongs to the domain of other institutions in the UN system (ECOSOC, UNDP, World Bank, IMF, etc.). So far, there have been no exclusively positive sanctions decided on by the Council. There are examples of a mixed approach where conditions are specified for ending negative sanctions and initiating support to post-war reconstruction. This was seen in the international diplomacy at the ending of the war on the Taliban regime in Afghanistan in 2001.

However, the focus on negative actions may also stem from the fact that the UN system in general and the Security Council in particular are called into action when situations have already become difficult and severe. It is a common hypothesis that positive sanctions are more useful in earlier stages of conflict, and that later periods are more suitable for negative actions. That would imply that in the studies of conflict prevention, for instance, the utility of positive sanctions could be an important concern. However, some researchers dispute this and would give a larger role for positive actions.[5] Such arguments were also important during the Cold War when positive actions were seen as ways to reduce tensions and develop détente.[6] However, there are few systematic studies on this particular point, and particularly not on the conditions after the end of the Cold War. It might sometimes be implied or made part of typology, for instance as 'non-coercive measures'.[7] In the Eliasson ladder of conflict prevention, actions to positively stimulate parties belong to the first steps in the early phases of conflict.[8] Also, much work on positive sanctions has concerned interstate relations, thus pointing to the need to explore also intrastate conflict situations, which, after all, have taken a larger share of attention on the international agenda since 1989.

This means that there is an important field to explore and this chapter is devoted to a discussion on the utility of positive measures: under which conditions are they likely to be important and how do they function, compared to negative sanctions. In this way, their potential role in international peacebuilding can be elucidated.

Positive sanctions: what are they?

Early in the sanction study the focus on negative measures was observed. There was a need to explore the potential of the logical opposite, positive sanctions.[9] It has also been observed in the study of many negotiation situations between a sanctions sender and its targets that the lifting of sanctions can serve as an incentive for achieving compliance.[10]

This, then, has been regarded as an inbuilt reward in sanctions. By imposing negative sanctions the sender is at the same time suggesting that there is a possible positive outcome: 'if you only comply we will then restore what we have just taken away.' It may well be true that this is a way that a sanctions episode works and that the lifting of the sanctions is an incentive for actors to comply in the end. It has been reported, for instance, in the case of sanctions on Yugoslavia that the hope of having them removed was a major reason for Serbian President Milosevic to cooperate with the negotiations and treaties of Dayton in 1995.[11]

This is, however, not what we could include as positive sanctions. It is simply the continuation of negative measures, and the gradual easing of them still means the relationship is at the negative end of the spectrum of measures. Moving back to level zero, the *status quo ante*, is not adding something to the parties and their interaction. It is analytically important to make a clear distinction between these forms. This, of course, does not preclude the use of both in a political situation, but they are different and may have a different impact.[12] It makes it also possible to compare these measures to one another, as they are independently defined.

It could also be argued that the existence of a particular relation (exchanges of goods, services, cultural visits, diplomatic links, etc.) is a type of positive sanctions in itself and serves to legitimize a particular regime or its behavior. Some may see that as a reason for reducing relations, so as to make clear there is no positive legitimization going on. In order to separate sanctions measures from such continuous operations, the use of sanctions has to be a deliberately undertaken action with a clear and explicit motive. This makes clear that the issue of dependence is a separate matter and belongs to the study of international structures, rather than specific actions.

A problem is, of course, how to determine level zero or '*ex ante*': if the relations have been frozen for many years and then are gradually improved, should *ex ante* then refer to the moment when some warming takes place (i.e. the measures become a positive move) or to the 'normal' situation that prevailed before the freezing took place (in this case it is a relaxation of negative sanctions). This time element has not been adequately addressed in the literature so far.

In the writings on positive sanctions, there is sometimes a preference for posing the terms 'sanctions' and 'incentives' against one another, arguing that this divide between negative and positive action becomes clearer. However, as we have just considered, although moving towards zero could well be an incentive for the targeted side, it is still part of the negative spectrum of actions. Thus, the term 'positive sanctions' is more straightforward, although less elegant. It will be used here, although the literature on 'incentives' is highly pertinent.[13]

Thus, we define positive sanctions as measures which add something (a resource, recognition, a membership, etc.) to a targeted actor beyond what exists at point zero. A negative sanction is a measure which deprives the targeted actor of something (resources, recognition, membership status, etc.) of what it had at point zero. This means that promises and threats are part of the situation, but also that they do not include the actual act of adding or depriving the actor of anything until after point zero.

To this formulation needs to be added that an act of sanctions is tied to an expectation that the targeted actor is to comply with explicit demands. These may have been set up earlier or clarified at the time of the imposition of the sanctions measures. This is customary for negative sanctions and the same logic applies to positive sanctions. As exemplified above, entangling another actor through a web of linkages is common in history. It can be seen as integration, while in a more asymmetric condition it may become dominance or imperialism. However, the sanctions actions we are interested in have specific demands attached to them. The purpose is to make an actor change behavior in a particular critical situation. The change, furthermore, is expected to be of lasting quality. Whether it will result in dependence or not, is, however, not necessarily of the immediate concern to the parties. Thus, positive sanctions are those measures which add something (a resource, recognition, a membership, etc.) to a targeted actor beyond what exists at point zero in expectation of compliance to a specified demand (or demands). The formulation 'in expectation of' leaves out the requirement of an explicit conditionality, without entirely excluding it, however.

With this in mind, different typologies of positive sanctions can be surmised. Table 15.1 is a starting point. Baldwin's original list on positive sanctions included mostly economic measures, which is to be expected in a work dealing with economic statecraft. Cortright adds a number of measures, drawing from a broader spectrum but also including the dimensions that have been added to international security following the end of the Cold War. Table 15.1 thus is illustrative, but not exhaustive.

A key consideration is also that positive measures are coupled to policy changes. In his case study, Lawson gives an example: the Gulf countries offered a large-scale economic compensation scheme in exchange for a ceasefire agreement in the Iran–Iraq War. The proposal was rejected by Iran, but constituted a deliberate effort to use a substantial positive sanction instrument. It not only adds to the categories

Table 15.1 Positive sanctions: possible measures

In the field of economics
Extending most-favored nation status
Making tariff reductions
Making direct purchases
Extending subsidies to exports or imports
Providing export or import licenses
Guaranteeing investments
Encouraging capital imports or exports
Extending favorable taxation
Granting access to advanced technology
Giving debt relief
Increasing assistance in development, reconstruction, compensation
Granting access to international economic organizations

In the field of international security (narrowly defined)
Extending diplomatic and political support
Initiating military cooperation
Giving security assurances
Pushing for membership in military organizations (alliance)

In the field of security (broadly defined)
Extending environmental and social cooperation
Intensifying cultural exchanges
Giving support for citizen diplomacy
Opening for membership in democratic international organizations

---

Source: Building on work by D. Cortright, 'Positive Inducements in International Statecraft', speech to the June 2000 Fraser Forum; and Baldwin, 1985. The verb forms are meant to convey the notion that the sanction measures move positively from level zero.

of positive sanctions, but also shows that such ideas receive serious consideration in high-level politics.

Table 15.1 does not include promises, as we do not see them as a separate category. Nor is the lifting of negative sanctions included as a positive measure as explained above. Furthermore, a number of the measures deal with matters that are potential, in the sense that the government will not be the one that actually makes use of a particular incentive. Opening up the society for more trade will benefit the economy as a whole, if there are actors (businesses, entrepreneurs) able to actually exploit the opportunities. It provides little for the targeted actor, the state itself, however. If the offer is coupled to a policy change in the targeted country, the cost of that may not easily be offset by increased opportunities for the business sector to trade with the sender. For the targeted government, it may in fact mean less control or even less revenue, for instance if the demand is a tax reform or a costly scheme of land redistribution. This suggests that measures which include subsidies, debt relief and, perhaps, membership, will be those most attractive to target governments. It adds to their resources and to their standing domestically. Such measures can help ease budget deficits. They may also include a transfer of resources that the cabinet members themselves can benefit from.

The measures of Table 15.1 are also conceived in an interstate relationship. For instance, States that are admitted into an organization or have their tax revenue affected, etc. However, the international security agenda has changed, and consequently we need to develop a different typology. The headings in Table 15.1 can be of some help. This is also in line with much recent UN sanctions experience. It has concerned matters of removing undemocratic governments (Haiti), ending of wars (Angola, Yugoslavia, Sierra Leone, Liberia, Eritrea–Ethiopia) and fighting terrorism (Libya, Sudan, Afghanistan, Al-Qaida). Only a few of these are traditional interstate situations. Applying them in intra-state situations may lead to problems. For instance, offers of military cooperation, security guarantees or diplomatic support may mean propping up a particular actor in an internal dispute. This means that the sanctions and the senders are taking a position in an internal conflict. There may also be moral complications. For instance, to actually remove a government with the help of positive sanctions may mean paying a leading figure for leaving the country. There is at least one reported experience of this from Haiti in the 1980s. Personally attractive arrangements were proposed to Mr Savimbi, leader of the rebel group UNITA in Angola, in the middle of the 1990s. If agreed, it might have ended a war and spared a country of years of death and destruction. At the same time, it may have put Mr Savimbi out of reach of national law. Such actions do not add to the reputation of positive sanctions, although they may be effective. They are carried out in the shades of truth and publicity. They become particularly illegitimate if they are coupled to amnesty for crimes in civil wars or in suppression of human rights.

This means that positive sanctions have to meet the same standards as other measures. They have to be effective; they also have to be able to withstand the scrutiny of the public and of international conventions.

Having specified the measures that are central to the debate, let us proceed to see how positive sanctions work, according to the studies that exist and then develop a new typology of positive sanctions that could be more applicable to present conditions of international peace and security

Positive sanctions: how do they work?

The field of positive sanctions is still in an early stage of development. Published work builds on examples and crude typologies. There are few systematic studies where a number of cases are compared in the search for regular patterns. The theoretical underpinnings are drawn from a diverse set of sources. For instance, Crumm[14] points out that in the field of economics there has been more consideration given to the impact of positive sanctions.

Crumm studied 40 cases of Soviet uses of incentives towards India in the 30-year period from 1953 to 1983. Twenty-two of the cases are defined as 'at least moderate success'. This is more successful than would be expected. The incentives consisted of the provision of scarce goods (delivered and/or sold on special terms), for instance in the field of advanced military technology. The author observes that when the Soviet Union tried to change India's behavior in areas where India had a strongly held different view, the success rate was lower.[15] Crumm finds that the incentives worked particularly well when they were consonant with the norms on which the relations were built. They cemented the connection, but when the Soviet Union raised demands that were incompatible with these norms, which included a strict adherence to non-interference, relations became strained. Furthermore, the author finds a declining utility in the incentives, and argues that they may be more effective if they are used sporadically. Thus, oil deliveries at certain intervals was a tool that strengthened the relationship. Also, India's needs of spare parts for earlier military deliveries were important throughout the period, whereas other goods may have lost their value in this regard. The author also observes that incentives helping to break an existing monopoly by providing an alternative to the targeted state (in this case, Soviet assistance to sectors strongly monopolized on the world market by Western countries) are attractive. In this regard, the offer of military assistance and technology made the Soviet alternative useful to India's policy makers, as the West blocked access to similar goods and services.

In this way, Crumm is able to indicate some areas in which the use of positive, economic sanctions may succeed in changing behavior. Also limits are clarified. A typical constraint is the fundamentality of the demand. As would be expected with any policy tool, it is more difficult to change strongly held beliefs than matters which are seen as more instrumental or expedient. Furthermore, the operation of the world market is important. In cases of negative sanctions, it is the ability to evade sanctions through the world market that constitutes a problem. In the case of positive sanctions, the ability to avoid some of the blockages of that market made India more willing to maintain and develop its relations with the Soviet

Union. The way the two types of sanctions function may not be that different, in other words.

This comparison can be pursued further. Newnham is one of the first to systematically compare different types of measures, be they negative or positive sanctions. In an analysis of 32 cases of negative and positive sanctions sent from Germany towards Russia/Soviet Union and Poland from around 1850 to 1990, Newnham finds that there were 8 negative sanctions – all unsuccessful – and 24 positive sanctions, of which 22 were regarded as successful. Success is estimated from the point of view of the initiator. Many of the incentives concerned economic matters, something Germany with its strong economy clearly could deliver to the others. The cases involve, for instance, the historical deal that led to the reunification of Germany in 1990: this was agreed to by the Soviet Union in return for a large economic scheme including housing in Russia for returning soldiers. This agreement certainly was a major turning-point, shaping Europe in ways which often only are seen to be possible through pressures, wars and conquests. It requires close scrutiny, of course, to search for alternative explanations to understand the way in which generalizations can be drawn from this case. As Newnham has a long perspective and can see repetitions of successful uses of positive sanctions, this work is an important addition to the literature.

At the same time, the author notes that on issues which concerned border revisions, positive incentives did not make either Poland or Russia consider real changes.[16] These are definitely fundamental issues to these two countries (as they would be to any state), and in this case it was the tangible outcomes of the Second World War. The inclusion of East Germany into the Federal Republic probably was less challenging to Poland and Russia, given the conditions of the deal, than actually changing the map. Of course, to the East German leadership, the prospect of merging into West Germany may have been less attractive. For them it was a fundamental loss, but their position was entirely eroded by the popular will expressed with the opening of the Berlin Wall. These are important contextual factors to bring to an understanding of the strength and the limits of positive sanctions.

Newnham makes a further, important observation, namely that positive sanctions serve to develop a constituency in the target country. Certain groups were likely to benefit from the implementation of positive measures and they were favorably disposed to making necessary concessions in return for economic support. Newnham points to the surprisingly positive view of the conservative Soviet military establishment to the agreement. This is a factor that relates to the effect of rewards: some will be attracted, others will not. This means that the recipient will be divided on how to deal with the situation. This is an important contrast to negative sanctions, which often serve to strengthen the regime internally, as observed already in 1967 by Galtung and repeated since then for other situations.

Newnham's work points to the need for sanctions strategies that may consist of both negative and positive sanctions, or as some prefer to call it: sticks and carrots. Dorussen and Mo[17] have used leading sources on economic sanctions and studied the period from 1914 to 1997. They observe that the combination of positive and negative sanctions is common, actually in 35 percent of the comparable cases (note that the terms are defined independently as mentioned in the first section of this chapter). They also find that negative measures are more common than positive ones. Positive sanctions are more effective if there is a low level of interdependence between the sender and the target, whereas negative sanctions achieve the goals of the sender if there is a higher level of interdependence. For intermediate levels the combination of both types of measures are the most effective. The authors conclude that the two types of sanctions should be seen in combination and also be studied together, rather than separately, as has so far been the case.

This means that there are reasons to contemplate ways in which different sanctions can be combined. It remains to consider how they will work if this is translated into the intra-state conflict situations that have dominated the agenda of the post-Cold War period. Also, we should relate this to the idea of targeting sanctions, in line with the theme of the present volume, rather than considering the entire country as the one to impose sanctions on. In the sanctions studies reviewed, this has not been an important element in the data effort, but there are clues pointing to the significance of this.

Towards a positive sanctions strategy

In this overview, we have seen that there are experiences of positive sanctions and that they are achieving changes in government policies. In fact, this may be more of a standard approach than is normally envisaged. For instance, in June 2003 US Secretary of State Colin Powell commented on the upcoming elections in Cambodia, saying that the US would resume aid to the country if it were the case that the elections were run fairly. This was regarded by a leading opponent of the government as 'a strong message'. It suggested a relaxation in the US negative sanctions policy. Whether it also could be regarded as a positive sanctions strategy depends on whether we regard the pre-1997 level as the '*ex ante*' to refer to, or if it would be the post-election 2003 position. Either way, it was probably intended as an incentive for improved behavior.

However, the idea of positive sanctions can also be used in finding ways out of international negative sanctions. To some it may serve to confuse the picture. For instance, speaking on Zimbabwe, Dr Siphamandla Zondi of the Africa Institute of South Africa in August 2003, said that the Southern African Development Community (SADC) should link up with the international community to reward Zimbabwe with positive sanctions for every positive step taken. Such sanctions could, for instance, include convening a donors' conference or lifting the sanctions imposed by the United States and the United Kingdom.[18] The suggestion is one of a tit-for-tat approach: for everything positive by the target, there is another positive step by the sender. It would serve to change the dynamics of a situation that could threaten to deteriorate. However, it may also illustrate that it can be difficult for a committed international community (in this case the USA, EU and the Commonwealth) to change from one type of action to another.

These are typical examples in the contemporary world. Although stemming from different parts of the world, both the cases mentioned deal with internal political affairs, matters of elections, democratization and the ambition of incumbent elites to maintain control. It is for such situations that sanctions need to be relevant, not only for the interstate relations.

This suggests that we need to move one step further in the discussion on positive sanctions. As is the case with negative sanctions, they can be targeted. Most of the positive measures in Table 15.1 are drawn from a traditional way of conceiving sanctions: they are largely measures that are thought to affect an entire country or its economy. Even if this were to succeed, the effects of such sanctions could be of limited interest to governments that are more concerned about their own (private) situation. As long as they can maintain control, they will also have sufficient reasons to resist, particularly if the senders' demands include their leaving office. The gains accruing to targets from tariff reductions may be indirect at best, although of benefit to others in the society. They are not the immediate beneficiaries of such positive sanctions. Furthermore, drawing from the conclusions on how positive sanctions work, we note that positive sanctions may affect different parts of the society differently. Some will be more willing to change policy in order to retrieve the gains from the resources offered. The targeting of the positive sanctions, thus, becomes highly interesting and needs further elaboration.

In most cases of the 1990s, making the government change its course of action has been the demand. It would mean that other targets than the governments should be considered for positive sanctions. This includes ways to improve the conditions for the opposition. In cases where the issue of contention is one of human rights violations, repressive practices, fear of civil war, actual pursuit of civil war, or intervention in the 'internal affairs' of other countries, this is a logical target for positive actions. In such cases, the idea would be to stimulate pressure on a particular government to bring about a change in government policy (or in the composition of the cabinet) from domestic actors. This could include actions by political parties, independent trade unions, professional organizations, religious communities, environmental organizations or others in the vast array of actors in the non-governmental community. If a change is to enhance democratization rather than replacing one repressive regime with another, this becomes particularly important. This is alluded to in Table 15.1, which includes the idea of supporting citizen diplomacy. It needs to be developed further, however, by elaborating on measures that are targeted specifically at either the government or the non-governmental organizations. Table 15.2 suggests such measures for conflicts inside states.

Table 15.2 points to the significance of targeting positive sanctions. The measures are likely to be different if they are aimed at the government, the opposing community or at both sides. An important lesson from the sanctions debate of the last decade is that only targeted sanctions are likely to be internationally acceptable. It remains to be shown that they are more effective than the undifferentiated, comprehensive type of sanctions that were typical of the Cold War era, however.

Table 15.2 Targeted positive sanctions in internal conflicts

Targeting government ('regime')
Offering international organization membership
Extending external assistance for policy change
Making high-level visits after policy change

Targeting non-governmental community ('opposition')
Internationalizing the issue
Extending external support for organization activity
Receiving opposition representatives officially

Targeting 'both' sides
Hosting international conferences
Providing constitutional advice
Extending electoral assistance
Organizing transitional peacekeeping activities
Extending economic support (trade, investment, aid)
Developing compensation schemes

Furthermore, sanctions now have to build on a clear understanding of the type of conflict that the senders enter. In intra-state conflicts this means a government facing an organized opposition. Measures can target either of these sides, but there are also some that could be deliberately targeted at both. Table 15.2 includes some examples but is by no means exhaustive.

The UN sanctions history has included cases where some differentiation has been made. For instance, only the government in Rwanda is allowed to import weapons to the country, i.e. armed opposition is barred from further arming itself. It has been more common that negative sanctions has targeted opposition groups such as RUF (in Sierra Leone) or UNITA (in Angola). Here, it is argued that the targeting could be for democratic opposition, but with positive measures.

Is is also possible to develop a sanctions strategy that consists of both positive and negative sanctions. The Stockholm Report gives examples of possible targeted negative sanctions.[19] They are targeted on individuals and organizations that maintain the regime in place. If these measures are instituted at the same time as targeted positive sanctions – the recipients being other than the government (the civil forces opposing the government) – there will be additional reasons for a government to reconsider its policies. This becomes a more differentiated sanction approach to intra-state conflicts. It has some support from the studies presented, but has not really be brought to an empirical test in particular situations. The two mentioned above, Cambodia and Zimbabwe, could be objects of study. The lessons drawn from the targeting of negative sanctions are probably applicable, for instance that support from the region in which the targeted country is located may be crucial for the message to be convincingly communicated to targeted leaders as well as opposition.

The use of positive sanctions should be on the agenda for researchers as well as for policy makers. It remains to be explored and the appropriate international agent for such actions also needs to be considered. Some of these measures may be difficult for the Security Council to consider. They may be more appropriate in a regional context or for the donor community. It is also not always clear that an active opposition would like to have such outside support; it may serve to undermine its position domestically. This has to be part of the studies and the pre-assessments that are necessary before any international action is contemplated.

Notes

1 F. Hoffmann, 'The Functions of Economic Sanctions: A Comparative Analysis', *Journal of Peace Research*, 4 (1967), pp. 140–160.
2 For instance, where food aid was such a tool, see R. L. Paarlberg, 'Using Food Power: Opportunities, Appearances and Damage Control', in M. Nincic and P. Wallensteen (eds) *Dilemmas of Economic Coercion: Sanctions in World Politics* (New York: Praeger, 1983), pp. 131–154.
3 P. Collier, 'The Failure of Conditionality', in C. Gwin (ed.) *Perspectives on Aid and Development*, Overseas Development Council Series (Baltimore: Johns Hopkins University Press, 1997), pp. 51–77.
4 Art. 41 of the Charter says that Security Council action 'may include' negative sanctions, suggesting other possibilities. The exemplification refers only to negative measures, however, as the sentence continues 'complete or partial interruption of economic relations and of rail, sea, air, postal, telegraphic, radio and other means of communication, and the severance of diplomatic relations'.
5 R. E. Newnham, 'More Flies with Honey: Positive Economic Linkage in German *Ostpolitik* from Bismarck to Kohl', *International Studies Quarterly* 44 (2000), pp. 73–96.
6 C. E. Osgood, *An Alternative to War or Surrender* (Urbana, IL: Illini Books, 1962) and L. Kriesberg, *Constructive Conflicts. From Escalation to Resolution* (Oxford: Rowman & Littlefield, 1998, 2002).
7 M. Lund, *Preventing Violent Conflicts: A Strategy for Preventive Diplomacy* (Washington, DC: USIP Press, 1996).
8 P. Wallensteen and F. Möller, *Conflict Prevention*, Uppsala Peace Research Papers No. 7, 2003.
9 J. Galtung (1967, 1983), 'On the Effects of International Economic Sanctions: With Examples from the Case of Rhodesia', reproduced in Nincic and Wallensteen, 1983, pp. 17–60.
10 D. A. Baldwin, *Economic Statecraft* (Princeton, NJ: Princeton University Press, 1985).
11 R. Holbrooke, *To End A War*, Revised edition, (New York: The Modern Library, 1999), pp. 252, 259, which discusses the role of heating oil and gas for Belgrade during the negotiations.
12 F. H. Lawson, 'Using Positive Sanctions to End International Conflicts: Iran and the Arab Gulf Countries', *Journal of Peace Research* 20, 4 (1983), pp. 311–328. Newnham, 2000. H. Dorussen and Y. Mo, 'Opposites Attract? The Use of Sanctions and Incentives in International Politics', Paper presented at Uppsala University, Department of Peace and Conflict Research, February 2003.
13 For additional arguments in favor of the term 'positive sanctions' see Newnham 2000, pp. 74–96. D. Cortright and G. A. Lopez (eds) *Economic Sanctions: Panacea or Peacebuilding in a Post-Cold War Era?* (Boulder, CO: Westview Press, 1995), add to the vocabulary by introducing the concept of 'positive incentives'.

14 E. M. Crumm, 'The Value of Economic Incentives in International Relations', *Journal of Peace Research* 32 (1995), pp. 313–330.
15 Crumm, 1995, pp. 318–319.
16 Newnham, 2000, pp. 90–94.
17 Dorussen and Mo, 2003.
18 Zim needs time frame, 14/08/2003 16:06, News 24.com.
19 P. Wallensteen, C. Staibano and M. Eriksson, *Making Targeted Sanctions Effective: Guidelines for the Implementation of UN Policy Options*, Department of Peace and Conflict Research, Uppsala University (Stockholm: Elanders Gotab, 2003).

SELECTED BIBLIOGRAPHY*

Mikael Eriksson

Stand alone publications, reports or papers by publishers or institutions

International sanctions in general

Ahmed, Samina and Cortright, David. *South Asia at the Nuclear Crossroads, U.S. Policy Options Toward South Asian Nuclear Proliferation: The Role of Sanctions and Incentives.* Managing of the Atom Project at Harvard University, the Fourth Freedom Forum, and the Joan B. Krock Institute for International Peace Studies (Notre Dame: University of Notre Dame, 2001).

Amini, Gitty M. *A Larger Role for Positive Sanctions in Cases of Compellence?* Working Paper no. 12, Center for International Relations (California: University of California, 1997).

Bethlehem, Ronnie, Kane-Berman, John, and Mogoba, Stanley. *Sanctions and the Alternatives* (Johannesburg: South African Institute of Race Relations, 1988).

Brierly, James Leslie. *Sanctions* (London: Grotius Society, 1932).

Brzoska, Michael (ed.). *Design and Implementation of Arms Embargoes and Travel and Aviation Related Sanctions: Results of the 'Bonn–Berlin Process'.* German Foreign Office in cooperation with the United Nations Secretariat (Bonn: International Center for Conversion, 2001).

—— (ed.). *Smart Sanctions: The Next Step: The Debate on Arms Embargoes and Travel Sanctions within the 'Bonn–Berlin Process'.* BICC, Bonn International Center for Conversion, no. 6 (Baden-Baden: Nomos Verlagsgesellschaft, 2001).

Cortright, David and Lopez, George A., with Wagler, Julia, Conroy, Richard W. and Dashti-Gibson, Jaleh. *The Sanctions Decade: Assessing UN Strategies in the 1990s* (Boulder, CO: Lynne Rienner, 2000).

Dietrich, Christian. *Hard Currency: The Criminalized Diamond Economy of the Democratic Republic of the Congo and its Neighbours.* Occasional Paper no. 4, Partnership Africa Canada (Ottawa: Partnership Africa Canada, 2002).

Elliot, Kimberly Ann. *Towards a Framework for Multilateral Sanctions* (Atlanta: Carter Center, 1996).

Gazzini, Tarcisio. *Sanctions Against Air Terrorism: Legal Obligations of States.* Conflict

---

*For a more complete bibliography please see our website, <http://www.smartsanctions.se>

Studies, no. 290 (London: Research Institute for the Study of Conflict and Terrorism, 1996).
Michailovi'c, Kosta (ed.). *Sanctions: Causes, Legitimacy, Legality and Effects: Proceedings of the Round Table Held on 14 and 15 June 1994*. Presented to the Sixth Meeting of the Department of Social Sciences, held on 20 September 1994 (Belgrade: Serbian Academy of Sciences and Arts, 1995).
Minear, L., Cortright, D., Wagler, J., Lopez, G. A., and Weiss, Thomas G. *Toward more Humane and Effective Sanctions Management: Enhancing the Capacity of the United Nations System*. Occasional Paper no. 31, Thomas J. Watson Jr Institute for International Studies (Providence, RI: Brown University, 1998).
Mitchell, John V. *Companies in a World of Conflict: NGOs, Sanctions and Corporate Responsibility*. Papers from a workshop organized in Oslo by the Royal Institute of International Affairs (London: Royal Institute of International Affairs, 1998).
Mitrany, David. *The Problem of International Sanctions* (London: Oxford University Press, 1925).
Nossal, Kim Richard. *Rain Dancing: Sanctions in Canadian and Australian Foreign Policy* (Toronto: University of Toronto Press, 1994).
Osada, Masako. *Sanctions and Honorary Whites: Diplomatic Policies and Economic Realities in Relations between Japan and South Africa* (Westport, CT: Greenwood Press, 2001).
Ross, John F. L. *Neutrality and International Sanctions: Sweden, Switzerland and Collective Security* (New York: Praeger, 1989).
Sparrow, Gerald. *Sanctions* (London: British Commonwealth Union, 1969).
Stremlau, John. *Sharpening International Sanctions: Towards a Stronger Role for the United Nations*. A report to the Carnegie Commission on preventing deadly conflict (New York: Carnegie Corporation, 1996).
Tomasevski, Katarina. *Between Sanctions and Elections: Aid Donors and their Human Rights Performance* (London: Pinter, 1997).
Wallensteen, Peter (ed.). *International Sanctions: Theory and Practice. Proceedings of the Nordic Conference on Sanction Research, Sigtuna, Sweden, April 27–28, 1968*. Report 1 (Uppsala: Department of Peace and Conflict Research, 1969).
Wallensteen, Peter, Staibano, Carina and Eriksson, Mikael (eds). *Making Targeted Sanctions Effective: Guidelines for the Implementation of UN Policy Options*. (The Stockholm Report.) Department of Peace and Conflict Research, Uppsala University (Stockholm: Elanders Gotab, 2003).
Webster, Charles Kingsley. *Sanctions: The Use of Force in an International Organisation* (London: David Davies Memorial Institute of International Studies, 1956).

United Nations sanctions and League of Nations

Bhatia, Michael V. *War and Intervention: Issues for Contemporary Peace Operations* (Bloomfield, CT: Kumarian Press, 2003).
Boggs, George T. and Paxman, John M. (eds). *The United Nations: A Reassessment – Sanctions, Peacekeeping, and Humanitarian Assistance* (Charlottesville: Virginia Legal Studies, 1973).
Brüderlein, Claude. *Coping With the Humanitarian Impact of Sanctions: An OCHA Perspective* (New York: United Nations Office for the Coordination of Humanitarian Affairs, OCHA, 1998).

Burci, G. L. 'The Indirect Effects of United Nations Sanctions on Third States: the Role of the Article 50 of the Charter', in *African Year Book of International Law*, vol. 2 (Norwell, MA: Kluwer Academic, 1994).

Burciul, Barry A. *United Nations Sanctions: Policy Options for Canada* (Ottawa: Department of Foreign Affairs and International Trade, 1998).

Conlon, Paul. 'Mitigation of UN Sanctions', in *German Yearbook of International Law*, vol. 39. Universität Kiel, Institut fûr Internationales Recht (Berlin: Duncher & Humbolt, 1996).

—— *Sanctions Infrastructure and Activities of the United Nations: A Critical Assessment* (Carnegie Commission on Preventing Deadly Conflict, Task Force on Economic Sanctions, 1995).

Cooper, Andrew F., English, John, and Thakur, Ramesh C (eds). *Enhancing Global Governance: Towards a New Diplomacy?* (Tokyo: United Nations University Press, 2002).

Cortright, David and Lopez, George A. *Sanctions and the Search for Security: Challenges to UN Action* (Boulder, CO: Lynne Rienner, 2002).

Doxey, Margaret P. *United Nations Sanctions: Current Policy Issues*. Center for Foreign Policy Studies (Halifax: Dalhousie University, 1999).

—— *International Sanctions in Contemporary Perspective*, second edition (New York: St Martin's Press, 1996).

van Genugten, Willem J. M. and Groot, Gerard A. de (eds). *United Nations Sanctions: Effectiveness and Effects, Especially in the Field of Human Rights* (Antwerp: Intersentia Law, 1999).

Haass, Richard N. and O'Sullivan, Meghan L. (eds). *Honey and Vinegar: Incentives, Sanctions and Foreign Policy* (Washington, DC: Brookings Institution Press, 2000).

Hanlon, Joseph and Omond, Roger. *The Sanctions Handbook* (New York: Penguin Books, 1987).

Hoskins, Eric. *The Impact of Sanctions: A Study of UNICEF's Perspective* (New York: UNICEF Office of Emergency Programmes, 1998).

Knight, Andy W. *The United Nations and Arms Embargo Verification* (Lewiston, NY: Edwin Mellen Press, 1998).

Manning, Charles Anthony Woodward. *Sanctions Under the Covenant*. Montague Burton International Relations Lecture (Nottingham: University College, 1936).

Martin, Lisa L. and Laurenti, Jeffrey. *The United Nations and Economic Sanctions: Improving Regime Effectiveness*. Paper, UN–USA International Dialogue on the Enforcement of Security Council Resolutions (New York: United Nations Association of the United States of America, 1997).

O'Sullivan, Meghan L. *Shrewed Sanctions: Statecraft and State Sponsors of Terrorism* (Washington, DC: Brookings Institution Press, 2003).

Rowan-Robinson, H. *Sanctions Begone!: A Plea and a Plan for the Reform of the League* (London: Clowes, 1936).

Sarolea, Charles. *The Policy of Sanctions and the Failure of the League of Nations* (London: International Publishing, 1936).

International economic sanctions

Alerassool, Mahvash. *Freezing Assets: The USA and the Most Effective Economic Sanctions* (New York: St Martin's Press, 1993).

SELECTED BIBLIOGRAPHY

Askari, Hossein. *Economic Sanctions: Examining their Philosophy and Efficacy* (Westport, CT: Praeger, 2003).

Baruch, Bernard M. *The Making of the Reparation and Economic Sanctions of the Treaty* (New York: Harper & Brothers, 1920).

Bienen, Henry and Giplin, Robert. 'Evaluation of the Use of Economic Sanctions to Promote Foreign Policy Objectives'. Unpublished paper, Boeing Corp., 1979.

Biersteker, T. J., Eckert, S. E., Halegua, A., Reid, N. and Romaniuk, P. *Targeted Financial Sanctions: A Manual for Design and Implementation – Contributions from the Interlaken Process*, the Swiss Confederation in cooperation with the UN Secretariat and the Watson Institute for International Studies, Brown University (Providence, RI: Watson Institute, 2001).

Carter, Barry E. *International Economic Sanctions: Improving the Haphazard U.S. Legal Regime* (Cambridge: Cambridge University Press, 1988).

Chan, Steve and Cooper Drury, A. (eds). *Sanctions as Economic Statecraft: Theory and Practice* (New York: St Martin's Press, 2000).

Clark, E. (ed.). *Boycotts and Peace*. A Report by the Committee on Economic Sanctions (New York: Harper & Brothers, 1932).

Cortright, David and Lopez, George A. (eds). *Smart Sanctions: Targeting Economic Statecraft* (Lanham, MD: Rowman & Littlefield, 2002).

Cortright, David and Lopez, George A. (eds). *Economic Sanctions: Panacea or Peacebuilding in a Post-Cold War World?* (Boulder, CO: Westview Press, 1995).

Daoudi M. S, and Danjani M. S. *Economic Sanctions: Ideals and Experience* (London: Routledge & Kegan Paul, 1983).

Doxey, Margaret P. *Economic Sanctions and International Enforcement* (London: Macmillan for the Royal Institute of International Affairs, 1980).

—— *Economic Sanctions and International Enforcement* (London: Oxford University Press, 1971).

—— *Economic Sanctions: Past Lessons and the Case of Rhodesia*. Behind the Headlines Series, vol. 27, no. 2 (Toronto: Canadian Institute of International Affairs, 1968).

Drezner, Daniel W. *The Sanctions Paradox: Economic Statecraft and International Relations* (Cambridge: Cambridge University Press, 1999).

Evans, Clark (ed.) and Butler, Nicholas Murray (chair). *Boycotts and Peace: A Report by the Committee on Economic Sanctions* (London: Harper & Brothers, 1932).

Haass, Richard N. and O'Sullivan, Meghan L. (ed.). *Economic Sanctions and American Diplomacy* (New York: Council on Foreign Relations, 1998).

Hayes, John Philip. *Economic Effects of Sanctions on Southern Africa* (Aldershot: Trade Policy Research Centres, 1987).

Hufbauer, Gary Clyde, Schott, Jeffery J. and Elliott Kimberly, Ann. *Economic Sanctions Reconsidered. History and Current Policy*, second edn (Washington, DC: Institute for International Economics, 1990).

Hufbauer, Gary Clyde, Schott, Jeffrey J. and Kimberly, Ann Elliott. *Economic Sanctions Reconsidered: History and Current Policy*. Institute for International Economics (Washington DC: MIT Press, 1985).

Hufbauer, Gary Clyde, Schott, Jeffrey J. and Kimberly, Ann Elliott. *Economic Sanctions in Support of Foreign Policy Goals* (Washington, DC: Institute for International Economics, 1983).

Leyton-Brown, David (ed.). *The Utility of International Economic Sanctions* (New York: St Martin's Press, 1987).

SELECTED BIBLIOGRAPHY

Losman, Donald L. *International Economic Sanctions: The Cases of Cuba, Israel, and Rhodesia* (Albuquerque: University of New Mexico, 1979).
Malloy, Michael P. *Economic Sanctions and U.S. Trade* (Boston: Little: Brown, 1990).
Martin, Lisa L. and Laurenti, Jeffrey. *Coercive Cooperation: Explaining Multilateral Economic Sanctions* (Princeton: Princeton University Press, 1992).
Miyagawa, Makio. *Do Economic Sanctions Work?* (New York: St Martin's Press, 1992).
Moorsom, Richard. *The Scope for Sanctions: Economic Measures Against South Africa* (London: Catholic Institute for International Relations, 1986).
Nincic, Miroslav and Wallensteen, Peter. *Dilemmas of Economic Coercion: Sanctions in World Politics* (New York: Praeger, 1983).
Potter, Pitman Benjamin. *Sanctions and Security: An Analysis of the French and American Views* (Geneva: Geneva Research Center, 1932).
Preeg, Ernest H. *Doing Good or Feeling Good with Sanctions: Unilateral Economic Sanctions and the US National Interest* (Washington, DC: Center for Strategic and International Studies, 1999).
Reisersen, Tormod. *Macroeconomic Impacts of the Sanctions Against South Africa*. NUPI no. 548 (Oslo: Norwegian Institute of International Affairs, 1996).
Renwick, Robin. *Economic Sanctions* (Cambridge, MA: Harvard University Center for International Affairs, 1981).
Simons, Geoff. *Imposing Economic Sanctions: Legal Remedy or Genocidal Tool?* (London: Pluto, 1999).
Ströberg, Karin. *Prospects for Success in International Interventions: The Examples of Economic Sanctions and Peace Enforcement* (Stockholm: Defence Research Establishment (FOA), 2000).
Taubenfeld, H. J. *Economic Sanctions: An Appraisal and Case Study* (New York: Colombia University, 1958).
Wallensteen, Peter. *A Century of Economic Sanctions: A Field Revisited*. Uppsala Research Paper, no. 1 (Uppsala: Department of Peace and Conflict Research, 2000).
Weiss, Thomas G., Cortright, David, Lopez, George A. and Minear, Larry (eds). *Political Gain and Civilian Pain: Humanitarian Impacts of Economic Sanctions* (Lanham, MD: Rowman & Littlefield, 1997).

International law

Brown-John, C. Lloyd. *Multilateral Sanctions in International Law: A Comparative Analysis* (New York: Praeger, 1975).
Gowlland-Debbas, Vera (ed.). *United Nations Sanctions and International Law. The Graduate Institute of International Studies*, vol. 1 (The Hague: Kluwer Law International, 2001).
—— *Collective Responses to Illegal Acts in International Law: United Nations Action in the Question of Southern Rhodesia*. Legal Aspects of International Organization, no. 11 (Dordrecht: Nijhoff, 1990).
Highley, Albert E. *The First Sanctions Experiment: A Study of League Procedures* (Geneva: Geneva Studies, 1938).
Krasno, Jean, Hayes, Bradd C., and Daniel, Donald C. F. (eds). *Leveraging for Success in United Nations Peace Operations* (Westport, CT: Praeger, 2003).
Scott, James Brown. *The Spanish Conception of International Law and of Sanctions*. Carnegie Endowment for International Peace. Division of International Law. Pamphlet Series, 54 (Washington, DC, 1934).

INDEX

Abdallah, Ould 128
Afghanistan 4, 10, 11, 21, 31, 33, 35, 41, 45–6, 48, 68, 69, 149, 182, 183, 184, 230, 231, 234
African (Banjul) Charter on Human and Peoples Rights 189
aid 230
Ajello, Aldo 136, 141
Albania 152
Al-Qaida xv, 21, 22, 24, 31, 33, 41, 45–6, 48, 49, 68, 149, 156, 168, 182, 183, 184, 185, 190, 194, 201, 234
American Convention on Human Rights 189
American Court of Human Rights 186
Angola 10, 20, 31, 33, 41, 42–3, 48, 69, 151, 152, 182, 185, 209–10
Angola Monitoring Mechanism 147–8, 153, 154
antidumping 161
Arab League 155
Aristide, Jean-Bertrand 41–2, 155
arms trade 61, 178
arms embargo 11–12, 17, 18, 35, 48, 60–1, 155, 169–70, 185; against Afghanistan 45; against Angola 42; against Burma/Myanmar 111; against Ethiopia and Eritrea 46; against former Yugoslavia 11, 39, 40; against Liberia 46; against Rwanda 43; against Sierra Leone 44; against Somalia 40; against the Taliban 45; national end-use certificates and 75–90
ASEAN 112, 114
assessment, pre- 101–3
Aung San Suu Kyi 113
aviation sanctions xiv, 17, 18, 61
Azerbaijan 7

Balkans 10
Bagaza, Jean-Baptiste 132
Belarus 108, 109–11, 119
Belgium 128
Berewa, Solomon 214, 218
bin Laden, Usama 24, 45, 168, 183
blacklisting 182, 183–5, 194, 195, 198, 199
Blix, Hans 146
Bonn International Center for Conversion (BICC) 17
Bonn-Berlin Process 15, 17–18, 19, 22, 23, 24, 25, 63, 64
Bonn-Berlin Report 26, 27, 60
Bosnia and Herzegovina 10, 39, 151
Brahimi, Lakhdar 69
Brahimi Report 197
Bulgaria 39, 83, 152
Burma (Myanmar) 7, 108, 111–14, 119, 120, 121
Burundi 126–42
Bush, George W. 7
Buyoya, Pierre 127, 130, 132, 135, 136–7, 139, 140, 141–2

Cambodia 6, 33, 34, 47, 239
Cameron, Iain 23
Canada 71, 223
capacity building 18, 28, 49–51, 63, 172–3, 178–9
Carbah, Francis M. 216, 220–4, 225
Cedras, Raul 155
certificate of origin 44, 48, 154
Chihuri, Augustine 117
China 109, 113, 114
Chirac, Jacques 117, 136
Christopher, Warren 131
COMESA 118, 134, 135

247

commodity sanctions 48
Comprehensive Anti-Apartheid Act (US) 6–7
comprehensive sanctions 27–8
conditionality 230
Conference for Security and Cooperation in Europe (CSCE) 15
conflict diamonds 48, 150–1
conflict prevention 231
Convention on the Financing of International terrorism 183
corruption 12
Cortright, David 207
Counter-Terrorism Committee (CTC) 25–6, 28, 45, 48, 61, 63, 65, 68, 70–1, 73, 156, 167–79, 183
Counter-Terrorism Executive Directorate (CTED) 46, 156
Croatia 39, 151, 152
Cuba 4, 7, 13, 230
cultural embargoes 97
customs 149

delisting 19–23, 193, 198
democracy 111
Democratic Republic of Congo (DR Congo) 21, 31, 34, 35, 48, 49, 126, 134; Zaire 43, 129
diamond: bans 10, 12, 42, 44, 45, 46, 48, 61–2, 212–13; conflict 48, 150–1; rough 44, 46, 61–2, 213
Diamond High Council 150–1
diplomatic sanctions 42, 44
Dominican Republic 42
Djibouti 40
drugs 178
drug trafficking 3
dual-use goods 38, 61, 97, 146

East Timor 69
ECOMOG 44, 49, 50, 152
Economic Community of West African States (ECOWAS) 44, 152–3, 212, 215
Egypt 230
El Baradei, Mohamed 145
elections, Belarus 110
end-use certificate 60, 76–90
Estaing, Giscard d' 104
Ethiopia and Eritrea 21, 31, 34, 35, 40, 46, 48, 49, 170
EU Common Foreign and Security Policy (CFSP) 98, 103, 109

EU Framework Decision on Freezing of Assets 200
European Convention on Human Rights (ECHR) 189, 191–3, 196, 201
European Court of Human Rights (ECtHR) 186, 187, 188–9, 191, 192, 197, 201
European Court of Justice 97, 101, 103, 201
European Security and Defense Policy (ESDP) 95
European Union (EU) xiii, 39, 49, 151–2; arms embargoes 97; financial sanctions 97, 100; sanctions 4, 76, 95–105, 108–22; targeted sanctions 108–22; targeted trade sanctions 99; travel bans 97, 116
Expert Panel 27, 42, 44–6, 100; Angola 69; Liberia 26, 34, 47, 148–9, 150, 153, 214; Sierra Leone 148, 149, 212, 214, 225; Somalia 27, 40–1

Fall, Ibrahima 69
Financial Action Task Force (FATF) 61, 114
financial sanctions 15, 16, 17, 23, 26, 35, 57–8, 61, 168–9, 185, 186
Former Soviet Union (FSU) 4, 6
Fowler, Robert 42, 65, 69, 71, 72, 147, 154
France 72, 82

General Agreement for Tariffs and Trade (GATT) 146
Generalized Scheme of Tariff Preferences (GSP) 99
genocide 4, 43, 139–40
Germany 15, 82, 236
Ghana 215
Golley, Omrie 216, 217–20, 225
Greenstock, Sir Jeremy 71

Haiti 4, 10, 20, 31, 33, 41–2, 47, 48, 95, 154–5, 209
human rights 48, 104, 115–16, 134, 151, 181, 182, 185–8, 193
humanitarian: assessment 23, 72; consequences 3–4, 141, 216–17; costs 207; exception 36, 37, 153, 197; missions 38, 67, 70, 71–2
Hungary 152
Hussein, Saddam 7, 145

implementation 50, 57–64, 71–2

INDEX

incentive 230, 232, 235, 236
India 4, 7, 113, 114, 235
Indonesia 109, 114
inter-governmental organizations (IGOs) 144, 153
Interlaken Process 15, 16–17, 19, 22, 23, 24, 58, 61, 63, 64
Interlaken Report 23–4, 25, 26, 57
International Air Transport Association 148–9, 154
International Atomic Energy Agency (IAEA) 38, 145–6
International Civil Aviation Organization (ICAO) 148–9, 154
International Court of Justice (ICJ) 197
International Covenant on Civil and Political Rights (ICCPR) 186, 187
International Criminal Court (ICC) 198
International Criminal Tribunal for the former Yugoslavia (ICTF) 197–8
International Crisis Group 136, 141
International end use document (IED) 75, 79–90
International Labour Organization (ILO) 159
international law 181–201
International Maritime Organization (IMO) 149–50
International Monetary Fund (IMF) 230
international organizations (IOs) 144–56
Interpol 147–8; Weapons and Explosive Tracking System (IWETS) 148
Iran 4, 7, 13, 233
Iran–Libya Sanctions Act (ILSA) (USA) 7
Iraq xv, 20, 23, 31, 32, 35, 104, 145–6; invasion of Kuwait 10; sanctions against 4, 10, 15, 16, 27, 37–8, 48, 95, 145, 155; travel ban 209–11
Israel 230
Italy 82

Japan 114

Kabbah, Ahmed Tejan 44, 212
Kenya 43, 134, 136, 170
Khmer Rouge 6, 47
Kimberley Process 62
Korea 6
Kosovo 39, 40, 211
Kuruneri, Christopher 117
Kuwait 10, 35, 37, 210

League of Arab States 155
legal rights 181–201
Liberia xv, 10, 20, 23, 26, 31, 32, 34, 46–7, 48, 49, 63, 152–3, 182, 183, 184, 212–13; Panel of Experts 148–9, 150; travel ban 213–16
Liberia Committee 24–5
Libya 4, 7, 10, 11, 13, 20, 31, 32, 35, 41, 48, 145, 208–9, 234
lists, listing 19–23, 118, 121, 197
Lockerbie (Scotland) 41
Lopez, George 207
Lukashenko, President Alexander 109, 110, 111

Macedonia (FYROM) 39, 152
Malaysia 114, 116
Malinga, Joshua 116
Mangwana, Paul 117
military: expenditure 79–83; production 82; *see also* arms trade
Milosevic, Slobodan 40, 231
Minani, Jean 133, 137
Mkapa, Benjamin 135, 138
Model Law 17, 18, 58
money laundering 147, 178, 184; *see also* Financial Action Task Force (FATF)
Monitoring Mechanisms 26
Montenegro 100
Mubarak, Hosni 44
Mugabe, Robert 115, 116, 117–18, 119, 207, 211
multilateralism 11
Myanmar *see* Burma

Ndadaye, Melchior 127
Ndarubagiye, Leonce 132
Nigeria 83
Niyonsaba, Ambroise 137
non-governmental organizations (NGOs) 15, 37, 50, 126, 139, 141
non-state actors; entities 22
North Korea 6
North Atlantic Treaty Organization (NATO) 39, 100, 152
nuclear proliferation 3, 4, 145, 178; *see also* weapons of mass destruction
Nyangoma, Leonard 137, 138
Nyerere, Julius 127, 128, 129, 130, 135, 137, 138, 139, 140

Oil-for-Food Programme (OFFP) 38

249

INDEX

Organization for Security and Cooperation in Europe (OSCE) 38, 39, 49, 100, 110
Organization of African Unity (OAU) 126, 155
Organization of American States (OAS) 154–5, 186
Oxfam 82, 83, 84

Pakistan 4, 7, 68
peacekeeping missions 71
Pinheiro, Paulo Sergio 134, 135
Poland 236
positive sanctions 229–40
Powell, Colin 237
pre-assessment 101–3
private sector 59, 60
procedural and substantive rights 185
Project Hindsight 81
property rights 186, 188, 191–3, 196
proportionality 191–2
punishment 78, 229

Razali, Ismail, Tan Sri 112, 113
regional organizations 151–5
reward 230, 231
Romania 7, 152
rough diamonds 44, 46, 61–2, 213
Rukingama, Luc 133
Ruprah, Sanjivan 222
Russia 4, 236
Rwanda 10, 20, 31, 33, 35, 43, 48, 49, 50, 51, 126, 128, 139–40, 239

safeguards: legal 182–3, 188, 194, 195, 200, 201; national 198; procedural 188, 189–91, 194, 197, 200
Sanctions Assistance Missions (SAMs) 39, 47, 49, 50, 100, 151–2; SAM Communication Centre (SAMCOMM) 39, 152
Sanctions Committees 22, 37, 42, 50, 59, 60
Sanctions Coordinator 65–74
Sankoh, Foday 44
Savimbi, Jonas 10, 12, 42, 43, 44, 168, 234
SCOO 159–61, 162
secondary sanctions 46
September 11, 2001 xv, 7, 45, 68, 183
Serbia 100
Sierra Leone xv, 10, 21, 31, 33, 35, 44–5, 46, 48, 49, 50, 51, 148, 151, 152–3, 182, 183, 185, 190, 209, 212–13, 239
small arms 75

Smith, Ian 36, 208
Somalia 10, 20, 31, 32, 35, 40–1, 48, 49, 50, 51, 170
South Africa 6–7, 31, 32, 35, 36–7
Southern African Development Community (SADC) 115, 154, 169–70, 237
Southern Rhodesia 31, 32, 36, 51
Soviet Union: collapse of 3, 6; sender 235; target 4
Spain 82
sport bans 97
Stockholm Process 15, 18–19, 22, 24, 27, 58, 64, 75, 169–70, 172, 237
Stockholm Report 26, 101–2, 119, 172, 239
Sudan 7, 21, 31, 33, 35, 44, 48, 118, 170, 234
Sweden 15, 23, 82, 83, 188; Swedish 22
Switzerland 15, 16

Taliban xv, 4, 21, 22, 24, 31, 33, 41, 45–6, 48, 49, 68, 149, 168, 182, 183, 231
Tanzania 136, 140, 141, 170
targeted sanctions xiv, 11–12, 19, 57–64, 144–56, 168–72, 178–9
targeted trade sanctions 99, 104
Taylor, Charles 10, 12, 41, 47, 48, 150, 168, 212–13, 215, 220, 221, 222, 223, 224
technical assistance 175–8
terrorism 3, 25, 35, 45, 48, 70, 147, 173–5; see also Counter-Terrorism Committee (CTC)
Terrorist Exclusion List (TEL) authority 219
Thailand 113, 114
timber sanctions 10, 12, 47, 48, 62
trade sanctions 12, 47
transparency 24
transportation sanctions 11
travel bans 17, 18, 24–7, 97, 170–1, 185, 207–27, 173; against Belarus 110, 111; against bin Laden 45; against Burundi 129; against Liberia 46, 47; against Libya 11; against Sudan 44; against Zimbabwe 116; EU 97, 116; list 118; sanctions 11, 61, 186

Uganda 6, 141, 170
Ukraine 39
UNESCO 133–4, 135
UNITA (National Union for the Total

INDEX

Liberation of Angola) 10, 20, 22, 26, 31, 33, 35, 41, 42–3, 47, 48, 69, 147–8, 150, 152, 153, 154, 168, 182, 183, 190, 207, 210, 234, 239
United Kingdom 82, 237
United Nations (UN): Charter 37, 58, 75, 96, 167, 192–3, 208, 230; Department of Humanitarian Affairs 134; Department of Political Affairs (DPA) 73; High Commission for Refugees (UNHCR) 136; International Commission of Inquiry (UNICOI) 43, 48; Preventive Deployment Force (UNPREDEP) 39–40; Secretariat 17, 18, 51, 65, 73; Security Council (UNSC) 10, 15, 16, 27, 31, 32–4, 43, 44; Special Commission (UNSCOM) 37–8, 145
United States sanctions: effectiveness 7–9; frequency of 3, 4, ; role of Congress and domestic politics in 6–7
Universal Declaration on Human Rights (UDHR) 186
UNMOVIC 38, 145
Uppsala University 18

Vietnam 230
Visa/s: bans 11, 99, 111, 116, 207, 210; EU 97, 99
Volpe, Harold 141

Ward, Curtis 70
Wassenaar Arrangement 61, 76, 77–8, 85, 146–7
Watson Institute 17
weapons of mass destruction 83, 104, 145, 178, 210
Western European Union (WEU) 38, 39, 152
Working Groups on Sanctions 18–19
World Bank 131
World Customs Organization (WCO) 149
World Diamond Council 150–1
World Trade Organization (WTO) xiii, 98, 159–63, 181; Appellate Body 159; Dispute Settlement Body (DSB) 159, 162, 163; sanctions 161–2; Understanding on Rules and Procedures Governing the Settlement of Disputes (DSU) 159

Yugoslavia, Federal Republic of 10, 20, 31, 32, 38–40, 47, 48, 49, 50, 100, 231
Yugoslavia, former 11, 151

Zaire 43, 129
Zimbabwe 6, 35, 47, 108, 115–21, 208, 211, 237, 239
Zondi, Dr Siphamandla 237

eBooks – at www.eBookstore.tandf.co.uk

A library at your fingertips!

eBooks are electronic versions of printed books. You can store them on your PC/laptop or browse them online.

They have advantages for anyone needing rapid access to a wide variety of published, copyright information.

eBooks can help your research by enabling you to bookmark chapters, annotate text and use instant searches to find specific words or phrases. Several eBook files would fit on even a small laptop or PDA.

NEW: Save money by eSubscribing: cheap, online access to any eBook for as long as you need it.

Annual subscription packages

We now offer special low-cost bulk subscriptions to packages of eBooks in certain subject areas. These are available to libraries or to individuals.

For more information please contact webmaster.ebooks@tandf.co.uk

We're continually developing the eBook concept, so keep up to date by visiting the website.

www.eBookstore.tandf.co.uk